A Century of Foreign Investment
in the Third World

The late twentieth century witnessed a dramatic upsurge in foreign direct investment in the Third World. In this book, Michael J. Twomey explores both the origins and the impact of this trend.

Based on thorough statistical analysis *A Century of Foreign Investment in the Third World* presents comprehensive case studies of policy in 'metropolitan' countries and of the experiences of 'host' countries throughout Africa, Asia and Latin America. The findings reveal that foreign direct investment in – and therefore control over – third world countries was relatively higher at the beginning of the century than at its end.

The book's main innovation is its broad data set which uses a common frame of reference to make comparisons across historical, geographical and political boundaries. With its wide geographical and historical focus, this book makes an important contribution to current debates on dependency theory.

Michael J. Twomey is Professor of Economics at the University of Michigan, Dearborn. His previous publications include *Multinational Corporations and the North American Free Trade Agreement* and *Modernization and Stagnation: Latin American Agriculture into the 1900s.*

Routledge Studies in International Business and the World Economy

A Century of Foreign Investment in the Third World

Michael J. Twomey

London and New York

First published 2000
by Routledge
11 New Fetter Lane, London EC4P 4EE

Simultaneously published in the USA and Canada
by Routledge
29 West 35th Street, New York, NY 10001

Reprinted 2001

Routledge is an imprint of the Taylor & Francis Group

© 2000 Michael J. Twomey

Typeset in Baskerville by Wearset, Boldon, Tyne and Wear
Printed and bound in Great Britain by Biddles Short Run Books, Kings Lynn

British Library Cataloguing in Publication Data
A catalogue record for this book is available from the British Library

Library of Congress Cataloging in Publication Data

Twomey, Michael J.
   A century of foreign investment in the Third World/Michael J. Twomey
      p. cm. — (Routledge studies in international business and the world
      economy; 20)
   Includes bibliographical references and index.
   1. Investments, Foreign—Developing countries—History—
   20th century. I. Title. II. Series.
HG4538.T94 2000
332.67′3′091724—dc21

                                                            00–036596

ISBN 0–415–23360–7

Contents

Tables

Graphs

List of abbreviations and currencies

Technical terms

FI	Foreign Investment
FDI	Foreign Direct Investment
Non-RR FDI	Non-railroad Foreign Direct Investment
GDP	Gross Domestic Product
K	Capital stock
K/O	Capital output ratio
FSC	Free Standing Company
IDP	Investment Development Path

International organizations

IMF	International Monetary Fund
OECD	Organization for Economic Co-operation and Development
UNCTAD	United Nations Conference on Trade and Development
UNCTC	United Nations Center on Transnational Corporations
UN-ECLA or ECLAC or CEPAL	United Nations Economic Commission for Latin America and the Caribbean

Geographical entities

AOF	French West Africa
AEF	French Equatorial Africa

Publications

CEI	*Changing Economy of Indonesia*
CIIP	*Canada's International Investment Position*

Currencies   The "£" indicates the British Pound Sterling, while, for example, "E£" is Egyptian pounds. United States dollars are generally indicated by "US$" because several countries use "$" to indicate their currencies. The Japanese Yen is "¥" and was also used to indicate values in colonies such as Korea and Taiwan. The French Franc is indicated as "FF." The "R" is the Brazilian Real (plural, Reais).

Other Conventions   In some tables, "n.a." will be used to indicate that a specific datum is not available. However, when several items cannot be presented and repetitive n.a.'s would reduce legibility, blank spaces will be used. A billion is 1,000 million.

1 Introduction

Major themes

Does foreign direct investment occupy a larger role today in the economies of the Third World than it did at the beginning of the twentieth century? Specifically, do foreigners now own more of the Third World's productive assets? What can be said about the timing of the expansion of the foreign-owned capital stock in the colonies, and how does that differ by which country was the metropolitan power? How important was the achievement of independence in affecting the amounts of foreign direct investment (hereafter, FDI) in the previously colonial areas? What lies behind the late twentieth-century surge in FDI, and will it last?

These questions motivate the analysis in this book. This a timely investigation, with the current wave of relaxation of restrictions on FDI, the end of the Cold War, and sufficient period having passed since the ending of the colonial era to allow those complex times to be viewed with some perspective. The end of a century invites us to take a longer, more historically informed look at contemporary economic issues such as foreign investment. We push this by attempting a wide geographical coverage – Africa, Asia, and Latin America – one that is simply not present in the historical literature, even if contemporary economic analysis has no qualms about jumping such boundaries. Also revealing the author's economics background is the decision to begin the analysis before World War I and occasionally before 1900, downplaying the historians' practice which typically treats the Great War as the definitive watershed.

Our major focus is on foreign direct investment – that which the foreigners control. Nevertheless, the analysis of the experiences of both host countries or source countries requires that we also incorporate data on total foreign investment (hereafter FI), including loans as well as FDI. The analysis of loans to third world countries would inevitably lead us to look at the several debt crises which have been so frequent in the second half of the century. But that is a different story, and so our main interest will be on FDI. The economic framework which informs the organization of the material and the empirical analysis is a mainstream approach deriving from the work of John Dunning and Raymond Vernon. Their insights provide a vision of how FDI affects source and host countries, and what factors produce changes in FDI, in both sets of countries. Our model in comparative, quantitative economic history is Raymond Goldsmith.

It may be useful to place our interests in the context of the major writings on foreign investment. One of the most important approaches to the study of foreign investment has been the measurement of its rate of profit. As will be mentioned below, this had often been part of a broader analysis of the costs and benefits of foreign investment, especially in colonial contexts.

The broad currents of Marxist writings may have influenced some of the questions which are asked here, but they are not present in the formal analysis in the following chapters. Another possibility was to follow the lead of numerous scholars from the Third World, who look to Dependency Theory for conceptual guidelines. A common element of both the Dependency school(s) and the mainstream approach of Dunning, *et al.* is their association of more FDI with increased impacts in other sectors of the economy. For Dunning this may mean more technology inflows, for many Dependency and Marxist analysts this may imply reduced prospects for growth and development. One book cannot resolve that debate. Our goal is to contribute to the discussion by investigating where FDI has been large or small, in order to orient other studies which perhaps unconsciously assumed an unwarranted conclusion to that essentially empirical question.

This study's data on FDI for the first half century typically come from sources working in and on the industrial countries. Subsequently, especially after 1970, most of the data comes from the international organizations such as the World Bank and the United Nations, whose sources are the third world countries themselves. There are many problems in working with the available statistics on FDI, which will be acknowledged subsequently. There are some efforts underway at improving the generation of current data. We attempt to build bridges between the better measured data for the contemporary period and that before 1950, when the historical foundations were being established.

One other introductory comment relates to the geographical coverage – the Third World. Canada and Australia are certainly not third world countries, but are included here for purposes of comparison. The received wisdom at the end of the century is that the term Third World has lost much of its usefulness. The term itself was a child of the Cold War, when the First World signified the industrial, capitalist countries, the Second World referred to the socialist countries of the Soviet bloc, and the Third World was everywhere else – with a few countries like Vietnam and Cuba straddling one fence, while others such as South Africa, Israel and certain parts of Europe straddled the other. But the end of the Cold

War and the growing differentiation of Third World countries are rending this term obsolete, along with its predecessor, developing countries. For example, Singapore and Saudi Arabia have very high per capita income levels. The newly industrializing countries have a distinct identity in the mind of the general public, as well as of specialists at the World Bank and in academia. We will also note later how countries like Korea, Taiwan, Mexico, Chile and Brazil are fledgling exporters of direct investment. On the plane of international politics, China and India are reasserting themselves as powers in their geographical regions, and beyond. The other side of the coin of increased divergence is the stagnation of several countries, most notably in Africa. Furthermore, the disintegration of the Soviet bloc has increased the number of capital scarce countries with the potential of becoming industrial exporters. We will not propose an alternative classification scheme. The solution of the World Bank, listing countries by income levels, using somewhat arbitrarily defined categories (upper middle income, low income except China and India, and so on) is certainly practical, if not otherwise analytically helpful.

Our intention is to use two twentieth-century terms to describe what may well turn out to have been predominantly a twentieth-century phenomenon. The Third World is indeed a construct of the second half of the century. Moreover, we will also argue that foreign direct investment between the First World and the Third World is also quickly becoming dated, for two reasons. First, this direct investment has resulted primarily because of dramatic differences between first world and third world countries in technological capabilities, or nationalistic governmental policies, an abundance of certain raw materials, or markedly different wage levels. One of the results of this diversification of the Third World is that some of the FDI that these countries receive has come from other third world countries, not just the traditional sources. Furthermore, some third world countries are now exporters of portfolio capital. Secondly, the mode of FDI is evolving. Improved technological and administrative abilities imply that contractual arrangements with the multinational firms no longer cede total control to the latter, in terms of domestic participation in design and production, what products will be produced, and where and how they will be marketed. This does not necessarily imply the elimination of dependency, but it demands that our evaluation of it be updated.

Outline of the book

Chapter 2 begins with a survey of several strands of the major theoretical and empirical works on foreign investment and FDI. The distinction between direct and portfolio investment is introduced, and different related versions of Dunning's eclectic model, Vernon's product cycle hypothesis, and Narula's Investment Development Path are described. Historical work on Free Standing Companies, investment groups and expatriate investment function are then presented, as variations on the central phenomenon of FDI. From this point we investigate aspects of colonialism, and whether or how being a colony might have affected the amount of investment – portfolio or direct – sent to an area. The chapter ends with some observations about measurement issues.

The third chapter provides an overview of global trends in foreign investment during the twentieth century, and then moves to more specific analyses of the countries which were the major sources of capital for the Third World; the United Kingdom, France, the United States, Belgium, the Netherlands and Japan. For some time the sun did not set on the British and French empires, and those countries receive the most attention. The other countries on the list had only one or two formal colonies. Of course the foreign investment of the United States became dominant in the Third World by mid-century. We are cutting corners here, of course, by not including either Germany, Portugal, or other European countries, but the expectation is that we have covered most of the important countries. The two major factors in this chapter are the evolution of the metropolitan countries' treatment towards their colonies, and the impact of the World Wars and the 1930s Depression.

The next three chapters provide a series of short analyses of the experiences of individual countries of the Third World, and as such form the core material of this book. Comparisons will be made of foreign investment and FDI to local population, GDP, trade and, where possible, the stock of capital. For most countries the population numbers are known well enough for the accuracy required here, and the data on FDI/person basically serve as a check for the other series. Our major innovation is to utilize the results of a significant body of recent research on historical trends of GDP to compare FDI stocks to that variable. The tables in the middle three chapters also include ratios where the denominator is trade – the average of exports and imports – particularly as a substitute for those years where no GDP estimates are available. The shakiness of the data on the capital stock suggests that primary reliance should be placed on trends in the ratio FDI/GDP over time or across countries. Data on the relative size of the stock of foreign investment is also presented, even though our major interest is direct investment. These country studies are grouped geographically; first Africa, then Asia, and finally Latin America. This does not make for a smooth flowing narrative. One alternative selection criteria, sorting by colonial power, only makes sense for the ex-colonies of Britain and France, and not the other three metropolitan countries, and would certainly mix an odd group of countries which during this century were always independent. Moreover, as will be demonstrated, the fact of having been a colony had relatively little to do with the end of century situation with regard to foreign investment.

Chapter 7 attempts to gather up these disparate results and provide some comparative analysis. The topics that are confronted are those of the start of this introductory chapter: who had more or less investment, why did it change, and the impact of colonial status. One theme that is appended is a section on railroads during the first third of the century. Similarly, the end of the century issue of privatization and new forms of FDI are discussed. The chapter ends with a summary of the overall argument, and risks some comments about projections for the future.

Acknowledgments

Over the years I have received helpful comments from several researchers, whom I would like to acknowledge here. Morris Altman, Camron Amin, Ricardo Bielschowsky, Catherine Boone, Victor Bulmer-Thomas, Michael Chege, Ben Gales, Reinaldo Gonçalves, Jean-Francois Hennart, Thomas Lindblad, Angus Maddison, Carlos Marichal, Rory Miller, Michael Monteon, Rajneesh Narula, Irene Norlund, Trithankar Roy, Keetie Sluyterman, Colin Stoneman, William Summerhill, Tom Tomlinson, Steven Topik, Pierre van der Eng, and Mira Wilkins all responded warmly and generously to questions about their own work and the areas that they have studied.

My ideas have been influenced by a conference on Latin American Economic History at Bellagio, Italy, for which I thank its organizers, John Coatsworth and Alan Taylor, the commentator on my paper, Gabriel Tortella, and the other participants, particularly Alan Dye, Anne Hanley, Nanno Mulder, and Gail Triner. Special thanks to André Hofman and Lance Davis, who generously shared not only their insights but also important and unpublished data.

Dedication

Many of us who lived during more than half of the twentieth century are still having difficulty assimilating the impact of all the dramatic events that occurred during it. A less dramatic, but more personal recognition of the passage of time is the realization that I began my professional career more than three decades ago, teaching economics at the Catholic University in Lima, Peru. At many times while working on this book I reached back for support and inspiration to the memories of personal cordiality and high professional standards for intellectual freedom in academic research that were espoused and maintained by my colleagues there, of whom I especially remember Máximo Vega-Centeno, Adolfo Figueroa, Rufino Cebrecos, Ivan Rivera, as well as José María Caballero, Michel Delbuono, and Juan Antonio Morales. These fond recollections were warmly revived during a most welcome stay in Michigan by my ex-officemate Guillermo Rochabrún together with his wife Teresa Oré and their son Marcelo. To all of them and with best wishes for the continuing success of their work, I dedicate this book.

2 Conceptualizing and measuring foreign investment

This chapter reviews several models of foreign investment, beginning with very basic textbook models, and subsequently incorporating newer versions which are refined to incorporate specific historical cases or contemporary phenomena. The theoretical discussion leads to various comments about measurement issues, relating to foreign investment and the national economic aggregates to which it is compared. These questions are broadly described here and then addressed in subsequent chapters of the book.

Theoretical perspectives

The simplest and probably the earliest model explaining foreign capital flows claims that they are a function of the return to capital – interest rates. In this story, capital flows respond to interest rate differentials, continuing until these are eliminated. Typically, the wealthier country has lower interest rates, because of its abundance of capital and loanable funds. In a simple before-and-after scenario, interest rate differentials exist because of controls in capital markets, and relaxation of those controls leads to capital flows – foreign investment. Slightly more complex versions, building off the same basic principles, implicitly speak of potential interest rate differentials arising because of different rates of saving and investing in the several countries. A standard example is the belief that "young" countries at the beginning of the twentieth century had insufficient savings compared to their investment opportunities, and therefore turned to the "old world" for savings, which materialized as foreign investment. A recent treatment along these lines is Taylor and Williamson (1994).

One reason for creating theoretical models is to generate predictions of the effects of economic processes. Thus, as a standard textbook exercise, foreign capital flows which result from interest rate differentials will raise income in the receiving, or host country, and lower domestic income in the sending, or source country (Salvatore 1998: 375). In addition, the distribution of income will be affected. Wages and/or employment will rise in the receiving, or host country, while the return to capital will fall there, with the opposite effects occurring in the sending country. World income and efficiency will both rise. Such a prediction jars with the received wisdom of most writing on third world areas – particularly historical work, not to mention literature in the Marxist traditions. The mathematical rigor of the model does not hide the fact that, as a description of concrete reality, it is terribly simplistic. That observation is different from saying that the model is wrong; the theorist's task is to simplify down to the key factors in a given situation.[1] The theoretical models can be made indefinitely more complex, starting off with allowing for repatriation of the earnings of the foreign investment, through conversion of loans into consumption, side effects on exchange rates, and by explicitly giving the analysis an inter-temporal dimension. Even though such extensions inevitably multiply the range of possible outcomes to the theoretical exercise of the impact of foreign investment, the standard vision of international economists remains that such investment is beneficial to the recipient country.

The next level of sophistication categorizes capital flows as direct or portfolio. Direct investment is associated with control, usually identified empirically by having achieved ownership of a certain fraction of the outstanding equity of a company, such as 10 or 25 per cent. In contrast, portfolio investment involves loans at fixed rates of interest, most often to governmental entities, and provides no managerial control. There is a strong tradition in British economic history to identify a presumed preference for portfolio finance as a symptom of an aversion toward risk and a general lack of entrepreneurship.

The distinction between portfolio and direct investment only gained wide acceptance after World War II, when international capital markets were dominated by investments from the United States, whose overseas capital flows were indeed measured according to that conceptual scheme. Nevertheless, the identification of control with ownership of equity, and not with portfolio lending, is often questionable even in the British case, as discussed by Edelstein (1982: 33–7). Further confusion arises because at the beginning of the twentieth century the term direct investment was applied to funds that firms raised outside of financial markets, typically "directly" through reinvestment of profits, or perhaps through financing by immigrants. The early investigators who based their estimates of foreign investment on data from the financial markets would not have possessed concrete information on direct investment as it was then understood, and often relied on asserting the equivalent of "everyone knows" that it was small.[2]

Several examples from the end of the twentieth century could be mentioned of situations for which the portfolio/direct dichotomy is inadequate. Lending agencies, such as commercial banks or the International Monetary Fund, continually exercise a degree of control by means of a potential threat not to extend credit to a firm – or national government – which engages in undesirable actions. Recent changes in international capital markets have facilitated transactions in the stock of companies using another country's currency, generating what is termed foreign equity flows. The growth of franchising, particularly in services such as hotels or fast food chains, does not necessarily involve capital flows, but certainly produces very visible symptoms of a foreign presence.

Furthermore, the distinction between portfolio and direct does not lend itself easily to empirical studies explaining why one mode was chosen over the other. Now, it was the case that most foreign investments by US businesses involved direct ownership of assets overseas, and US portfolio investment was sent to governments, so the particular question of choice of mode of investment received little attention. In particular, it took some time for researchers to suggest factors besides interest rates, or less aversion to risk, that might explain direct investment. Investigators initially attributed that latter role to the kinds of dynamic factors explaining domestic investment – the "investment accelerator" – but this was unsatisfactory in its application to the external sector.

Dunning's "eclectic model" of FDI

Beginning with Charles Kindleberger's espousal of the posthumously published dissertation of his student Stephen Hymer, scholars have sought an explanation of foreign direct investment distinct from that of portfolio loans, focusing attention on factors derived from the industrial organization literature. One of the more popular versions is John Dunning's "eclectic model" of direct investment. Also known as the OLI model, it posits that a firm will invest overseas when it has either an Organizational advantage (trademark, production technique, entrepreneurial skills, returns to scale), or the intended investment site has a Locational attraction (existence of raw materials, low wages, special taxes or tariffs), and the firm prefers to Internalize these advantages by producing abroad, as opposed to indirectly profiting from its advantages by producing through a partnership arrangement such as licensing or a joint venture. The OLI model was considered to be especially appropriate to the post-World War II foreign investment of US manufacturing corporations. The emphasis on competitive advantages having been created by technological superiority or greater willingness to take entrepreneurial risk was also attractive to scholars looking for factors to explain the relative decline in the British economy after 1914. Furthermore, in contrast to our first mentioned model, in this framework, the market rate of interest would be relatively unimportant. The focus on aspects treated in that area of economics known as industrial organization parallels a broader reappraisal of the contributions of that literature to international economics, in what is known as the "new" trade theory. Perhaps the leading theorist in these efforts is James Markusen; illustrative of this work is Zhang and Markusen (1999).

Returning to our theoretical observations on the benefits and costs of foreign investment, it is the case that Dunning's conceptualization introduces new factors into the evaluation of direct investment, while the analysis of portfolio investment remains the same as before. An organizational advantage facilitates the transference of technology or some special skills, and in some sense is an exportation of a service. As such, FDI improves the overall welfare of both the sending and the recipient countries, while still having distributional effects. However, in this theoretical model, not all the net impacts associated with FDI are positive. For example, a locational advantage may have been generated by host country protectionism, as was often the case with "tariff factories" in Canada and post-World War II Europe, for which case the welfare evaluation of FDI is less clear. Similarly, some FDI results from government subsidies or tax benefits, not the direct effect of market forces, and may well be part of a process which according to a market-based theoretical analysis would make the country worse off. Another, less strictly economic example is the belief that some FDI currently is being directed towards countries with lower environmental standards. It should also be recognized that organizational advantages can have political origins, ranging from tariff privileges for overseas firms to military protection and intervention by the multinational company's home country. Such actions were not limited to the era of "gunboat diplomacy", of course, when they stimulated the criticisms of people like J.A. Hobson and Lenin.

Overall, insights such as the OLI framework do not easily lend themselves to mathematical modeling, and it is difficult to envision the model as a whole being subjected to a statistical test. In contrast to the simple textbook model of foreign investment discussed above, one implication of the industrial organization approach is that the amounts of FDI will differ by sector of the economy, because the influence of the OLI factors are quite sector specific. Nevertheless, although we know that government policies affect FDI, the empirical dimensions of such stimuli or controls do not lend themselves to direct measurement. Moreover, Dunning himself has continually modified the core set of insights; recently classifying FDI as market seeking, efficiency seeking, or resource seeking. John Dunning's influence is very broad on this subject; for example he has been a senior advisor to the United Nations group working on this area, initially referred to as the United Nations Center on Transnational Corporations, with headquarters in New York, and more recently attached to UNCTAD in Geneva. This group has made important advances towards the generation of internationally comparable data on investment stocks and flows, and their publications are a key source for numerous tables in this work.

The Product Cycle and the Investment Development Path

The distinction based on control opened the analysis to considerations of foreign direct investment focusing on the transference of some technical skill or advantage, payment for which would be realized in profits or licensing fees. One of the earliest academic treatments of this process was Raymond Vernon's "Product Cycle Hypothesis." The insight here was to take the business school's standard textbook version of a product cycle, wherein innovation eventually leads to standardization, and expand it by arguing that these cycles will involve countries beyond the one where the initial innovation occurred, eventually leading to a geographical relocation of production as those other countries develop the technological capacity which, combined with their presumably lower costs of labor, allows them to be competitive. A key contributor to the growth of overseas production could well be multinational corporations. Indeed, Mira Wilkins has coined the term "The American Model" to describe the process wherein overseas investment is made by multinational manufacturing firms which had initially developed a product at home, and subsequently entered tariff protected overseas markets by establishing production there (Wilkins 1988).

An important extension of product cycle literature has been recently presented by Dunning's student Rajneesh Narula. In his dissertation, Narula hypothesized what he called an Investment Development Path, in which increases in income, technology, and physical capital lead a country from an initial position of net inward investment to one of net outward investment. Narula's contributions were both theoretical and empirical; with regard to the latter, he argued that each country's path will be affected by its resource structure, market size, role of government, and the development strategy which is followed. In this model, a country's overall net FDI position results from the net effect of separate cycles, corresponding to primary products, manufactured goods, and services. Although data availability restricted the empirical work in his dissertation to cross-sectional analyses of a group of predominantly developed countries, he was able to demonstrate (Narula 1996: 45 ff) the hypothesized inflection of the net investment position, which is the key aspect of the cyclical description.

One import historical illustration of Narula's scheme is the railroad sector. It turns out that the early development of railroads in the Third World received a significant amount of financing from overseas, and that this sector has experienced a very marked cycle of foreign investment; with the aggregate position rising during the late nineteenth century, and disappearing by the middle of the twentieth century. Two types of technological change contributed to the displacement of the foreign investment in railroads, which might be described as demand and supply side. On the demand side, the expanded use of automobiles and trucks led to reduced use of railroads. With regard to supply, improved domestic skills led to the displacement of foreign by local entrepreneurs; sometimes this resulted from conscious government policies, such as a nationalization of the rails. In general, for the case of railroads, as with several others, the cyclical pattern of the net foreign investment position will be generated not only by market forces but also by government policy.

The obsolescing bargain

A rather different approach to enriching the dynamic conceptualization of the FDI process is the literature on the obsolescing bargain, for which a good source is Bergsten, *et al.* (1978). The core idea, also attributable to Raymond Vernon, is to describe the agreements between host countries and foreign investors as a bargain which is subject to negotiation not only at the initial signing, but also subsequently. The evaluations of costs and benefits to the agreement will change for both groups over time. In sectors such as petroleum and mining, very large ("lumpy") investments have to be made before production begins. After those expenditures have occurred, the multinational has little alternative but to stay and attempt to recuperate costs. The host country, on the other hand, might well wish to raise taxes or otherwise increase perceived benefits for local interests. In the words of Bergsten, *et al.* (1978: 131), "Once the investments were made and the mines or wells successfully working, however, such long-term agreements could not be enforced without the use of gunboats (or the covert equivalent of gunboats) by the home governments of the investors." The realization by all parties that these are the effective "rules of the game" will lead them to structure their negotiating strategies accordingly. The emphasis on bargaining in a situation of uncertainty leads the economic analysis away from one whose solution in terms of prices or returns is determined by a simple, well-defined, market equilibrium.

This literature commanded attention during the 1970s, the major period of nationalizations of extractive industries in third world countries. Two key elements in the greater relevance of this sector were the growing ability and willingness of the host governments to confront the multinationals, and the increasing availability of alternative sources for the services that the original multinationals provided. Another, perhaps less spectacular example of dynamic bargaining has occurred with third world governments' efforts at attracting manufacturing FDI, especially in export oriented activities. The case of automobile production in Mexico has received insightful analysis by Bennett and Sharpe (1985). They point out how the strategies of both the government and the transnational automobile companies evolved over time. Their analysis of the nature of the alliances between the government and local industrialists, labor unions, and foreign companies provides an important link to the substantial literature written within the framework of dependency theory. A parallel analysis is that of Samuels (1990), who looked at automobile subsidiaries in Brazil, analysing how their responses to such government pressures varied according to different characteristics of the firms and their overseas parents. It is the mark of a useful economic model that its framework can be used for both macro- and micro-level analyses. Moreover, these studies of automotive industries in third world countries describe a leading sector of end of the century manufacturing FDI. One lesson from them is how the various agents in the bargaining processes have been able to adjust their strategies to allow for a series of shorter term agreements, allowing all sides to accommodate their newly revealed needs in subsequent rounds.

Free Standing Companies

Over the last decade or so, economic historians have proposed several conceptual schemes for the analysis of foreign investment during the period before World War I. In contrast to "The American model" according to which a firm grows at home prior to expanding abroad, and finances that investment with its own funds, the more frequently encountered situation before World War I, according to Mira Wilkins, was that a firm was developed in one country by the nationals of another country – particularly Great Britain – who used their connections back home to generate funding, channel technological expertise, find markets, and so on. Such a firm, which Wilkins christened a Free Standing Company (FSC), had minimal control from the home country, and its "lean management" led to the characterization of its home headquarters as little more than a brass plate on a door in "the City". One direct and important implication of this insight was that much of what had been characterized as British portfolio investment – bonds raised for overseas firms – might well be considered direct investment, as it involved British control. Academic discussion of the FSC has argued that the consideration of internalization (as in Dunning's OLI framework) in the FDI decision must be expanded.

Subsequent research, reviewed in Wilkins and Schröter (1998), has established that the majority of British overseas firms were indeed of the FSC type. The FSCs were especially important in raw materials, public utilities, plantation agriculture, banks, and railroads – practically everything except manufacturing. Although it had been thought that the FSCs had short life-spans unless they evolved institutionally, it has been shown that several have had a long life-span. Although Wilkins initially focused on British and American investments, it has been shown that other countries engaged in this type of investment, particularly Holland and Belgium, in their colonies. Unfortunately, the historical experience of France has been less researched in this regard.

However, scholars such as Chapman (1998) have proposed a revision of

Wilkins's model that would incorporate the fact that many of these firms operated as parts of investment groups, sharing directors in London (including a well-connected, retired Member of Parliament), technicians knowledgeable about the relevant problems, and financial agents whose blessings the market required beforehand. Indeed, the attention on investment groups has further widened the scope of inquiry, as the Managing Agency Houses fit this description quite well. Although these are often considered a relic of a mercantilist past, of interest mainly to specialists on places such as colonial India, it has also been pointed out that the organization and functions of Japanese conglomerates, such as the *zaibatsu* and *keiretsu*, are quite similar. Moreover, we will see that this concept is also appropriate for the Korean *chaebols*, as indeed for investment clustered around *grupos*, or economic groups, in several Latin American countries.

Expatriate investment

Another analytical extension of the study of FDI is the category referred to as expatriate investment. An expatriate is someone who, although a longtime resident, is in some relevant sense a "foreigner" in the territory where the investment occurs, either in a legal sense due to citizenship somewhere else, or perhaps due to the persons being distinguished by race or religion from the local population. The most important example will be immigrant settlers from the colonial power. The conceptual distinction between foreign and expatriate investment will be tricky to operationalize empirically, because it may depend on a judgement of the entrepreneur's intentions regarding residency. One useful, but obviously problematic indicator is whether or not the firm is registered locally. A helpful procedure for separating expatriate investment from FSCs might focus on the source of financing of the firm. Nevertheless, because the political reaction against foreign investors has generally been a function of the overall size of their total capital in a country, not simply of FDI, we will attempt to identify these other manifestations of foreign involvement.

The fact that many investors from the United Kingdom ultimately stayed in the United States, Canada, Australia or New Zealand is commonplace, hardly deemed worthy of note. A parallel situation occurred with people from Spain, Italy and France, who settled in Latin America. With minor exceptions, this also passes without comment.[3] However, the typical experience of colonies in Africa and Asia was that, after attaining independence, there was pressure to "indigenize" the "foreign" firms, including those of settlers. In extreme cases, this has led to the expulsion, or worse, of the erstwhile settlers. Thus the process of decolonization sometimes made foreign that which was local, in the sense of having been created locally using domestic labor and capital. The Union of South Africa may turn out to be an important exception.

However, European settlers were not the only outsiders to have been exposed to this hostility. In the Mediterranean area, it is well known that Armenians, Greeks, Jews, "Levantines" and other ethnically or religiously identified peoples have had similar experiences. Similarly, there was a brief and intense period of Japanese settlement in Taiwan, Korea and ultimately China, which produced a very strong backlash. Another noteworthy example of expatriate investment, not directly involving colonialism, has been that of Chinese and Indians in southeast Asia and parts of east and southern Africa. As will be noted in subsequent chapters, at different times during the twentieth century a nationalistic reaction has also been directed at these groups; investment by ethnic Chinese being particularly targeted. Some of the cases of non-colonial settler investment illustrate that the definition of who is "a foreigner" is neither uniform nor fixed. Historical forces converted settlers into foreigners in places as diverse as Algeria, Uganda and Indonesia, and the expulsion or flight of those people had major impacts on their erstwhile home countries.

Early in the century, expatriate investment had been important in several areas, although by the end of twentieth century, it was basically non-existent. In some cases, the owners became citizens or in other ways ceased being outsiders, no longer distinguished from the rest of the local population. A related story is that expatriate enterprises were taken over by firms from the home country, meriting the new classification as FDI. The other, less congenial outcome was that settlers' capital was taken from them or simply destroyed, typically as part of a colony's independence movement and its sequels. Our case studies will encounter several examples of the first and third processes, with only non-quantifiable hints of the second process.

The Third World and colonies

On the eve of the First World War, about half of the population of the areas we now call the Third World resided in colonies – almost all the areas of Africa, much of Asia, and scattered places in the Caribbean. Similarly, roughly half of the output of the Third World was produced in colonies.[4] Any study of foreign investment in the Third World during the twentieth century must address the issue of colonialism – without getting absorbed by it. While Belgium, Japan, the Netherlands and the United States had one or two formal colonies during the twentieth century, both the British and the French empires spanned the globe, and their situation is more complex. Spain and Portugal also possessed colonies, but those cases will not be considered in this book. One pair of questions we will address is whether being a colony resulted in increased or decreased FDI during the formative era, and if the colonial legacy impacted investment levels during the subsequent period of independence.

The largest number of colonies was in Africa, and indeed the "scramble" for Africa after the Conference of Berlin in 1884–85 marked the start of what is referred to as the second phase of western Europe's imperial-ist expansion. There was considerable diversity in the exact juridical status of the areas to be referred to as colonies, especially inside the British and French empires. One result of the First World War was the transference of Germany's colonies in Africa, Asia and the Pacific into protectorates, most of them governed by France and Britain. The Ottoman Empire was similarly dismembered. Another distinct category is the self-governing colonies of Britain, a term nearly synonymous with that of "areas of white settlement". Of Britain's dependent colonies, India was a special case, due to its size, per-ceived benefits to the United Kingdom, governance structure in London, coexistence of princely kingdoms, and so on. For France, Algeria was the most important overseas possession, in terms of both trade and investment, and also as an area of French emigration. Moreover, it was an overseas department whose (French/European) residents enjoyed complete status of French citizens. Nevertheless, ultimate authority affecting Algeria con-cerning military, economic, social issues resided in Paris.

Moving beyond the broad category of colony, historians also describe several independent countries as being part of an informal empire, and only appearing to have political and economic autonomy, while being under the effective control of some hegemonic country. In Asia, China and Thailand are the important cases of countries struggling to maintain autonomy, something Japan had successfully achieved by the start of the twentieth century. While the United States only had one formal colony, the Philippines,[5] many commentators would include large parts of Latin America and the Caribbean in America's informal empire; this would seem difficult to deny for a country such as Cuba. Another example would be Egypt at the beginning of the century, which was alternatively asserted to be in the British, French, or the Ottoman empire, or at least in their sphere of influence. The Rhodesias were part of the business empire of the British South Africa Company.

One reason for special mention of colonies is the expectation that foreign investors would prefer to place their capital in areas of their own country's sphere of influence, where preferential treatment might be assumed. In cases characterized by such preferential treatment, or at least the impression that it occurred, we might further hypothesize a strong reaction against foreign investment when independence was achieved.

Colonial policy and FDI

The writing of comparative colonial history is an important service indus-try with its own product cycle; this author's generation was very much influenced by the writings of D.K. Fieldhouse and A.G. Hopkins. One fun-damental issue is the link between foreign investment and colonialism.

Many commentators have asserted that colonial expansion was motivated by a need for investment opportunities. Such a position has often been attributed to Vladimir Lenin and to J.A. Hobson, the latter a distinctly non-Marxist British economist whose works influenced the Russian revolutionary. Fieldhouse argued forcefully against this economic interpretation of the expansion of imperialism[6] into the Third World; in Chapter 3 we will review the relatively familiar result that the major part of FDI has indeed circulated among the industrial countries, and not toward the Third World.[7] As noted by Eckstein (1991) among many others, the downplaying of this strictly economic content of the rationale for imperialist expansion encourages the incorporation of a broader range of political, cultural, and other explanatory factors. For example, Aldrich (1996) reviews the motivations of French colonial policy, in which the sparse economic gains actually obtained must have played a minor role compared to an elusive promise of future gains, strategic considerations, and France's "civilizing mission"; a list to which Henri Brunschwig would add that of strengthening French pride. In spite of the activities of an influential colonial lobby in France, Aldrich (1996: 90) concludes that "Not until the second or third decade of the twentieth century did anything approaching consensus reign ... that empire was basically a 'good thing'." More broadly, we are led to expect inconsistency of policy towards the colonies, specifically in terms of economic issues such as subsidizing infrastructure and settlement programs. Indeed, a comparative study of the political economy of colonial policy might well reveal higher priorities being placed on facilitating human migration than on that of the migration of capital.

A related topic in the debates about the desirability of late nineteenth-century colonial empires, which continues to receive close attention in the literature today, is the profitability to the metropolitan countries of their overseas possessions. An aspect of immediate relevance to commentators of the day was the amount of trade with the colonies. In addition, we can perhaps now see more clearly that the profitability of private sector investments was dependent on the amount of social infrastructure in place, thus giving rise to debates as to who would finance that infrastructure. Railroads were the most important example, resulting in cases of public or private ownership, foreign or domestic. The landmark study of the issue of profitability for the case of Great Britain, Davis and Huttenback (1986), reveals the importance in such a calculation of the question of imperial subsidies, and particularly those for defense. These authors conclude "The British as a whole certainly did not benefit economically from the Empire. On the other hand, individual investors did." (page 306). The distributional impact of colonialism inside the metropolitan countries is evidently beyond the scope of this work. Nevertheless, the question of subsidies for businesses will have to be confronted, however unsatisfactorily, as one of the determinants of foreign investment. The colonial histories possess many other similarities, with regard to the subject of investment by outsiders, in such areas as the importance of free-standing companies and expatriate investment, the general lack of infrastructural investment, the weak growth of manufacturing, and so on. The differences in the socio-political traditions of the metropolitan powers were translated into similar variations of the amounts of government assistance to their nationals in the colonies, as well as tariff policies and credit mechanisms.

The metropolitan countries' policies affected investment in their colonies both directly and indirectly. Establishment of the rule of law, and provision of social as well as economic infrastructure were key contributions to growth and development, and were correspondingly emphasized by defenders of colonialism. In a less positive light, it is now widely recognized that most colonial powers explicitly gave their nationals a privileged position *vis-à-vis* their colonial subjects. These advantages ranged from explicit preference for production licenses, export and import rights, loans, to tax benefits and expropriation of locally held land. People from the metropolitan country were often governed by a different legal system. Somewhat more subtle biases would involve programs for education and training. Needless to say, the evaluation of the policies creating these advantages has been a source of debate, then as now. It would appear that France, Belgium, and Japan engaged in this more actively than did Great Britain, the Netherlands, or the United States. Even in the latter cases a disposition towards *laissez faire* faded as distinctions were made between investors from allied, as opposed to hostile countries; for example, investment from Japan became subject to increased discrimination as that country's industrial prowess grew.

In terms of loans, almost all borrowing by or in the name of colonial governments took place in the financial markets of the mother country. It is not clear if this resulted in higher financing costs for the colonies, as the colonial link could be interpreted as lowering risk to the lender. The case of private sector loans, and a potential bias in favor of entrepreneurs from the mother country over those from the colony, is also very controversial. One can certainly find Indian companies borrowing in London at an early date, yet in this case it must be acknowledged that the primary source of loans was the agency houses. Although the literature has not yet generated empirical measures of the cost to the colonies of the discrimination in favor of the home financial market, the belief in its existence was an important motivation for independence movements.

Policy with regard to land ownership certainly affected foreign investment. Colonial governments instrumented policies designed to remove natives from their land, not only making the land available to the colonial settlers, but also providing unemployed workers for them. The development of plantations (large, centrally run, export oriented farms with a resident, virtually landless, native labor force) was important in British East Africa, particularly Kenya, and in French Equatorial Africa; the process in South Africa was even more encompassing.

One of the classic debates in economics regards tariffs, and the advisability of using protectionism to restrict imports and thereby stimulate the growth of domestic industry. For many years, Britain had followed free trade at home, and correspondingly imposed that policy on its colonies. The situation was different in the French empire, where the colonies gave preferential treatment to imports from France. In both cases, of course, the assertion has often been made that these policies inhibited the development of locally run manufacturing industries, although for our purposes it might be difficult to argue that these policies were explicitly designed to stimulate metropolitan investment, and ultimately any analysis becomes overly complicated when attempting to infer intentions. A similar case can be made with regard to tax policy; tax rates often differed, according to whether one was a native or a colonial, and company taxes were often paid in the metropolis to its benefit (Fieldhouse 1971: 614). The French used these mechanisms as a means of pressuring the natives to assimilate to French culture, and citizenship, which would be indicated by renouncing native religion, language, clothing and so on. This approach would evidently have had larger effects in settler colonies, although encouraging investment by expatriates rather than foreign direct investment. The cases of the Netherlands, Japan, and Belgium are rather notorious in this regard. Interestingly, one does not find in the literature much conversation about colonial regulations stifling a domestic financial market.

Many colonies, particularly in Africa, had not reached a high state of industrial development upon attaining independence. The development of infrastructure was incomplete, domestic channels of savings and investment were incipient, and many politicians and commentators felt that there was still a need for outside investment.[8] India might be considered a counter-example. Although the subcontinent still suffers from major gaps in infrastructural development, by independence there had already developed significant domestic capacity in manufacturing, and the local financial system generated funds for British and native entrepreneurs.

The broadest issue on colonialism is its impact on the growth of output. In his study of the experience 1870–1913, W. Arthur Lewis, a future Nobel Prize recipient and no friend of colonialism, concluded:

> In general, it is not possible to say how much difference colonial status made to the rate of economic growth. Several countries which became colonies after 1870 grew faster after colonisation than before, and only one (the Congo) actually experienced a decline. But since all countries, colonies or not, did better after 1870 than before (except the core [UK, US, France, Germany] and the sugar colonies) this proves nothing.

> (Lewis 1978: page 213)

Lewis noted that colonial status was an obstacle for industrialization, although, "... [this] in much of Africa and Asia would still only have been a marginal issue," (ibid). He also argued that while the metropolitan countries had been criticized for greedily developing the colonies as sources of cheap raw materials, the more appropriate evaluation would be to criticize them for so ineffectively developing their agricultural and mineral potential. He is most critical of colonialism for its restriction of human development potential, beginning with a "shock of colonial subjugation", and leading to a hindrance of "the development of a native modernising cadre", both through racist policies which placed a "colour bar" against "educated young people", and eventually "diverting much brilliant talent" into anti-colonial struggles (page 214).

There were parallel but essentially independent evolutions in attitudes toward the colonies, converging perhaps only after World War II with the period of decolonization. Around 1900 the dominant attitude in the empire countries was still disregard, as more important things were happening elsewhere. The "scramble" for Africa, events in Asia, especially China, gradually changed that. The Dutch moved from a plantation policy (the "culture system") to the "Ethical Policy" which recognized a larger governmental role in the development of infrastructure. A landmark for the British was Joseph Chamberlain's period as Secretary of the Colonies, disrupting the default position that a colony should be self-financing. Albert Saurraut as France's Minister of the Colonies had a similar effect in the 1920s. Independence movements were given an unexpected boost by the experience of the First World War. France was clearly unable to control Indo-China. People from the colonies were mobilized to man the armies of both sides. The need to encourage growth in colonial areas became more evident. The Japanese government's position about the role of its colonies also evolved from envisioning them as providers of raw materials to sources of manufactured goods.

Just as the "American model" of FDI had misled observers into erroneously considering FSCs as portfolio investment, so can we also note other limitations inherent in a conceptualization primarily created from that perspective formed at mid-century. The "Anglo-Saxon" viewpoint inherently assumes separate roles for the private sector and the state. However, particularly in colonial times, the state was a major player in both financing and operating enterprises. As these were nominally owned and operated by people from the mother country, these enterprises might well be considered foreign direct investments. We will see that a significant part of total finances made available to French firms came from the state, and that the fusion of private and state was even stronger in the Belgian Congo and in Japanese investments in Manchuria. Similarly, in the early years of the century, when railroads dominated private sector lending, and were in turn subject to numerous subsidies and price control schemes, there was no clear cut-off in the riskiness between railroad equity and debentures.

Measuring and comparing the size of FDI

The strand of the classic economic literature on foreign investment that will be most important to us – with key authors such as Paish, Jenks, Feis, Kindersley, Cleona Lewis and Rippy – investigated the empirical question of how large it was, and where it was located geographically. Some of these authors also provided disaggregations of foreign investment totals. The focus of this work was generally the source countries, investigating for example the question of the effect of foreign investment on the source country's balance of payments. At the start of the inter-war period this question also attracted attention because of its link to the issue of war-debt settlements (Staley 1935; Moulton and Lewis 1925). A related theme attracting writers from practically all the European imperial countries was whether or not the colonies represented a drain on metropolitan finances. The treatment of defense expenditures was often the determining factor in their calculations. More fundamentally, the work alluded to above focused on the industrial countries, both as sources and as recipients of funds, and very little has been done to survey trends of FDI in the Third World.

Our central task will be to study the size of foreign investment for a broad cross-section of the Third World, providing where possible a century of observations. This focus on the quantitative aspect does not ignore nor negate the political discussions that have dominated the literature on foreign investment in the Third World. Rather, our intention is to facilitate such discussions of foreign control in particular, by providing a series of benchmark estimates of this variable, or some close proxy, for a variety of countries and time periods. When available, disaggregated FDI will be examined, as well. Countrywide ratios of FDI to GDP or to the capital stock disguise the fact that FDI tends to be concentrated in certain sectors in third world countries, and trends in the countrywide ratios often respond more to differences in sectoral growth rates, rather than changes in sector specific foreign ownership.

The analytical economic models which were briefly noted above are not particularly useful for the big question – whether or not FDI is good for the host country, or even for the source country. Dunning's eclectic model has a marked microeconomic focus, which does not directly address such a broad welfare issue. It is the case that a high fraction of the works that are critical of multinationals, from an anti-capitalist or Marxist position, adopt a very broad economy-wide or macro perspective, making the confrontation of these two approaches quite difficult. Two competing views are that FDI indicates a transfer of technology and improvement in competitiveness – and as such is good for the host country, to which is contrasted the hypothesis that FDI is harmful because it provides the source country some control over the host country, and opportunities for exploitation. This is not a debate which will be entered into here; the contrasting positions are mentioned simply to motivate the analysis. For both paradigms, more FDI means more of the effect under discussion.

Given that the fundamental task of this book is to measure and compare the size of FDI in a number of third world countries during the twentieth century, we turn to discuss which measures can be used in these comparisons. One major choice which was made early in this project was to focus on stocks, rather than flows of foreign investment. The rationale was two-fold: the desire to look at the sectoral distribution and impact of FDI, for which flow data are quite inadequate; and a belief that early (pre-1950) data on FDI flows did not include reinvested profits, and that it would be difficult to know when the balance of payments methodology was updated. The downside of this choice is the fact that any estimated stock variable is plagued with problems such as inflation and depreciation, to which should be added the issue of the appropriate exchange rate. The empirical side of any study of foreign investment is so loaded with pitfalls that the temptation is to begin – or end – each paragraph with an apology, but this recourse will be used sparingly.

Because foreign investment typically involves transferring funds from one currency to another, a question arises about which exchange rate to use. For several decades the use of the market exchange rate for making cross-country comparisons has been questioned, and now a significant body of research has investigated the biases. One of the consistent results of the World Bank's so-called ICP project has been that market exchange rates undervalue products – and income – from third world countries. There has resulted from this work an alternative mode of comparison, using a non-market exchange rate which is calculated on the basis of relative prices of a large number of individual products. Indeed, we will use a key work in this effort, Maddison (1995), which compares different countries' series of real GDP using this methodology. Nevertheless, this monograph will utilize market exchange rates in most of our calculations, for three reasons. First, the practical consideration is that alternative ICP exchange rates do not exist for many countries included here. Secondly, most of our data on foreign investment has already been converted using market exchange rates. Finally, there is currently little reason to suppose that the distortions between market and equilibrium exchange rates in the 1990s can be considered constant in historical work.

When making comparisons across countries and over time, several candidates come easily to mind as indicators of the relative size of foreign investment. There have been many presentations, over the years, of comparisons of per capita values of FI or FDI. Examples would include Staley (1935: 14), Frankel (1938: 170), up to Pamuk (1987: 138).[9] These results will be reviewed, and more estimates provided, in the chapters that follow. What the OLI perspective would suggest we look for is a measure of payments for technology transferred; such data do not exist calculated in an appropriate and uniform manner. The anti-FDI school focuses on foreign control – of the total economy, or perhaps of key sectors such as manufacturing or foreign trade. An approach common to both would be the share of foreign capital in total capital, FDI/K. This is certainly scaled to the size of the national economy, and several observations on this ratio will be presented. Nevertheless, the measurement problems are severe, as will be outlined below. Our solution is to rely on an intermediate variable, GDP, for the comparisons of the size and importance of FDI, so that the following chapters present numerous observations on the ratio FDI/GDP. The attraction of using GDP is that data on it are available for many countries, much of that being of recent vintage, especially as a result of the work of Maddison and his co-workers on several third world areas.

Capital and the capital–output ratio

How well does GDP reflect the size of the economy? There are several arithmetical identities linking our variables – FDI, FDI/person, FDI/GDP, and FDI/K – these are portrayed in Table 2.1. Because, for example, FDI/GDP equals FDI/person divided by GDP/person, we know that these two FDI series will move in parallel only if GDP/person is relatively constant. Similarly, in comparing different countries, FDI/person will provide similar rankings to FDI/GDP only if levels of GDP/person are the same. The same comments can be made about FDI/GDP; it is a good indicator of FDI/K, when the ratio K/O is constant across countries or over time. In short, FDI/person is an accurate proxy for FDI/K, in cross country or time series studies, when the two intermediate variables, GDP/person and K/O, are approximately constant. One of the findings of this work is that the dispersion among countries' levels of per capita income is large when compared to that of their levels of per capita foreign investment, limiting the usefulness of FDI/person for studies of foreign dominance. We will see below that K/O ratios are not constant, nor do they change uniformly with higher incomes. Thus, as a proxy for foreign ownership of the domestic capital stock, FDI/person is doubly flawed.

Let us turn to the link between FDI/GDP and FDI/K, which according to the formula in Table 2.1, is the ratio of the capital stock to total output, known as the capital-output ratio, often written as K/O. The capital stock is very difficult to measure, for several of the same reasons as the stock of FDI. However, much effort has been directed to measuring the capital stock, and particularly the capital-output ratio, which some decades ago had been a focus in studies of economic growth. Much of the life's work of the late Raymond Goldsmith was devoted to issues of measurement of physical and financial capital, and we are indeed fortunate that we can turn to Goldsmith (1985) for an authoritative summary of efforts at measuring the capital stock, and what they imply about the capital-output ratio. Three factors are to be considered; measurability, constancy, and comparability across countries.

Table 2.1 Indicators of the relative size of foreign investment

Variable	Relation to previous variables
Nominal FDI	
Real FDI	= Nominal FDI ÷ Price index
FDI/capita	= Real FDI ÷ Population
FDI/GDP	= FDI/capita ÷ GDP/capita
FDI/K	= FDI/GDP ÷ K/O ratio

In countries with abundant data, the preferred method of measuring the capital stock is called the perpetual inventory method, in use since the 1950s, having been developed by such leaders of the field as Goldsmith and Simon Kuznets. Briefly, the investigator deflates each year's investment flows by an appropriate price, and after adjusting for depreciation, sums the resultant series to obtain the net capital stock. There is a long-standing discussion about what would be the appropriate price index for such a procedure, which is often resolved by a lack of alternatives. A short-cut simply sums the series on annual investments from a country's national income accounts, ignoring depreciation. A second type of approach uses census data on capital stock, for which the informants were presumably asked to provide an estimate of their company's worth, with all the inherent dangers of such a procedure. What might be termed the third place methodology involves estimating the stock from information on taxes where the assessment rate is believed known. Finally, one can utilize the estimates of so-called well informed people. Although this seems highly dubious, it played an important role in the path breaking work of Jacob Viner on Canada.

For his broad international comparisons of measures of the capital stock, Goldsmith uses a three-fold classification; what we might call business and government assets, reproducible tangible assets, and (total) tangible assets. The business and government category consists of buildings and machinery, and indeed were often estimated using data on machine production and imports, and the output of construction companies. Reproducible tangible assets adds on to this group the value of residences, inventories, and consumer durables. Finally, total tangible assets adds on to reproducible tangible assets the value of land. In round numbers, the averages in Table 2.2 indicate that the distribution of tangible assets for developed countries before World War I was one third land, one third business and government fixed assets, one sixth residences, and one sixth other. Thus we see that, even in industrial countries, the assets of businesses and the government form a small part of the national total. This leads us to presume that FDI will also amount to a small fraction of total capital, as it will be limited to businesses and, in certain cases, land. The process of industrial growth did reduce the share of land in total tangible assets; according to Goldsmith (1985: Table 5) its ratio fell from 45 per cent

Table 2.2 Distribution of tangible assets: eight developed countries, 1913 (percentages)

Total	100	
Land	32	
Agricultural		20
Other		12
Reproducible Assets	68	
Equipment and Other Structures		35
Dwellings		16
Inventories		7
Livestock		3
Consumer Durables		5

Source: Author's calculations using Goldsmith (1985: Table 5).

Note
Numbers may not sum due to rounding errors.

in 1850 to 22 per cent in 1939. Note also that livestock and inventories comprised over one fifth of the total for businesses and the government, and did not decline nearly so much with improved transportation and communication. These data will serve as useful guidelines for our subsequent analysis of data in the Third World.

Corresponding to Goldsmith's three specifications of the capital stock are three measures of the capital output ratio. The data in Table 2.3 are separated into three geographical groupings; the early industrializing countries – Europe and the US, two late industrializers – Japan and South Africa, and two developing countries – India and Mexico. Let us first discuss the comparisons across countries at a given point in time. One question to ask of the data on K/O ratios is how much they vary between countries. As can be seen in Table 2.3, sizeable differences occur between countries that we might believe had similar income levels and productive structures, even when measured as consistently as was possible for one investigator and his colleagues, using the available national data sets.[10] Moreover, the data in Table 2.3 do not suggest a uniform relation between K/O and average income level, across countries at a particular point in time. A positive relation would be expected on basic economic principles, as richer countries substitute capital for more expensive labor. When land is included in the definition of wealth, the explanation could simply be differences in allotments of land per person, but this finding also occurs when land is excluded. Another potential explanation is structural differences, examples of which would be the heavily capital intensive mining in South Africa, or methodological differences in the valuation of residences. The conclusion about the cross-country differences of K/O ratios cautions us against assuming that a higher FDI/GDP ratio necessarily implies a higher ratio of FDI to total capital.

Let us now turn to the time trend of the K/O variable. At a theoretical level, one hypothesis would predict that this will rise over time, due to a presumed declining marginal productivity of capital. A practical consideration argues that the K/O might fall – many countries began the century with a large amount of railroads, which were relatively capital intensive. It is easy to imagine scenarios in which technological change would cause the K/O to fall.

Turning to Goldsmith's data in Table 2.3, we see that the average K/O ratio in today's developed countries fell consistently from 1850 up through 1965 when land is included in the measure of capital, while the

Table 2.3 Capital output ratios

Year	Europe & US (average)	Japan	South Africa	India	Mexico
Net tangible assets					
1875	6.1	6.3		2.6	
1895	5.2	6.2		3.3	
1913	5.2	5.4	5.2	3.5	
1929	4.6	4.9	4.2	5.9	2.9
1939	4.4	4.1	4.1	6.2	2.4
1948	4.1	4.0	3.8	4.3	1.8
1965	3.7	5.1	3.8	4.4	2.2
1978	4.5	4.6	4.3	. 5.2	2.6
Net reproducible tangible assets					
1875	3.6	3.4		1.6	
1895	3.4	3.3		1.8	
1913	3.6	3.1	3.7	1.6	
1929	3.5	2.7	3.2	2.4	2.0
1939	3.5	2.7	3.1	2.4	1.8
1948	3.2	1.4	3.0	2.2	1.2
1965	2.9	1.7	3.0	3.0	1.7
1978	3.7	2.3	3.5	3.9	2.1
Non-residential structures, equipment, inventories, and livestock					
1875	2.3	2.2			
1895	2.1	2.0			
1913	2.4	2.2	3.1		
1929	2.3	2.0	2.5		1.4
1939	1.7	2.1	2.5		1.2
1948	1.9	7.1	2.2	1.6	0.9
1965	1.7	1.2	2.2	1.8	1.1
1978	2.2	1.7	2.7	3.0	1.3

Source: Author's calculations using data in Goldsmith (1985), Tables 16, 17 and 18, respectively.

Notes
Coverage of Europe includes Belgium, Denmark, France, Germany, Great Britain, Italy, Norway and Switzerland. The third set of data includes France, Germany, Great Britain, Italy and Norway. Data in the first column are unweighted averages.

two indices which exclude land tended to fluctuate with no discernible trend. For the second grouping of countries, the K/O fell for Japan and South Africa when land is included in the numerator, and also when land was excluded. Goldsmith (1985) only included two third world countries, India and Mexico. The capital output ratio rises in India until 1939, independently of the inclusion of land.[11] The Mexican K/O falls and then rises during the period covered in the Table, so a distinct mixture of capital deepening and technological change is involved here. Overall, this evidence is not very encouraging in our quest for a presumptive pattern in the capital output ratio.[12]

In the 1950s the newly formed United Nations Economic Commission for Latin America analysed the growth experience of several countries in the region in a series of country specific monographs. As part of what was then state-of-the-art macroeconomic programming, capital stocks, and the capital output ratios were measured – several of these will be discussed in Chapter 6. Recently, Hofman (1992 and 2000) has updated that work, presenting for the period since 1950 similar calculations derived from a rigorous application of the perpetual inventory methodology, more uniformly applied to the national data. One of his results is that the K/O ratios have tended to rise – the average for his sample of Latin American countries grew by between one third and one half over the period 1950 to about 1990, depending on the specification of capital. Hofman's calculations do not indicate a reduction of the cross-country dispersion of K/O ratios over time. Moreover, his clear exposition reveals the sensitivity of the resulting K/O ratios to issues of specification, such as gross or net capital stocks, inclusion or not of residences, and which set of prices (national or "international") are used. The thoroughness of that presentation facilitates our comparison of the results of several other studies, using his estimates as benchmarks.

Broader geographical coverage to the measurement of capital output ratios is provided in a recent article by King and Levine (1994). As a by-product to their study of the importance of capital in economic growth, these authors calculate the K/O for about 100 countries in the post World War II era. With regard to third world countries, four general conclusions can be highlighted. First, the average K/O was in the range of one to two. Secondly, the K/O rose over time, at less than 1 per cent per year. Thirdly, the values for the K/O in Latin America were similar to those calculated more carefully by Hofman, and correspondingly were less than those resulting from the ECLAC studies of the 1950s. Finally, the K/O was smallest in Africa, with an average level of 1.4 for all countries.

Further measurement issues

The country that has the most documented statistics about its outward foreign investment is the United States. One of the notable results illustrated in Table 2.4 about the aggregate balance sheet of US foreign investment is that total assets of these firms are significantly larger – by a factor of four in 1989 – than either the value of current plant and equipment, or the amount invested in these firms by foreigners. Although cash and inventories are only one sixth of total assets, they are two thirds of net plant and equipment. Finally, it is worth emphasizing that over half of the owners' equity was financed through retained earnings. Such a result indicates that estimates of FDI flows based on scanty information from the balance of payments will seriously understate the amount of FDI.

A related question is the constancy of the ratios between FDI and other indicators of foreign business. For the United States, the standard measure is the "historic value" of the FDI position; the accumulation of balance of payments flows, including new capital from the country, intercompany flows, and reinvested earnings. Since the 1960s there have been censuses taken every five or so years of US overseas firms, called benchmark surveys, that complement the data on the FDI position with statistics on sales, total assets, employment, among others. Moreover, since 1982 there have been attempts to adjust the series on "historic value" of FDI to take into consideration the effects of inflation and changes in market valuations. The basic answer derived in Table 2.5 from the US benchmark surveys, is that the ratios between these various indicators are not particularly constant, nor do they reveal any simple trend over time. Curiously, neither of the two indicators calculated by the Department of Commerce with the intention of adjusting for changes of prices and exchange rates, the "market value" and the "current value" of FDI, appears to have more stable ratios than does the "historic value" of FDI. Some major sectoral differences can be mentioned as well. Taking the ratio in 1989 of Net

Table 2.4 Combined balance sheet for US foreign affiliates, 1989 (billion US $)

Assets			Liabilities and Owners' Equity		
Total	1,330		Total	1,330	
Current	674		Debt and Other	838	
Cash		75	Owners' Equity	492	
Inventories		128	Stock		230
Receivables and other		471	Retained Earnings		257
Net Property, Plant			Other		6
and Equipment	331				
Other	324				

Source: US Department of Commerce (1991: Table II.B 3).

Notes
Data refer to nonbank affiliates of non-bank parents. The gross (i.e. undepreciated) figure for Property, Plant and Equipment is $586 billion. That part of Owners' Equity which is attributable to foreigners is called the Direct Investment Position. In 1989 the total corresponding to non-bank affiliates of non-bank parents was $356 billion.

Table 2.5 Ratios of key aggregates for United States overseas firms, 1966–1994 (per cent)

	1966	1977	1982	1989	1994
Property, Plant & Equipment/FDI	89	98	115	93	n.a.
Sales/FDI	214	466	472	361	286
Sales/Assets	86	134	125	97	74
FDI-Market/FDI	n.a.	n.a.	109	219	174

Sources: United States Department of Commerce (1975a, 1981, 1986, 1991, 1997). Data refer to non-bank affiliates of non-bank parents. "FDI-Market" is Market Value of Direct Investment Abroad, taken from the *Survey of Current Business*, July 1996 and July 1998; this series begins in 1982.

Note
"n.a." indicates not available. The denominator in lines 1, 2 and 4 is the "historic value" of FDI. The coverage for 1966 is not completely comparable to that of later years.

Property, Plant and Equipment to historic FDI, for example, high values (>200) are obtained for Mining and Petroleum, while Finance and Wholesale Trade have values less than 40. In general, one presumes that these differences can be easily explained – banks and warehouses do not have much physical capital – but their magnitude is such as to further complicate the understanding of trends in aggregate ratios.

Final comments

Several schemes have been suggested for describing and categorizing foreign investment; that which dominates in this work is the disaggregation into direct and portfolio, where the former is identified with control and entrepreneurial risk, and is assumed by many scholars to imply technological transfer. This distinction is not easily operationalized in the data, and differences exist in practice by country. The scheme chosen here responds to practice and data availability of the dominant foreign investor in the second half of the century, the United States; in other cases the distinction will be between business and government recipients. Recent trends will suggest that the portfolio/direct scheme is losing relevance as the century ends and new modes of investment are adopted.

Data problems are recognized as being formidable. Many sources of data on FDI are ultimately based on balance of payments information, and omit both reinvested profits and investments financed from local sources in the host country. Beyond that, data on the accumulated value of FDI is difficult to adjust for inflation and depreciation, as happens with any series on capital stocks.

Not much effort was made to motivate a study of the relative size of foreign investment. Indeed, most discussions of foreign investment tend to assume the author's conclusion – that foreign investment is either beneficial or harmful. Our approach is to assume the importance of the issue of size, while adopting an agnostic position on the question of net effect of FDI, taking a step back from that discussion, attempting to establish benchmarks on size and trends, which will then allow further research to differentiate cases more realistically.

Notes

1 At the beginning of the twentieth century, most observers – of whatever economic school – agreed that Britain and other foreign investors had excess capital.
2 See the examples in Platt (1986: pp. 54–5).
3 Díaz Alejandro (1970: p. 63) notes that resident aliens in Argentina had nearly equal rights as citizens, and fewer duties – maintaining their foreign nationality allowed them to avoid the draft. The textile industries around the Mexican state of Puebla involved significant French expertise; these people remained after the unsuccessful experience of the Emperor Maximilian. Something similar happened to Spaniards in Cuba during the nineteenth century.
4 Based on the population and GDP data in Maddison (1995), with interpolations of GDP estimates for omitted countries based on the regional averages. Independent countries included Latin America, Egypt, China, Thailand, and Turkey. Maddison's coverage is weak for sub-Saharan Africa and the Middle East. However, these calculations are most sensitive to the inclusion and classification of China and, to a slightly lesser extent, the Indian subcontinent. Exclusion of both these areas maintains a roughly even split between colonies and independent countries, either in terms of population or total GDP.
5 The list of US overseas territories could be expanded to include Alaska and Hawaii, which eventually became states, and Puerto Rico, Guam and other islands, but the Philippines is the only US colony whose data will be analysed in this book.
6 Except when referring to specific writers or their works, in this book we will avoid the use of the term imperialism as an analytical construct, in recognition of the fact that it has been utilized by so many authors in such different ways as to rend it virtually useless.
7 Fieldhouse was subsequently criticized as exaggerating the intellectual link between Hobson and Lenin, although the review of that literature by Eckstein (1991) reaffirms the validity of Fieldhouse's specific point.
8 Several contemporary authors coming from a Marxist tradition can also be cited in support of this proposition. Tomlinson (1993: p. 19) mentions Bill Warren and Geoffrey Kay, reporting the latter's comment that "Capitalism created underdevelopment not because it exploited the underdeveloped world but because it did not exploit it enough." This book will not directly engage that debate. Revisionist in a different direction is the suggestion by Cumings (1984: p. 489) that Japanese policies in Korea led to the latter's *overdevelopment.*
9 Other authors, not cited specifically to save space in the bibliography, are Colin Clark, the Woytinskys, along with the several United Nations publications in the 1950s. The United Nations' UNCTC/UNCTAD only began including estimates of the ratio of FDI stocks to GDP in its *World Investment Reports* during the late 1990s.
10 A contemporary of Goldsmith whose work was often cited at the time, but is hardly remembered today, was Robert Doane. In Doane (1933 and 1957),

there are presented estimates of national wealth for about 30 and 50 countries, respectively, in the latter book even disaggregated by sectors. That author's references and methodology are not detailed. As it turns out, comparisons of the data in Doane (1957) on output (p. 194) with that on assets (pp. 202–3) suggests that he assumed constant sectoral K/O ratios for many of those countries for which the availability of data was not good. Evidently his results cannot be used to analyse aggregate K/O ratios, nor the growth of capital stocks.

11 One puzzle in the Indian case is that the K/O ratio for net reproducible tangible assets is already so high in 1875. More questions will arise from the investigation of railroads in Chapter 7, which suggests that this sector reached its highest relative importance in the nineteenth century. In other countries, the K/O fell after the rest of the economy started to grow relative to the railroads.

12 One initially hypothesized pattern was that agrarian societies with a small amount of industrial capital but perhaps a healthy agricultural export sector might have during the first years of foreign investment, a modest level of FDI/K, a low K/O, and a correspondingly high FDI/K. The data on India and Ghana provide only modest support for this scenario.

3 The major source countries

The presentation of the data on foreign investment in this chapter begins with world totals, which is followed by a series of presentations on the aggregated data for the major investing countries. Although our basic interest is the Third World, a prior review of the evolution of investment from the individual source countries permits an overview of major trends while suggesting explanatory factors. Greater attention will be placed on the first half of the century, for which data from the Third World are less available, with the additional benefit that this focus allows us to search for common experiences among the colonies. This sets the stage for the discussion in the later chapters of the data for individual host countries.

Global overview

The twentieth-century path of world investment by source countries is traced in Table 3.1, where for convenience the data are deflated by the price deflator for US GDP.[1] The United Kingdom had provided the largest amounts before World War II, while the United States has been the biggest source of foreign investment (FI) since mid-century. British investments had about the same level in 1938 as they had attained in 1913, although the intervening period saw much destruction and loss during the World War I period, and recovery during the 1920s. France's overseas investments suffered a steep decline after World War I, due to default in Russia, and to the post-war inflation which affected its unindexed bonds. France has not returned to its pre-World War II prominence as an external investor. The declines of investments due to war losses are evident for Germany and Japan, as is their subsequent recoveries. The acceleration of foreign investment after 1980 is quite remarkable.

Table 3.2 provides a parallel view of FDI data. One fact that can be deduced from the table is that there are considerable differences among the countries in terms of the fraction of their foreign investment that is attributable to direct investment, and that this pattern has not changed significantly over the long run. In particular, the United States always preferred direct investment, while the United Kingdom and Switzerland

Table 3.1 Outward foreign investment stocks, by source countries, twentieth century (US$ billion at 1900 prices)

	1913	1929	1938	1950	1980	1990	1995
World total	36.7	22.3	30.4			219.7	362.6
Australia		0.1	0.1			2.5	4.1
Belgium	0.8	0.7	0.7		1.8	8.2	11.2
Canada	0.2	0.6	1.0	0.5	2.8	6.7	8.7
France	7.3	1.7	2.1			10.7	28.3
Germany	4.7	0.5	1.5		4.6	18.1	30.0
Italy		0.1	0.1		1.1	6.7	13.7
Japan	0.2	0.5	0.7			44.8	53.3
Netherlands	1.6	1.1	2.7			9.9	16.6
Sweden		0.2	0.2			3.5	5.9
Switzerland	1.0	1.0	0.9			14.2	23.7
UK	16.1	8.7	12.7	1.7	11.0	34.4	52.2
US	2.8	7.1	6.4	5.3	24.5	60.0	115.0

Sources: 1913, Total, and for France, Germany, United Kingdom, and the United States from Woodruff (1967: Table IV–3); data for Belgium, Japan, Netherlands and Switzerland from Staley (1935); for Canada from Viner (1975: 94). 1929, from various pages of Staley (1935), except Canada which is from the *Historical Statistics of Canada* series F176 and F177. Total is author's summation. 1938, total from Woodruff (1967), individual countries from Lewis (1948). 1950, for Canada from *Historical Statistics of Canada*, series F176 and F177; for United Kingdom from Bank of England (1953), United States is author's calculation based on *Survey of Current Business* September, 1967, p. 40. 1980–1995, from *International Financial Statistics Yearbook*, 1998, using that source's subtotals for direct and portfolio investments. World totals are the sums for these countries only.

Note
Nominal values converted to US dollars at the current exchange rate, and deflated by the US GDP deflator.

tended to rely on portfolio-type loans. Of course, the ongoing work on free-standing companies, investment groups, *et al.*, is leading to a re-evaluation of that distinction during the first third or so of the century. Contrary to stereotype, Japan's overseas assets in the post World War II era have been predominantly portfolio type investment. The overall ratio of FDI to FI at the end of the twentieth century is slightly less than one half.

An essential task in this book is the presentation of comparisons of ratios of foreign investment to various indicators of the size of the economies of the host or source countries. Looking at the size of overseas investment compared to the source economies' levels of GDP, some important differences emerge from the results in the previous two tables. These data for FI/GDP and FDI/GDP are presented in Table 3.3 and Table 3.4. There is a general trend of a U-shaped pattern in each of these variables for the source countries. Greater data availability allows us to note a drop by half of FDI/GDP between 1938 and 1960. Most FDI takes place among industrial countries, but the data to be presented later with regard to the recipient countries will also reveal this U-shaped pattern. The decline is more marked for total foreign investment, and is quite

Table 3.2 Stock of outward FDI by source countries, twentieth century (US$ billion, 1900 prices)

	1913	1929	1938	1950	1960	1971	1980	1990	1995
World total	11.5		14.6		15.7	29.4	41.9	102.9	156.1
Australia					0.0	0.1	0.2	1.7	2.0
Belgium					0.3	0.4	0.5	2.3	3.4
Canada	0.1	0.2	0.4	0.3	0.6	1.1	2.1	4.7	5.7
France	1.4		1.4		1.0	1.2	2.1	6.1	18.4
Germany	1.2		0.2		0.2	1.2	2.7	7.0	11.2
Italy					0.3	0.5	0.6	3.2	5.3
Japan	0.2	0.5	0.9		0.1	0.8	1.8	11.2	11.6
Netherlands	0.7		1.5		1.6	2.4	3.7	6.3	9.1
Sweden					0.1	0.4	0.5	2.7	3.4
Switzerland					0.5	1.6	1.8	3.7	7.0
UK	5.2		5.8	1.0	2.5	4.0	7.0	12.9	15.3
US	2.1	3.6	4.0	3.6	7.7	14.1	18.9	40.9	63.8

Sources: FDI: for 1913 and 1938, all countries from Dunning (1983: Table 5.1) – in which Japan should be $200, not $20 – except the Netherlands, for which both years are taken from Gales and Sluyterman (1993: 65); 1929, Canada from *Historical Statistics of Canada,* series F176, datum for Japan summed from host countries, from Kaneko (1982) and Remer (1933), US data from Lewis (1938); 1950, for the United States, US *Department of Commerce* (1960: 91); 1960, these countries from Dunning (1983) – Belgium, Canada, France, Germany, Japan, Netherlands, UK, US, and these countries from Stopford and Dunning (1983: Table 1.2) – Australia, Italy, Sweden, Switzerland; 1971, all countries from Stopford and Dunning (1983: Table 1.2); 1980–1995, all countries from *World Investment Report* 1997.

Note
Nominal data converted to US dollars at current exchange rate, and deflated by the US GDP deflator.

accentuated for the United Kingdom and elsewhere in Europe. Moreover, the decline is quite small for the United States, where, indeed, the ratio of either FI or FDI to GDP is rather smaller than that of most of the other countries. Another important point is that the United Kingdom was not the only country to invest "heavily" overseas, as indicated by the ratio of its investment to GDP. Switzerland and the Netherlands had ratios of FI/GDP as high as Britain's, and the levels of France and Belgium were also appreciable. When the investment ratios are expressed with capital stock in the denominator (from Goldsmith: 1985), the ranking of countries remains basically the same; the differences in capital output ratios are not so large as to reverse these rankings determined when GDP is in the denominator. Furthermore, the decline of outward foreign investment stocks, relative to capital, was quite general. To illustrate the order of magnitude involved, the ratio of the stock of outward FDI to total domestic capital in the United Kingdom in 1913 was about 20 per cent; in 1973 the highest level for the industrial countries was 8 per cent, in Switzerland, and those for the United Kingdom and the United States were 4 and 3 per cent, respectively.

One final introductory comparison relates to the fraction of the world's

Table 3.3 Outward FI/GDP, various source countries, twentieth century (per cent)

	1913	1929	1938	1950	1980	1990	1995
Australia			6			15	24
Belgium	65	57	46		17	75	84
Canada	9	21	38	10	12	21	31
France	119	29	33			16	38
Germany	44	6	6		6	22	26
Italy			2		3	11	26
Japan	12	14	16			27	21
Netherlands	58	88	163			63	86
Sweden						27	53
Switzerland	165	99	75			112	159
UK	150	88	84	15	23	63	96
US	9	15	12	6	10	19	33
Average					9	24	33
Index (1938 = 100)	184	78	100			111	167

Sources: FI, from the sources listed in Table 3.1. GDP: for 1913, all countries from Goldsmith (1985), except Netherlands, from Mitchell (1992), and Canada, from Buckley (1985: Table 2.1); 1929 and 1950, Canada from *Historical Statistics of Canada*, series E61, United States data from Goldsmith (1985); 1938, Belgium, Germany, Switzerland, United Kingdom and United States from Goldsmith (1985), and Australia, France, Japan, and Netherlands from Mitchell (1992); 1971–1995, all countries from various *International Financial Statistics Yearbooks*.

Note
The average is the ratio of the sums of FI and of GDP, for those countries for whom the source reports the data for 1980. The average ratios for 1990 and 1995, for all countries in this Table, are 26 and 36, respectively. The index is calculated by dividing the total real FI by the GDP for these countries in Maddison (1995); the 1995 datum was approximated by applying to the 1990 datum the growth of the index of real GDP for the OECD countries, from the OECD's *Main Economic Indicators*, September 1998.

total FI and FDI which is received by third world countries. With regard to foreign direct investment, only about one fifth of total stocks are currently located in the Third World. In other words, FDI is concentrated among the developed industrial countries, not only as sources, but also as recipients. See the first row in Table 3.5. Indeed, the higher income third world areas receive a disproportionate amount of FDI – over half is in Latin America. To analyse trends, we will use GDP as a scalar. The Table again indicates upward trends in FDI into the Third World, relative to income in either sending or receiving countries, for the last decades of the twentieth century. Thus, the stock of FDI in third world countries represented about 2 per cent of the GDP of the source (developed) countries in 1990, and almost 9 per cent of the GDP of the host (developing) countries – the difference is attributable to the higher aggregate income of the industrial countries. Total outward FDI from the source countries at the end of the century was about 12 per cent of their aggregate GDP. It might also be noted that the virtual eruption of investment into mainland China during the 1990s significantly affects the world totals. More than half of the investment into China comes from Hong Kong or countries in south-east

Table 3.4 Outward stock of FDI divided by domestic GDP, twentieth century (per cent)

	1913	1929	1938	1950	1960	1971	1980	1990	1995
Australia					1	1		10	12
Belgium					12	8	5	21	25
Canada	6	7	14	6	6	7	9	15	20
France	23		21		6	5		9	25
Germany	11		1		1	3	4	8	10
Italy					3	3	2	5	10
Japan	11	14	21		1	2	2	7	5
Netherlands	82		91		89	35	25	40	47
Sweden					3	7		22	30
Switzerland					21	38		29	46
UK	49		38	9	15	17	15	23	28
US	7	8	8	4	6	8	8	13	18
Average							6	11	13
Index (1938 = 100)	121		100		49	56	58	108	143

Sources: FDI: 1913–1971, from the sources listed in Table 3.2. 1980–1995, from the *International Financial Statistics Yearbook*, 1998. GDP: as in Table 3.3.

Note
The index is calculated by dividing the total FDI by the GDP for these countries in Maddison (1995); the 1995 datum was approximated by applying to the 1990 datum the growth of the index of real GDP for the OECD countries, from OECD *Main Economic Indicators*, September 1998. The "Average" is the ratio of the sums of FDI and of GDP, for those countries for whom the source reports the data for 1980. The average ratios for 1990 and 1995, for all the countries in this table, are 12 and 16, respectively. Although the methodology utilized by the *International Financial Statistics* differs from that of the *World Investment Report* and the *International Direct Investment Statistics Yearbook*, the only country for which a major difference was noted was the United States; the *International Financial Statistics* providing the (higher, current) replacement values, and the other two sources reporting the accumulated historical cost. For 1990 and 1995, using the lower values would reduce the ratio FDI/GDP for the United States to 7 and 10, while reducing the average ratios to 9 and 10.

Asia which are not typically considered industrial, developed countries. This indicates a limitation of the traditional identification of capital exporters with developed countries.

With regard to the global distribution of total foreign investment, the expanded coverage in the International Monetary Fund's 1998 *International Financial Statistics Yearbook* indicates that several of the wealthy countries are currently net capital importers, and that the principal exporters are Germany, Japan, and Switzerland. A more precise description of the net position of some of the other countries would require attention to details that are of less relevance to us here; there is a question of short-term deposits, the role of key currency countries, intermediate financial centers, and so on. In other words, the deep financial integration of the industrial countries makes it difficult to ask what fraction of world lending is received by the Third World. For these reasons we will not attempt a presentation of world debt paralleling the data on FDI in Table 3.5. Of course, the capital importers receive funds not only from other industrial countries, but also from the Third World. The image of capital flight from an unstable third world country being invested in liquid government debt of a rich industrial country is a convenient example, but the causes of the phenomenon it illustrates are undoubtedly more complex and diverse.

Table 3.5 does report the trend in the ratio of third world debt to its GDP, and this has risen from 5 per cent in 1970 to almost 30 per cent in 1995. As the century ended, the accumulated debt of the Third World was almost double the amount of FDI it had received. In 1971, the accumulated amount of long-term debt was about 10 per cent less than the amount of its inward FDI. Third world debt has risen more in absolute amounts, and at a more rapid rate, than has its inward FDI since 1950. We have not been able to find an authoritative series on total third world debt for the period between World War II and 1971, so we are not able to state when the low point of the ratio debt/GDP was reached. Presumably a major contributor to the lack of information was the unsettled status of the debt of the colonies as they were gaining independence. In addition,

Table 3.5 Selected global and Third World indicators of the size of FDI and debt, 1970–1995 (percentages)

	1970	1980	1985	1990	1995
A. Third World Inward FDI/World Total FDI		22	28	20	28
B. World Outward FDI Stock (Gross)/World GDP		4.9	5.9	8.1	9.9
C. Developed Country Gross Outward FDI/Developed Country GDP		6.5	7.5	9.8	11.8
D. Developed Country Outward FDI (net)/DC GDP = Third World Inward/Developed Country GDP	2.0	1.4	2.3	2.1	3.6
E. Third World Inward FDI/Third World GDP		4.3	8.1	8.7	15.4
F. Third World Inward FDI/Third World GDP	6.0	3.6	n.a.	8.3	15.1
G. Third World Debt/Third World GDP	5.3	15.7	n.a.	28.3	28.3

Sources: A: World Investment Report (1997: Annex Table B.3); B: *World Investment Report* (1997: Annex Table B.6); C: *World Investment Report* (1997: Annex Table B.4) and OECD *National Accounts Volume 1*, 1997, adjusting for Mexico and Turkey; D: FDI for 1971 from OECD (1973), and *World Investment Report* (1997: Annex Table B.3), GDP from OECD *National Accounts Volume 1*, 1997, adjusting for Mexico and Turkey; E: *World Investment Report* (1997: Annex Table B.6); F: FDI for 1971 from OECD (1973), and *World Investment Report* (1997: Annex Table B.3), GDP from *Global Development Finance* (1997: 190), first year is 1970; G: Debt and GDP from *Global Development Finance* (1997: 190), last year is 1996.

Notes
It was not possible to eliminate intermediaries, such as Hong Kong or the tax havens in the Caribbean. The indicator of debt that is used here and in subsequent tables is "Long-term debt"; data on total debt stocks, including short term debt, is about one quarter higher.

this period saw an evolution of the mode of financial transfers to the Third World, with the phasing out of not only foreign aid and grants, but also of the practice of subsidizing loans. Finally, it should be emphasized that most of the developing countries' debt was governmental debt;[2] this accounted for 85 per cent of the accumulated long-term debt in 1996, according to *Global Development Finance* (1998: 160). Although there have been some important cases of third world private enterprises entering into the global bond markets, the order of magnitude of this phenomenon is small.

As a benchmark for future comparisons, Table 3.5 provides for the entire Third World an end-of-century average ratio of total foreign investment to GDP of 50 per cent, while the ratio of FDI/GDP was 15 per cent. This should be kept in mind when looking at the individual country experiences.

Looking at individual source country data for 1990 of this geographical distribution (FDI to advanced industrial versus to third world countries), Table 3.6 illustrates the pattern that most of the continental European

Table 3.6 Indicators of the relative importance of outward stocks of FDI and Third World FDI in 1990, and the geographical distribution of FDI, major OECD countries

	FDI ÷FI	FDI ÷GDP	Third World FDI ÷GDP	Geographical distribution of total FDI:			
				Third World total	Latin America	Africa	Asia
Australia	66	10	1	14	7	0	6
Belgium	28	21					
Canada	71	14	2	14	9	0	4
France	58	9	1	6	2	2	2
Germany	39	9	1	9	6	1	2
Italy	48	5	1	14	10	2	2
Japan	25	10	3	30	13	2	15
Netherlands	64	35	4	11	7	1	3
Sweden	80	21	3	12			
Switzerland	26	27	5	19	15	1	2
United Kingdom	37	22	4	18	9	3	5
United States	68	7	2	23	17	1	6
Average	46	11	2	19	11	1	6

Sources: FDI, FI and GDP are taken from the *International Financial Statistics Yearbook*, 1998. The total and geographical distribution of FDI was calculated from various issues of the *International Direct Investment Statistics Yearbook*. Turkey was included in Asia; to the extent possible, investment into South Africa was excluded. Investment into countries of the Middle East, such as Saudi Arabia and Israel, was not included.

Note
Imprecisions result from the existence of geographically "unallocated" investments, and investments into tax havens such as the Cayman Islands. The average is the ratio of the sums for the individual countries. Blank spaces indicate data are not available.

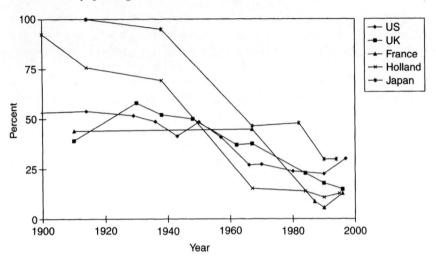

Graph 3.1 FDI to the Third World as percentage of total FDI, by source country

Sources: United Kingdom: Paish (1911), Kindersley (1933), Bank of England (1950 and 1958), *Board of Trade Journal*, 23 September 1980, *British Business*, 2 March 1984, *International Direct Investment Statistics Yearbooks*; France: Woodruff (1967), *International Direct Investment Statistics Yearbooks*; United States: Lewis (1938), US Department of Commerce (1960), *Survey of Current Business*; Netherlands: Gales and Sluyterman (1993), *International Direct Investment Statistics Yearbooks*; Japan: Lewis (1948), OECD (1972), *International Direct Investment Statistics Yearbooks*.

countries had only a small fraction of their total FDI in the Third World, and that this ratio was successively larger in the United Kingdom, Switzerland, the United States, and Japan. Extending that analysis backwards in time, and as a preview of subsequent case studies, Graph 3.1 indicates that the experience of a reduction of the fraction of FDI going to the Third World was quite widespread during the middle third of the twentieth century, and that this ratio may have only recently begun to rise. When investment into the Third World is expressed as a ratio to source country's GDP, the highest fraction obtained in Switzerland, with the Netherlands and the United Kingdom also above average. It will be commented below that much of this investment into the Third World by the Netherlands goes to the Netherlands Antilles, from whence it is reinvested elsewhere.

One of the factors to be taken into consideration is the geographical variable as a determinant of the distribution by source and receiving countries. Table 3.7 suggests some orders of magnitude for the net effects of two influences, what might be termed geographical block and colonial heritage. Thus western Europe dominates in Africa, and the United States in Latin America. Both Japan and Europe have a strong presence in Asia. The dominance of investment by the European metropolitan powers in

Table 3.7 Third World countries: percentage distribution of inward investment stock, by major investing areas, circa 1990

	Western Europe	Former European Colonial power	US	Japan	ASEAN	Reference year
Asia						
China	10		16	7	64	1987
India	70	52	20	$<\frac{1}{2}$		1988
Indonesia	16	6	6	18	12	1988
Korea	13		28	52	4	1988
Malaysia	27	16	6	20	38	1987
Philippines	15		55	14	10	1989
Taiwan	13		32	27	17	1988
Thailand	15		24	37	21	1988
Vietnam	58	22		14	16	1989
Latin America						
Argentina	48		42	1		1989
Brazil	48		28	9		1989
Chile	19		45	3	1	1990
Colombia	17		71	1		1990
Ecuador	19		54	1		1990
Honduras	5		81	7		1989
Mexico	25		63	5		1990
Peru	46		22	3		1990
Venezuela	29		52	4		1990
Africa						
Algeria	37	5				1995
Egypt	50		17	5	2	1995
Ghana	100					1993
Côte d'Ivoire	99			1		1993
Kenya	99			1		1993
Liberia	12		4	84		1993
Nigeria	55		29			1993
Senegal	80	60		20		1993
Tunisia	73	23	1			1994
Tanzania	92	53		3		1993

Sources: UNCTAD *World Investment Directory*, Volumes 1, 4, and 6.

Notes
Blank spaces indicate that the data are not available, not necessarily that the item is zero.

their former colonies tends to be strong, and could be inferred for certain African countries for which the breakdown is not provided in the source.

In light of the emphasis in the OLI model of sectoral specific factors in the determination of FDI stocks, which the case studies in the subsequent chapters will investigate, it is disappointing that information from the source countries on the sectoral breakdown of their total FDI into the Third World is quite scarce. Indeed, the only source of such a breakdown is OECD

Table 3.8 Sectoral distribution of FDI into the Third World by source countries, 1967

	Total (million US$)	Agric.	Percentage distribution Mining	Petrol.	Manuf.	Services
Total	33,135	6	11	33	29	21
Australia	100	30	15	10	24	21
Belgium	613	10	13	2	53	22
Canada	1,454	0	15	2	17	66
France	2,689	14	14	32	27	13
Germany	1,018	1	5	4	83	7
Italy	696	1	3	27	63	6
Japan	700	3	8	11	61	16
Netherlands	1,694	1	1	77	16	4
Sweden	180	0	37	0	59	3
Switzerland	565	0	2	0	51	46
UK	6,582	15	8	31	23	23
US	16,703	3	12	38	26	20

Source: Author's calculations based on OECD (1972).

(1972); its data for 1967 are portrayed in Table 3.8. Petroleum received about one third of total FDI; the share of manufacturing was about one quarter of total FDI, and services was one fifth. These ratios typify the FDI portfolio of the three biggest investors of that time – the United States, United Kingdom, and France – while for the other countries a larger variety of patterns is evident. Apparently the only source country regularly publishing this breakdown is the United States; its data will be analysed below.

FDI in services

The fastest growing area for FDI is the service sector. There is no widely accepted precise definition of services; one characteristic is that there is no physical product changing hands. Examples are wholesale and retail trade, communications, banking and finance, business services such as legal, consulting, accounting, and personal services such as tourism, education and health. The management of railroads and other public utilities was an important service activity in the past. The presence of holding companies has been constant.

According to UNCTC (1989: 8), services accounted for about 20 per cent of world FDI stocks in the early 1950s, about 25 per cent in the 1970s and about 40 per cent in the mid-1980s. About two thirds of the growth of service FDI occurred in finance and trade-related activities during that decade. This probably underestimates the importance of the globalization of services, as joint ventures, franchising or other types of sub-contracting characterize parts of this sector, especially such visible examples as fast food restaurants and hotel chains. Nor is this all horizontal investment, with just another branch of a bank or real estate office in another country.

Companies in major growth areas such as automobiles and electronics need wholesale offices and elaborate retail chains in the economies to which the firms wish to export their products.

Several factors explain the growth in service FDI. Easing of restrictions in host countries is obviously important, particularly in the area of banking and financial services. More broadly the communications revolution facilitates the flow of information which is essential in these activities. In most industrial countries the service sector is the fastest growing sector, so it is not surprising that foreign investment in this area is also thriving.

One question that arises is whether or not this trend towards a concentration of FDI in services also occurs in the Third World. With regard to one of the source countries, the United States, it is the case that the share of services in FDI into the Third World closely parallels that to the industrial countries, from 1929 up to the end of the century.[3] This was not altogether expected, because during that time period the share of total US FDI accounted for by the Third World fell from half to one quarter. However, it is the case that banking and finance in the Caribbean tax havens (Bermuda, Netherlands Antilles, etc.) comprise one third of US service investment in the Third World. Because these areas are not the final users, it could be argued that some adjustment should be made. However, a similar adjustment would have to be made for non-final users in the industrial world (Switzerland, Luxembourg, United Kingdom, etc.), and resolution of this problem is beyond our interests and abilities. Finally, it could be noted that this author has not found similarly disaggregated data for Japan.

What do the data from the host countries say? One convenient compilation is the several volumes of the *World Investment Directory*, which classifies according to three sectors, primary secondary and tertiary. The average fraction of total FDI represented by services around 1990 are: Africa, 40 per cent; Asia, 29 per cent; Latin America, 34 per cent – weighting each country equally. Moreover, this host country data certainly do not indicate a strong increase in the share of services, as was indicated by the global figures cited above. Perhaps the growth is limited to the financial sector, which is not reported by the host countries.

Foreign Portfolio Equity Investment

During the last decade of the twentieth century, a new mode of foreign investment began to have an important impact on selected international markets in the Third World. Called Foreign Portfolio Equity Investment (FPEI), it consists of purchases of non-controlling amounts of equity investment through a variety of new financial instruments. Because of their recent introduction, these forms of investing are still relatively small in aggregate, and concentrated in a few countries. Because they indicate new directions for the global marketplace, it is worth describing them.

The description that follows is taken from the 1997 *World Investment Report,* which is one of the few treatments of the subject.

Conceptually, the FPEI is in the middle between FDI and portfolio investment, in that it is non-controlling and equity investment. More tellingly, it is generally believed that those who invest in these markets are making short-term commitments, which would not involve technology transfer. The mode of investment involves individuals channeling their savings through institutional investors such as pension funds or country funds, and may well involve transference of ownership without a flow of currency across borders. Yet certainly they benefit the host country by increasing total funding for investments. The FPEI has grown as a result of financial liberalization in a relatively small subset of third world countries, which are often referred to as emerging markets. Indeed, outside observers often believe that if a country is willing to allow this type of investment, then the economic and political authorities in the country are making an unusual commitment to financial openness and economic stability.

Over the decade 1986–1995, about US$150 billion was generated in FPEI in emerging markets, according to the 1997 *World Investment Report.* However, the increase in the stock of FDI for these countries was more than three times as large, and the total increase in Third World debt was over US$1 trillion, according to the *World Debt Tables.* So the significance of FPEI is mostly symbolic, in the most aggregate sense. However, for countries such as Mexico, Thailand, Argentina, Brazil and Indonesia the relative importance of the FPEI has been much larger. At the time of this writing, the big question is whether or not the emerging market economies will be able to sustain the short-term volatility that appears to be endemic with this type of investment. History affords several examples of other innovations which have failed.

British investment

Great Britain was the world's most important source of foreign investment at the start of the last century, remaining so until the Second World War. The measurement and analysis of her investment position began with the pre-World War I work of George Paish, which will also serve as the point of departure for this discussion. His total of £4 billion for British capital overseas at the start of the war has been widely utilized by several generations of both scholars and polemicists, in spite of the methodological drawbacks that he himself acknowledged.[4] What is perhaps the most thorough recent study of British overseas investments before World War I, Davis and Huttenback (1986: 41), presents a range of estimates of the accumulated total from £4.1 to £6.6 billion, seeming to prefer the lower number. Platt (1986) argued strenuously for a downward revision of Paish's estimate by almost one fourth; responding to him, no less an authority than Feinstein (1990) has reaffirmed the essential validity of Paish's original estimates.

This total for overseas capital of £4 billion is equivalent to US$20 billion. The total for British FDI used above in Table 3.3 is US$6.5 billion, or less than half that amount. Both the United Kingdom and France had less than half their overseas capital in FDI, with the fraction being smaller if we omit FDI in railroads. Unfortunately, the source for the series on FDI from the source countries, Dunning (1983), does not provide any details permitting further disaggregations, and so we turn to the original sources for its construction.

Table 3.9 presents the data for the first half century of total, sectoral, and regional distributions of British overseas capital. Loans to governments and municipalities in 1913 accounted for about 30 per cent of total investment, and capital in railroads accounted for about 35 per cent. Thus the category we label "other businesses" has the remaining third; its total of £1 billion is basically consistent with Dunning's FDI total mentioned above, attributing the difference to some direct investment in railroads. It should be clear that it is particularly difficult to identify who controls railroads; candidates are the directors, the stock holders, the banks that channel new loans to them, or the host country's government which subsidizes them and controls their rates. Certainly a significant part of the disagreement about the relative distribution between portfolio and direct investment revolved around the issue of control of these railroad investments. A similar problem, of smaller magnitude, pertains to investment in public utilities. Beyond that, the short-cut identification of non-railroad foreign business investment with non-railroad foreign direct investment appears satisfactory, and opens the door to further analysis. The geographical breakdown is shown below. Using Stone (1999), the disaggregation of accumulated capital in 1914 in the private non-railroad sector in the Third World is: utilities, 22 per cent; finance and shipping, 29 per cent; raw materials 33 per cent and manufacturing industries only 16 per cent. The next year for which a sectoral disaggregation of British FDI into the Third World can be attempted is 1967, using OECD (1972: 13) – and manufacturing still accounts for less than a quarter of the total, whereas petroleum is now over 30 per cent. With regard to the mode of financing British capital abroad, Stone (1999) indicates that debentures were 68 per cent of the total raised over 1865–1914, with the following sectoral breakdowns: railroads, 69 per cent; utilities, 62 per cent; finance, 27 per cent; raw materials, 18 per cent; industry, 38 per cent. Referring to 1929, Kindersley (1931: 380) reported that share capital accounted for more than half of capital for all companies, and more than two thirds for companies outside of railroads.

Table 3.9 also reveals two important trends, the dramatic decline of the nominal value of capital in railroads, and a subsequent decline in loans to governments.[5] It turns out that the amount of funds in "other business"

Table 3.9 British capital overseas, twentieth century (million current £)

	1913	1930	1938	1950	1957	1962
Total	3,714	3,185	3,545	2,019	2,102	
Government & Municipals	1,107	1,440	1,521	789	707	
Railways	1,521	788	836	180	75	
Other Business	1,086	957	1,188	1,050	1,320	4,515
Europe, US, Japan	992	389	525	371	357	
Settler Colonies	969	1,287	1,273	762	771	
Africa	} 997	105	179	179	266	
Asia		683	598	234	229	
Latin America	756	662	793	297	140	

Sources: 1910, Paish (1911); 1913, Paish (1914); 1930, Kindersley (1933); 1938, Bank of England (1950); 1950 and 1957, Bank of England (1958); 1962, *Board of Trade Journal,* 23 September 1970, and Bank of England, *Quarterly Bulletin* March 1964, p. 32.

Notes
Settler colonies: Australia, New Zealand, Canada, and South Africa. The distribution for railways in 1950 is estimated using that for 1948. The 1962 data include oil companies, of the value of £1,110 million. No effort was made to assign the "non-classifiable" investments for 1950 and 1957.

investments remained rather stable in comparison, until after the Second World War. Thus the most important contributor to the decline in the British foreign investment for the first half of the century was the displacement of railroad investments. Over half of those railroad investments had been placed in the United States and Canada, whose residents were gradually purchasing these bonds from holders overseas. India, Argentina, and other third world areas had a bit over one third of British railway investments before the Great War; their stories are related in the following chapters. The message from this data is that the greatest single part of the decline in British capital is a function of relations between the United Kingdom and other industrial countries.

The distinction between direct and portfolio investment has played an important role in discussions of British economic performance over the century, with some commentators interpreting the high fraction in portfolio investments as revealing a lack of entrepreneurial, risk-taking behavior, and thereby a flaw in the character of British capitalists, contributing to the country's relative decline. An important contribution to a revisionist view was provided by the recalculation of the relative importance of direct and portfolio investment of Svedberg (1978), finding the former to be much larger than had been generally accepted. As noted elsewhere, the work of Mira Wilkins and others on Free Standing Companies also suggest that these portfolio investments reflect entrepreneurial, risk-taking behavior. This emphasis on the importance of railroads in the emerging economies of a century ago further suggests that the major decline of British foreign investment was not directly attributable to weak entrepreneurial spirit. Nevertheless, we leave for others the evaluation of the importance of this finding in the broader historical debate about British capitalism.

Trends in British direct investment

The trends of British FDI are presented in Table 3.10, accepting the category of business investment as a useful approximation to FDI, and omitting railroads. These data suggest that the Third World accounted for a rising fraction of British FDI up to around 1950, when reaching almost two thirds of total. Since then, its share had fallen rather severely to only about 22 per cent in 1981; the OECD data in the *International Direct Investments Yearbooks* indicate that the Third World's share of total British FDI has continued to fall since then. That British investors have recently preferred Europe and the United States over the Third World reflects the

Table 3.10 United Kingdom: non-railroad FDI, twentieth century (million current £)

	1910	1930	1938	1948	1962	1971	1981
Total	884	957	1,198	921	3,405	6,667	28,545
Europe, US, Japan	136	154	293	139	757	2,267	14,778
Settler Colonies	397	295	232	218	1,403	2,616	7,141
Third World	351	489	536	498	1,230	1,796	6,239
as per cent of total	40	51	45	54	36	27	22
Geographical Distribution:							
Africa	49	51	123	116	412	595	1,911
Asia	151	282	198	209	541	713	2,617
Latin America	151	157	215	163	277	489	1,711
Political Status:							
Colonies	108	251	306	259	928		
Independent	243	238	230	239	302		

Sources: Author's calculations. 1910, from Paish (1911); 1930, from Kindersley (1933); 1938, Kindersley (1939) and Bank of England (1950); 1962, from *Board of Trade Journal*, 23 September 1970; 1971 and 1981, from *British Business*, 2 March 1984.

Notes
Data for 1910 is used here instead of the previous table's 1913, because Paish did not provide as thorough a disaggregation, by sector and country, for the latter year. Non-Railroad Business Investments for the years 1910–1948, calculated by subtracting government loans and railroad capital from total capital. Oil, banks, and insurance are excluded from the FDI data from 1962 on. The value of overseas oil companies in 1962 was £1,110 million, according to Bank of England, *Quarterly Bulletin* March 1964, p. 32. The total value of FDI in 1981, including these three sectors, was £43 billion; its distribution was quite similar to that indicated here. The Third World's share of British FDI in 1994 was about 18 per cent, according to OECD *International Direct Investments Statistics Yearbook* 1995. The geographical distribution of railroad capital in 1938 was approximated using also the breakdown given in Kindersley (1937); the totals for the two years were almost identical. The allocation of investment between Africa and Asia in 1930 and 1938 is imprecise due to Kindersley's category of "other".

general trend among industrial countries. The data also indicate that fewer funds were invested in the colonies than in Latin America and other independent countries before World War I, but that subsequently investment into the latter areas stagnated, while the amounts in the dependent colonies increased, tripling in nominal terms, although starting off from a low initial level.

Also worthy of note is the nominal decline in British FDI (excluding railroads) in the major settler colonies of Canada, Australia, New Zealand and South Africa during the first half of the century, and a robust recovery since then – which disappears when the comparison is made to the host country GDPs. We argue in the corresponding country studies that the first phase reflected growth in local expertise, displacing the foreign entrepreneurs. In stark contrast to the decline in FDI in several parts of the Third World after about 1960, this is generally not attributable to nationalist policies, and only in Canada can a role be identified for a substitution of British by American investors.

The disaggregation of British FDI by regions and political categories, leads to some interesting comparisons when weighted by the level of British GDP; these are presented in Table 3.11. The spectacular decline in FI/GDP, from 155 per cent in 1910 to 19 per cent in 1948, is mirrored by the decline in FDI/GDP from 43 per cent in 1910 to 9 per cent in 1948. There is reason to believe that measurement problems understate FDI in 1948, subse-

Table 3.11 Britain's outward stock of overseas investments as a percentage of British GDP, 1910–1994

	1910	1930	1938	1948	1962	1971	1981a	1981b	1994
FI/GDP: Total	155	75	71	19	31				
FDI/GDP:									
Total	43	23	24	9	13	13	11	17	26
Third World	17	12	11	5	5	4	2	3	5
Colonies	5	6	6	3	4				
Independent	12	6	5	2	1				
Settler Colonies	19	7	5	2	6	5	3	4	3

Sources: FI and FDI from the sources in Table 3.10; 1994, from OECD *International Direct Investments Statistics Yearbook* 1995. GDP from Mitchell (1988) and the *International Financial Statistics Yearbook*. The FI for 1962 is taken from the Bank of England's *Quarterly Bulletin*, March 1964, and refers to private long term capital overseas.

Notes
The Settler Colonies are Canada, Australia, New Zealand and South Africa. Thus, our category of (other) Colonies includes India and what Davis and Huttenback (1986) refer to as the Dependent Colonies. There is a significant methodological break in the coverage of total overseas capital before and after 1957, so the series is not continued here past 1962. The two columns for 1981 correspond to FDI without, and with oil, which is about one fourth of total British FDI. The 1994 data would appear to include oil, judging by a comparison of the data for 1987 in *British Business* 29 September 1989 and the OECD publication. The breakdown of British investment in Africa, between South Africa and the rest, was approximated by this author.

quently the data indicate that this ratio stayed low. It is quite evident in the Table that British direct investment into the Third World has always been small compared to the size of the total British economy. The ratio of British FDI into the Third World divided by British GDP declined rather continuously between its pre-World War I high point, and the low level reached around 1970–80, from which it has increased marginally since.

A census of British capital overseas was taken in 1962, replacing the previous series which had been produced by Kindersley and the Bank of England. Comparison of the new data for 1962 with the previous stock data for 1957 and certain balance of payments flows suggests that the aggregate data from the previous Bank of England series was low by between one third and one half of the new total. Nevertheless, adjusting upward the mid-century ratios for FDI/GDP in Table 3.11 by those fractions does not alter the message that British investment into the Third World at that time was a much smaller fraction of total GDP than it had been at the beginning of the century.

French overseas investment

France had the second largest overseas investment portfolio in 1914, after the United Kingdom. At that time, Europe was her main investment area, and the biggest single overseas market for French capital had been Russia. About one fifth of French capital was in Latin America, only one tenth in the French empire, and one twentieth in the Ottoman empire. Inside the Empire, northern Africa – Algeria, Tunisia and Morocco – received more than all of sub-Saharan Africa and Indo-China combined. The First World War represented a major blow to French overseas investment, not only because of the repudiation of the Russian debt by the new Soviet government, but also because payment on French bonds was set in nominal terms, while prices in France rose by a factor of five. Colonial areas received a growing fraction of investment in the inter-war period, but after the late 1950s, Europe again retained preference.

At the beginning of the century, over half of overseas capital was composed of loans to governments, and railroads absorbed another 15 per cent, leaving about one third to other private enterprise stocks and bonds (France, Ministère des Finances 1902). This distribution is similar to that of Great Britain, and distinct from those in the United States and, presumably, Germany, the Netherlands and Belgium. However, just as research on Free Standing Companies and Investment Groups is forcing us to revise our interpretation of British financial market data, suggesting that it previously understated the importance of entrepreneurial investments, so this categorization of the French data may also be in need of revision. One additional problem is the need to re-evaluate the role of the French government, both as subsidizer of private business, and in its own role as entrepreneur. Unfortunately, that work has not yet appeared. In its absence, we will treat business investment as direct investment, whether its financing came from stocks, bonds, or government transfers.

A broad outline of the trends of French overseas investment over the century is displayed in Table 3.12. In 1990, about half of the stock of French overseas investment was direct investment as that term is currently understood, and the Third World then received only about 5 per cent of that direct investment. Neither the availability nor the consistency of the data on most of the rest of the century is good, but the following comments attempt to describe several parts of the historical picture.

The value of the foreign investment, at constant prices, fell between pre-World War I and either 1929 or 1938, by a larger percentage than had occurred in the United Kingdom. The biggest decline was in Russia – complete default, and in the rest of Europe. The real value of the funds in what is now called the Third World also fell by more than half, which, being a smaller drop than that of French investments in Europe, meant that the Third World's share of the accumulated French foreign investment rose from about one quarter in 1914 to over half in 1938.[6] There was a decline in Latin America's share of French capital, in both absolute and relative terms. The real value of FI and FDI in the empire rose after 1914. Thus, for the first half of the century, there was a marked upward trend in the proportion of overseas assets placed in the empire, rising from 10 per cent in 1914 to 30–40 per cent in 1929, and 40–50 per cent in 1939 (Marseille 1984: 103). The most important political figure in this redirection of French investment towards the empire was the Minister of the Colonies, Albert Sarraut, whose developmentalist rhetoric of *mise en valeur* defined French thinking from the early 1920s until decolonization began.

Effective political movements against the French had begun in Indo-China before the beginning of World War II. Armed struggle there and in Algeria discouraged post-war private investment in these two areas, which had been the largest recipients of French capital. Thus for about a decade after the Second World War, the major location of new French colonial investment activity was in sub-Saharan Africa. The combination of decolonization and France's entry into the European Common Market combined to reorient the country's investment away from the former empire, while also reducing its overall ranking worldwide.

An indication of the dramatic size of government transfers to the colonies is provided in Table 3.13. The most famous of these programs was known as FIDES. These were similar to what later became known as foreign aid projects. An important political difference was that the recipients were colonies, not independent countries. It could also be assumed that the FIDES involved more outlays for infrastructure, compared to many aid programs which were oriented towards immediate consumption needs. The major increase in these programs occurred after World War II, when it was much higher than the increase in private investment. Their existence and magnitude indicates one problem in applying a term such

Table 3.12 French overseas investment, twentieth century (million US$ in 1900 prices)

	1900	1914	1929	1938	1958	1960	1967	1971	1980	1990	1995
Foreign Investment	5,800	7,165	1,681	2,131						10,682	19,370
FI-Third World	1,100	2,732		1,273							
FI-Africa	400	633		553							
FI-Asia	50	831		498							
FI-Latin America	650	1,267		221							
FI-Empire		619	968	1,141							
FI-Aust, NZ, SA	350	238		55							
FDI-Total		1,386		1,384		964	1,249	1,247	2,079	6,153	8,810
FDI-Third World		1,589		1,118			560			398	
FDI-Africa		484					360			105	
FDI-Asia		286					102			139	
FDI-Latin America	440	879		131			97			153	
FDI-Empire		300	546	668	971						
FDI-Non-Empire	680	1,290		450							

Sources: FI: 1900, 1914, 1938 total FI and its geographical distribution from Woodruff (1967); 1929, Staley (1935: 527); the series on FI-Empire from Marseille (1984: 105), summing data on funds to Colonial Societies and loans to governments; 1990 and 1995 from the *International Financial Statistics Yearbook*, 1998. FDI totals: 1914–1960, Dunning (1983: 87); 1967 and 1971, Stopford and Dunning (1983: Annex Table 1.2); 1980–1995, from *World Investment Report* (1997: Annex Table B.4). FDI for the Third World is the sum of the sub-totals for empire and non-empire for 1914 and 1938, and for 1967 and 1990 the sum of those for Africa, Asia (excluding Japan and Australia New Zealand), and Latin America. FDI: for Latin America, 1900–1938, Rippy (1948: 59, 63, 67; for Africa and Asia in 1914, summing the non-empire data listed below, and the breakdown of empire investments (Marseille 1977: 105) according to the distribution in Marseille (1977: 388). FDI in the non-empire parts of the Third World, sums the above data for Latin America with amounts for Turkey, Egypt and China. Turkey in 1900 from Pamuk (1987: Table A3.3); 1913, from Pamuk (1987: 66); 1938, from Lewis (1948: 305). Egypt – corresponding to the years 1902, 1914, 1933, Crouchley (1936: 48, 172, 95). China from Hou (1965: 17, 20 and 13). FDI in the Empire 1914–1958: summing the sub-periods from Marseille (1984, 105). FDI for Africa, Asia and Latin America: 1967 from OECD (1972); 1990 from OECD *International Direct Investment Statistics Yearbook* 1996.

Notes

Data were converted to dollars at the current exchange rate, and deflated using the US GNP deflator. Both Woodruff and Dunning provide data from a broad set of sources, without always specifying the exact reference. The most obvious inconsistency in these figures is that of FI and FDI in Latin America. Probably the most important inconsistencies are between the world total and that of the Third World in 1914, and the world total and that of the empire for 1960 and 1958, respectively. As discussed in the text, it seems unlikely that this could be explained simply as Dunning using a strict definition of FDI, having excluded loans to private businesses.

Table 3.13 Accumulated French capital in the Empire (million gold francs)

	1914	1929	1939	1958
Marseille (1984: 105)				
Total	6,493	9,025	13,753	25,743
Budget Transfers	2,424	2,656	3,195	} 19,359
Loans to Colonial Gov'ts	2,098	2,774	6,163	
Private	1,971	3,595	4,395	6,384
Sum of Private and Loans	4,069	6,369	10,558 (1940)	
Marseille (1977: 388)				
Total	4,161		20,964	
Private	1,276		15,979	
North Africa	854		9,921	
Indo-China	231		2,793	
Sub-Saharan Africa	191		2,793	
Public	2,884		4,986	
North Africa	1,713		2,393	
Indo-China	426		1,007	
Sub-Saharan Africa	746		1,586	

Sources: Marseille (1977: 388); Marseille (1984: 105).

Notes
Sub-Saharan Africa includes AOF, AEF, Madagascar and "others". The totals for 1940 in Marseille's 1977 book are here converted from 1940 Francs to 1914 Francs by dividing by 14. For the period 1940–1958, the datum in the table in the 1984 book is interpreted here to combine both loans and budgetary transfers; the presentation in that book is somewhat ambiguous. The data taken from the 1984 book are added together without any correction for losses, repayments, or depreciation. Marseille acknowledges the roughness of this procedure. The series for private investments is capital issues by colonial societies (*Émissions des sociétés coloniales*), implying that reinvested corporate profits and settler capital are not included. As discussed in the text, several alternative estimates are available: Public funds to Algeria in 1914 might be FF2000 million instead of Marseille's FF1181 million, according to Meynier (1981: 63). The datum on French private capital in Algeria in 1914 appears to exclude settler capital, while that for 1940 seems to include them, making their direct comparison invalid. In the section on Algeria in Chapter 4, it is argued that settler capital was three or four times the size of capital raised from France. Southworth (1931: 99) estimated total outstanding market value of French colonial stocks and bonds in 1929 – public and private sectors, Algeria included – at FF16 billion, or the equivalent of FF3.3 billion gold.

as capital abroad in the different contexts of France and Britain. In principle, funds for FIDES involved a balance of payments outflow, but no obligation for repayment. In a British or American context, capital abroad would normally be identified with private capital or loans to the government.

Before World War II, Sub-Saharan Africa received a very small amount of French overseas capital, and even a small amount of colonial capital, however defined, as indicated in Table 3.2 and Table 3.13. Although this large and diverse area did not receive a significant amount of foreign investment in absolute or even per capita terms, we will argue in Chapter 5 that this is not true when measured against other indicators of the size of the national economies.

There were important differences in the operation and vision of French and British colonialists in Africa, which left imprints after independence. The general case of the French colonies in sub-Saharan Africa is that the break with the mother country was less complete. Incorporation into the Franc zone meant utilizing a common currency, thus maintaining the link to the metropole and minimizing the role of country-specific central banks. On a broader scale the granting of independence occurred without the violence which accompanied several British and Portuguese ex-colonies. At an official level, the links between the newly independent governments and France were warmer than in the case of Britain – or indeed Portugal. This led to a situation where much of the foreign investment in the newly independent countries involved French government parastatal entities.

Issues in the measurement of French colonial investment

One of the complicating factors affecting the study of French foreign investment is inflation. This is typically handled by deflating the flows during each period, say a year, by that year's price index, and summing the deflated components. Because of the importance of inflation in France, this procedure is well established, and has in fact been followed by the vast majority of writers, although one's faith in data deflated by a factor of 154 is inevitably lessened.[7]

A more substantive issue is the one treated immediately above, the greater variety of modes of transferring capital overseas, especially to colonies. We have also seen that the existence of expatriate investment complicates interpretation of the data. For example, in later chapters it will be noted below that the amount of investment by French settlers in Algeria was not only larger than the amount of capital investment sent there from France, but was probably larger than the amount of French investment in rest of the empire. However, our data will suggest that French settlers in Indo-China did not dominate that area's economy as much as did those in North Africa.

The best single source for analyses of the French overseas empire[8] is the work of Jacques Marseille (1974, 1977, 1984). One important but problematic source is a survey that was carried out for the Vichy government in the middle of World War II, one of whose goals was to provide a high total of French investment abroad (*"des chiffres aussi élevés que possible"*) to strengthen their bargaining position in case of a German victory in the war. Marseille (1977: 388) presented a total for French private capital in the empire in 1940, based primarily on the Vichy survey, that was double the estimate of business capital subsequently reported in his doctoral dissertation, (Marseille 1984: 105). Unfortunately, the source for the latter, the *Annuaire Desfossés*, only permits geographical separation of Indo-China, and most pointedly not of Algeria, which alone accounted for over 40 per cent of the total in Marseille (1977). The data on Indo-China in the Vichy study has subsequently been studied by Brocheux and Hémery (1995), whose results indicate that the amount of investments from retained profits was two thirds again higher than simple equity flows, that non-corporate investment was about half of equity, that the exaggeration due to the price index was of the order of 16 per cent. The total value of French investment in Indo-China in 1940 was over three times the value measured by capital emissions. This latter is the measurement most often appearing in the literature, used for Indo-China by Bernard (1934), Callis (1942), and Lewis (1948).

The total for French capital in the empire in 1938, provided by Lewis (1948: 304) is only one tenth the corresponding total for the French empire in 1940, given by Marseille (1977: 388). While not denying an element of exaggeration by the Vichy administration, our explanation for the differences between the totals places more emphasis on factors such as expatriate investment and reinvested earnings. As such, the preferred vision of total FDI would be closer to the totals reported in Marseille (1977).

The United States

At the beginning of the twentieth century the United States had the largest stock of inward foreign investment in the world. Its outward foreign direct investment was geographically concentrated into its neighbors – Canada, Mexico, Cuba and other places in the Caribbean. The various estimates included in Lewis (1938) suggest that there were small amounts of portfolio investment in the early years, but direct investment always dominated; indeed, until the 1980s. The United States emerged from the First World War as a net creditor, and of course played an important role as an exporter of non-commercial capital to governments during and after the two world wars.

The basic quantitative description of US investment is relatively familiar, and was outlined in the tables presented earlier in this chapter. The long run pattern of outward US investment, relative to GDP, is traced in Graph 3.2. In addition to the low amount of portfolio compared to direct investment during the first half of the century, also familiar is the mid-century decline – and a rather striking increase after 1980 – in portfolio investment. In comparison, the ratio of FDI/GDP appears to rise only slightly. These results occur using either US GDP or the US capital stock in the denominator.

It is curious that, although the work reported by Lewis and others popularized the distinction between portfolio and direct foreign investment, the US government in its official publications has not utilized the category

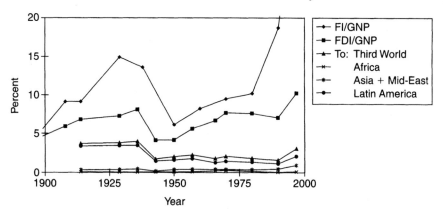

Graph 3.2 United States: foreign investment/GDP, twentieth century

Sources: FI: 1897–1929, Lewis (1938); FI: 1950, 1960 and 1970, sums FDI and loans – from various *Survey of Current Business*; 1980–1997, summing FDI and Portfolio investment from *International Financial Statistics Yearbook*, 1998. FDI: 1897–1935, Lewis (1938); 1938, Dunning (1983); 1950 and 1957, United States Department of Commerce (1960); 1966, US Department of Commerce (1975a); 1970–1997, various *Survey of Current Business*, using the "historic cost" valuation. GNP or GDP: 1900–1960, *Historical Statistics of the United States* (1975b); 1970–1997, *International Financial Statistics Yearbook*, 1998.

"portfolio investment" for decades. For private assets abroad not classified as direct investment, the *Survey of Current Business* lists amounts of foreign securities (stocks and bonds), claims reported by banks, and claims reported by non-banking concerns. These categories include items such as trade credits which should not be considered portfolio investment. Recall also that the debt crises of the 1980s and 1990s involved excessive short-term bank debts, which had escaped surveillance by officials from the IMF and the US Treasury precisely because they were short term. In the United States, as in many other capital exporting countries, the total of overseas assets is more than double that of foreign direct investment.

The evolution of total FDI/GDP for the United States is evidently the result of distinct geographical trends. Investment into Europe and Japan has grown dramatically since 1950, while that into the settler areas of Canada, Australia, New Zealand and South Africa has stayed relatively constant, as a fraction of US GDP. The Third World passed from being the most important area for US investment before World War I, to the smallest area in the 1970s; since then its share has started to rise somewhat. The trends in US FDI into the Third World are dominated by that of FDI into Latin America and the Caribbean, as shown in Graph 3.2. Note the declining relative importance of this area after the 1930s, and its very recent recovery in the 1990s. Neither Africa nor Asia has ever received a significant fraction of US overseas FDI, and even the Middle East with all its petroleum never accounted to more than about 6 per cent of the total US overseas stock. The recent wave of liberalization of FDI regulations has stimulated US FDI not only to Latin America, but also to Asia, including China. Nevertheless, the amounts are not large, compared either to total FDI or to US GDP.

Of the various investing countries, the United States provides the best historical data on FDI stocks, disaggregated by sectors. Using this, Table 3.14 reveals several important trends in the relative shares of US FDI into the Third World over the century. FDI in agriculture has declined, falling from one fifth of the total in 1929 to an insignificant fraction today. Mining was over one third of the total before the Great War, and is now less than 5 per cent. The series for petroleum and manufacturing present peaks in the mid-1950s and 1982, respectively. Unfortunately, the reported growth of the finance sector distorts the other results in the Table, as over three fourths of that amount has been placed in tax havens in the Caribbean and elsewhere, from which it was evidently been rein-vested, but the US Department of Commerce does not report its ultimate location. At the start of the century, the "other services" sector includes important amounts of railroads, particularly in Mexico. Beyond the issue of whether funds in railroads should even be considered direct invest-ment, the early decline in the relative importance of "other services" is clearly exaggerated by the inclusion of that particular item. Finally, we note the temporary distortions in petroleum in the mid-1970s, and in the finance sector in the early 1980s, are presumably to be associated with actions taken by the OPEC countries in the first case, and with the third world debt crisis in the second case.

The marked decline in the share of US investments into the Third World experienced by two raw materials categories – agriculture and mining, together with the beginnings of a decline in petroleum, will be explained as corresponding to the product cycle phenomenon referred to as the Investment Development Path. Of course the shifts in the distribu-tion of the investment of even the major source country do not necessarily imply similar changes in domestic ownership ratios in the host countries, for which more detailed analysis of individual cases will be presented in the forthcoming chapters. It should also be noted that the rising share of manufacturing FDI causes the sectoral profile of US FDI in the Third World to mirror fairly well that of US FDI in the developed industrial countries, as far as can be ascertained – given the importance of the tax havens. Two further comments merit inclusion. First, Africa and many parts of Asia have never received much US FDI, and certainly have only minimal amounts of manufacturing FDI from that country. Secondly, we are unable to judge the relative importance of two distinct motivations for the rise in manufacturing FDI – whether it is market seeking or resource seeking, in terms of Dunning's terminology. While US manufacturing firms in Europe and Japan are presumably producing for the local markets, the hypothesis would be that there has been a change in

Table 3.14 Sectoral distribution of US FDI in the Third World, twentieth century

	Ag	Mining	Petrol	Manuf.	Services	
					Finance	Other
1897	18	24	7	1	50	
1914	18	39	13	3	26	
1929	21	20	19	8	32	
1936	14	22	19	8	37	
1943	14	13	24	12	36	
1950	10	13	38	15	25	
1957	6	13	46	14	2	19
1966	1	12	36	25	9	17
1977	1	6	5	39	32	17
1982	1	4	40	44	−4	16
1989	1	3	15	38	31	12
1994	0	3	13	28	38	17
1998		3	11	27	38	21

Sources: Author's calculations, based on Lewis (1938), US Department of Commerce (1960, 1975a, 1981, 1986, 1991, 1998), and the September 1999 *Survey of Current Business*.

Notes
The measure used was the "Direct Investment Position," and the firms are "non-bank affiliates of non-bank parents." The geographical distribution of this measure for agriculture and mining in 1989 and 1994 was estimated by using the ratio of Third World/Total for Assets. The 1998 datum for agriculture and minerals is assumed to sum to 3 per cent, these are not separately listed in the *Survey of Current Business*.

perspective for US businesses in the Third World, for whom the attractions of price competitive export platforms are increasingly important. The quantitative dimensions of this phenomenon are not yet known.

Belgium

Belgium's colonial experience was limited to one area, the Congo, more familiar as Zaire, but currently named the Democratic Republic of the Congo. Beginning its colonial life as the personal property of King Leopold II, the Congo was formally ceded to Belgium as a colony in 1908, near the end of Leopold's life. After World War I, the adjoining ex-German colonies of Ruanda and Burundi were appended to it. Although Belgian dominance of the formal economy was as complete as that of probably any other European colony, European settlers were of comparatively small importance, and the major European activity was export-oriented mining.

Data on Belgium's overseas investments are scarce; we do know from the tables presented earlier in this chapter that the ratio FI/GDP before World War I was relatively high, in comparison to the other European countries. Staley (1935: 534) comments that Belgium served as an entrepôt for funds from other countries (especially France), and that Russia was a favored pre-war investment area. The corresponding table in Lewis

(1948) indicates that the Congo had one quarter of Belgium's total overseas capital in 1938, an amount equaled by Latin America, where it was concentrated in public utilities in Argentina. Schröter (1998: 325) argues that Belgium was an attractive place for entrepreneurs to raise capital because of its liberal corporate law, low taxes, and a well-developed financial market. He uses these aspects to explain the existence of a large number of Free Standing Companies.[9] With regard to the latter, Schröter reports that Europe had over half of Belgian investment by 1930, and that Latin America hosted almost as many as did the Congo. He also acknowledges, without further attempt at explanation, the contrast with the case of the Netherlands, a country with similar structural characteristics, but most of whose investment was in its colony. Furthermore, that author's reading of the evidence is that the fraction of Belgian firms active in the Congo that should be classified as Free Standing Companies was no different than in other third world areas. The Belgian companies in the Congo were concentrated into four financial groups, and the Belgian government was itself a major shareholder in the largest, the Société Générale.

Belgium, together with Luxembourg, retains its major role as an international financial center. Although it is difficult to identify the geographical distribution of its current FI or FDI, the supposition is that these are predominantly oriented towards Europe.

The Netherlands

At the beginning of the twentieth century, perhaps half of Dutch investment was directed towards the Third World, mostly into the area now called Indonesia. Of course Amsterdam had been a center for international trade and finance for centuries, so that the institutions for foreign investment were already long established. The broad outline of the magnitudes of foreign investment, total and direct, are suggested in Graph 3.3. Post-World War II levels of foreign investment/GDP are much lower than pre-war, and the Third World now receives a much smaller fraction than before that war. The major center of investment in the Third World had been Indonesia, then known as the Dutch East Indies. Latin America had also received some 5 per cent of total pre-World War II investment, according to Lewis (1948). The data in Gales and Sluyterman (1993) suggest growth of FDI outside of the East Indies during that period, while at the same time overall foreign investment was declining compared to GDP.

The political movements associated with Indonesian independence in the 1940s led to the massive emigration of Dutch settlers, and the loss to the Dutch of virtually all that investment. Currently Latin America receives about two thirds of Dutch FDI into the Third World, although much of that goes to the Netherlands Antilles, from where it is presumably reinvested and the ultimate destination is not recorded in the available official statistics.

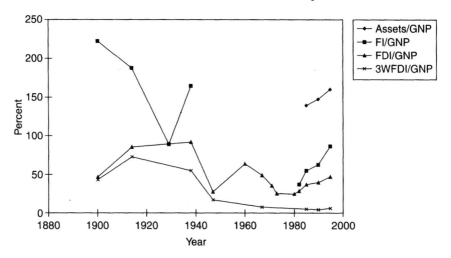

Graph 3.3 The Netherlands: foreign investment/GDP, twentieth century

Sources: Foreign Assets 1985–1995, *International Financial Statistics Yearbook*, 1998. Foreign Investment: 1900, 1914, 1938, 1947, 1973, Gales and Sluyterman (1993); 1929, Staley (1935); 1982–1995, *International Financial Statistics Yearbook*, 1998. FDI: 1900–1947, 1973, Gales and Sluyterman (1993); 1960–1971, Dunning (1983); 1980–1995 *International Financial Statistics Yearbook*, 1998. FDI into the Third World: 1900–1947, Gales and Sluyterman (1993), allowing for investment outside Indonesia, according to Lewis (1948); 1967, OECD (1972); 1985–1995, *International Direct Investment Statistics Yearbook*. NNP/GDP: 1900–1947, Mitchell (1992); 1960–1995, *International Financial Statistics Yearbooks*.

Note
Staley's estimate for 1929 appears to be low, because there is little reason to accept a temporary decline in FI/GDP.

One historical question is the mode of that investment during the first half of the century. In a pair of publications, Gales and Sluyterman (1993 and 1998) have argued that about half of Dutch direct investment in Indonesia was similar to what is called the Free Standing Company, and that "Most of the remainder consisted of investment by companies registered in the East Indies and managed by expatriates." (1998: 296). Indeed, their description of the Indonesian case illustrates well the continuity between free standing company and expatriate investment, while downplaying the importance of the "American model" of direct investment arising from firms initially established in the home country.

Japan

Although it had re-entered the world economy only in the second half of the nineteenth century, Japan already had become a net overseas creditor by the end of the First World War. Moreover, due to its military victories in wars with China and Russia, it also possessed by that time significant overseas colonies and possessions. Japan's major investments in the Third World were not in its formal colonies but in nominally independent China – in Manchuria and along the coast. Smaller amounts of Japanese capital were sent to Korea and Taiwan, where it dominated those local economies.[10] There were also small investments in places such as Hawaii, the south Pacific, and the continental United States. Japan's foreign investments expanded rapidly during the inter-war period, and of course were lost after 1945. In spite of widespread destruction during the war, the recovery of the Japanese economy was quite rapid, and since about 1960 there has been a tremendous expansion of foreign investment, mostly loans. When compared to the size of the home economy, Japan's overseas investments before World War II were much higher than the post-World War II era.

These two waves of foreign investment are depicted in Graph 3.4. As was indicated in the tables earlier in this chapter, a comparatively high fraction of Japan's total FDI has always been directed towards third world countries, and a higher fraction of her FDI goes to Asia than is the case for other major source countries. For a time in the 1960s, Latin America had more Japanese investment, but after 1980 Asia regained prominence as the receiving area.

Japan's rapid progression from an isolated country in 1850 to a major regional power by 1920 of course astonished contemporary observers. Accompanying this unexpectedly rapid growth of output was an evolution in the orientation of its policies toward its colonies, with a major switch occurring in about 1920. Korea and Taiwan were initially viewed as producers of scarce foodstuffs; rice in both countries, sugar in Taiwan and soybeans in Korea. The attraction of Manchuria was both strategic and economic – a source of several raw materials. The Chinese market was the ultimate goal of the Japanese strategists, as it was also for the Europeans. In both Korea and Taiwan, the early policy of the Japanese authorities was to discourage the development of industrial production which would compete with home manufacturing, thus limiting investment by *zaibatsu* (Peattie 1984: 32–33; Duus 1984: 159; Ho 1984: 356). As Japan's Pacific War expanded with the invasion of Manchuria and the spread of the conflict to other parts of China, the usefulness of Korea and Taiwan as complementary industrial producers became clearer, so that policies were accordingly modified, and colonial manufacturing grew more rapidly. Some historians see the origins of post-war growth in the ex-colonies in their pre-war development of manufacturing, which had some native as well as Japanese entrepreneurs.

The colonies were also viewed as an outlet for surplus population. In 1940 the number of Japanese residents in the colonies was 3.6 per cent of the population of Japan itself, and ranged from 2 to 6 per cent of the populations of Manchuria, Korea and Taiwan.[11] Peattie (1984: 89–90) notes that the settlers' social background was similar to that of the *pieds noirs* in

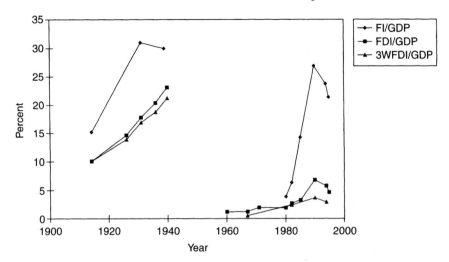

Graph 3.4 Japan: foreign investment/GDP, twentieth century

Sources: FI: 1914, 1929 Moulton (1931); 1926, 1931, 1936, *Estimates of Long Term Economic Statistics*, Volume 14, Table 16; 1938, Lewis (1948); 1939 sum of totals for China (including Manchuria), Korea, and Taiwan, from Chapter 5 of this book; 1980–1997; *International Financial Statistics Yearbook*, 1998. FDI: 1914–1940, the sources for Korea, Taiwan, and China, in Chapter 5; 1960–1973, Dunning (1983); 1980–1997, *International Financial Statistics Yearbook*, 1998. FDI to the Third World: 1967, OECD (1972); 1982–1995, *International Direct Investment Statistics Yearbook*. GDP: 1914–1940, *Long Term Economic Statistics*, Volume 1, Table 1; 1960–1997, the *International Financial Statistics Yearbook*.

Notes
Virtually all FDI for the pre-World War II period was to the Third World. Dunning's reported FDI for 1980 was double that of the OECD and the IMF; this may be a price valuation problem, rather than inconsistent sources. One of the reasons that some of the FDI totals for the pre-World War II period are higher than the same year's figures for FI is because the former include locally financed investment, while the latter is estimated on Japan's balance of payments data.

Algeria; semi-skilled workers, technicians, farmers. He also points out that Japan was initially a capital scarce country, which helps explain the low levels of foreign lending, to colonies or elsewhere. Japan's willingness to transfer funds to its colonies for their development is more reminiscent of the French than the British experience.

The institutional arrangements of Japanese investments during the colonial era also merit further comments. The major investment in China, called the South Manchurian Railway, was in fact a mixture of economic activities centered around a railroad which had been ceded as part of a war indemnity, and functioned as an enclave in a region geographically remote from the traditional growth centers of that country. The other investments in China, as well as those in Korea and Taiwan, do not appear to have been generated by companies developing at home and then expanding abroad, as in the "American model". Although these have not received much attention in English language publications, it would appear that they fit somewhere between Free Standing Companies and expatriate investments. Because Japan was not an important exporter of capital, and these activities seemed to have obtained a large part of their funds from Japanese controlled local sources as well as retained profits, the latter description may well be more accurate.[12] Most of these firms were registered in the colonies. The term "expatriate" understates the degree of controlled exercised from Japan, due to its physical closeness of its colonies, in contrast to the Asian or sub-Saharan colonies of the European powers.[13]

Another characteristic of Japanese business is the dominance by conglomerates, which before the war were called *zaibatsu,* and now are referred to as *keiretsu* or *kigyo shudan.* These are composed of many nominally independent firms, and have at their core a major bank and a general trading company, or *sogo shosha.* The degree of diversification of these entities is greater than that of the multi-divisional firms of the United States and Europe, and it should be clear that the potential for exclusionary or monopolistic practices is also greater. The *sogo shosha* success has led some, such as Abe (1997), to suggest that this holding company form of organization may supplant the corporate managerial institutional forms that have evolved in the other industrial countries. Some also conjecture that the *sogo shosha* are not reproducible in contexts culturally different from Japan, and thus standard development path or evolutionary type thinking is in error. This is a familiar discussion about which most predictions will be wrong, so none will be proffered here. With regard to the trading companies, we note that, as the name indicates, their activities are fundamentally centered around organizing trade, which for the big companies involves foreign trade, and a physical, institutional presence in overseas markets. Secondly, being members of large conglomerates, the range of products provided is quite large. The standard story is that these Trading Companies arose soon after Japan was re-inserted into the global economy in the latter nineteenth century, because the country had little experience with foreign trade and international markets, and the Japanese government and some major businesses felt they were being exploited by the western trading companies. Many had predicted that these companies would become obsolete as industrial capital became more influential than commercial capital; such is the story told of trading firms in Europe, but evidently this has not happened.

The *sogo shosha* are also important for this work because they have been the key co-ordinators in developing raw material production for Japanese industry, either indirectly through joint ventures, or using Japanese FDI. Their importance introduces several problems with the data on Japanese FDI: they may underestimate the amount of overseas production that is controlled by Japanese interests, mis-attribute the managerial links between domestic and foreign enterprises, or over-estimate the amount of production originating in service activities.

More broadly, the existence and importance of trading companies, whether in Nigeria in 1900 or in England in 1990, inevitably complicates empirical work. The basic motive for looking at the assets of a company is to get an idea of that company's production and employment potential; surely this is less valid here. For a similar reason, it is less appropriate to speak of a geographical location of a trading company's assets, nor is the volume of a trading company's sales any reflection of that company's productive capacity. Of course, the same qualifications hold for banks, which is why some statistical reports on FDI exclude financial institutions.

Finally, it should be noted that the growth path of Japanese investment, dominated by service activities, for which the *sogo shosha* and financial institutions are responsible, is rather distinct from that of the United States over the last half century. More US investment was directed towards manufacturing. Some of this was tariff jumping, for which investment in the European Union is the prime example. Protectionist regulations against Japanese autos and electronics are causing similar effects. More recently, both countries have moved towards export oriented manufacturing investments, located in third world countries.

Concluding comments

Several major patterns emerge from the preceding data, most importantly a mid-century decline in the ratio of outward stock of foreign investment – total or direct – to the GDP of the source countries, and a recovery of FDI/GDP to a level significantly lower than had been achieved before World War II. This finding will be reflected in a similar U-shaped pattern of the ratio of inward FDI to GDP in the case studies of practically all of the third world countries in the subsequent chapters. Of course these results are not completely parallel. Although the source countries are the same in the two periods, there were substantial changes in their relative importance. In addition, there has been more rapid growth in the industrial countries' GDP, which tends to lower the FDI/GDP ratio for the source countries. More importantly, there has been a concentration of FDI after mid-century, with less going to the Third World, and more flows among the industrial countries, which evidently lowers for the Third World the ratio of the inward stock of FDI to GDP. In the early 1990s, the industrial countries had placed about one sixth (an unweighted average) of their outward FDI into the Third World. In virtually all investing countries, that ratio was higher at the beginning of the century. Furthermore, as the tables in this chapter have indicated, and will be analysed in more detail in the subsequent chapters, for most countries there had been a tendency to concentrate their overseas investments in their colonies up to World War II. Thereafter, with independence, investment into third world areas declined in relative terms, and in certain well-known cases, in absolute amounts as well.

Also worth noting is a tendency towards convergence of the ratio of source countries' outward FDI/GDP, to a level somewhat less than 20 per cent. For these countries, the average ratio of their FDI stocks in the Third World to their own GDP has fallen to a bit above 2 per cent. This latter ratio is largest for Switzerland and the Netherlands – where we may be seeing reinvestment of funds originating elsewhere – and smallest in Germany and Italy, typically thought of as EU-oriented economies. Levels for Japan and the United States are about 3 per cent. As fractions of their domestic fixed capital stock, or of their net wealth, those numbers would be divided by two or four, respectively. Whatever else can be said about the foreign direct investment of the industrial countries into the Third World, it is not the case that this is large compared to the size of their own domestic economies.

Notes

1 Fortunately most of our results are expressed as ratios to GDP or the capital stock, because the issue of the appropriate price deflator is very tricky. Not only is there a question of which country's prices to use, but it is also the case that local purchases – property, construction, and local materials – often accounted for more than half of total costs. Thus the frequent use of a price index for manufactured exports (e.g. from the UK) would seem inappropriate.
2 More precisely, the term is "public and publicly guaranteed" long-term debt. One factor encouraging the rapid rise of debt after about 1970 by third world parastatals and the private sector has been guarantees by their home governments, and an implicit belief on the part of the lending banks that their governments would be willing to bail them out in an emergency.
3 Data from the United States Department of Commerce (1960, 1975a, 1981, 1986, 1991), and recent *Survey of Current Business.* It is interesting to note that in the 1982 Benchmark Survey, the FDI position in finance in the Third World is a negative $13 billion (the first Third World Debt Crisis), and the entire FDI in services was $10 billion. Thus the statement in the text is not valid for the FDI position in that year, although it is for assets or sales.
4 Several problems can be identified, some conceptual and some operational. Funds raised in British markets outside of the City would not be included; there is an issue of funds which originally came from other countries, and utilized the London market for its convenience and efficiency. There would be gaps between money "authorized" and actually "called". In moving to the estimation of the outstanding amounts, there is no way of accounting for the repayment of loans. Furthermore, there is no inclusion of the increment of firms' investments abroad using their internally generated funds.
5 During the period 1918–1939, loans raised by colonial governments on the London market summed £144 million, while the British government's grants and aids to the colonies amounted to £35 million (Constantine 1984). It would appear that British foreign aid was smaller in absolute and relative amounts than French aid during this period.
6 Newmarck's 1914 estimate, reported in Moulton and Lewis (1925) and Staley (1935), and the 1938 data in Woodruff (1967) which is based on Lewis (1938).

Higher fractions for the pre-World War I date are reported by Woodruff, or implicitly if the estimates for Latin America of Rippy (1948) are used.

7 Poquin (1957: 189, footnote 4). Evidently, the correction depends on which price deflator is selected. In round numbers, French prices increased over five times between 1914 and 1929; between 1914 and 1940 the index was 14. See also Suret-Canale (1971: 163), Picquemal (1957), and Bloch-Laine (1956: 109). One source of debate about the Vichy survey is the index used to reflate current values to 1940 prices.

8 Recall that juridically, Algeria was not a colony, but an overseas part of France, so it was typically not included in data on colonial foreign trade and investment. Sub-Saharan French Africa was divided into AOF and AEF (west and equatorial French Africa). Data for Togo and Cameroon were appended, inconsistently to that of AOF and AEF. Although it was governed separately, data for the island of Madagascar is sometimes included in totals for tropical Africa.

9 This also leads to the provocative comment (Schröter 1998: 325) that many firms registered in Liechtenstein, the Cayman Islands, and so forth are contemporary versions of Free Standing Companies.

10 Referring to 1938, Lewis (1948) attributes 92 per cent of Japanese overseas assets, i.e. including loans, to Asia, and 86 per cent to China itself.

11 The ratio of Japanese to total population in Kwantung Province and South Sakhalin in northeastern China was much higher (one third), but these were smaller and less important economically (Kaneko 1982: 35).

12 Kaneko (1982: 42) presents data for 1920 on Japanese companies in Korea, Taiwan, and Manchuria in which surplus reserves and retained profits amount to about one fourth of paid up capital.

13 Duus (1995) has an insightful discussion of the distinction between emigrants and colonists, and how the latter were preferred by Japan's leaders, because of their continued loyalty to the interests of the home country. Peattie (1984: 14) utilizes the distinction drawn by Hannah Arendt between European overseas colonial empires and their "continental imperialism" involving geographically close areas (Ireland to England, Poland to Germany) where similar cultural heritages were invoked, and argues that the Japanese case had more in common with the latter situation.

4   Africa

The order of presentation of the African countries will follow a political/geographical sequence, starting in the northeast with Egypt, and then the three ex-French colonies of the Maghreb – Algeria, Morocco, and Tunisia. The other ex-French colonies from south of the Sahara are studied next, with detailed data for any year prior to 1970 available only for the Côte d'Ivoire. Two isolated cases are then considered, that of independent Liberia, and that of Belgium's only colony, the Congo.[1] Finally, Britain's colonies are considered in three groupings – west, east, and southern Africa.

In this and the next two chapters, tables have been prepared for each country or colony, with the goal of providing three indicators of the relative amounts of foreign investment, total and direct. The first indicators are FI/person and FDI/person, and are presented in terms of US dollars in 1900 prices. The second set of indicators are FI/GDP and FDI/GDP, and are presented as percentages; no effort is made to distinguish between GDP and GNP. Finally, to complement the ratios with respect to GDP, and fill in the gaps for those countries/periods where these are not available, FI/trade and FDI/trade are calculated, where "trade" is the average of the value of exports and imports. For a small number of countries, estimates are available for the capital stock and perhaps even its distribution, which are also presented and analysed at the end of each country's case study.

Egypt

There are several advantages in beginning our survey of Africa with the case of Egypt. Its political status was somewhere between that of a dependent colony, like so much of sub-Saharan Africa, and an independent country, as in most of Latin America. The country has benefited from the attention of serious economic researchers for several decades, so that we have a good set of data on foreign investment, and some pre-World War II estimates of national income.

The beginning of the twentieth century saw Egypt recovering from external debt problems, enjoying a boom created from cotton exports grown on newly irrigated land. The country also benefited economically from the First World War, through both the expansion of trade and the local investment of accumulated profits. Egypt's process of attaining political independence, throwing off its status as a British protectorate, and pursuing a nationalist development strategy during the inter-war period, foreshadowed many of the problems that most colonies would experience after World War II. One important step was the development of a national banking system, led by the Bank Misr, as well as institutions devoted specifically to agricultural and industrial growth. The National Bank of Egypt passed into Egyptian control and functioned as a central bank after 1951. Another noteworthy step in the country's slow journey along a nationalist development path was the revision in the late 1930s of what was referred to as the Capitulations, agreements which had given to foreigners special legal and tax treatment, thereby encouraging foreign ownership (Tignor 1984). One is struck by the cosmopolitan nature of the country's business elite on the eve of Nasser's takeover, which subsequent events were to reverse dramatically. The counterpart of that observation is that some part of the reduction in overseas ownership before the coup had been simply a reclassification of the owners from being foreigners to being the equivalent of what could be termed residents with strong foreign ties.

As indicated by Table 4.1, Egypt had relatively large amounts of foreign investment at the turn of the century, which continued to grow up to World War I. FDI was much less than total foreign investment, and the size of the subsequent decline in loans was much larger than that of FDI. The calculated values of the ratio FDI/GDP are similar to those of several Latin American countries during the 1930s.[2] In retrospect, we see that foreign ownership levels in the rest of the economy outside the Canal were not high at mid-century. Several factors contributed to the relative decline of foreign investment before Nasser; the development of the domestic stock market and banking institutions, the removal of the Capitulations, war-time bonanzas during both World Wars favoring Egyptian entrepreneurs, limits on the spending of the local authorities by the Debt Commission, and so on. The post-1914 decline in the value of foreign holdings of stock was roughly counterbalanced by an increase in Egyptian holdings. This replacing of holdings overseas by that of residents of Egypt was most noticeable with respect to the land companies and other financial institutions. In a series of measures, President Gamal Abdel Nasser nationalized the Suez Canal, foreign holdings, and much of the private sector. FDI inflows did not resume until the 1970s. The century ends with levels of FDI/GDP that are similar to those before World War I.

The decline in foreign investment between 1914 and 1950 had not resulted in an acceleration of manufacturing investment by Egyptians. Indeed, it was the reaction by Nasser's government to a perceived lack of domestic response that led to the period of extensive state entrepreneurship.[3]

Table 4.1 Egypt: relative size of inward foreign investment stocks, twentieth century

	1902	1914	1934	1938	1948	1970	1980	1990	1995
FI/capita	60	63	18	14	8	8	35	42	38
FDI/capita	12	29	10	10	5	$<\frac{1}{2}$	5	12	12
FI/GDP	122	105	44	44	14	19	79	116	98
FDI/GDP	23	48	23	33	10	1	11	32	30
FI/trade	695	683	277	249	66	118	180	275	272
FDI/trade	134	310	148	188	48	12	48	145	163

Sources: Population: 1900–1950, author's extrapolation of estimates in McEvedy and Jones (1978); 1970–1995, the *International Financial Statistics Yearbook*. Foreign Investment, total and direct: 1902–1934, Crouchley (1938: 273), where FDI is securities held abroad by foreigners, excluding the Suez Canal, for which data is given in Radwan (1974: 279–80); 1938, Lewis (1948), subtracting E£20m for the Suez Canal; 1948, Issawi (1954: 207–8); 1970–1995, loans from *World Debt Tables*; 1971, FDI from OECD (1973); 1980–1995, FDI calculated by adding on to the 1971 datum the accumulated flows (from 1975) indicated in various issues of *World Investment Report*. GDP: 1902 and 1913, using the above population figures and the per capita GDP estimates of Sherbini and Sherif in Issawi (1963: 34); 1934 and 1938, using the 1938 estimate of the Egyptian National Planning Committee cited by Issawi (1963: 34); 1948, Hansen and Marzouk (1965: 319); 1970–1995, from various issues of the *World Debt Tables*. Trade (average of exports and imports): 1902–1934, Crouchley (1938); 1938–1948, Mitchell (1995); dollar values of exports and imports for 1970–1995 from various issues of *World Debt Tables*.

Note
Foreign investment in railroads was minimal, according to data in Crouchley (1936).

The political evaluation of Tignor (1998) is that the ideological leanings of those behind the 1952 military coup did not predestine them towards nationalization of all foreign holdings, nor indeed of the larger firms in the private domestic sector. The Free Officers had seized power and deposed King Farouk in 1952, quickly declaring a land reform. However, Nasser's consolidation of his position as leader was gradual, and he was to nationalize the Suez Canal Company only four years later, in 1956. Indeed, it was some five years after the Suez crisis that massive nationalizations occurred, accompanying the Socialist Laws of 1961.

Who was affected by those nationalizations? Those most affected were not Europeans. First of all, the agrarian reform was aimed at a political class – people linked to the royal family.[4] Although most people in this group were in some sense foreigners, and their ouster certainly appealed to nationalist feelings, it would be easy to exaggerate a parallel to the post-independence hostility later directed towards European settlers in the ex-colonies in Africa or Asia.[5] In any event, the estimates assembled by Tignor (1998: 167) indicate that two thirds of the total value of the properties taken over by the Egyptian government between 1952 and 1961 was accounted for by the land reform and the Socialist Laws of 1961; neither of these had significant impact on Europeans.

The most famous foreign property in Egypt was the Suez Canal; its construction had been completed in 1869, but by 1875 control had passed completely to British and French investors. The canal had been run by a private company – *la Compagnie Universelle* – whose stock was predominantly held overseas. The indemnization eventually paid for the canal was £23 million, when the market value of the Company's stocks had been £70 million. Moreover, the amount of liquid assets owned by the Company, and untouched by the nationalization, was £62 million – this latter was the basis of a successful finance company, owned and operated in Europe. Tignor further reports estimates of the value of other British, French and Belgian property taken over during this time, summing to £236 million, of which £166 million was officially desequestered, or returned. For the outstanding claims totaling £71 million, the price paid was £51 million. These data reveal an order of magnitude of the value of non-corporate investments. Apparently some multinationals owned by Americans and other foreigners were not touched, particularly in the petroleum industry.

The statistics for Egypt are reliable enough that one can suggest overall trends in foreign ownership of national wealth. The data are included in Table 4.2. A first point is that the value of land was always over half of the total, and that the value of the Suez Canal was less than 5 per cent of total Egyptian wealth. Beyond that, the data suggest a decline in the ratio of accumulated foreign business investment to total reproducible assets, from about 30 per cent in 1914 to about 10 per cent in 1948. For all the crudeness of the basic data on total assets, it is clear that these results are dominated by an absolute decline in the nominal value of foreign holdings during the first third of the century, which is well surveyed in the standard works of Crouchley, Issawi, and – most recently – by Tignor. During the period after 1938 inflationary trends make the data even less reliable, but from other sources we know that there was little outside investment around that time.

With the passing of time, Egypt's relations with its neighbors in the Middle East have changed, and the Nasserite vision has faded as well. There is a parallel in the responses to the policies of Nasser and Sukarno, two key third world leaders at the 1955 Bandung conference. In both cases, the nationalizations decreed by the fiery radicals in the late 1950s have been essentially completely reversed. At the end of the century, official attitudes in Egypt are welcoming to foreign investment, and one of its growth areas has in fact been petroleum.

Algeria

Algeria was the most important overseas territory for French capital and French colonization. The area was invaded and conquered by France in 1830. Settlement accelerated after the Franco-Prussian war of 1870, when the area received French citizens relocated from Alsace-Loraine, which had been lost as a result of that war. Indigenous Algerians[6] fought for

Table 4.2 Wealth and foreign investment in Egypt, 1914–1948 (million E£ current)

	1914	1929	1936	1943	1948
Land	~365	600	~470	660	~935
Housing	~60	150	~114	170	~235
Private Enterprise	~100	~100	~100	180	330
Government	~60	~75	~90	140	~160
Total Wealth	~585	~925	~775	1,100	~1,660
Total Wealth, Non-Land	~220	~325	~310	440	~730
FI	157		110		100
FDI	71	~70	~50		~80
Ratios:					
FI/Total Wealth	27		14		6
FI/Non-Land Wealth	71		36		14
FDI/Total Wealth	12	8	6		$<\frac{1}{2}$
FDI/Non-Land Wealth	32	22	16		14
CPI (1938 = 100)	76	107	95	233	267

Sources: 1914: Wealth items from Topuz (1948), except government assets, which is this author's estimate. FI and FDI – Suez Canal excluded – from Crouchley (1936). Housing based on the estimates by Eid and Cressaty for 1907 and 1912, from Minost (1931). 1929: Minost (1930 and 1931); 1936: Total for land and housing, and foreign investment, from Topuz (1948); 1943: Adler (1943); 1948: Total for land and housing, and foreign investment, from Topuz (1948); CPI from Mitchell (1995).

Notes
The "~" indicates an approximation by this author, based on the information in the sources. Topuz (1948) estimated FI/Wealth at 30 per cent in 1914, and 7 per cent in 1948. Private enterprise estimated from the data on Joint Stock Company stocks and debentures, in Crouchley (1936) and the *Annuaire Statistique*. Government estimated from the series on irrigation in Radwan (1974: Table 2–1) and railroads, from the *Annuaire Statistique*. The disaggregation of land and buildings (propriete bâtie) for 1936 and 1948 was based on the 80 per cent in both Minost and Adler. The FI data in Topuz are not completely consistent with those from Crouchley or Lewis (1948). Adler's disaggregated estimates, in £E million, were: industry and commerce 70, mines 10, private non-corporate 40, inventories 60. He also made adjustments for Egyptian holdings abroad.

France during World War I, by which time a significant two-way migratory flow had been established, with important consequences on local social institutions. French settlers progressively took control of the best land in Algeria, and a thriving export trade developed, most notably in wine and other agricultural products. After World War II, discontent with French rule developed into armed struggle, complicated by growing sentiments for independence on the part of the settlers. The independence of Algeria in 1962 was followed by a massive flight out of the country of French and other Europeans. This is not reflected in aggregate figures of foreign investment, because at the same time commercial production of petroleum was beginning in the southern part of the country, attracting with it new money that the government was more than willing to accommodate.

The political history of independent Algeria has been marked by an inability to reach an accord accommodating the historical influences of its diverse cultural and religious heritage. After independence, the regimes of Presidents Ben Bella and Boumedienne took increasingly more assertive stands against the foreign oil companies, increasing state owner-ship while relying on joint ventures, sub-contracting, or other non-majority ownership alternatives. The heady nationalism of the first years of the OPEC price increases further discouraged investors, as has domestic political and religious violence during the last decade or so.

Because it was juridically part of France, and generally not included in the contemporary statistics for "colonies", a term such as foreign invest-ment was generally not used to describe French capital in Algeria, and data on this subject are less available than the importance of the topic war-rants. Moreover, because it was a settler colony, there is the problem of distinguishing between funds generated by European settlers inside the country from those brought in from overseas. Let us proceed to the basic outline of the historical pattern of foreign investment, which is presented in Table 4.3. The level of external business capital, our approximation to FDI, is not particularly high in 1914, relative to estimated GDP. Lacking a decent economic census, our understanding of the situation even at mid-century is hazy, as indicated by the inconsistency in the estimates for 1938 and 1940 in the Table. One item that does stand out in Table 4.3 is the low level of FDI after 1970, which responds to the increasingly hostile political stance of the various post-independence governments. At the

Table 4.3 Algeria: relative size of inward foreign investment stocks, twentieth century

	1914	1938	1940	1955	1970	1980	1990	1995
FI/capita	48	15	73	89	14	87	62	55
FDI/capita	15		57	59	3	6	3	2
FI/GDP	103	27	130	160	24	45	46	83
FDI/GDP	32		102	106	4	3	2	4
FI/trade	296	92	470	574	81	125	211	262
FDI/trade	94		369	383	15	9	10	11

Sources: Population: 1900–1950, author's extrapolation of estimates in McEvedy and Jones (1978), subsequent years from issues of the *International Financial Statistics Yearbook*. Foreign Investment: 1914, Marseille (1977: 388) for total and private investment; 1938, Lewis (1948), including both Algeria and Tunisia; 1955, FDI sums the 1940 datum and the post-war increase estimated by Picquemal (1957: 74), while the total FI includes the "public invest-ments" from Bobrie (1956: 425); 1970–1995, loans from the *World Debt Tables*; 1971 FDI from OECD (1973); 1980–1995 FDI adds on to the 1971 datum the accumulated sums given in *World Investment Report*, 1997. GDP: 1914–1955, authors's interpolations of estimates reported in Amin (1966, 104); 1970–1995, from various issues of the *World Debt Tables*. Trade (average of exports and imports): 1913, Lamartine Yates (1959); 1938–1962, Mitchell (1995); dollar values of exports and imports for 1970–1995 from various issues of *World Debt Tables*.

Notes
The GDP data for 1955 in Amin (1966) closely approximates contemporary reports in the United Nations. Non-railroad FDI in 1914 was less than half of the total FDI, according to Meynier (1981: 64), so a value of non-railroad FDI/GNP of 16 was used for that year in the statistical work in Chapter 7.

same time, the rise of the measures of total foreign investment reflects increases in loans, which had been borrowed because of the troubled state of the economy. These eventually produced several experiences with debt problems and macroeconomic stabilization programs.

Marseille (1977) presents estimates of foreign investment (total and private) for 1914 and 1940. Because the report for the Vichy authorities on French overseas capital only encompassed French colonies, Algeria was not included in that comprehensive review, so other sources must be relied on, whose comparability to the Vichy data is also open to question. Marseille (1977) states that his sources for pre-World War I Algeria are Meynier and Bobrie, without providing specific citations. The very large estimates he presents for Algeria in 1940 come from an encyclopedia article, written by E. Morard, a top-ranked government economic official. However well informed that official may have been, it is in the nature of that publication that no references were provided. So we will now turn to some of the other sources of information about private and public investments in Algeria, both to clarify Marseille's data, and to draw out further details about these investments.

The pre-World War I levels of foreign business investments in Algeria are analysed by Meynier (1981: 64). He reports a total corporate investment from France of some FF520 million, of which one third was in banks and insurance companies, and about half in mines and railroads. Non-French corporate investment was 11 per cent of that of the French, concentrating especially in mines. The French in Algeria provided an amount of corporate investment which was only 5 per cent of that coming from the metropole, with banks and agriculture each receiving about one fifth; evidently the *colons* preferred non-corporate investment. The Vichy survey had estimated that some 80–90 per cent of the private investment in Indo-China, Africa and other French colonies (outside of north Africa) was through corporate investment, as opposed to individual investment (Marseille 1974: 416).

More information is available about public expenditures. The task of collecting the varied accounts on this item, whether funded from France or from Algeria, was originally performed by Douël (1930). The authorities gave Algeria a significant amount of fiscal autonomy in 1900, so that year marks something of a discontinuity in the data. With regard to funds allocated to Algeria's colonial government, Meynier (1981: 63) presents sub-totals in three major categories for the period up to 1914. The interest rate guarantees for railroads were FF700 million, loans to the colonial and local governments[7] were FF400 million, and budgetary transfers for investment was FF950 million. Although several of these publications have a disturbing lack of precise references, it may be correct to infer that Marseille's estimate of FF1,181 million for French public capital invested in Algeria incorporates Meynier's first two categories, while excluding budgetary transfers, which were quite sizeable.[8]

As was pointed out in the previous chapter, labeling as debt the funds transferred from France to the local colonial government is probably not appropriate, as there was not an automatic assumption that these funds would be repaid. As such, the comparison is stronger to post-World War II foreign economic aid, in that these funds typically passed some sort of examination of economic feasibility, and were often a major source of finance for capital formation. Moreover, Table 3.13 indicated that these transfers were especially important after World War II.

The fiscal record of Algeria is sufficiently well documented that it can illustrate the importance of government capital formation, its subsidies for private sector investments, and other links between the government and private companies. As a point of reference, the estimated nominal value of Algeria's 1910 GDP was FF2,100 million. Bobrie (1976: 1231) presents a total for public expenditure on productive assets, outside of railroads, in Algeria for the period 1850–1900, totaling FF781 million. This apparently includes what would be considered normal upkeep and repairs, which for three years (1904, 1907, 1909) listed in locally available issues of the *Annuaire Statistique* would seem to be about 40 per cent of the total, so we could estimate the government's non-railroad capital formation before 1900 at FF450 million. Demontès (1922: 93) states that public expenditures on ports and other maritime services had totaled FF134 million by 1900, only to have increased by FF36 million by 1922, and the amount invested in irrigation works was said to be about FF20 million. The totals in Douël (1930) for public works and extraordinary expenditures between 1901 and 1913 was FF275 million and FF173 million, respectively.[9] All of these sum up to about FF1 billion, as the accumulated governmental expenditure before World War I on capital formation outside of railroads.

Capital formation by railroad companies – both public and private – is estimated in Hara (1976: 206) for the period up to 1914, at FF665 million, which compares well with the earlier total in Poggi (1931: 579) of FF789 million. With regard to subsidies and interest rate guarantees to private railroads, Bobrie (1977: 182) provides a table indicating that the accumulated public expenditures on these items, up to World War I, was FF924 million. In summary, railroads accounted for half of the actual amounts of social investment, and the government spent about as much on subsidies to the railroad companies as it did on all investments in other sectors. In contrast, the funds actually generated by the stockholders in the private railroads were quite small. Further underscoring the point that government expenditures were narrowly focused in sectors not benefiting the local population, Bobrie (1976: 1230) estimates that defense and railroads accounted for fully three fourths of total public expenditure in Algeria. Finally, echoing a theme emphasized in the literature on India, the Algerian railroads were criticized for not serving to develop the areas occupied by the indigenes.

An important issue for Algeria as elsewhere is the size of capital and its distribution, and this can be approximated for the pre-World War I period. The estimates of private wealth of Oualid (1910a and 1910b) are presented in Table 4.4. After adjusting Oualid's data for cash and deposits at financial institutions, and adding in the previous paragraph's estimates of government and railway capital, we arrive at an estimate of fixed reproducible wealth of FF5 billion, and of fixed wealth (including land) of FF6.5 billion. Comparing the fixed reproducible wealth to the current value of Amin's (1966: 101) estimate of 1910 GDP, FF2.1 billion,[10] results in an implicit capital output ratio of two and a half, which is only slightly higher than what is suggested by other countries' experiences, implying that we have the correct order of magnitude.

Table 4.4 Distribution of fixed reproducible wealth in Algeria, 1913 (million French francs)

	Total	European	Indigenes
Land	1,543	799	744
Land minus correction for improvements	1,089	398	691
Private Reproducible Wealth:			
Agriculture, including Land Improvements	1,239	730	524
Urban Buildings	2,426	1,949	477
Total Private Reproducible Wealth	3,665	2,678	1,001
+ Government Assets	1,000		
+ Railroads	665		
= Total Fixed Reproducible Wealth	5,330		
Total Fixed Wealth = Land (unimproved)			
+ Total Fixed Reproducible Wealth	6,419		
Private Capital from France			
Invested in Algeria	547		
Ratios to Total Fixed Reproducible Wealth (TFRW):			
Settler Wealth/TFRW		40	
FDI/TFRW		10	
Indigenes' Wealth/TFRW		19	
Government + Railroads/TFRW		31	
Total		100	
Non-railroad FDI/TFRW		5	
Addenda:			
Cash and Deposits at Financial Institutions:		497	
Total Private Wealth, as reported by Oaulid:		5,251	

Sources: For private wealth, Oualid (1910a and 1910b). French private capital from Marseille (1977: 388). Government fixed assets; author's calculations, based on Bobrie (1976: 1239) and others – see text. Railroads from Hara (1976: 206).

Note
Settlers' wealth calculated as the difference between Europeans' wealth and private capital from France. The separation of land improvements from total land is estimated as the difference between actual and the average value of land in cereals; values given in Oualid (1910b). Non-railroad FDI in 1914 is approximated here as half of the total FDI, following Meynier (1981: 64).

Thus emboldened, we will use Oualid's estimates to examine the distribution of wealth between indigenous Algerians, settlers, foreign firms, and the government in pre-World War I Algeria. According to the data in the Table, the government owned 30 per cent of the total, and indigenes held 20 per cent. European settlers and foreign firms together owned half of the physical wealth of Algeria, with settlers owning 40 per cent of domestic capital. For comparison, Amin (1966: 119) estimated that 47 per cent of the national income was received by non-Moslems in 1955, when non-Moslems made up about 10 per cent of the population. Although concrete data are lacking for the middle of the century, either before or after independence, it is commonly asserted that Europeans controlled large scale production in urban activities, and that "... (to) local capital was left only the small and medium-sized industries ..." (Bennoune 1988: 73), a situation which was to have been changed, much too late, by the *Plan de Constantine* announced by De Gaulle in 1958.

The amount of wealth attributed by Oualid in 1910 to Europeans was almost five times as large as the sum of capital actually sent to Algeria by French (or European) businesses, according to Marseille (1977) and Meynier (1981), as indicated in Table 4.4. Even very generous allowances for errors in measurement cannot keep us from concluding that the settlers were much more important sources of investment funds in Algeria, than were the institutions in France.[11] One implication of this is that the low level of the ratio of non-railroad FDI to national wealth in Table 4.4 – only 5 per cent – severely understates the total European domination of the economy, because of its omission of settler wealth. The fraction of total fixed reproducible wealth owned by Europeans was close to one half, the government had about 30 per cent, and indigenes possessed about one fifth of Algeria's wealth.

We are less fortunate on the subject of total capital around the time of World War II. As mentioned, Marseille (1977) uses the estimate of French capital by Morard (1948) of FF149 billion for 1940. In contrast, the total foreign investment for 1938 in Lewis (1948: 304) was only FF4.9 billion. The phrasing in Morard strongly suggests an interpretation that investment by settlers was included in his total; this would certainly not have been included in the figures reported by Cleona Lewis. Indeed, the latter's sub-total for the business sector was limited to corporate issues over the years 1924–1938. The Morard total is equivalent to about 10 billion gold francs, using the standard index for deflation. Interpreting the Morard data to be total non-indigenous capital – that is, including settler and government, as well as French overseas investment – implies a doubling of that variable compared to the pre-World War I estimate of Oualid in Table 4.4, which is rather surprisingly in line with the increase of Algeria's real output, as reported in Amin (1966: 101), thereby supporting our interpretation that the Morard total refers to all French (or European) capital in the colony. This implies that the data on French capital in

Algeria, for the years 1914 and 1940 from Marseille (1977: 388), involve quite distinct coverages – the first excluding settlers, the second including them. Unfortunately, there do not appear to be any estimates of total capital in Algeria in 1940, or some other separate calculation of that owned by indigenes, so that a calculation similar to that of the previous paragraph of the fraction of total foreign ownership is not possible. The availability of similar data for the contemporary period has not improved since independence.

Morocco

It goes without saying that the area immediately south of Gibraltar has long had a European presence. At the beginning of the twentieth century, Morocco was in the French sphere of influence, and would become a French protectorate in 1912. There was a rapid increase of lending to Morocco in the early years of the century, which was part of the European powers' geo-strategic competition leading up to the Great War. Independence was achieved in 1956, after a process that was less violent than what was to occur in neighboring Algeria.

The comments of Swearingen (1987) on French policy in Morocco are valid for most other French colonies, as well. He cites A.S. Kanya-Forstner on "the enormous disparity between the hopelessly unrealistic objectives of French policy makers and the actual results of their policies". Furthermore, those policy makers reflected conflicting ideologies and economic interests towards Morocco. Finally, the achieving of independence did not generate a clean break into "before" and "after" periods in that country's historical development. Only in the early 1970s was a Moroccanization program announced, but subsequent events suggest it was not vigorously implemented, and was effectively dropped after a decade.

The time paths of the ratios of FI and FDI to GDP, as revealed in Table 4.5, indicate that debt and direct investment had very different trajectories. With regard to direct investment, there was an initial increase at the start of the century, a plateau at a level of 20 to 30 per cent from then until independence, followed by a slow decline, and a very recent rise in that ratio to about 10 per cent. As the enthusiasm accompanying independence gave way in light of the meager economic achievements, Morocco increased foreign borrowing. This has given rise to debt payment problems, and forced her rulers to adopt IMF type stabilization programs.

Because direct French political influence was later in Morocco than the other two Maghrebian countries, the settler population was relatively smaller there. The most important agricultural export was citrus fruits; an item which was not produced by French farmers. This lessened protectionist sentiment in France, and only with the expansion of the European community and competition with producers in Spain did market access become problematical. Moreover, after independence, land previously

Table 4.5 Morocco: relative size of inward foreign investment stocks, twentieth century

	1902	1914	1938	1940	1957	1970	1980	1990	1995
FI/capita	1	13	27	22	35	13	39	54	46
FDI/capita	$<\frac{1}{2}$	4	11	6	17	3	2	3	6
FI/GDP		44	53	43	76	29	49	95	81
FDI/GDP		18	29	15	36	6	2	5	10
FI/trade	40	156	703	676	408	135	174	276	215
FDI/trade	18	49	296	178	194	29	8	13	27

Sources: Population: 1900–1950, author's extrapolation of estimates in McEvedy and Jones (1978), subsequent years from issues of the *International Financial Statistics Yearbook*. Foreign Investment: 1902, 1914, 1938, Guillen (1977: 400); 1940, Marseille (1977: 328); 1957, Belal (1976: 36); 1970–1995, loans from the *World Debt Tables*; 1971, FDI from OECD (1973); 1980–1995, add on to the 1971 datum the accumulated FDI inflows from *World Investment Report* 1997. GDP: 1914–1940, author's extrapolation of estimates in Amin (1966, 101); 1957, *International Financial Statistics Yearbook* 1976; 1970–1995, from various issues of the *World Debt Tables*. Trade (average of exports and imports): 1904, 1913, 1938, 1940, from Mitchell (1995); 1957, from *International Financial Statistics Yearbook* 1976; dollar values of exports and imports for 1970–1995 from various issues of the *World Debt Tables*.

Notes
Amin's earliest estimate of GDP is for 1920. Guillen's data refers to French capital; his source for the 1914 datum, Fidel (1915), indicates that almost all the external capital was from France. Fidel also estimated FDI in 1902 at four times the amount which Guillen reported. It is not clear if any of this represented railroad capital. The data on foreign investment for 1938 in Lewis (1948) is about one third less than that of Guillen. Lewis includes investment from the Netherlands and the United States, and these were quite small compared to French investment. Guillen also reports the French government's grants to cover balance of payments, whose inclusion would raise the 1938 FI data here by about two fifths.

Belal's 1957 datum used here for FDI is actually externally financed private investment, which presumably includes bonds and perhaps some expatriate investment. Only about half of Guillen's reported foreign private investment in 1938 was direct investment, the other half being loans to governments and corporations. Ayache (1956: 145) cites an article which reports French holdings at double the total used here for foreign investment. OECD (1972) reports a total FDI for 1967 in Morocco which in nominal terms is only one fourth the private investment provided by Belal for 1957, and the OECD mentions that settler investment might raise their total by another fourth. The *World Investment Directory* provides a series on the local currency value of FDI, from 1970. Use of this series and the local currency value of GDP results in the following ratios of FDI/GDP for 1970–1995: 7, 6, 6, and 12.

owned by settlers – one seventh of total land, three fourths of the highly productive sector[12] – was gradually transferred to Moroccans, as expatriates moved to the cities, or returned to Europe. The King and his newly independent government did not institute nationalist-motivated expropriations, in either the urban areas or the cities, partially out of fear of increasing the flight of the Europeans, as well as from a feeling that such actions would also be used against them and their local allies.

The available data offer few clues in regard to overall distribution of the means of production. Belal (1976: 36) offers an estimate of cumulative finance during the period of the protectorate. According to his data, the relative roles of foreign and domestic financing were about equal, as were the weights of private and public capital formation. In this case, at least, the indigenous sources appear to have had significant importance.

Tunisia

In several ways, the background history of Tunisia is midway between that of Algeria and Morocco. Tunisia became a French protectorate in 1881, roughly halfway between the incorporation of Algeria and Morocco. The fraction of domestic income received by non-indigenous people in 1955 was 47 per cent in Algeria, 33 per cent in Morocco, and 43 per cent in Tunisia (Amin 1966: 119). After Tunisia gained independence in 1956, her policy stance towards France could be described as somewhere between that of these two fellow Maghreb countries.

The data in Table 4.6 on indicators of the relative size of foreign investment in Tunisia suggests that it has been low and relatively steady throughout the century. In terms of comparisons with the above two countries, Tunisia had fewer resources to attract French capital and settlers, and the ratios FDI/GDP were correspondingly lower. The recent upturn of FDI/GDP has been higher than that of other countries in the region, in part because of closer ties between this country and Italy.

French sub-Saharan Africa

Several broad comments will be presented initially about the aggregates for the French sub-Saharan colonies before independence. Only for Côte

Table 4.6 Tunisia: relative size of inward foreign investment stocks, twentieth century

	1914	1940	1970	1980	1990	1995
FI/capita	22	44	25	60	64	72
FDI/capita	6	19	6	13	16	23
FI/GDP	43	57	51	51	78	77
FDI/GDP	11	25	12	11	20	25
FI/trade	201	528	178	106	149	143
FDI/trade	50	231	44	23	38	46

Sources: Population: 1914, 1940, author's interpolation of estimates in McEvedy and Jones (1978); 1970–1995, various issues of *International Financial Statistics Yearbooks*. Foreign Investment: 1914, Thobie (1982: 111); 1940, Marseille (1977: 388); 1970–1995, sum of loans and FDI – loans from *World Debt Tables*. FDI: 1914, Thobie (1982: 111); 1940, Marseille (1977: 388); 1971, OECD (1973); 1980–1995, adding on to the datum for 1971 the subsequent inflow, as indicated in the *World Investment Report*. GDP: 1914 and 1940, author's interpolation using estimates in Amin (1966: 101); 1970–1995, various *World Debt Tables*. Trade (average of exports and imports): 1914, 1940, Mitchell (1995); 1970–1995, various *World Debt Tables*.

Notes
The part of Foreign Investment corresponding to loans is public capital. The data on foreign direct investment stock in the *World Investment Report* are quite similar to those for Tunisia in the *World Investment Directory*, 1996.

d'Ivoire can country specific data be presented for the colonial period, while we have data on several countries after 1970. The scattered estimates for the colonial period are only disaggregated to the level of two large groups, West and Equatorial (or Central) Africa, and are summarized in Table 4.7. Per capita levels of investment were small, and most funds

Table 4.7 French sub-Saharan Africa: relative size of inward stocks of foreign investment, 1914–1995

	1914	1936	1938	1940	1958	1970	1980	1990	1995
French sub-Saharan Africa									
FI/capita	6	9	4	17		12	30	32	31
FDI/capita	1	4	2	11	7	6	6	4	4
FI/GDP						44	59	96	124
FDI/GDP					30	23	11	13	17
FI/trade	508	539	277	2,652		146	147	286	297
FDI/trade	72	209	125	1,740	178	75	28	40	41
French West Africa									
FI/capita	4	5				11	27	28	28
FDI/capita	1	2				5	4	3	3
FI/GDP						41	61	102	121
FDI/GDP						18	9	10	11
FI/trade	263	331				145	160	277	310
FDI/trade	89	152				65	23	26	29
French Equatorial Africa									
FI/capita	14	17				16	36	42	39
FDI/capita	4	5				10	10	9	9
FI/GDP						50	57	87	130
FDI/GDP						31	16	19	29
FI/trade	902	920				146	128	304	276
FDI/trade	240	260				92	35	65	61

Sources: Population: 1914–1950, interpolated from the estimates in McEvedy and Jones (1978); subsequent years from various issues of the *International Financial Statistics Yearbook*. FI and FDI: 1914, Thobie (1982: 111); 1936, Frankel (1938); 1938, Lewis (1948); 1940, Marseille (1977); 1958 FDI from Suret-Canale (1972: 384), citing a study on business investment. For subsequent years, FI is the sum of Debt and FDI. Debt for 1970–1995, from various issues of the *World Debt Tables*. FDI for 1971 from OECD (1973); for 1980–1995, from *World Investment Report*. GDP: 1958, from the United Nations *Yearbook of National Account Statistics*, 1967, interpolating some of the individual country data; 1970–1995, from various *World Debt Tables*. Trade (average of exports and imports): 1914–1940, Frankel (1938) and Mitchell (1995); 1958, United Nations *Yearbook of National Account Statistics*, 1967; 1970–1995, from *World Debt Tables*.

Notes
For Marseille and Frankel, FDI was taken as funds for the private sector; in Lewis, FDI was funds other than government debt. As explained in the discussion of Table 4.8, the data Marseille reported for 1940 are much higher than those of either Lewis or Frankel, and would appear to be an exaggeration. Frankel's data for 1914 are about 20 per cent lower than Marseille's. Dresch (1979: 187) estimated commercial capital in 1914 in French sub-Saharan Africa at about double the level used here. Less than one tenth of the FDI in 1940 was in railroads. It would be incorrect to label as loans or debt, the funds transferred to the colonies under programs such as FIDES, as no repayment was expected. However, for purposes of comparison, the accumulated value of these grants, from 1947–1958, equaled 67 per cent of the sub-Saharan French Africa's GDP in 1958 (Maldant 1973: 96, 110).

initially went to the colonial governments. Although income estimates apparently do not exist for any point before 1950, the comparisons of foreign investment to trade suggests levels not that different from other parts of the Third World. Once again, although investment per person was low, it was probably also true that per capita income was low, so that ratios of FDI to GDP are much closer to average. Furthermore, business investment grew relative to total investment before 1940, as suggested not only by the Vichy data for 1940 reported in Suret-Canale (1972) and Marseille (1977) – which the previous chapter argued was an exaggeration – but also from the other sources for the mid-1930s, such as Frankel (1938) and Lewis (1948). As measured by our ratios, FDI was higher in equatorial Africa than in west Africa during the colonial period, and remains so today, buoyed up particularly by petroleum and mining. FDI continued to dominate total foreign investment into the 1950s, although in the years after independence, foreign borrowing dominated. After 1970, FDI fell compared to GDP, achieving a small recovery only in the 1990s.

French investment in sub-Saharan Africa in the late 1930s provide the clearest specific example of the wide range of estimates available from highly respected sources about that area. The data are presented in Table 4.8, and we see that the numbers reported by Marseille are several times

Table 4.8 Comparison of estimates of foreign capital in French sub-Saharan Africa, 1936–1940 (million current US$)

	Total	Public	Private	
			Listed	Non-Listed
1936: *Frankel*				
All Sub-Saharan Africa	352	217	119	15
West and Equatorial	258	158	87	12
West	152	82	62	7
Equatorial	106	76	25	5
Togo and Cameroon	93	56	32	4
1938: *Lewis*				
Sub-Saharan Africa	189	103	86	
West and Equatorial	173	99	74	
Togo and Cameroon	16	4	12	
Madagascar	71	53	18	
1940: *Marseille*				
West and Equatorial	962	331	631	
Madagascar	344	84	260	

Sources: Frankel (1938: Table 28) – converted at 5$/£, Lewis (1938: 342), Marseille (1977: 388) – converted at 0.0228$/F.

Notes
It is not clear if Togo and Cameroon are included in the data for West and Equatorial Africa (AOF and AEF) reported by Marseille. The categories here termed "private" for Lewis, include corporate issues and direct investment. Although Madagascar is geographically and historically distinct, and was governed separately, for convenience it is sometimes included in listings for Africa. Frankel did not include Madagascar in his tables.

the size of the estimates of Frankel, whose numbers are half again larger than those in Lewis. The gaps are biggest for private investment, and are much too large to be explained merely by the coverage of the estimates; Lewis reported funds raised in capital markets, while the Vichy report used by Marseille would have included expatriate capital, for example. Although one's inclination is to take the result of the person most directly informed, Frankel, which happens to be the middle estimate, there are few concrete reasons for selecting among them, thus restricting our ability to generate trustworthy comparisons for the period of French colonialism.

The distribution of foreign investment in 1940 was the following: agriculture and forestry (31 per cent), mining (8 per cent), industry and construction (13 per cent), transport (4 per cent), and trade and finance (43 per cent), according to the Vichy survey (Suret-Canale 1971: 162). This last-mentioned sector included the trading companies, whose presence in the area antedates colonial control. Indeed, one could speculate that a major contributor to the differences between the Vichy results and those of Frankel or Lewis is that the former's methodology more fully accounted for these companies, who dominated the region's economy. Also noteworthy is the reversal in the relative importance of investments into the public and private sectors, which occurred in several colonies, according to Marseille (1977). Private investment in railroads was not strong, nor, indeed, had much public money been spent on rails. More generally, infrastructural development was more limited here than in French colonies elsewhere, or than in the British colonies, leading some commentators to suggest that French Africa had too little, rather than too much imperialism. The grand concessionary companies of French Equatorial Africa (AEF) were particularly notorious for their treatment of African workers, as were their British and Belgian counterparts in the neighboring colonies.

During the inter-war period increased attention began to be paid to these colonies, under the influence of Albert Surraut. For tropical Africa, this trend increased immediately after World War II. More funds were made available, both as loans and as grants, through programs known as FIDES and FAC. Because French tradition has a weak separation between the state and the private sector – especially for French companies in the colonies – the separation of grants, loans, and private investment is difficult. According to Suret-Canale (1972: 389), French government aid and investment was four times the value of private sector investment in tropical Africa, between 1945 and 1958. The same source states that the major change in the distribution of private French investment in 1958, compared to 1940, was an increase in industry and mines by about 15 per cent each, and a corresponding decline elsewhere, especially in agriculture.

One unusually detailed set of data is that collected by Suret-Canale (1987), which measures the value of enterprise capital in 1970 for about a dozen ex-colonies, further classifying it in terms of foreign and domestic, public and private. According to his estimates, summarized in Table 4.9,

Table 4.9 Distribution of enterprise capital in ex-French African colonies, 1970 (percentages)

	Private		Public	
	Domestic	*FDI*	*National*	*Foreign*
Grand Total	1	56	13	30
West Africa	1	64	16	19
Mauritania	0	58	4	38
Senegal	0	76	13	11
Mali	0	4	89	8
Côte d'Ivoire	2	79	12	7
Haute Volta	1	58	28	13
Niger	1	50	26	24
Dahomey	3	30	59	8
Togo	1	65	27	6
Central Africa	1	48	10	41
Tchad	0	64	33	3
Rep. Central Africa	1	75	22	2
Congo	0	23	21	56
Gabon	0	44	3	53
Cameroon	4	77	10	9

over half of such capital was private sector foreign investment.[13] Moreover, more public or state capital was owned by foreign governments than by the newly independent national governments. Because this is limited to enterprise capital, the amounts involved are small relative to national GDPs, typically about one quarter, where we would expect the ratio of total capital to GDP to be greater than one.

Individual country data become available starting about 1970. Several countries are listed in Table 4.10, where for economy of presentation the ratios with respect to trade are not included. Several points can be commented. First, there is a general trend for government debt to increase. Secondly, the FDI/GDP levels are not large, in general. These levels have little correlation with the official position of their governments toward foreign investment, indicating that in many countries such a position has not been uniformly maintained. There is little manufacturing investment, and the raw material projects are dominated by the totals for minerals (including petroleum). Beyond that, one notes greater investment in countries bordering the ocean, responding to ease of transportation and the attraction of certain agricultural products.

Côte d'Ivoire

For many years, the Côte d'Ivoire was considered a post-colonial success story, with high growth rates of output and employment, whose key was an openness to foreign trade and investment. In many ways, the colonial

Table 4.10 French sub-Saharan African countries: foreign investment trends, 1970–1995

	1970	1980	1990	1995		1970	1980	1990	1995
Cameroon					Niger				
FI/capita	10	29	33	41	FI/capita	3	15	13	11
FDI/capita	6	5	6	6	FDI/capita	1	4	2	2
FI/GDP	30	46	66	132	FI/GDP	9	36	73	98
FDI/GDP	18	9	12	19	FDI/GDP	4	9	12	18
Chad					Republic of the Congo				
FI/capita	3	8	7	10	FI/capita	45	106	122	34
FDI/capita	1	3	3	3	FDI/capita	20	24	17	18
FI/GDP	16	56	61	115	FI/GDP	84	116	199	213
FDI/GDP	6	20	23	33	FDI/GDP	37	26	27	113
Côte d'Ivoire					Senegal				
FI/capita	20	76	67	65	FI/capita	15	23	27	25
FDI/capita	10	8	6	5	FDI/capita	9	5	4	4
FI/GDP	39	74	157	174	FI/GDP	39	50	63	81
FDI/GDP	20	8	14	13	FDI/GDP	23	12	9	13
Mali					Togo				
FI/capita	9	8	17	17	FI/capita	9	39	22	22
FDI/capita	$<\frac{1}{2}$	$<\frac{1}{2}$	$<\frac{1}{2}$	$<\frac{1}{2}$	FDI/capita	6	8	5	5
FI/GDP	74	41	97	117	FI/GDP	41	103	87	129
FDI/GDP	2	1	1	3	FDI/GDP	25	22	19	27

Sources: Population from various *International Financial Statistics Yearbooks*. FI calculated as the sum of debt and FDI, with debt taken from the *World Debt Tables*; 1970 FDI taken from OECD (1973); 1980–1995, calculated by adding on to that datum the accumulated inflows, as reported in various issues of the *World Investment Report*. GDP from *World Debt Tables*.

legacy was typical; agricultural exports dominated the economy while there was only a small group of French agriculturists, so that foreign control was strongest in the commercial sector, infrastructural development in transport was not as extensive as in the neighboring British colonies. Forced labor had not been utilized as much as in French Equatorial Africa, as the demand for it was not generated by either mining or colonials' farms. The transference of power was led by Félix Houphouët-Boigny, a one-time planter whose control of the political system continued for three decades after independence. His preferred strategy was to seek accommodation with French interests in the country, in marked contrast to leaders in nearby Guinea and Ghana.

The two major export crops were coffee and cocoa; Gbagbo (1982: 127) indicates that the fraction of coffee production in European hands had fallen from 80 per cent in 1934 to 3 per cent in 1960, corresponding not so much to a displacement of the Europeans as to a phenomenal growth of African production. Apparently cocoa production was always dominated by Africans.[14] Amin's estimates of the distribution of national income by nationality, summarized in Table 4.11, suggested a shift in favor of the foreigners; this was an important part of his analysis that was critical of post-World War II capitalist development. Nevertheless, during the

1970s it became increasingly clear that economic production in Ivoirien control was growing in step with national GDP indicators. Representative of this position is the summary in Rapley:

> Ivoirien capitalism is alive and well, thriving and dynamic ... Côte d'Ivoire's economy is not a battleground between domestic and foreign capitalism ... Ivoirien capitalists never sacrificed control of the state in this [development] process nor have they struggled to resist foreign domination. Rather than see Ivoirien capital as dependent on foreign capital, it is more fruitful to see the two as interdependent, ... in a sort of symbiotic relationship.
>
> (Rapley 1993: 98)

One of the bases of this view is revealed in the second set of data in Table 4.11; during the decade of the 1970s, the percentage distribution of ownership of major firms shifted dramatically from foreigners to Ivoirien

Table 4.11 Côte d'Ivoire: indicators of foreign/Ivoirien distribution, 1950–1991

	Distribution of Income		
	1950	1965	
Foreign	24	32	
Ivoirien	76	68	
of which:			
Autoconsumption	38	17	

	Distribution of Enterprise Capital		
	1970	1981	1991
Public:			
Total	19	65	53
Ivoirien State	12	65	53
French and Others	7	0	
Private:			
Total	81	35	47
Ivoirien	2	9	9
French	57	16	20
Other	22	11	17

Sources: Income distribution calculated from data in Amin (1967: 298–9). Distribution of capital in Suret-Canale (1987: 469) and Chevassu (1997: 68).

Notes
The total value of enterprise capital in 1970 amounted to about one fourth that year's GDP, much lower than would be expected. Because there had not been much inflation, another explanation is that these data represent a small part of the country's total capital. The percentage distribution of capital in Chevassu for 1981 is very close to that reported by Suret-Canale for 1982. The latter does not provide totals; and Chevassu's nominal totals for 1981 and 1991, for manufacturing industry alone, amount to about one tenth of the corresponding year's GDP. His reported foreign capital data are significantly less than the domestic equivalent of the dollar figures of FDI in the *World Investment Report*; part of this discrepancy is attributable to the 1980 devaluation.

control, even while the absolute amount of foreign investment did not fall. Houphouët-Boigny pursued a policy of Ivoirization in terms of government employment and industrial ownership and the workforce, which neither eliminated the foreigners nor alienated them.

Events since 1980 have tarnished the glow of the Ivoirien success story. The immediate symptoms were the slowing down of growth, and the need for structural adjustment programs; in the background were the evident vulnerability of reliance on a few raw material exports, and the unwillingness of the Ivoirian state to cede control or privatize parastatal enterprises. Control by private sector-based Africans of the urban-based activities had not grown appreciably by 1991, as indicated in Table 4.11. Disappointment in the Ivoirianization of commerce is discussed in Boone (1993). More broadly, her analysis contributes to an approach which makes an interesting contrast with the one cited above, centered in a doubt or disappointment that "[Y]esterday's planters of coffee and cocoa invest[ed] their profits shrewdly to become today's industrial capitalists." Instead, "... the state itself remains the main source of private fortunes, local capital is thoroughly subordinated to foreign capital, and that indigenous business interests are ensnared in the clientilistic networks of the regime". (Boone 1993: 67) In sum, the post-colonial experience of Côte d'Ivoire has confounded supporters and critics from both ends of the ideological scale.

Liberia

Because it was an independent country throughout the century, the experience of Liberia offers a potentially interesting contrast with other countries in the region. For several decades the country was governed by a clique composed of descendants of Africans who had been taken to America in slavery, and subsequently freed and returned to Liberia. This group, which had no links with the local population, eventually turned to repressive measures to maintain themselves in power, and did little to improve the country.

Starting in the 1920s, the Liberian economy was dominated by the Firestone Rubber Company, which farmed large plantations.[15] After World War II the country's dominant activity became metal mining and exporting, in which Japanese interests have recently become paramount. There had been little government borrowing before the 1950s. Development in the non-export sector has remained minimal, as the export activities had an inherently enclave productive process, their fiscal impact was minimal because of the unusually favorable tax regime that those companies faced, and there was a lack of an orientation toward development on the part of the successive governments. No railroad system was constructed, and rural infrastructural development had not been pursued.

Although per capita levels of foreign investment were not high before

1950, the evidence provided in Table 4.12 indicates that the ratio of FDI to trade was in fact relatively large, which indeed supports the conventional wisdom about foreign dominance. With the expansion of mines after 1950 the dominance of FDI became even higher in statistical terms, although what effectively happened is that the foreign controlled export enclave became more capital intensive. This situation persisted into the 1970s, until civil unrest made measurement of macroeconomic variables sporadic.

In spite of much government interest in expansion of manufacturing, only a very small fraction of the foreign investment has been placed in this sector. For example, Firestone always resisted the establishment of a tire factory in the country. Even the development of other agricultural exports has been slow. In general, the fraction of foreign ownership of the means of production is not directly measurable, because of the lack of national censuses. However, there is nothing in the literature to suggest the exist-

Table 4.12 Liberia: relative size of inward foreign investment stocks, twentieth century

	1929	1938	1950	1962	1970	1980	1990	1995
FI/capita		11			62	40	62	50
FDI/capita	4	9	7	84	41	15	37	29
FI/GDP					118	76	231	
FDI/GDP			45	189	78	29	136	
FI/trade		567			211	140	718	
FDI/trade	395	473	82	439	141	53	424	

Sources: Population: 1929–1938, author's estimates, based on reported later trends; 1950–1995, *International Financial Statistics Yearbook*. Foreign Investment: 1938, Lewis (1948); 1970–1995, summing FDI and loans; the latter using debt from various *World Debt Tables*. FDI: 1929, 1950, from United States Department of Commerce (1960); 1962, McLaughlin (1966: 66); 1970, OECD (1973); 1980 level is not given in the *World Investment Report*, and was taken as equal to the 1970 level; 1990 and 1995 are the sums of the 1970 datum, and total inflows reported in the *World Investment Report*. GDP: 1950, McLaughlin (1966: 183); 1962, calculated as the average for 1960, in McLaughlin (1966: 32) and 1965, from *International Financial Statistics Yearbook*; 1970–1989, from various *World Debt Tables*. Trade (average of exports and imports): 1929–1950, Mitchell (1995); 1962, *International Financial Statistics Yearbook*; 1970–1989, various *World Debt Tables*.

Notes
The population estimates for 1925 and 1950 in McEvedy and Jones (1978) are significantly higher than those reported for 1950 in the *International Financial Statistics Yearbook*, and so were not used. McLaughlin (1966: 183) indicates that the GDP estimate for 1950 is very rough. One reason for the lack of data for the 1990s would be armed conflict in the country. The low level of FDI/trade in 1950, compared to that ratio for 1938 or 1962, illustrates what is hopefully an extreme example of the limitations of the methodology employed in this manuscript. Several non-quantitative indicators would suggest that there was no absolute or relative decline of the size of foreign direct investment in 1950. One reason for an exaggerated fall in FDI/trade in 1950 was the rapid rise of the nominal value of trade, with exports rising dramatically in both price and volume with new products coming on line. One also presumes that prior to 1950, the Firestone Company had expanded using retained profits, which were not recorded in the valuation of FDI, thus also contributing to a drop in the value of FDI/trade.

ence of an important local agricultural, industrial, or even merchant class
(see McLaughlin 1966: 119). With regard to domestic rubber production,
data in McLaughlin (1966: 25, 27) would suggest that independent (local)
farmers only produced about one fifth of the total around 1960. For
several years, internal strife in the country has impeded any significant
improvement in these conditions.

Zaire

A creation of the Berlin Conference of 1885, the Congo Free State was the
privately owned fiefdom of King Leopold II until 1908, when it was ceded
to Belgium, shortly before the king's death. Two unfortunate aspects of
the Leopoldian legacy are a tradition of forced cultivation and corvée
labor, and a weak separation of the public and private sectors, to the
benefit of the latter, which was initially dominated by Belgian business and
financial elites.[16] Also established in those early years was the colony's
domination by the mining sector, relegating to settler agriculture a secondary role. The lack of settler resistance to independence was an important aspect of the decolonization process, as was the fact that Belgium's
paternalistic policies had hindered the formation of an indigenous political elite. Upon the granting of independence in 1960 a period of political
instability occurred, finally resolved with the assumption of power by
Mobutu Sese Seko in 1965, who ruled until his death in 1997. Mobutu's
reign motivated the introduction into the economic lexicon of the word
kleptocracy. Since his death, the country has been racked by civil war.

During the first half of this century, there was a significant amount of
foreign investment in the Belgian Congo, primarily in railroads and
mining. At the same time, government borrowing was not large, even
though significant guarantees were given to large foreign companies. As
shown in Table 4.13, the real value of foreign investment per person grew
steadily up until the early 1930s, declined somewhat for a decade, and
rose rapidly during the 1950s. The level of FDI/person fell during the
period of uncertainty associated with the achievement of independence,
and the subsequent periods of Africanization/Zairianization. The table
also indicates that FDI was also high when compared to GDP – using the
crude estimate of the latter generated by the central bank[17] – or to trade,
which was more accurately measured. Furthermore, after independence,
as FDI has shrunk in importance, the amount of foreign borrowing
increased, leading to debt payment problems in the late 1970s, which
became increasingly chronic thereafter.

Because of the significant inflation of the Belgian Franc during the
colonial era, it was standard practice to adjust nominal values of assets by
an appropriate price index, and we are fortunate to have estimates of the
real value of capital stock and foreign investment in the country. These
are presented in Graph 4.1, calculated in per capita terms (US$ at 1900

Table 4.13 Zaire: relative size of inward foreign investment stocks, twentieth century

	1900	1914	1929	1935	1938	1953	1970	1980	1990	1995
FI/capita		14	34	44	23	66	7	18	15	12
FDI/capita	4	10	28	34 ⎫		46	5	3	1	1
Non-RR FDI/capita			5	15 ⎬ 14						
FI/GDP			202	343	125	192	25	52	114	192
FDI/GDP			171 ⎫			135	16	10	9	15
Non-RR FDI/GDP			91 ⎬	245	79					
FI/trade		1,614	830	1,854	962	435	101	199	363	510
FDI/trade	544	1,103	703 ⎫			307	65	36	29	40
Non-RR FDI/trade		628	373 ⎬	1,324	607					

Sources: Population: 1900–1953, interpolated from the estimates in McEvedy and Jones (1978); 1970–1995, *International Financial Statistics*. FI is the sum of loans and FDI. Loans: 1914, 1928, 1936, Frankel (1938: Table 28); 1938, Lewis (1948); 1953, BBCCBRU (1955: 295); 1970–1995, various *World Debt Tables*. FDI: 1900, estimated by deflating the 1914 datum by the 1900–1914 growth of total capital stock in Huybrechts (1970: Annex Table 1); 1914–1935, Van de Velde (1936: 191); 1938, Lewis (1948); 1953, BBCCBRU (1955: 292); 1970, OECD (1973); 1980–1995, calculated by adding to the 1970 stock the cumulated inflows reported in *World Investment Report*, 1997. Railroad investments from Van de Velde (1936: 88), and Frankel (1938: 407). GDP: 1929–1953, BBCCBRU (1956); 1970–1995, various *World Debt Tables*. Trade (the average of exports and imports): 1900, Mitchell (1995); 1914, 1929, 1935, Frankel (1938); 1953, Mitchell (1995); 1970–1985, various *World Debt Tables*.

Notes
During the colonial period, Rwanda and [B]Urundi were often included in the total for the Belgian Congo; in terms of trade they represented only about one twentieth of the total. Although Frankel's 1935 datum for FDI is very similar to that of Van de Velde, he preferred a much higher total for 1914, equivalent to US$16 in 1900 prices. The Table's decline in reported investment between the levels in 1935 and 1953, as compared to that of 1938, results from the inconsistency due to different methodologies in the sources: Van de Velde (1936) and BBCCBRU (1955) have reflated values, while Lewis (1948) did not. In fact, the BBCCBRU (1955: 293) would raise the 1953 total (estimated by the Ministère des Colonies) by another third, as they used a different deflator.

prices) and as a fraction of GDP. The graph highlights how an increase in estimated per capita income causes a divergence in the paths of the indices deflated by population or GDP after the early 1930s; per capita levels stay constant, while K/GDP and FDI/GDP fall by almost half. The series on the stock of capital from BBCCBRU (1956) has a value similar to that of FDI in Huybrechts (1970), reflecting the belief that indigenous capital formation was minimal. Variations in the relative size of the two indexes presumably respond to the precariousness of deflating nominal values during high inflation eras. Although most of the raw data are not available, this result presumably arises from the use of different price indices, and greater attention to depreciation by the Central Bank. Nevertheless, the two sources both portray consistent trends.

According to Peemans (1975: 181), the distribution of assets in 1958 was very skewed along racial lines; Europeans comprised 1 per cent of the

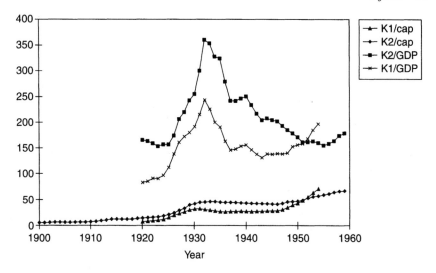

Graph 4.1 Belgian Congo: trends in the capital stock and FDI, 1900–1960

Sources: Population: author's interpolation of the data in McEvedy and Jones (1978); K1 capital stock from BBCCBRU (1956); K2: FDI from Huybrechts (1970); GDP: BBCCBRU (1956).

population, received 42 per cent of national income, controlled 82 per cent of the firms, and possessed 95 per cent of total assets. One of his major sources, the Central Bank's estimate of capital stock, essentially ignored the African subsistence farming sector. Although we discuss else-where other cases of third world countries where this assumption is quite misleading, it can be argued that it is more defensible here. First, the Belgian Congo was predominantly a mineral producing colony, and the value of European agricultural companies was only 15 per cent of total corporate stock in 1953 (BBCCBRU 1955: 296), having been 10 per cent in 1912 (Peemans 1975: 182). Furthermore, there are reasons to believe that the value of subsistence farmers' assets was smaller than that of the European farmers. Peemans (1975: 181) notes that "... various measures were taken, at least until 1945, to hamper indigenous economic initiative". The same message is put in slightly different terms by Ndongala (1982: 267): "In contrast to the English and French colonial agrarian policy, which encouraged Africans to cultivate their soil for their profit, the Belgian colonial policy consisted in favoring the development of the pro-duction of large plantations, directed by commercial societies or Euro-pean colonists" (my translation). Of course, very little hard data are available for the subsistence sector. One source is Lefebvre (1955), who presents data on the extension of land cultivation by indigenous vs. Euro-pean farmers, by crops. The Europeans produced on just one third of the land. About half of the cropland of the Africans was devoted to manioc and corn, and the Europeans clearly dominated, but did not monopolize, land producing exported products such as vegetable oils, coffee and rubber. In summary, although Africans worked most of the land, they produced the less capital intensive crops, and had minimal access to funds with which to invest in agricultural capital.

The estimated share of the government in the total capital stock in the 1950s was about 20 per cent, while parastatals accounted for 10–15 per cent, depending on the methodology utilized (BBCCBRU 1955: 301). In light of the above comments, this suggests a round figure for private sector, non-African ownership of total assets at two thirds. Although this may seem high, note that the estimated level in the colony for 1953 of FDI/GDP, 135, was actually even higher, compared to other entities analysed in this book. As a check, recall our the arithmetical identity between the two variables, FDI/K = FDI/GDP ÷ K/GDP. At mid-century, the capital output ratio (K/GDP) in the colony was almost two (1.9 in 1953), having declined from earlier (less reliably estimated) levels of three or higher in the 1920s (BBCCBRU 1956: 107). The capital output ratio was high, compared to that of other countries, because the two major economic activities, mining and railway transportation, were much more capital intensive than agriculture or even industry.

Belgian economic influence was all-encompassing during the colonial period. At mid-century, investment by non-Belgian foreigners only accounted for about 10 per cent of the total FDI (BBCCBRU 1955: 301). With regard to the issue of expatriate investment, Schröter (1998) downplays the fact that a significant amount of Belgian investment in the colony was in fact registered locally – half, according to the Congo's Central Bank (BBCCBRU 1955: 301) – as opposed to registration in Belgium. Schröter points out that this pattern started to emerge after World War I, and specifically asserts that control was not necessarily exercised at the place of registration, so that transferal of registration to the colony did not imply a lessening of control from outside.

Note should also be made of the high propensity to finance investments out of retained earnings. One unpublished study estimated this to have accounted for only 18 per cent of total funds before 1938, while the Central Bank calculated that this was the mode of financing 47 per cent of accumulated investment up through 1953 (BBCCBRU 1955: 293–4). The early post-World War II years would logically have seen high rates of reinvested profits, as credit was scarce and prices for Belgian Congo exports were also very high. In particular, Matukama (1988: 54) cites a study indicating that 74 per cent of Zaire's corporate investment was self-financed between 1950 and 1970. Van der Steen (1977) comments on the successive investment programs attempted by President Mobutu during the first years of independence, which ultimately were unsuccessful in stimulating new domestic private sector savings and investment.

The literature on the Belgian Congo also emphasizes the high degree of concentration of economic power; for example Peemans (1975: 183) cites studies concluding that four financial groups controlled almost 70 per cent of the economy in 1950, which was down slightly from the proportion that those same groups dominated in 1932. There is much debate about the continuity in the concentration of power between the colonial period and during the Mobutu regime. An important example is the copper mines. As recounted by Katwala (1979), a major foreign enterprise, UMHK, was nationalized in 1966. The resulting claims and counterclaims were resolved by an agreement giving control over marketing to a firm related to the UMHK, while ownership and control rested with a government parastatal, GECOMIN. Most commentators, of whatever political orientation, view arrangements such as this as leading to the worst of both worlds, in which power was increasingly concentrated in a rentseeking political establishment, whose mismanagement led to what Nzongola-Ntalaja (1986: 4) called the breakdown of the socio-economic infrastructure. In such a context only the largest and politically most powerful foreign firms were not driven from the scene. Although our data in Table 4.13 probably do not accurately trace the withdrawal of foreign investment, there can be no doubt as to the existence of this phenomenon.

British Tropical Africa

When investigating trends in foreign investment in British Africa, it is first necessary to treat separately the investment in southern Africa, which followed a different dynamic, and accounted for three fourths of the continent's total at the beginning of the twentieth century. We will first examine the evidence on British foreign investment in East and West Africa, sometimes referred to as tropical Africa, before examining South Africa and the Rhodesias. For East and West Africa, investment and output data are rather scattered, and even population estimates for the early period are quite rough. The available information for the entire century is summarized in Table 4.14. East and West Africa received about the same amount of investment in relative terms, before the achievement of independence around 1960. In both sub-regions, the decline of the investment ratios had begun well before independence.[18] After midcentury, the West African countries have received more of both FI and FDI.

The early levels of foreign investment per capita were rather low, and before the 1930s most of this was direct investment. One intriguing fact revealed by the table about the pre-1950 experience is the high levels of the ratio of investment to trade. Although GDP and capital stock estimates are not generally available, the implication from the trade ratios is that the corresponding ratios of FI and FDI to GDP or total capital would also be high. This is not surprising. Indeed, just as there had been little indigenous

Table 4.14 British West and East Africa: relative size of inward foreign investment stocks, twentieth century

	1900	1914	1935	1938	1950	1962	1970	1980	1990	1995
British West Africa										
FI/capita	7	8	10	4	1		8	10	20	22
FDI/capita		6	6	1	1	3	5	4	4	7
FI/GDP					6		19	17	141	173
FDI/GDP					5	15	11	7	31	59
FI/trade		317	441	203	29		131	43	331	367
FDI/trade		222	245	82	24	86	81	17	74	126
British East Africa & Sudan										
FI/capita	7	6	17	3	1		5	13	15	14
FDI/capita		6	5	2	<½	3	1	1	1	1
FI/GDP					5		22	49	97	
FDI/GDP					3	8	5	4	4	
FI/trade		440	797	159	29		97	189	463	387
FDI/trade		425	226	82	16	36	23	15	21	23

Sources: Population: 1900–1938, author's interpolations based on data in McEvedy and Jones (1978); 1950–1995, *International Financial Statistics Yearbook*. Foreign Investment and FDI: 1900, subtracting new series (1900–1913) in Frankel (1938: Table 26), from estimates for 1913 (which provides a total for East and West together); 1913, in West Africa, Paish (1914: v); and for East Africa, Frankel (1938: 150); government loans from *Statistical Abstract of the British Empire, 1931*; 1950, estimated by summing data for the United Kingdom and the United States, from Bank of England (1952) and US Department of Commerce (1960), respectively; 1962, summing UK and US data, from *Board of Trade Journal* (September, 1971) and various issues of the *Survey of Current Business*; 1970, summing government loans from *World Debt Tables* and FDI from OECD (1973); 1980–1995, from *World Investment Report*. GDP: 1950 and 1962, using United Nations *Yearbook of National Account Statistics* 1957, and the *International Financial Statistics Yearbook*, 1988; 1970–1995, various issues of the *World Debt Tables*. Trade (average of exports and imports): 1913–1935, Frankel (1938); 1938–1962, Mitchell (1995); 1970–1995, various issues of the *World Debt Tables*.

Notes
With the exception of the early estimates of FI and FDI, the regional sub-totals are the author's calculations based on data for individual colonies/protectorates. The geographical regions were selected to avoid the high investment areas of southern Africa, including the Union of South Africa and the Rhodesias, but inclusion by the sources of Sudan, Rhodesia, and Cameroon was not always consistent. According to Paish (1911), there was no private investment in railroads in West or East Africa in 1910.

development of machine-based production, nor was there significant local accumulation of physical capital as currently conceived. So, our expectation is that the ratio of FDI to the total capital stock would be very high. We turn now to a discussion of trends in individual countries, selecting cases from West and East Africa, before finally turning to southern Africa.

Ghana

One of the few British colonies for which estimates of the pre-Depression era level of total product exist is the Gold Coast in west Africa, now known as Ghana. At the turn of the century this area underwent significant change, due to the expansion of export-oriented cocoa production and mining, facilitated by the government-financed construction of railroads. According to the estimates of Szereszewski (1965: 149), per capita GDP – including traditional products – increased by 43 per cent over 1891–1911, at a very healthy rate of 1.8 per cent/year. During this period, the fraction of total output accounted by non-traditional production rose from 17 per cent to 43 per cent. That author also estimated (1965: 92) a doubling of per capita real GDP between 1911 and 1960, while the estimates of Omaboe (1960) suggested that 15 per cent of that increase occurred between 1911 and 1930, and of course the increased price of gold during the 1930s would also have benefited the Gold Coast. With such a strong economic base, predominantly in the hands of Africans, there was much hope for the future of the country upon its achieving independence in 1957 under Kwame Nkrumah. However, he was overthrown in 1966, a victim of bad politics, unsuccessful nationalistic economic policies, and a drastic decline in the price of the major export product, cocoa. Much of the country's subsequent history has been characterized by political and economic instability.

The data in the accompanying Table 4.15 indicate that even in per capita terms, the amount of foreign investment in Ghana was high during the colonial period. The major reason is the amounts of capital invested in mining. That the initial levels of FDI/GDP were not so large is simply a result of the higher levels of per capita income. Our calculations suggest a long-term decline in the relative importance of foreign investment, and direct investment, from the start of the century up through 1990. Very recently there has been a sharp increase, but regional macroeconomic problems continue to scare away foreign investors, in spite of an open attitude of Ghana's policy makers. We might also note in the table that there is a hint of an increase in FDI/GDP during the 1950s, which would agree with other information about the reduced economic opportunities during World War II, and strong growth during the 1950s.

Ghana is one of the few sub-Saharan countries for which estimates exist of the value of the domestic stock of capital. To be more precise, Szereszewski (1965 and 1966) did not include capital for traditional activities, although he did include land improvements for cocoa production, which had only recently begun to expand at the beginning of the twentieth century. It can be argued that traditional farming for local consumption did not involve much capital, particularly if this is conceived as items with a useable life of several years. Although Szereszewski still ignored the value of residential housing, it may be useful information. He estimated non-traditional capital in 1911 at just under £14 million. Our reading of Paish suggests a total of FDI at that time of £12 million. However, the resultant ratio FDI/K is too high, as Szereszewski indicated that half of domestic investments had been spent on railroads and cocoa, neither of which qualifies as FDI in our terms (railroads were government funded).

Table 4.15 Ghana: relative size of inward foreign investment stocks, twentieth century

	1911	1935	1938	1950	1962	1970	1980	1990	1995
FI/capita	29	33	15			17	14	13	16
FDI/capita	24	20	11	2	7	6	4	2	3
FI/GNP	75	87	43			37	38	59	96
FDI/GNP	60	52	31	5	14	13	11	10	20
FI/trade	353	333	193			156	135	260	301
FDI/trade	282	206	141	18	77	54	41	45	64

Sources: Population: 1900–1950, author's extrapolation of estimates in McEvedy and Jones (1978), subsequent years from various issues of the *International Financial Statistics Yearbook*. Foreign Investment (the sum of loans and direct investment): 1911, FI estimated to be £15m and FDI at £12m, based on the total for West Africa from Frankel (1938), that region's sectoral breakdown for 1910 in Paish (1911), supplemented by information in Szereszewski (1965) and Ndoma-Egba (1974); 1935, total and business ("private") from Frankel (1938); 1938 and 1950, total and business estimated by disaggregating the data for West Africa in Bank of England (1950 and 1953) according to the breakdown given in Frankel (1938); 1962, FDI taking UK from *Trade and Industry* November 15, 1973, that for the US is the average of the data for 1957 and 1967, from US Department of Commerce (1960) and OECD (1972), adjusting the sum upwards by accounting for other countries as per OECD (1972); for 1970–1995, loans from *World Debt Tables*; 1971, FDI from OECD (1973); 1980–1995, adds to the stock of FDI in 1970, the increments given in various issues of United Nations, *World Investment Report*. GDP: 1911, Szereszewski (1965); 1935 and 1938, using the 1930 estimate from Omaboe (1960); 1950 and 1962, *International Financial Statistics Yearbook*; 1970–1995, *World Debt Tables*. Trade (average of exports and imports): 1913–1935, Frankel (1938); 1938–1962, calculated from Mitchell (1995); 1970–1995, from various issues of the *World Debt Tables*.

Notes
All FDI was non-railroad. The 1911 FDI estimate appears high when compared to Szereszewski's estimate of total capital stock (£13.8 million), at least half of which was government or otherwise locally owned.

Part of the explanation for the inconsistency is that our mining estimate based on Paish (and Frankel) is too big; another factor would be the inclusion in Paish's data of the non-fixed capital assets of the trading companies, which should not be compared to estimated physical capital.[19] So the conclusion must be limited to affirming that the pre-World War I ratio of FDI/K was less than half. As would be expected from the other data in Table 4.15 on FDI/capita or FDI/GDP, the ratio of FDI/K fell between 1911 and 1960, by when it was only 7 per cent.[20]

For the early years of the century, the foreign ownership varied starkly by activity; cocoa production was in the hands of Africans, some of whom had recently immigrated into the country, as Polly Hill so presciently studied. The gold mines were owned and run by Europeans. Railroads accounted for about one quarter of fixed capital, and were financed by the government. Most of international trade was controlled by foreign companies, and this sector saw progressive consolidation into the United Africa Company, which itself became controlled by Unilever.

Nigeria

Apparently there are no estimates of GDP nor GDP/person for Nigeria for the period before 1950. Indeed, population estimates for the colony are poorer than they are for Ghana. In the late pre-independence period, Nigeria had three times the aggregate GDP of Ghana, but something like half the per capita income level.[21] The data in Table 4.16 suggest that Nigeria's experience with loans and FDI followed a path similar to that of Ghana, although starting out at a lower level in per capita terms. The pre-World War I levels are not large when comparing to average trade levels. Before petroleum came to dominate Nigeria's exports, her agricultural production and exports were more diverse than those of Ghana, the mining sector was less important, and more in the hands of Nigerians, and like Ghana its foreign trade was dominated by Europeans. Both countries had important railroad systems. Neither country had much manufacturing.

Mars (1948: 57) presents an estimate of Nigeria's capital stock of £79 million for 1942, and its disaggregation by owner into foreign (25 per cent), government (29 per cent), and Nigerian private (46 per cent). But he gives no hint of the source or methodology for his data. He certainly was familiar with Frankel's work, and his datum for foreign owned capital is arguably consistent with the latter's (£20 million versus £37 million; allowance taken for depreciation and non-fixed assets of the trading

Table 4.16 Nigeria: relative size of inward foreign investment stocks, twentieth century

	1913	1935	1938	1950	1962	1970	1980	1990	1995
FI/capita	3	8				5	10	24	19
FDI/capita	2	4	2	1	2	4	4	6	7
FI/GDP						17	15	162	195
FDI/GDP				4	14	12	6	37	71
FI/trade	313	578				130	37	337	365
FDI/trade	188	310	230	24	97	93	15	77	133

Sources: Population: 1900–1950, author's extrapolation of estimates in McEvedy and Jones (1978); subsequent years from issues of the *International Financial Statistics Yearbook*. Foreign Investment (the sum of loans and direct investment): 1913, FI estimated to be £20m and FDI at £12m, based on the 1913 total for West Africa in Frankel (1938), the sectoral breakdown for 1910 in Paish (1911), supplemented by information in Szereszewski (1965) and Ndoma-Egba (1974); 1935, total and business ("private") from Frankel (1938); 1938 and 1950, total and business estimated by disaggregating the data for West Africa in Bank of England (1950 and 1953) according to that region's breakdown by colonies in Frankel (1938); 1962, the Bank of Nigeria's *Economic and Financial Review* December, 1981; 1970–1995, loans from *World Debt Tables*; 1971, FDI from OECD (1973); 1980–1995, the accumulated inflows of FDI are given in various issues of the *World Investment Report*, which are added to the stock for 1971. GDP: 1950 and 1962, *International Financial Statistics Yearbooks*; 1970–1995, from various issues of the *World Debt Tables*. Trade (average of exports and imports): 1913–1935, Frankel (1938); 1938–1962, Mitchell (1995); 1970–1995, from various issues of the *World Debt Tables*.

companies).[22] It might also be supposed that his estimate of government capital stock was based on relatively well documented levels of expenditure. The reason for questioning his data is that the total would appear to be quite incompatible with the 1950 estimate of GDP, about £600 million (United Nations 1958), and our current understanding about the evolution of capital-output ratios.[23] The implication would be that Mars underestimated domestic capital, hence exaggerating the relative size of foreign ownership.

Kenya

This East African country holds special interest. Kenya has fertile land and good rainfall, and benefited at the start of the twentieth century from the railroad constructed from the coast through it into Uganda. Its physical setting made Kenya an important settler colony, but unlike the other such dependent colony in British Africa, South Rhodesia, it did not have significant mines. But scenic beauty was not the only attraction for outsiders; there were several laws and policies favoring the white settlers and discriminating against native Africans, which have been succinctly reviewed by Deininger and Binswanger (1995). After World War II there was a brief period during which official British policy still attempted to continue these policies, basing the colony's growth on settler agriculture. However, the events during the 1950s known then as "The Emergency", and now as the Mau Mau uprising, produced a reversal of the pro-settler policy, so that much of the land previously "scheduled" only for whites was subsequently sold and transferred to indigenous Africans. Independence came in 1963. Although President Jomo Kenyatta characterized the newly independent country's policies as African Socialism, his government was in fact quite open to foreign investment. Tourism has been a major area of investment, but in addition many multinationals have chosen Nairobi as the site for their regional offices.

Current levels of FDI/GDP are not high by international standards, and are much lower than earlier in the century. The basic data on Kenya are presented in Table 4.17, to which Table 4.14 above allows an approximation for 1913, based on combined totals for East Africa. While the FDI/GDP ratio may have declined by about 5 per cent between 1970 and 1995, the corresponding increase in total foreign investment – due to loans – has been 50 per cent. For the half century from 1930 to 1980, the available data leave us with an impression of a gradual decline of the ratio FDI/GDP in Kenya, that probably began even earlier.

Can the result of a decline in FDI/GDP be reconciled with the widespread impression of a flood of foreign investment into Kenya, after World War II and especially after independence? Support for an affirmative answer has several components. First of all, and quite mechanistically, GDP grew even faster than did FDI. This was not so much a nominal

Table 4.17 Kenya and Uganda: relative size of inward foreign investment stocks, twentieth century

	1935	1962	1970	1980	1990	1995
Kenya						
FI/capita	14		10	16	15	12
FDI/capita	4	4	3	3	2	1
FI/GDP			39	43	80	84
FDI/GDP		25	15	8	11	11
FI/trade	549		112	118	241	211
FDI/trade	174	86	37	21	31	26
Uganda						
FI/capita	14		4	4	7	8
FDI/capita	4	1	1	$<\frac{1}{2}$	$<\frac{1}{2}$	1
FI/GDP			10	54	53	60
FDI/GDP		8	3	5	1	6
FI/trade	549		68	171	444	317
FDI/trade	174	30	19	16	12	31

Sources: Population: 1935, author's extrapolation of estimates in McEvedy and Jones (1978); subsequent years from issues of the *International Financial Statistics Yearbook*. Foreign Investment (the sum of loans and direct investment): 1935, total and business using the combined data for Kenya and Uganda from Frankel (1938); 1962, estimated for each country projecting up from the amount from the United Kingdom in the *Board of Trade Journal* September 1970, and the UK's 1967 share of each country's total FDI, in OECD (1972); 1970–1995, loans from the *World Debt Tables*; 1971 FDI from OECD (1973); 1980–1995, FDI from various issues of the *World Investment Report*. GDP: 1962, *International Financial Statistics Yearbook*; 1970–1995, from various issues of the *World Debt Tables*. Trade (average of exports and imports): 1935, Frankel (1938); 1962, Mitchell (1995); 1970–1995, various issues of *World Debt Tables*.

Notes
West (1965: 33) estimated the Kenyan GDP at £8.8 million for 1935, which is slightly higher than the estimate of private listed capital for Kenya and Uganda combined, in Frankel (1938, Table 28). Although we lack a breakdown of foreign investment by territories, we might conjecture that the FDI/GDP ratio for Kenya in 1935 was between 50 and 75 per cent. Moreover, Frankel also estimated settler capital at that time at somewhere between £4 and £20 million.

growth due to inflation as an acceleration of the growth of real GDP; not only of GDP/capita but also of population, for the latter has attained one of the highest rates in the world. Furthermore, there is an illusion created by not separating direct investment from loans, for example in the official data cited by Leys (1975: 118). There is also an issue of perception: some of the new investment was in consumer goods whose advertising increased its impact on a less sophisticated public. It should also be remembered that during this time European farmers were selling their farms and relocating to the cities – this process was probably not picked up in the data. In addition, as noted below, the expansion of East Indian Kenyans into manufacturing heightened the impression of Africans being surpassed by outsiders. Finally, it should be emphasized out that although FDI inflows maintained a high level compared, for example, to pre-World War II years, the acceleration of FDI inflows had pretty much stopped by the mid

1970s, resulting in a subsequent decline in the ratio of the stock of FDI to GDP. Rather more ominous was the above noted acceleration of foreign borrowing, which led to several episodes of debt crises and unsuccessful stabilization programs.

The existence of a sizeable settler population in a colony relatively open and attractive for foreign investors leads to a consideration of the overall distribution of assets. At the twilight of the colonial period this can be approximated for all parts outside of the African rural sector. For fixed agricultural capital in 1958, Ord (1962) reported £28 million owned by European farmers resident in the colony, and £11 million by overseas firms. The non-agricultural private sector had £51 million owned by over-seas companies (£40 million from the United Kingdom), and £74 million owned by residents, of which £29 million was in the hands of Europeans. These estimates are supported by an estimate, using British data, of the value of the stock of foreign direct investment in a range between £30–50 million.[24] In a subsequent publication also referring to 1958, Leys (1975: 42) suggested that plantation agriculture (foreign companies) had a value of £25–30 million, and raised the estimate for European settler farms to £40–45 million. Ord placed the African ownership of industrial assets at only three million pounds,[25] with the other £40+ million being owned by Asians. Thus, the European settlers controlled almost as much wealth as did the foreign firms, with most of the rest of private sector capital, about one quarter, in the hands of residents of Asian descent. Inventories and livestock were estimated at £86 million, and urban housing at £26.5 million (Ord 1962).

The value of government assets was not similarly measured, but Swain-son (1980: 36, 111) cites unpublished estimates by Ord which indicate a gradual decline of the importance of the public sector in total gross capital formation, from 44 per cent in the mid-1920s, to 25 per cent in the mid-1950s. Thus we might raise the datum on total capital in Ord (1962: 238) of £250 million (net physical assets, excluding African agriculture), by one third, for a round total of £330 million. The colony's 1958 GDP was estimated to be £208 million, and the resulting capital output ratio of over 1.5 is credible, especially given the attention paid to depreciation in the census.

There have been few efforts at measuring the wealth of black African farmers, and the presumption is that their capital accumulation had been small,[26] as was their share of national income.[27] They had been dispos-sessed of their ancestral territories in the central highlands, their ability to enter into the national and international markets had been restricted by the settlers, and in particular the European-run credit agencies paid them little attention.[28]

While African agriculture has flourished since independence, so has urban growth, in both industry and services. In the latter sector a domin-ant role has been played by Kenyans of Indian descent, whose forebears had arrived as indentured workers before World War I, or indeed had been involved in trading at various ports of the Indian Ocean for centuries. Himbara (1994: 6) argued that Kenyan capitalists of Indian descent "... spearheaded the industrialization process from the 1940s onwards. For the black segment of the Kenyan capitalist class, it was confirmed that they remained numerically and strategically inconsequential..." More recently, Chege (1998: 209) has provided "... evidence that credit for Kenya's economic achievements is more widespread and more race neutral". This issue of ethnicity had important implications for independent Kenya's efforts towards "Africanization" of management positions as well as control of enterprises, and is further complicated by the fact that some Kenyan born Asians retained citizenship in the country of their ancestors.

Uganda

Foreign investment has always been relatively smaller in Uganda than in Kenya, as Table 4.17 also indicates. Indeed, the one major British project in colonial Uganda was the government financed railroad, the motive for which was predominantly strategic – protecting the headwaters of the Nile. Settler agriculture was not nearly as successful in Uganda as it had been in Kenya, and hopes in the colony as a British controlled source of cotton did not materialize. It will be recalled that with the accession to power of Idi Amin, Uganda's relations with most industrial countries reached terrible lows, from which the country is only now beginning to emerge.

The path of the investment ratios in Tanzania is rather similar to that of Uganda, and will not be pursued here. In the former country a well-articulated motivation for autarchic policies was presented by the government of its first president, Julius Nyerere. The natural resource endowment of Tanzania is much poorer than that of its erstwhile colleagues in the East African Union, providing another reason for the lack of interest by foreign investors.

Union of South Africa

The Union of South Africa was established in 1910. The development of diamond mines had already initiated fundamental changes in the economic trajectory of the area during the 1860s, and the gold mines were to assume that leading role in the 1880s. One central aspect of the economic history of South Africa is the move beyond raw material exports at the turn of the century, to develop a manufacturing sector, which by the 1950s had more fixed capital than mining. The high average income of South Africa and the several similarities of its productive structure to that of countries in Europe make it difficult to categorize the country in terms of

First or Third World, while, for that reason, making the country's story all the more interesting.

Like settler colonies elsewhere, South Africa had received a large amount of British overseas investment; fully three fourths of the accumulated amount in Africa in 1914. Much of that investment had been in mining, as well as in speculative land companies oriented toward mining. The long-term path of foreign investment in South Africa involves a reduction of foreign investment from quite high levels at the beginning of the century, followed by a minor recovery recently. This is indicated in Table 4.18.

Because of the inherent nature of exploratory mining, the initial stages of the foreign investment in this sector in South Africa had more in common with Free Standing Companies and expatriate investment, than with the "American model" of FDI. Speculation played a major role in the first waves of mining, which is an aspect of entrepreneurship not emphasized in the FSC literature. However, what we prefer to emphasize is the fact that an important characteristic of the South African experience was the transference of the location of control, from London to South Africa. Localization is perhaps a more appropriate term for this process than indigenization, as European settlers retained control.

Table 4.18 Union of South Africa: relative size of inward foreign investment stocks, twentieth century

	1900	1913	1935	1938	1956	1962	1970	1980	1990	1995
Inward Investment										
FI/capita	157	202	145	57	82	53	65	101	52	65
FDI/capita		140	83	35	45	16	41	49	14	18
FI/GDP		235	138	56	70	55	50	45	36	41
FDI/GDP		163	79	34	38	33	32	22	10	11
FI/trade		667	594	255	246	306	226	146	144	190
FDI/trade		461	307	154	134	184	143	71	38	51
Outward FI/GDP					21	24	21	24	22	26
Outward FDI/GDP					6	8v	7	8	16	18
Net Inward FDI/GDP					32	25	24	14	−6	−6

Sources: Population: 1900–1938, author's extrapolation of estimates in McEvedy and Jones (1978), subsequent years from issues of the *International Financial Statistics Yearbook*. Foreign Investment and FDI: 1900–1935, Frankel (1938); 1938, Bank of England (1950); 1956–1995, various issues of the *Quarterly Bulletin of Statistics* of the South African Reserve Bank. GDP: all estimates from various issues of the South African *Statistical Yearbook*. Trade (average of exports and imports): 1913–1935, Frankel (1938); 1938–1962, Mitchell (1995); 1970–95, various issues of the *International Financial Statistics Yearbook*.

Notes
There were significant amounts of railroad trackage financed by private investors in the early decades of the century. However, since most of this was used only by the mining companies, separate data on it do not exist. Paish (1911: 180) reported a total of £9.4 million in railroad companies in South Africa, out of total investments in the private sector of £242 million. Use of these estimates results in non-railroad FDI/capita at 131, non-railroad FDI/GDP at 152, and non-railroad FDI/trade at 431.

The identification of the point at which, say, the mining sector should be considered South African as opposed to British is evidently problematic, given the country's Dominion status and the ease with which its leaders moved in British society. For example, Cecil Rhodes lived most of his adult life in southern Africa, including six years as Prime Minister of the Cape Colony, but he is typically described as a *British* imperialist. We will suggest placing that transition to local control during the period between the two world wars, which historians indeed recognize as one of growing nationalism in South Africa. Illustrative of this process is the case discussed in Innes (1984: 105–6) of how Ernest Oppenheimer, a German born member of the South African Parliament, successfully maneuvered to have the Diamond Control Act of 1925 give preference to *local* interests, characteristics to be determined by source of financing, residence of owners, and registration. One beneficiary was the recently formed Anglo-American Corporation – which Oppenheimer led – and which was registered inside the country. Soon after, Oppenheimer's group dominated the diamond syndicate, absorbing along the way the foreign registered De Beers, one of whose co-founders had been Rhodes. Incidentally, today Anglo-American is probably the biggest South African based transnational corporation. It could be pointed out that in his study of overseas investment, Frankel (1938) did not address the issue of location of control, but only of where the funds originated. One presumes that he would have found the distinction between domestic and imperial control quite artificial. In any event, it is certainly the case that discussions of the mines after World War II treat them as South African controlled.

Writing in London during the period we identify as that of localization of the South African mines, Kindersley (1935: 449) made the following general comment about companies financed by capital from Britain, but registered overseas: "In fact [their] growth ... indicated the diminished scope for the direct development of overseas territories by British skill and enterprise, and the desire of Dominion and foreign countries, after a certain stage, to proceed with further developments under their own management." Kindersley then went on to explain that the incidence of the British income tax had encouraged the growth of overseas registered companies. In addition, he highlighted the South African gold mines as the principal example of this class of firms, which were still "substantially owned and virtually controlled by British interests" (ibid). An important contributor to the localization of the mines had to have been the existence of a stock market in Johannesburg, well established before the twentieth century, which facilitated local financing.

To pursue this argument, two related points are made in Table 4.19. First, a significant amount of the total foreign investment in the country was in fact reinvested profits, as shown both in Frankel's data for the mines and in the official data for 1956, the year of the first foreign investment census. Secondly, inclusion of reinvested profits as well as short-term accounts bridges most of the gap between the amount of British FDI reported by the South African central bank, £556 million, and the corresponding total capital raised in England, reported by the Bank of England, at only £127 million. This suggests a similar interpretation of the gap in Table 4.19 between Frankel's estimate of British capital in South Africa and that reported by Kindersley in the mid-1930s. These two sources appear basically compatible, but reflect differing concepts of foreign investment, particularly because Frankel included reinvested profits. As such, Frankel's South African data should only be used with qualifications in discussions of FDI and capital exported from the United Kingdom, and the many studies which have not done so have exaggerated the amount of foreign investment in the country, by overlooking the process of relocation of control which was quantitatively so important.

The story for industry is quite different. Foreign investment in this sector grew dramatically after World War II. Previously, South Africa had experienced significant growth of local manufacturing. Several factors had contributed; tariffs, government parastatal corporations, a shared goal among the ruling elite of obtaining economic independence, and a strong raw materials led export economy, most notably gold during the 1930s. Unlike some east Asian NICs, however, South Africa has never progressed to the exportation of manufactured consumer goods using its "cheap" labor, rather its industrial exports have always been technology intensive, often related to capital goods in mining.

The availability of data for South Africa allows us to present calculations of the ratios of FDI to different measures of the capital stock and national wealth, which are illustrated in Graph 4.2. It would appear that the foreign ownership in 1913 is exaggerated. The reported amount of foreign investment in mining was more than double the reported value of the stock of fixed capital in that sector – the depreciated capital stock of mining in 1910 was £50 million in Franzsen and Willers (1959: Table 1), compared to British mining investment of £125 million in Paish (1911: 180). One explanation for this is the importance of the value of land, which is not included in a calculation of fixed (reproducible) capital, but would have absorbed some of the initial FDI outlay. In addition, exploration costs are probably not included in fixed capital, but presumably were included in the reported FDI totals. This exaggeration, which also occurs in other countries (e.g. Argentina, Venezuela) implies that the use of the ratio of FI or FDI to total fixed capital may overstate the importance of foreign control in the entire economy, particularly in mining and petroleum.

Because the statistical information available about South Africa is quite detailed, the period after 1956 can be analysed using official census data. The data shown in Graph 4.3 reveal strong differences by sectors in the degree of foreign control inside the country, with manufacturing, internal trade, construction, and mining having significant foreign control. Of

Table 4.19 British capital invested in South Africa, 1930s and 1956 (£ million)

1935a *Frankel*	Total	523.0		
	Public Listed Capital		224.1	
	Private Listed		250.8	
	Estimated Private Non-listed		47.5	
1935b *Frankel*	Accumulated capital in mines[a]	153.8		
	Loans: Total		51.5	
	Repaid			49.5
	Outstanding			1.9
	Profits Appropriated for Capital and Loans		80.0	
1936 *Kindersley*	Total[b]	248		
	Government and Municipal		103	
	Other		145	
	Mines			72
1938 *Bank of England*	Total[c]	199		
	Government and Municipal		99.1	
	Business		99.7	
	Shares			87.6
	Loans			12.1

1956 *Bank of England:* UK Securities to South Africa

Total:	155.0		
Government and Municipals		28.5	
Business		126.5	
Shares			113.7
Loans			13.3

1956 *Reserve Bank of South Africa:* Liabilities to United Kingdom

Total	865.6		
Direct		556.1	
Shares (nominal value)			148.0
Undistributed Profits[d]			220.0
Loans			32.2
Other[e]			155.9

Sources: Frankel (1938), Frankel (1967), Kindersley (1937), Bank of England (1950), Reserve Bank of South Africa *Quarterly Bulletin of Statistics: Supplement* (1958).

Notes
[a] Item is accumulated total capital with vendors at par; with vendors revalued is £203 million.
[b] Refers to South Africa and Rhodesia. As a potential comparison, note that the Bank of England's 1938 data on securities indicates £99 million for South Africa, and £73 million for the Rhodesias and Nyasaland. Kindersley had estimated the amount of British capital in South Africa (presumably also including the Rhodesias and Nyasaland) for 1930 at £224 million (Kindersley 1933: 200). It is also of interest to note that Staley (1935: 537) estimated total investment in the Union of South Africa in 1929 at US$1.3 billion, or about £267 million, by capitalizing the interest and dividend payments on long term capital, and comparing that total with "... incomplete international indebtedness data ...".
[c] For comparison, Lewis (1948) reports 1938 UK investments in South Africa and Rhodesia of £251 million, of which £109 million was government.
[d] Although the comparison is imperfect, it may be of interest to note that accumulated undistributed profits in the South African mines in 1956 was 183 million £ (Frankel 1967: 122).
[e] Includes branch balances, loans, mortgages, insurance, and short term obligations.

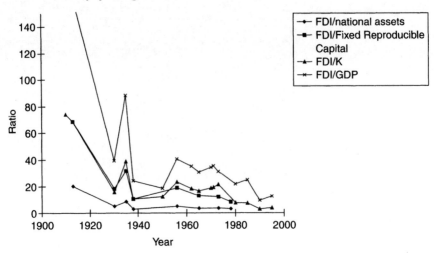

Graph 4.2 South Africa: foreign direct investment ratios, twentieth century

Sources: FDI: 1913, on the basis of Paish (1911 and 1914); 1930, Kindersley (1933: 201) –
apparently including investment in Rhodesia; 1935, Frankel (1938); 1938, Bank of England
(1948); 1956–1995, various issues of South African Reserve Bank *Quarterly Bulletin*, and the
South African *Statistical Yearbook*. National Assets and Fixed Reproducible Capital, Goldsmith
(1985). Capital Stock (K): 1913–1959, Franzsen and Willers (1959: Table III); 1956–1995, De
Jager (1973) and subsequent issues of South African Reserve Bank *Quarterly Bulletin*. GDP,
Goldsmith (1985), and the South African *Statistical Yearbook*.

course, the percentage foreign ownership of mining at mid-century had
already declined from earlier levels.

These observations suggest an upper bound on total foreign ownership
of domestic capital of less than 40 per cent at the start of the century.
According to the calculations of Franzsen and Willers (1959), mining and
manufacturing together amounted to about one fourth of total fixed
capital before World War I. For a rough calculation, if we take the following ratios of foreign ownership of capital in 1913: mining 100 per cent,
manufacturing 80 per cent, agriculture 50 per cent, railroads 10 per
cent, and zero elsewhere, then the overall ratio is calculated to be 33 per
cent. The quality of the aggregate data does not support an assertion
about trends between 1938 and 1955. However, given what is known of
ownership of mining companies, the declining trend after 1955 shown in
Graph 4.3 would seem to be valid.

One of the most important political events in recent South African
history was the ending of legal racial separation under the *apartheid*
regime. Campaigns of diplomatic and economic sanctions had been
brought to bear on the country to bring this about, with increasing impact
during the 1980s. At the time, there was considerable controversy in the
United Nations and in the OECD countries about the advisability of apply-

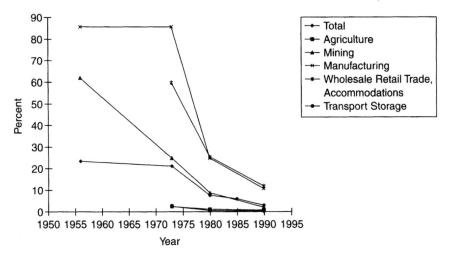

Graph 4.3 South Africa: foreign ownership by sector, 1956–1990

Sources: Author's calculations, based on FDI and the capital stock, total and by sectors, from several issues of the South African Reserve Bank *Quarterly Bulletin.*

ing sanctions, and debate continues today about their role in forcing a change in policy. During the 1980s, the nominal dollar value of the inward stock of FDI in South Africa fell by almost half, some $7 billion (*World Investment Report* 1998: 373). De Villiers (1995: 96) cites a governor of the South African Reserve Bank, who estimated a "politically induced capital outflow of $11 billion", over 1985–1988; the country was soon faced with a major debt payments problem. Although these numbers certainly suggest that sanctions had a significant impact, three other considerations should be mentioned. The exogenous changes in the capital account of the balance of payments were probably larger, and more rapid, through the changes in foreign loans than via shifts of FDI.[29] Secondly, because of the sophistication of domestic entrepreneurial skills, we would expect, along the lines of the Investment Development Path paradigm, that South Africa might well have been able to reduce some of its inward FDI independently of foreign pressures. Indeed, some of the reduction in the stock of FDI did not represent an elimination of the local production, but simply a paperwork change of ownership which left local management structure intact. Finally, De Villiers devotes an entire chapter to "The Sanctions of the Markets", which essentially attributes more power to markets than to individual boycotters. While that position does not negate the power of an effective campaign aimed at major international banks, which would then refuse to renew loans to a country, it does argue for the need of a careful examination of both political and economic factors, moving beyond a simple listing of data on inward stock of FDI.

A final aspect of the South African experience that is worth remarking is the growth in outward foreign investment. The data indicate that the country has been a net supplier of direct investment since 1986. Although as we have just seen, the impact of international sanctions against the apartheid system discouraged inward investment, that cannot be the entire explanation for the shift in the net position. The rising trend in outward direct investment is evident in the data for the 1970s, and of course the decline of inward investment – relative to GDP or to the aggregate capital stock – had already begun by 1913, with only a brief interruption during the 1950s.

Unfortunately, the official data do not provide a sectoral breakdown of the outward investment. In addition, the data indicate that the largest single recipient is Luxembourg, which of course is not the ultimate location of the investment. It is widely believed that mining is important – see Kaplan (1983). The development of a competitive advantage in those capital goods associated with mining was a precursor to investing abroad in these activities. Kaplan (1983) contrasted this country's experience with those of Argentina and India, but perhaps a more useful comparison would be with Australia and Canada, which have also expanded abroad in sectors related to their raw material exports. After reviewing what is known about the geographical location of the South African investment, Kaplan suggests several characterizations; a preference for investment in the industrially advanced countries – the United Kingdom and the United States; a preference for purchase rather than "greenfield" development, majority ownership, and investment in the area of a firm's domestic activity. The implication of this analysis is to downplay "capital flight" as a motive for FDI, and emphasize the pursuit of organizational advantages. The relatively high ratio of FDI over portfolio flows supports that interpretation.

North and South Rhodesia

The formal European colonization of the area now composed of Zambia and Zimbabwe began with the granting in 1889 of a charter for that purpose to the British South Africa Company, led by Cecil Rhodes. It was only in 1922 that a vote decided that this area was to be a self-governing colony, politically distinct from the Union of South Africa. The economic ties remained, however, especially in mining and industry, as well as railroad transportation. Although the British South Africa Company failed to discover a second Rand of abundant gold deposits, Southern Rhodesia did have other minerals, and certain crops flourished, particularly tobacco. Very rich copper mining developed in the northern part of what is now known as Zambia, not far from the copper producing areas of the Belgian Congo.

In the 1950s there was an attempted federation of North and South Rhodesia, together with Malawi/Nyasaland. At the dissolution of this Federation in the early 1960s, Zambia/North Rhodesia became governed by Kenneth Kaunda, a black African, while South Rhodesia produced a unilateral declaration of independence, under a defiant white leadership in what has been called the only (European-) settler led decolonization of this century. International sanctions contributed to a situation where this country's development was rather autarchic. Majority rule in Zimbabwe/South Rhodesia was finally achieved in 1980 under Robert Mugabe.

The available data summarized in Table 4.20 indicate that this area had very high levels of foreign investment early in the last century. This appears to be the case even allowing for the exaggeration due to accounting conventions in mining investments, such as the inclusion of exploration expenses. Expatriate investment cannot be separated out, but the fact that European settlement began rather late would suggest that this type of investment was not large, compared to the amounts in mining. Furthermore, although the foreign investment has declined relative to income (or trade) in both countries after the 1950s, the Table shows that it has stayed above levels in most other third world regions.

Zimbabwe

Of the two countries emerging from Rhodesia, Zimbabwe had the higher level of foreign investment. The analysis is made difficult because of the importance of the Union of South Africa as a source for that foreign investment. Perhaps the best informed scholar is Colin Stoneman, whose estimates, along with those of others, are conveniently summarized in Clarke (1980: 32). The accumulated amount of FDI in Zimbabwe in 1978–79 was between £1.2 and £1.6 billion, of which 30 per cent was from South Africa, and 50 per cent from the United Kingdom. At the going exchange rate, this was between US$2.2 to 2.9 billion. An estimate of total FDI more than double that amount is reported by the United Nations. According to two successive UN reports, UNCTAD (1993: 249; 1994b: 416), the inward stock of FDI in Zimbabwe fell by two thirds during the 1980s, about US$4 billion, although the most recent *World Investment Directory* and *World Investment Report*, and UNCTAD (1997) use a different data base, for which the decline in FDI stock is nowhere near that value. Stoneman had worked with UNCTAD, but has distanced himself from those estimates, in private communication with this author.

What is striking in Stoneman's calculations is that, notwithstanding the "inadequacy of the statistics", he estimated that "the domestic stake in productive enterprise" was 20–30 per cent of the total in 1945 (Stoneman 1976: 33–4) and one third in 1978–79 (Clarke 1980: 32), which are comparatively high levels. Consideration of post independence government investment might bring the foreign total down to slightly over one half.

Table 4.20 The Rhodesias/Zambia and Zimbabwe: relative size of inward foreign investment stocks, twentieth century

	1913	1935	1938	1950	1962	1970	1980	1990	1995
North and South Rhodesia									
FI/capita	109	91	66	14		45	45	35	30
FDI/capita		56	54	6	45	29	24	11	9
FI/GDP		341	243	55		75	72	108	135
FDI/GDP		210	202	23	104	50	40	35	41
FI/trade	1,534	839	598	107		187	178	272	245
FDI/trade		515	497	44	262	119	97	84	72
Zambia/Northern Rhodesia									
FI/capita						52	45	43	34
FDI/capita					33	24	9	9	8
FI/GDP						71	79	174	208
FDI/GDP					88	37	19	41	54
FI/trade						141	157	332	376
FDI/trade					190	66	33	68	86
Zimbabwe/Southern Rhodesia				*(1953)*	*(1963)*				
FI/capita				63	83	40	45	28	26
FDI/capita				45	53	32	36	13	9
FI/GDP				172	179	80	68	73	98
FDI/GDP				124	114	65	55	32	36
FI/trade				403	524	281	199	221	217
FDI/trade				290	333	227	160	98	79

Sources: Population: 1900–1950, author's extrapolation of estimates in McEvedy and Jones (1978); subsequent years from issues of the *International Financial Statistics Yearbook*. Foreign Investment (the sum of loans and direct investment): for "North and South Rhodesia" 1914 FI, Frankel (1938: 150); 1935 FI and FDI (business), Frankel (1938: Table 28); 1938 and 1950, Bank of England (1950 and 1953). Zambia's 1970 FDI as the value of mines given by Martin (1975: 195); the value for 1962 calculated by subtracting from that 1970 datum, the estimated accumulated investment 1962–1970, of US$80 million, based on information in various years of the *Mining Industry Year Books*; 1980–1995, the accumulated inflows, as given in the *World Investment Report* 1997. Zimbabwe's FDI for 1953–1979 from Clarke (1980: 32); 1990–95, calculated using the 1979 datum and the accumulated FDI inflows in the *World Investment Report* 1997. 1970–1995, loans are "Long Term Debt" from various issues of the *World Debt Tables*. GDP: 1935 GDP for "North and South Rhodesia" is double Frankel and Herzfeld's estimated "money income," as reported in Barber (1961); 1950–1963, for both countries the data are the official estimates, as reported in Mitchell (1995); 1970–1995, from various issues of the World Bank, *World Debt Tables*. Trade (average of exports and imports): 1913–1935 from Frankel (1938); 1938–1962 from Mitchell (1995) dollar values of exports and imports for 1970–1995 from various issues of World Bank, *World Debt Tables*.

Notes
The Frankel/Herzfeld estimate of £14.5 million for South Rhodesian income in 1935 did not include African produce sold, nor, presumably, on-farm consumption. According to the official estimates for the immediate post-World War II years, this totaled between 10–15 per cent of total income. Deane (1948) estimated 1938 income of Northern Rhodesia at £13.4 million, of which 12 per cent was African agriculture. It was not possible to isolate investments in railroads. The data on foreign investment for 1950 are clearly underestimates, not only because the Bank of England did not incorporate retained profits, but also because of the omission of investments from South Africa. These data are included only for comparison. The *World Investment Report* for 1993 reports a total of US$6.7 billion for the FDI stock in Zimbabwe in 1980, which is not compatible with any other information available, and so was not used here.

Zambia

If the history of Southern Rhodesia/Zimbabwe can be described as that of an area dependent on both the Union of South Africa, and, in turn, on Britain, then that of Zambia/Northern Rhodesia might also be described as the smaller fish. The initial interest of the Europeans in this area was basically to use it as a path to the flourishing copper mines in the Belgian Congo. It was not until the 1920s/30s that it was realized that Zambia had copper of its own in commercially viable levels, in an area bordering on the Congo referred to as the copperbelt. The area's production was dominated by copper; agriculture was not promising, and neither gold nor diamonds ever appeared.

The breakup of the Federation of Rhodesia and Nyasaland in 1963 represented a political divide which for Zambia soon resulted in independence under Kenneth Kaunda. The foreign companies were awkwardly positioned to confront the nationalism that his government represented, and investment inflows declined, a process which accelerated after 1969 when his government purchased half the stock of the mines. A tempering of attitudes has led to a notable increase in recent years, as indicated in Table 4.20.

Notes

1 Although this country is currently named the Democratic Republic of the Congo, we will refer to it by its previous and more familiar name of Zaire.

2 The difficulty in finding accurate data is indicated in the Egyptian case with regards to foreign investment totals immediately after World War II. The largest single investing country would have been the United Kingdom, yet the Bank of England (1950) lists total nominal capital of only £7 million in 1948.

3 A parallel with post-Ottoman Turkey in the 1920s and 1930s is evident, although the usefulness of such comparisons is limited by the political and economic importance of the Canal, as well as by Egypt's armed conflicts with Israel, Britain, and France.

4 Baer (1962: 230) has a table indicating that the percentage of privately owned land held by foreigners declined from 11 per cent in 1900 to 4 per cent in 1950.

5 In the words of Issawi (1963: 6), Egypt had been ruled by foreigners for 2,500 years. The most recent group was the Mamluks, of Turkish-Albanian origin.

6 Terminology is problematical. Writing before World War I, Oualid divided the entire population of Algeria into *Indigènes* and Frenchmen (or Europeans). Many European writers often further distinguished among Arabs, Berbers, and Kabyles, with a negative connotation for the first group and a positive one for the last. An important contemporary author, Charles Ageron, employs the term Algerian Moslems. Rejecting the term "natives" for its insensitivity to local history, as well as its racist connotations in other contexts, we will refer to indigenes or indigenous Algerians.

7 With regard to loans to the colonial (central) government, it is necessary to recall that Algeria did not receive any sort of fiscal autonomy before 1900, so that the accounting of such loans must begin after 1900.

8 The neatness of these categories is easily exaggerated. Funds for interest rate

guarantees would have released monies which could be used for other purposes, thus indirectly the guarantees acted as loans. Moreover, some significant fraction of loans to the government was spent on railroads. Furthermore, during the first decades of the twentieth century the railroads were absorbed by the government, with the amount of payment determined sometimes several years later.

9   The listing in Douël (1930) does not distinguish between current and capital expenditures, and some of the public works expenditures was spent on railroads, further contributing to making this estimate a rough approximation.

10   Deflating Amin's data, in 1955 Francs, by 150, as in Poquin (1957: 189).

11   Oualid (1910a and 1910b) used a methodology based on a study of wealth in France, whose authors were Lavergne and Henry. It is somewhat reassuring to note that the estimate Oualid attributed to those scholars of the value of physical capital in France in 1908, FF190 billion, is comparable to the recent estimate of tangible assets in 1913, FF253 billion, presented by Goldsmith (1985: Table A5).

12   Swearingen (1987: 143–4). That author goes on to point to concentration of land inside both the settler community and the natives, with their being a sizeable group of Moroccan elite which owned latifundia – extensive, low productivity farms.

13   The totals for private sector, foreign owned firms corresponds well with the FDI data in OECD (1973).

14   Recall that the political borders drawn by the Europeans divided many ethnic groups in West Africa. The growth of agricultural production in Côte d'Ivoire (as in Ghana) used labor from outside the immediate area, many of whom risked nationalist reactions against foreigners.

15   This company had long been established in the United States, and was seeking to develop a cheap source of raw materials, as a response to artificially high prices resulting from the Stevenson plan which had reduced production in Asia. Firestone's timing was similar to that of Henry Ford's, whose plantations in Brazil were not successful.

16   Peemans (1980: 261) speaks of Leopold's "... state apparatus in the colony which had all the features of the mercantilist epoch (monopoly of exploitation of the natural resources, extreme harshness of the methods used to mobilize manpower resources, confusion between private and public uses of State money)", while Fieldhouse (1965: 357) comments that "... this empire was nonetheless important in modern colonial history as a microcosm – almost a caricature – of evolving European attitudes to tropical dependencies". A rather different legacy is one of the best sets of data for the colonial era. This arises fundamentally because of the good records kept by the Belgian authorities, and the virtual absence of a domestic – African – role in the formal sector of the economy.

17   The series was calculated by adding (a) an assumed fixed per capita production on the part of subsistence farmers, to (b) the value of production in the formal sectors, which was adequately registered by existing statistics of exports, industrial production, trade and government employment (BBCCBRU 1956: 100). While this methodology cannot address the fundamental question of colonial history – the impact of Europeans on indigenous people – it may well satisfy our need of an indicator of overall production, given the recognizably small contribution of agriculture in this mining economy.

18   The sources differ in terms of magnitude and timing of the decline. The totals in Frankel (1938) are roughly double the estimates of Cleona Lewis. Comparison of the investment levels for West Africa for 1913 and 1948, reported by Paish (1914) and Bank of England (1950), would suggest a slight increase in

FDI hardly ahead of inflation, while Frankel's estimate for 1935 is about three times that of Paish's for 1913. The published, official estimates of British overseas investment do not disaggregate the sub-Saharan African territories before 1962.

19 After what are referred to as the Ashante wars, there was a boom in Gold Coast mining stocks, encouraged by exaggerated reports of a new Witwatersrand. Frankel (1938: 318–9) notes estimates of nominal capital of mining companies in 1901 of £25 million, of which £15 was issued. Recall that the estimate of FDI used above for Ghana in 1911–14 was £12 million. As an indication of the structure of a trading company's balance sheet, the UAC reports total capital in 1948 of £32.7 million, of which fixed capital (at cost) was only £3.4 million (United Africa Company 1949: 58).

20 Estimated total capital from Szereszewski (1963: 39). Cocoa accounted for 31 per cent of this total, and its value was calculated by imputation of a discounted stream of future earnings. A version of the perpetual inventory method was used for the estimation of the other capital stock items.

21 GDP data in United Nations *Yearbook of National Account Statistics*, 1957, and presented in per capita terms in United Nations (1959). Maddison (1995) also indicates that Nigeria's per capita GDP was half that of Ghana in 1950.

22 Recall that Frankel assigned to Nigeria all the capital from the trading companies such as the United Africa Company, biasing downward the estimated difference in FDI/capita between Nigeria and Ghana.

23 As a point of reference between the data on Ghana and that for Nigeria or other countries, it is useful to note that Szereszewski's estimates for Ghana imply a capital-output ratio of 0.7 for 1911, and 2.5 for 1960. Without commenting on the accuracy of these data, nor proposing any alternatives, it is important to note the magnitude of the increase which one well-informed scholar believed plausible.

24 British private investment into East Africa was estimated at £27 million for 1957 (Bank of England 1959), using the methodology which for other countries we have argued underestimates total foreign direct investment by up to one half. Kenya received three fourths of that region's total, according to the official United Kingdom census of overseas investment for1962. The United States had little interest in Kenya then, and while one presumes that there was some investment from Dutch and other trading firms, data are not available. The estimated value of the plantations probably included reinvested profits not reflected in the UK statistics.

25 The message that black Africans owned little is reflected in Leys (1975: 45), "... on the eve of independence, Asians probably owned nearly three-quarters of the private non-agricultural assets of the country".

26 A stimulating aspect of the study of Kenyan development relates to the growing realization of the importance of changes inside the African community's economy, whose origins are found to predate the arrival of British settlers, and whose effects had major impacts on the society that emerged with independence. Colin Leys was an important figure in this "Kenya debate"; a critical but perceptive summary of it is provided by Kitching (1985), while more recent contributions are mentioned in Chege (1998).

27 For 1957, the British Colonial Office estimated the share of subsistence income in Kenya's total income to be one sixth (United Nations 1959: 15).

28 After the Mau Mau uprising signaled the impending demise of white domination of the highland farms, efforts under the Swynnerton Plan to sell the settlers' farms required the generation of significant amounts credit to the African farmers in order to maintain the purchase price of those farms in benefit to the settlers.

29 Curtis (1991) provides further details about the several waves of disinvestment after the Sharpeville massacre of 1960, while mentioning government actions such as exchange controls that, while designed to reduce repatriation of FDI, probably channeled it out via higher dividends. He refers to the July, 1985 decision of Chase Manhattan to stop rolling over loans to South Africa as "... turn[ing] the wave of disinvestment into a flood", Curtis (1991: 199).

5 Asia and the Middle East

The presentation of the various case studies for Asia and the Middle East will proceed in alphabetical order. The exception is the oil exporters of the Middle East, which are handled separately because of the uniqueness of their history, and the common lack of pre-World War II macroeconomic data on GDP, FDI, or any indication of total capital stock. Australia is included as a country of recent settlement, and the breadth of experiences in Asia provides cases of colonies from five metropolitan powers, along with such independent countries as China and Thailand.

Australia

The economic history of Australia exhibits many of the characteristics of that of a country of recent European settlement. Foreign loans were very important, as we shall see below. For much of the twentieth century Australia's growth was led by raw material exports, directly or with minimal processing. The vigor of the economy was such that the negative consequences of protectionism did not completely stifle the development of a manufacturing industry which has more recently been able to survive the limited moves towards liberalization. There are some important differences between Australia and, especially, Canada, that relate to geography. Transport costs "down under" provided an additional protectionist shield for import substituting activities, while at the same time discouraging exports. Secondly, Australia had a more difficult time attracting immigrants from Europe and North America. Similarly, Australia's economy was less closely tied to that of the United States. Finally, the country has recently been forced to re-orient its long-run trade, investment, and immigration policies to more fully acknowledge its position as an Asian economy.

At the beginning of the twentieth century Australia had received a very large amount of per capita foreign investment, both portfolio and direct. Mining was an important area of FDI, and speculation in this sector had provided the country with a boom and bust cycle as the century began. FDI was much smaller than FI, due principally to the fact that all financing of railroads was directed through the government. Moreover, as Table 5.1 indicates, when the similarly high level of per capita income is taken into consideration, the calculated ratio of FDI/GDP is rather modest. Now, as the century progresses, the differences between the Australian and Canadian experiences become patent; there was no swelling of United States investments into Australia during the 1920s and the 1950s, as had occurred in Canada. Further differences from the Canadian experience, and something closer to the norm in, say, Latin America, are the decline in the value of FDI/GDP after 1960, and its recovery after 1980. This newer wave of inflows of FDI is more heavily weighted towards the service sectors, such as wholesale and retail trade, property, finance, and insurance. Table 5.1 also includes calculations of the foreign ownership ratio. It will be noted that these are at levels quite comparable to the situation in Canada, which is to say, lower than those of most of the other countries for which such estimates are presented in this book. This certainly contradicts the common stereotype that because a country has been open to foreign investment, it must be dominated by multinational enterprises.

Australia's external indebtedness was much reduced after World War II, and although it is currently a marginally net importer of capital, she does have significant external assets in both bonds and direct investment. Although Table 5.1 indicates that the country is also a net importer of FDI, there had to have been substantial outflows to enable the accumulated outward stock to reach 16 per cent of GDP within a span of 15 years. The areas receiving this investment have been either the immediate vicinity – Papua New Guinea and New Zealand, or the United Kingdom and the United States. In particular, the capital importing countries of ASEAN are an important but not major recipient of Australian investment, at 16 per cent in 1990 (Bureau of Industry Economics 1993: 76). As was shown in Table 3.4, Australia's ratio of outward FDI to GDP is close to the average of that for the advanced industrial economies.

One topic on which the official data shed minimal light is that of sectoral ownership ratios. As reported in scattered issues of the *Year Book Australia* (e.g. 1979), foreign ownership accounts for one third to one half of the total in manufacturing and mining, and a very low percentage of agriculture, transport, construction, and similar sectors. A topic for further research would be the relative weight of FDI versus settler capital in the development of the country, perhaps during the last third of the nineteenth century. In contrast to our analysis of the data for mining in South Africa, what we see of the Australian experience for this century suggests that FDI never dominated any major sector such as agriculture, mining or manufacturing.

China

China entered the twentieth century reluctantly, governed by an ageing dynasty unwilling to accept industrialization or many of the other social

Table 5.1 Australia: relative size of inward foreign investment stocks, twentieth century

	1900	1914	1929	1938	1947	1960	1970	1980	1990	1995
Inward FDI										
FI/Capita	308	275	300	229	207	143		276	662	887
FDI/Capita	79	70	65	33	57	87	86	145	239	260
FI/GDP	118	80	103	64	83	40		32	68	93
FDI/GDP	30	20	22	9	23	24	18	17	25	27
FI/trade	511	436	612	505	503	263		214	512	596
FDI/trade	132	112	133	74	139	159	135	113	185	175
FI/Wealth	134	109	115		18					
FDI/Wealth	7	6	5		5	4	4			
Outward FI/GDP								11	25	33
Outward FDI/GDP								3	15	19
Net Inward FDI/GDP								14	10	8

Sources: Population: 1900–1980, Maddock and McLean (1987); 1990–1995, *International Financial Statistics Yearbook* 1998. Inward Foreign Investment: 1900 and 1914, unpublished estimates kindly provided by Lance Davis; 1929, League of Nations *Balance of Payments, 1931–32*; 1938, summing UK investment from Bank of England (1950), and US investment from Lewis (1948); 1947, 1960, Wheelright (1963); 1980, Australian Bureau of Statistics (1989); 1990–1995, *Year Book Australia,* 1995 and 1998. Inward Foreign Direct Investment: 1900 and 1914, unpublished estimates kindly provided by Lance Davis (alternative 1); 1929, League of Nations *Balance of Payments, 1931–32*; 1938, summing UK from Bank of England (1950) and US from Lewis (1948); 1947, 1960, Wheelright (1963); 1970, *World Investment Directory*; 1980–1990, *Year Book Australia*; 1995, Equity in the series International Investment Position in *International Financial Statistics Yearbook*, 1998. Outward Foreign Investment and FDI: 1980–1990, *Year Book Australia*; 1995, *International Financial Statistics Yearbook*, 1998. GDP: 1900–1938, Butlin (1962); 1947, Maddock and McLean (1987); 1960–1995, various *International Financial Statistics Yearbooks*. Trade (average value of exports and imports): 1900–1938, Butlin (1962); 1947, *Year Book Australia*; 1960–1995, various *International Financial Statistics Yearbooks*. Real Tangible Wealth: author's interpolations based on Garland and Goldsmith (1959: 351) and Goldsmith (1985: 196).

Notes
There was virtually no FDI in railroads. The estimates for FI and FDI for 1914 provided by Lance Davis are quite consistent with the estimates of Paish (1911 and 1914). Lewis (1948) indicates that the Australian government reported a total for foreign investment about one third larger than that used here, which she was unable to explain. For the second half of the century, the official data on FDI includes reinvested profits. Wheelright (1963: 160) estimated the market value of 1960 FDI at over double its book value, the measure used here. There was a change in methodology in the estimation of FDI, which doubled the estimated stock of FDI for 1980. There was a more recent change, not incorporated here, which increased the data for the 1990s by about one quarter. Curiously, neither the series on the International Investment Position in the *International Financial Statistics Yearbook* 1998, nor the *World Investment Directory* report either of these revised sets.

and economic innovations broadly referred to as modernization. Competition among Great Powers for control over China led to the establishment of spheres of influence, in the hope of an eventual breakup of the country. The most visible results were the treaty ports, the separation of Taiwan in 1895, and the subsequent establishment of a foreign controlled puppet regime in Manchuria. After the fall of the Ch'ing dynasty and a brief Republican period, the country slid into an extended period of civil war, from which Mao Tse-tung eventually emerged victorious in 1949. Mao's version of Marxism/Leninism, with its emphasis on egalitarianism and self-sufficiency, and hostility toward foreign investment, deteriorated rapidly after his death in 1976. A basic unknown is the long-term commitment of the current government to policies of decentralization and greater openness towards markets, and, even, foreign investment. Thus, the twentieth century ends just as it began, with foreign powers anxiously maneuvering to position themselves to take advantage of the economic potential of the country, in which foreign investment may well play a key role, while a large bureaucracy nervously protects its own interests while implementing the directives from a distant and weak central government.

Although the political history is writ large and momentous, the twentieth century profile of the country as a recipient of foreign investment is not unusual, as indicated in Table 5.2. Not surprisingly, before World War II, total and foreign direct investment were low on a per capita basis. However, as fractions of GDP, or when compared to trade levels, these indicators are closer to average for third world countries. The sectoral distribution of investment is also rather typical, with railroads dominating, and cotton textiles being the only manufacturing activity of serious foreign participation. That the geographical distribution of the investment was concentrated on the coast and in Manchuria also was not particularly surprising, given the historical background sketched out above. One factor distinguishing China from most third world areas is the importance of Japan as a source of funds; her share of foreign investment in China rose from negligible in 1902 to 40 per cent in 1936 (Hou 1965: 17).

For the pre-revolutionary era, sketchy information on ownership is available for a few specific sectors, although an estimate of the foreign ownership of the nations total capital stock is not possible. For example, most of the railroads were foreign owned or financed. With regard to manufacturing, Hou (1965: 129) indicates that Chinese factories produced 65 per cent of value added for firms with more than 30 employees. Similarly, Feuerwerker (1995: 117) calculates that Chinese owned two thirds of total factory production for 1933. These authors and several others distinguish between modern and traditional sectors of the economy, associating foreign dominance with the former, but not the latter. In this regard, the case of cotton textiles is interesting. The growth of factory production has been well analysed by Chao (1977), and it turns out that Chinese-owned firms had over half of capacity up into the 1930s.[1] Of course, handicraft production of yarn fell from 76 per cent of output before 1910 to 26 per cent in the mid-1930s, while the share of hand looms in total output fell from 97 per cent to 66 per cent during that period (Chao 1977: Table 26). Thus, the broad picture is that, although foreign investment in manufacturing did grow before World War II, the major source of growing manufacturing output displacing handicraft production was that of locally controlled firms. In contrast to manufacturing,

Table 5.2 China: relative size of inward foreign investment stocks, twentieth century

	1900	1914	1931	1936	1980	1985	1990	1995
FI/capita	2	3	4	4	<$\frac{1}{2}$	1	3	9
FDI/capita	1	2	3	3	<$\frac{1}{2}$	<$\frac{1}{2}$	1	5
Non-RR FDI/capita	1	1	2	2				
FI/GDP	17	24	25	26	2	5	17	32
FDI/GDP	11	16	19	20	<$\frac{1}{2}$	1	4	18
Non-RR FDI/GDP	5	11	15	15				
FI/trade	473	500	552		20	39	109	146
FDI/trade	302	331	415		<$\frac{1}{2}$	10	26	83
Non-RR FDI/trade	131	233	335					

Sources: Population: 1900–1936, from Maddison (1995); 1980–1995, *International Financial Statistics Yearbook*. Foreign Investment: 1902–1936, Remer (1933) and Hou (1965); 1980–1995, calculated as the sum of FDI and Debt, with FDI from the *World Investment Report 1997*, and Debt from the *World Debt Tables*. Foreign Trade (average of exports and imports): 1900–1936, Mitchell (1995); 1980–1995, from the *World Debt Tables*. GDP: 1900–1936, calculated by deflating the dollar value of the 1970 GDP, from the *World Debt Tables*, using the indexes of GDP from Maddison (1995); 1980–1995, from the *World Debt Tables*. All were deflated by the US price index.

Notes
Manchuria's trade was not recorded by the Chinese authorities after the area was separated in 1931. Hong Kong and Manchuria included, 1902–1936. One alternative to estimating the early GDP levels is to utilize the estimates made by Liu and Yeh for 1933, as reported by Maddison (1995: 144). This lowers the estimated GDP by one third, correspondingly raising the FI/GDP and FDI/GDP ratios by that amount.

agriculture – accounting for two thirds of national output – never held much attraction for foreigners. Mining received a negligible amount of FDI (Hou 1965: 16).

Any review of Japanese investments in China must distinguish those in Manchuria from the rest of the country. Over three fourths of Japan's stock of overseas investment was in China in 1926, and a major fraction of it was located in Manchuria. Historians describe early twentieth-century Manchuria as a frontier society, because of its low population density and lesser levels of socio-economic indicators, partially the result of special treatment ordered by the Manchu rulers in Beijing. After Japan's victory over Russia in their 1905 war, the latter's railways were ceded to the former country, which subsequently ran the South Manchurian Railway Company as a semi-private activity, one that directly or indirectly controlled most of the subsequent investments in the region. Manchuria was always the dominant recipient of Japanese investment in China; this accelerated after the political events of 1931. One indicator of the magnitude of this investment is the increase in the ratio of FDI/GDP. Combining the data on real GDP from Chao (1983: Table A-1) and the real value of paid up capital and bonds in Manchurian corporations from Kinney (1982: Table 22), results in an increase of FDI/GDP from 39 per cent in 1931 to 112 per cent in 1940; half of this was in the transportation sector. This is the largest increase we have been able to document for any colony during the 1930s.

The thoroughness of Remer's study allows us some remarks about the size of expatriate investment before World War II. Kindersley estimated total British capital in China at £40 million, commenting that the total would "... be substantially increased if proprietary holdings by British nationals permanently resident [were] included", (1933: 200). Basing himself on several sources in and outside of China, Remer (1933: 403) estimated total British holdings at £244 million, fully six times the amount of foreign investment registered by Kindersley. With regard to mode of financing, Remer recounts (1933: 480) a conversation with the manager of the South Manchurian Railway Company, who estimated that one quarter of the value of the company had been financed by reinvested profits; Kinney's data for all sectors in Manchuria during the 1930s indicates a ratio of only 10 per cent, with paid up capital being the single most important source of finance.

The new regime under Mao was decidedly hostile toward foreign investment. A new policy towards foreign investment was proclaimed in 1979, three decades after the triumph of the Revolution. There have been several distinct policy innovations. One was an openness towards large multinationals, in the technologically difficult areas in raw materials, such as petroleum. The opening up of ports and coastal areas has been significant. The Special Economic Zones have had much success. The current government is willing to accept that these changes will increase geographical differences in income and other variables.

The tremendous inflow of foreign investments since 1980 has made China the host to the fifth largest amount of FDI in the world, and the largest in the Third World. Hong Kong is the nominal provider of over half the recent torrent of direct investments, but presumably much of this has originated elsewhere. Political difficulties impede a more realistic evaluation of the current situation, but some observers claim that Taiwan is the largest single source. Whatever the case, the importance of shared ethnicity among residents of Taiwan, Hong Kong, and the mainland distinguishes this case from that of any other around the globe.

India

The East India Company was chartered in 1600; a very early example of foreign investment from England. After the independence of what became the United States, India was the most important British colony for more than a century and a half, until she received her independence in 1947. The legacy of the colonial period's experience has led its successor states, India, Pakistan, and Bangladesh, to pursue nationalist policies resulting in some of the lowest levels of FDI in the world.

Before looking at the numbers, we should underline the importance of scale when discussing India. At the beginning of the twentieth century, India had the world's second largest population, and, according to Maddison (1995), the fifth largest GDP – after the United States, United Kingdom, China, and Russia/URSS. When looking at absolute values, commentators correctly described the sub-continent as having the largest amount of foreign investment in the Third World before World War I. However, that same investment resulted small, when scaled on a per capita basis, which could well be the appropriate perspective of a local development official. So, keeping in mind this question of scale, we now proceed to analyse the Indian data in some detail, taking advantage of the relatively good estimates on GDP, and even a long series of capital stock, as well.

The initial set of calculations is presented in Table 5.3. At the start of the twentieth century, the per capita levels of FI and FDI were evidently small, but because of the widespread poverty in the country, its levels of FI/GDP were closer to the middle of the range for the countries considered in this book. However, FDI/GDP was quite below average, basically because the large amount of foreign funds in railroads is considered portfolio – not direct – investment. There had also been significant amounts of borrowing by the government for other activities. This situation had changed dramatically by independence, when most of the foreign debt was paid off, many foreigners had sold out and left the country, so that the ratios of both FI/GDP and FDI/GDP were quite low. Moreover, since mid-century, FDI has been very small compared to the total size of the economy, as the political system remains quite opposed to any significant opening. However, the level of governmental borrowing has been allowed to rise, although not to levels anywhere near those of countries in Latin America and parts of Africa.

The Indian railroads were initially built by the private sector, using foreign funds, typically benefiting from governmental subsidies for construction and/or interest rate guarantees on their bonds. This situation gradually evolved into one of direct state ownership with private sector management, and after the 1920s, moved to one of state ownership and control, which was completed in the late 1940s. The case of the Indian railroads illustrates the problem with the dichotomy direct/portfolio investment, as both ownership and control – and the financial burden and entrepreneurial risk they represented – were in fact shared by both the government and the private sector, in portions poorly indicated by formal agreements. Fortunately for our purposes, the statistics for the railroad sector in India are easily isolated from those of the rest of the economy, so we need not investigate the evolution of the control of railroads.

During the long period of British rule in India, there developed two related modes of foreign investment which were quite distinct from the post-World War II "American model". One of the dominant channels through which Europeans carried out business in India and other parts of Asia was the so-called agency house; groups of bankers and merchants

Table 5.3 India: relative size of inward foreign investment stocks, twentieth century

	1911	1929	1938	1948	1960	1970	1980	1990	1995
FI/capita	7	4	4	1	2	3	2	2	5
FDI/capita	2	2	2	1	1	$<\frac{1}{2}$	$<\frac{1}{2}$	$<\frac{1}{2}$	$<\frac{1}{2}$
FI/GDP	35	28	37	3	12	17	10	11	29
FDI/GDP	10	13	19	3	5	2	1	1	2
FI/trade	378	310	551		144	391	100	103	179
FDI/trade	113	139	276		60	39	7	5	11
FDI/K	7	7	8	2	2	$<\frac{1}{2}$	$<\frac{1}{2}$		
FDI/(K + L)	3	2	3	1	1	$<\frac{1}{2}$	$<\frac{1}{2}$		

Sources: Population: 1900–1980, Maddison (1995); 1990–1995, *International Financial Statistics.* GDP: 1911–1938, estimates of NDP from Sivasubramonian (1997: Appendix Table 1A); 1948, B. Roy (1996: Table 17); 1960, *International Financial Statistics*; 1970–1995, various *World Debt Tables.* Foreign investment and FDI: 1911, Svedberg (1978: 774) taking Howard's estimate; 1929, Bose (1965: 496) taking Rao's estimate; 1938, Banerji (1963: 183); 1949 and 1960, Reserve Bank of India (1964: 64) – census dates are mid-1948 and end 1961; 1970–1995, various *Bulletins* of the Reserve Bank of India. Trade (the average of exports and imports, in US dollars): 1913, Lamartine Yates (1959); 1938, Mitchell (1982); 1960, *International Financial Statistics*; 1970–1995, *World Debt Tables.* Capital Stock (K): 1911–1939, calculated using the real values and the investment price index of B. Roy (1979); 1949 and 1960, the surveys cited in B. Roy (1996: 114); 1970, Goldsmith (1983); 1980, India Central Statistical Office (1988). Land values (L) taken from Goldsmith (1983), interpolating for 1911, 1949, and 1980 using the ratios of land/fixed assets for his benchmark years.

Notes
Data for 1948 and after refer to present day India; for previous years the coverage, in principle, is to undivided India. These sources do not list any appreciable foreign direct investment in railroads during this time period, as most railroad equity had already been exchanged for government annuities. There was virtually no private investment in railroads after independence. The discussion in Banerji (1963) and Bose (1965) can be interpreted as indicating that the Table's sources exaggerate the increase in FDI between 1911 and 1929, due to an underestimate of activities in 1911, both investment in rupee companies, and investment by non-British foreigners. Expatriate investment is included in the FDI data for the colonial period. The data from the Table's sources on sterling investments originating in Britain, are quite parallel to those reported by Paish, Kindersley, and the Bank of England. The post-1970 data from the *Bulletins* of the Reserve Bank of India are essentially identical to those of the *World Debt Tables* and *World Investment Report*, used in most other tables in this book. The initial report on the Census, Reserve Bank of India (1950: 225), listed a much larger amount of government liabilities than did the subsequent reports, e.g. Reserve Bank of India (1964: 64). This may be related to the issue of blocked sterling accounts; the value of the Bank's external assets in 1946 was larger than all the country's accumulated external liabilities, according to Reserve Bank of India (1950: 13).

whose activities in foreign trade had expanded into other domestic sectors, where they exercised financial and managerial control. Because agency houses were typically not joint stock companies, they left less documentation of their operations in the public record, making quantitative analysis of their activities more difficult. In particular, although it is presumed that most of their funds came from reinvested profits, there is scant data on this. The importance of personal relations in the agency house system created much hostility amongst nationalist groups, who believed themselves excluded for ethnic and racial reasons. There has been a lively and informative discussion in the recent literature comparing agency houses and the Free Standing Companies. Chapman (1998) vigorously affirmed the differences between these two groups, noting that while both had relied on portfolio as opposed to direct financing, the agency houses had stronger managerial links with the United Kingdom, often as part of investment groups. Nevertheless, participants in this debate are in agreement that both are quite distinct from the American model of FDI.

A related theme in the colonial economic history of India is expatriate investment, which in the subcontinent had a well-established outlet, through European ownership of locally registered, or "rupee" companies. In principle, an agency house is quite distinct from a rupee company, although in practice many of the same people dominated both entities. The long colonial presence would have led to the development of a sizeable foreign colony. One would expect this group to have been familiar with local conditions, and therefore to have played a large role in investment activities; the opposite hypothesis is suggested by the vision of expatriates living the luxury filled life in exclusive clubs. In any event, data on the foreign ownership and financing of the rupee firms were scarcely included in the standard studies of British overseas capital, such as those of Paish, Kindersley, and the Bank of England, for whom the major interest was actions that directly impacted the British balance of payments.

Fortunately, there have been several studies of both expatriate and sterling investment by authors whose primary interest is India. The big puzzle is the fraction of rupee companies controlled by foreigners, and part of the debate relates to the identification of control. For 1929 and 1939, the two studies cited by Goldsmith (1983: 78) and used above in Table 5.3, suggest that foreign registered companies were respectively three fourths and one half of foreign investment in the private sector. Similarly, Banerji (1963: 183) places foreign capital in rupee companies at about half of foreign private sector capital during the inter-war period. Chapman notes that the sterling companies got started really only in the 1890s, while agency houses had long played a key role in business dealings. The implication is that the sterling companies represented a less traditional mode of entrepreneurship. A parallel story is told with regard to agency houses; according to some, by 1939 local Indian agency houses controlled more capital than did the foreign houses (Goldsmith 1983: 121). Bagchi's description is worth repeating:

> At the beginning of the twentieth century, most of the capital employed in privately-owned enterprises [in India] employing modern techniques or modern methods of organization was under foreign – British – control. By 1939, the proportion of the capital invested in modern enterprises controlled by Indians had gone up substantially . . .
>
> (Bagchi 1972: 158)

Comparing Banerji's totals for 1938 with those from the 1948 foreign investment census of the Reserve Bank of India suggests that both types of FDI declined during the important decade 1938–1948, with the fall in sterling funds being larger, or at least better documented. Tomlinson (1979: 55) speaks of a slow decline of expatriate firms during the inter-war period. Misra (1991: 244) indicates two broad lines of explanation for the decline of the agency houses; the evolution of the international economy, which diminished the complementarity between the Indian and the British economies, and the growing inability of the colonial government in India to maintain privileges for the expatriates during that period. Thus, in contrast to the British settlements in self-governing colonies, the expatriate sector in India is interpreted here as smaller and less dynamic than that of the purely foreign firms, and of course only a small fraction of the expatriates merged permanently into the local society.

These findings on trends of FI and FDI can be placed in a broader macroeconomic context for India, because of the pioneering work of a few scholars estimating the size of the capital stock over the century. The key study is that for 1950 by Mukherjee and Sastry (1959), which is based on numerous government censuses and other reports. Both Mukherjee and Bina Roy have used those results to calculate earlier levels of the capital stock by projecting backwards, using data on imports (and domestic production) of capital goods, as well as information on the activities of construction firms and the use of cement, lumber, and other inputs. The resulting estimated levels of FDI/total capital, also presented above in Table 5.3, indicate that direct foreign investment accounted for a relatively small fraction of total capital, even before independence. Indeed, the ratio of FDI to total capital was always less than 10 per cent during the twentieth century. The reader is reminded that during the twentieth century, India's railroads received virtually no FDI, as that term is used here.

The first year for which disaggregated estimates on the domestic capital stock are available is 1948–49; these are shown in Table 5.4. The distribution by sectors is not particularly noteworthy, except in so far as it illustrates that the productive sectors typically attractive to foreign investors, such as manufacturing, mining, and plantations, accounted for a small part of total capital. This helps explain one other result in that table, the small aggregate ownership ratio in 1948. Given the displacement of foreign by national investors in certain industrial activities, and the broad decline of the agency houses, by mid-century the major part of foreign investment had left, and most of the sectoral foreign ownership ratios are very small, except for mining and petroleum, for which the underlying capital stock data is probably imperfectly disaggregated.

The question arises – how can we reconcile the contrasting images of the low foreign ownership ratios indicated by the data, and the solidly established vision of a sub-continent economically dominated by

Table 5.4 India: sectoral distribution of domestic capital, and percentage foreign ownership, 1949 and 1980

	Distribution of Capital		FDI/K
	1949	1980	1949
Agriculture, Forestry and Fishing	31	20	1
Mining & Petroleum	1	2	31
Manufacture	12	20	3
Railroads	9	5	0
Trade	10	5	2
Other Services and Utilities	10	15	2
Government		9	0
Dwellings	26	23	0
Total	100	100	2

Source: Author's calculations based on the capital stock estimates for 1949–50 of Mukherjee and Sastry (1959: 366), and for 1980 of the India Central Statistics Office (1988), and the data on the 1947–48 distribution of foreign direct investment in Reserve Bank of India (1964: 71).

Notes
The correspondence between the capital stock and foreign investment data is not perfect. For example, the capital stock data do not include petroleum, and it is not clear if the foreign investment in petroleum involves extraction, refining, or distribution. The sectoral levels of FDI/K for 1980 are not given here, as most are less than 1 per cent. For 1949–50, the category manufacture is composed of 8 per cent factory establishments, public and private, and 4 per cent small enterprises. Tea plantations are included here in agriculture. Mukherjee and Sastry do not have a category for central government. They do separate some public enterprises and infrastructure, which account for 6 per cent of the total. Although the treatment of investment by resident Europeans is extremely difficult, there is no information in the results of the 1948 Census (Reserve Bank of India 1950) which would dramatically alter the message that it was a small part of total capital.

foreigners? Because the latter's political control cannot be questioned, many observers would be surprised if it had not translated into economic control. One easy check on the credibility of the size of the estimates of the capital stock is to compare them to existing estimates of national income. For example, the pre-World War I capital output ratio, of about 1.4 in B. Roy (1996: 317) or Mukherjee (1995: 188), is certainly a credible order of magnitude. The basic explanation has to be that the modern sector was small, or to be more precise, that there was much more capital in the rest of the economy, as indicated in Table 5.4. Compare, for example, Findlay Shirras's statement to the India Industrial Commission in 1916 (*Parliamentary Papers* 1919, Vol. 19, 854), placing the 1913 level of capital invested in joint stock companies and government outlays at £500 million, with Bina Roy's estimate, repeated in Goldsmith (1983: 24), of reproducible assets at the equivalent of over £2,200 million. One explanation of the weakness of the modern sector was formulated at mid-century by Thorner, who argued that the economic policies associated with railway development "restrained, rather than facilitated the indigenous economic development of India", so that "the economy of India is backward not so much in an eighteenth century sense as in a twentieth century or 'modern' sense". (Thorner 1951: 396, 402). A contemporary reader sees this as a precursor of the "development of underdevelopment" thesis of André Gunder Frank; and indeed in Indian scholarship a similar idea is frequently rendered as "arrested development".

A political-economy contribution to the reconciliation of low foreign investment and high foreign control would be that the dominant agency house system allowed foreigners greater leverage than they exercised in other economies. When speaking of the origins of the agency system by some of the directors of the East India Company, Chapman (1998: 203) says: "They stumbled across a device by which they exchanged their name (reputation) and marketing expertise for 'agency' (in fact control) of local companies, often taking a small or token shareholding." Debate continues about the relative role of factors such as imperfect information versus oligopolistic constraint of the market, in the determination of the strength and influence of the agency houses, but the fact of widespread control is acknowledged by all sides.

Unfortunately, the scant data on sectoral disaggregations before World War II makes the investigation difficult to advance beyond the totals for capital, or the corresponding capital output ratio. In 1900 the government's share of reproducible tangible wealth was 14 per cent (Mukherjee 1995: 188). In terms of accumulated gross investments, agriculture accounted for 36 per cent over 1850–1900, and 26 per cent over 1900–1949 (B. Roy 1996: 347). The accumulated value of railroads, depreciated, would have accounted for about one tenth of the total capital stock. Taking out government, agriculture, and railroads, then, leaves about half the capital stock to be accounted for. Mining was not a major contributor to economic activity, and India did not export petroleum products. So, there must have been a significant fraction of the country's total amount of capital in services and manufacturing firms which were not joint stock companies. Family owned and financed factories certainly abounded. There is a suggestion of an inherently large amount of capital accumulated in the non-mechanized activities in the country, such as village handicrafts, which had not been displaced by the products of the industrial revolution. Recent research by T. Roy (1996) and others has shown some continuity during the late Victorian era for textile weaving (much less for cotton spinning), and this would appear plausible for other village activities, as well.

The importance of the chronological dimension for a description of the degree of foreign ownership is illustrated by the railroads. A comparison of the amounts of railroad capital in Morris and Dudley (1975) with Bina Roy's estimates of total capital, suggests that railroads reached their highest share of total domestic capital as far back as 1875. Moreover, in the case of railroads, it was government ownership that displaced foreign capital. In other cases, domestic entrepreneurs were the key actors. However, in the most important consumer industry, textiles, what was replaced was production from Lancashire – and indeed handicraft output – but not FDI in India.[2] A similar story would be told of the growth of iron and steel. The overall result is that although the Indian case up to independence affirms changes fueled by two key factors highlighted in the Investment Development Path model, improved domestic entrepreneurship and competitivity, foreign capital was not as seriously affected basically because it had not yet evolved to dominate the Indian economy.

Turning now to the post-independence period, it is widely acknowledged that FDI levels in India have remained low compared to other countries, and that this has resulted, in good part, from decisions consciously taken by the government. It might also be noted that the data on FDI generated by the Reserve Bank of India indicate that external loans to domestic firms are much higher, compared to equity investment, than in other countries. For example, in 1980, the ratio was eight to one (*Bulletin* April, 1985: 275). It is quite conceivable that this involves an indirect mode of investment. Nevertheless, in the exaggerated assumption that all those loans were in fact investments granting foreign control, the total FDI would still be small, relative to the size of the economy.

In 1991, the government of India instituted a series of measures to liberalize foreign trade and investment, as part of an IMF structural adjustment program. Bureaucratic red tape was cut, restricted areas opened up to investment, majority owned investment was encouraged, etc. These actions have "... liberalised the industrial policy regime in the country, especially, as it applies to FDIs beyond recognition". (Kumar 1998: 1323). This is a relatively new program, and as such we should not be surprised that the initial response has seen more commitments than actual investment of funds. Moreover, the claim is often made that administrative discretion remains as strong as ever, while many question the commitment to liberalization of a broad cross-section of the country's political parties. Kumar's analysis of these policy changes is that they have attracted market seeking FDI, in areas such as infrastructural services. However, efficiency-seeking FDI, which would use the country's low priced skilled and unskilled labor for export activities, has not yet come.

Indo-China

The area referred to as Indo-China includes the present day countries of Cambodia, Laos and Vietnam; the latter was subdivided into Annam, Cochin-China, and Tonkin. French economic expansion into Indo-China can be dated to the last two decades of the nineteenth century. The first big loan to the colony was made in 1898. It is often said that World War I revealed France's inability to govern effectively such a distant colony; during World War II the Vichy government's representatives collaborated with the Japanese, so that at the end of the war there was a political vacuum which, among other things, would have discouraged private investments by the French.

French economic policy towards its Asian colonies discouraged trade and investment from other colonial powers, revealing a stronger mercantilist orientation than in either Britain or the Netherlands. We might add that the standard treatment in the literature describes French interest in Indo-China as being a stepping-stone to China, which was considered vulnerable due to the collapse of the Manchu dynasty. Finally, note can be made of the lack of success of colonization in Indo-China; a combination of soils/crops, attitudes towards the natives and the lack of a frontier.

During the first half of the twentieth century, foreign investment expanded considerably, while still being affected by the cycles of war and depression. Analysts such as Bernard (1934) and Robequain (1944) noted that private investment increased significantly during the latter 1920s, and then declined dramatically during the Depression of the early 1930s, when the major source of new funds was once again the state. Several authors have pointed out that the low level of the colonial government's indebtedness was due in part to the strength of tax revenues, of which the "tax farming" of opium is now considered the most odious. There was extensive railroad construction, but with so much government involvement that it should not be referred to as direct investment. French leadership was key to the expansion of irrigated land in the Mekong delta region, which led to the expansion of rice cultivation. One theme which receives attention in Robequain, Callis, *et al.* is the competition created for the Europeans by ethnic Chinese, particularly in service activities such as commerce, banking, and the milling of rice, but – in contrast to the Dutch Indies, Malaya and Thailand – not as much in export activities such as tin mining. The participation of "native" Annamese in mining was described by Robequain (1944: 268) as "microscopic"; although in certain consumer industries (food processing, etc.) it was larger. French domination appears to have been stronger by size of firm, and not by economic sector. Banking may be an exception, although even here there was a sizeable informal banking sector, in rural and urban areas, dominated by non-French, essentially Chinese and Indians.

Table 5.5 indicates that pre-World War II foreign investments into Indo-China were always small on a per capita basis. However, this is not true when foreign investment is compared to levels of trade or national production. Although the estimate of output used in that table is very crude, there is less reason to question the trade data. After World War II the region continued to be convulsed by fighting, initially against France, and subsequently the United States. Peace returned to Vietnam in the 1970s. For some years, a savage civil war raked Cambodia. To the surprise of many observers, the current leaders of Vietnam have expressed considerable openness to foreign investment. The level of foreign borrowing has

Table 5.5 Indo-China/Vietnam: relative size of inward foreign investment stocks, twentieth century

	1914	1930	1938	1980	1990	1995
FI/capita	9	8	11		18	17
FDI/capita	4	7	7	$<\frac{1}{2}$	$<\frac{1}{2}$	3
FI/GDP		93	95			128
FDI/GDP		85	74	$<\frac{1}{2}$	4	32
FI/Trade	258	220	565		1,008	303
FDI/Trade	131	201	444		10	48

Sources: Population: 1914–1938, author's extrapolation of estimates in McEvedy and Jones (1978); 1980–1995, from issues of the *International Financial Statistics Yearbook*. Foreign Investment: 1914–1938, Callis (1942: 85), identifying FDI with business investment; 1980–1995, FDI from the *World Investment Report*, 1997, which are the sums of inflows from 1970; 1990–1995, loans from *World Debt Tables*. GDP: 1930, using estimate of gross value of output for 1931 from Bernard (1934: 14); 1938, Leduc (1954: 26); 1980–1995, from various issues of the *World Debt Tables*. Trade (average of exports and imports): 1914–1929, from Mitchell (1995); 1938, League of Nations *Balance of Payments* (1939); 1980–1995, dollar values of exports and imports from various issues of the *World Debt Tables*.

Notes
Data refer to all of Indo-China up through 1938, but only to Vietnam subsequently. The Callis data reported here exclude investment by Chinese. Foreign investment in railroads was not separated by Callis, but he states that private sector funding was small. The amount of FDI reported for South Vietnam for 1971 by OECD (1973) was US$160 million. Lacking any concrete information, it was decided to assume that this entire amount was lost to war and nationalization, and treat the FDI inflows for 1980 as starting from an initial FDI stock of zero. The 1938 output data in Leduc are a listing of sectoral gross outputs in the private sector, and so are only a crude estimate of GDP.

recovered strongly, and direct investment appears to have accelerated there during the 1990s.

The use of the investment data from Callis (1942: 85) for the three years 1914, 1930, and 1938 in Table 5.5 provides a minimal level of continuity. However, we must acknowledge that there is a range of estimates of foreign investment available in the literature, and we should consider specifically the results of the recent works of Marseille and his colleagues. The basic message is that Marseille and the Vichy enumeration indicate a more rapid growth of French business investment than does Callis, which we attribute to the more rapid growth of non-equity funding. The comparison of the data for 1914 is indicated in Table 5.6, while more detailed figures for the period just before World War II are shown in Table 5.7. It is convenient to look at the later period first, in which several components of our explanation can be found. The simplest item is the importance of exchange rate changes between 1938 and 1940; note the five-fold difference between the Callis/Lewis and Vichy totals as presented in French Francs, versus the difference in dollars of about two and a half. More important is the role of retained profits, which together with non-corporate investment was equal in size to equity and debentures in the Vichy enumeration. Apparently the archives only make available the

Table 5.6 Estimates of foreign investment in Indo-China, 1914 (million francs)

	Total	Government	Private
Marseille – a	657	426	231
Marseille – b			212
			358
Brocheux and Hémery	638	426	212
Callis	769	378	391
Robequain			492
Nørlund	910	418	492

Sources: Marseille (1977); Marseille (1984); Brocheux and Hémery (1995); Callis (1942); Robequain (1944); Nørlund (1994: 79).

Notes
The first line is Marseille's reporting of the Vichy evaluation. In Marseille (1974: 416), that enterprise total of FF231 million is further broken down into *Entreprise Sociétaires* (FF212 million) and *Individuelles*, (FF19 million). The two totals from Marseille (1984: 100) refer to the total in the *Annuaire Desfossés* for the *émissions d'actions et d'obligations* of the 70 French enterprises covered in the Vichy evaluation, to the total in the Vichy evaluation for the 70 French enterprises. The difference between the two figures may well be reinvested profits. Brocheux and Hémery (1995: 150) report the total for *Émissions d'actions des sociétes*. The data from Callis (1942: 85) is here converted at US$/FF0.192. The source for Robequain (1944: 161) is the Indo-Chinese Statistical Office. The time period covered was 1888–1918, but it is understood that there were few new firms established during World War I. Callis (1942: 77) believed that this datum included some government and other portfolio investment, and reduced it to FF376 million.

estimate of retained profits for 1940, so that no similar comparison is possible in 1914. Nevertheless, the comparison in Table 5.7 of the 1940 dollar value of equity and loans calculated for the Vichy enumeration, US$428, with the 1938 value of business investment in Callis, US$302, we still have a 40 per cent difference, this time with Callis's datum being low, which cannot be attributed to inclusion of retained profits and non-corporate investments in the first study, without denying the crudeness of the data in the second.

There are enough indications of capital stock for 1930 that we can attempt an overall evaluation of foreign ownership. Bernard (1934: 58–9) provides data on total investments by the French, of FF4 billion, and FF20 billion by indigenous people (*indigénes*), of which FF12 billion were in agriculture. These estimates are extended in Table 5.8 by inclusion of two other rubrics. Government capital is estimated by summing up a constant price series of government infrastructure expenditures. The size of Chinese capital was poorly understood, and, lacking any alternative, the data from Callis (1942) for a slightly later date is used. The data in Table 5.8 imply that the French owned around 15 per cent of the total capital in Indo-China in 1930; different ratios result from inclusion or exclusion of land. Rather than dwell on that, it is best to evaluate the quality of the underlying data.

Table 5.7 Estimates of foreign investment in Indo-China, 1938–1940

1938: (*Callis*)	*Total*	*Rentier*	*Business*			
US$	384	82	302			
Francs	9,600	2,050	7,550			
1938: (*Lewis*)	*Total*	*Gov't & Railroad*	*Direct*			
US$	394	162	232			
Francs	9,850	4,050	5,800			
1940: (*the Vichy enumeration*)	*Total*	*Gov't Loans*	*Total Private*	*Corporate Equity & Loans*	*Corporate Retained Profits*	*Non-Corporate Invest.*
US$	1,191	323	876	428	354	95
Francs	52,620	14,162	38,459	18,756	15,517	4,186
1939: (*Bernard and Bourgoin*)			*Private*	*Total Flows*	*Capital Profits*	*Retained*
Francs			33,400	18,000	15,400	
1940: (*Henri Lanoue*)					*Direct Profits*	*Retained*
Francs				11,644	2,044	

Sources: The first two sets of data come from Callis (1942: 85) and Lewis (1948: 335). The source for the last three sets of data is Brocheux and Hémery (1995: 147, 154).

Notes
Both Callis and Lewis mention, but do not include, US$80 million of investment by Chinese. Lewis converts at 0.04 US$/FF, which appears to be the exchange rate used by Callis as well. A major difference between these two may be the classification of some "guaranteed rails" which Lewis puts with the government. Lewis also indicates US$3 million of French investment into New Caledonia, and her US$3 million of US investment includes that into Siam/Thailand as well. The 1940 exchange rate used here to convert the Vichy data from francs to dollars is US$/FF0.0228. Brocheux and Hémery extend the information on the Vichy enumeration in Marseille by including more detail from the archive, and using a slightly different price deflator (so that Marseille's total for accumulated private investment in 1940 is FF39,198 million). All three sets of estimates given by Brocheux and Hémery summed a series of flow figures of investments or capital emissions, for which each year's current value had been deflated by a price index. The Vichy enumeration indicates that business debentures were only 5 per cent of stock. Although Vichy did not evaluate government investments, it is clear from the data in Lindblad (1998: Table 4.4) and Borcheux and Hémery (1995: Appendix Table II) that the total for loans closely approximates what would be the total for investments. The data listed for Bernard and Bourgoin is their "large" estimate. The datum on retained profits cited here from Lanoue is for the restricted period 1924–40. Each of the French sources refers to French investment only.

There is no explicit reference to the source for the data on indigenous capital, although the numbers for agriculture appear to be based on the study by the noted agronomist Yves Henry (1932), whom Bernard cites frequently.[3] There is a general supposition that indigenous capital in industry was small, as indicated by those data.[4] The indicated value of French enterprises, about 400 million piasters, is small. The datum in Callis (1942: 85) for business investment was US$255 million, or 638 million piasters at US$/piaster 0.4. Because Callis relied heavily on Bernard, Robequain, and the other standard sources of the day, the

Table 5.8 Foreign and domestic ownership of the capital stock in Indo-China, 1930 (million piasters)

Indigenous Ownership[a]	Crops[b]		1,200
	of which:		
	Land		950
	Agricultural Implements		250
	Livestock	300	
	Buildings	400	
	Industry, Commerce, etc.	100	
French Companies[c]	Total	393	
	Land in rubber, rice, etc.		143
	Non-agriculture		250
Chinese owned capital[d]	Total	200	
Government Capital	Total[e]	771	
	Railroads[f]		242
Indo-China: Total except land		2,271	
Indo-China: Total including land		3,364	

Ratios:		
French capital/total renewable capital:		17%
French capital/total capital including land:		12%

Sources: Author's calculations as explained below.

Notes

The 1930 exchange rate between the piaster and the French franc was 1 piaster = 10 francs.
[a] Bernard (1934: 59)
[b] Bernard's total of 1,200 million piasters is roughly divided between land and implements according to the proportions which Henry (1932: 656) provides for rice.
[c] Bernard (1934: 59), referring to French capital. Callis states (1942: 82) that non-French foreign investment is "very small". It should also be noted that Callis, using essentially the same sources as available to Bernard, estimated business investment in the colony at US$255 million for 1930, which at $US/piaster 0.40, equals 638 million piasters, which is 60 per cent higher than Bernard's figure.
[d] Using the 1938 estimate in Callis (1942) of US$80 million, converting at piasters/US$2.5.
[e] Calculated by summing a series of deflated values of the annual investment data in Lindblad (1998: Table 4.4) using the price deflator in Brocheux and Hémery (1995), the French WPI for 1915–1919, and estimating pre-1900 accumulated investments at FF100 million. For comparison, the straight sum in Landblad's Table 4.4 of public investment over 1900–1930 is FF491 million.
[f] The railroad datum is the sum of pre-World War I railroad investments (Thobie 1982: 166) and post-1920 investments in Brocheux and Hémery (1995: Appendix Table II), deflated as above. This methodology produces, for the period up to 1925, a total very similar to that reported in Pouyanne (1926: 209).

difference is puzzling. Use of Callis's figure of foreign investment would raise the ratio of FDI/reproducible capital to 24 per cent, instead of the 17 per cent in the Table, which gives a sense of the preciseness of these estimates.

Because Indo-China was the most important overseas French possession outside of North Africa, the experience of its government investments has special interest. This is especially true because the popularizer of the term *mise en valeur*, Albert Sarraut, had been Governor General of this colony before returning to Paris as Minister of the Colonies. The period after

1900 was conveniently summarized by Pouyanne (1926), and has been studied by a group at the University of Paris, some of whose data are reproduced in Lindblad (1998). Railroads accounted for one third of the accumulated stock of government investments in 1930, according to Table 5.8. Virtually all of the railroads were built under the auspices of the government, and the most expensive line was the Yunan line built into southern China, as part of a large strategical plan emanating from Paris. Hydraulic works accounted for about 15 per cent of total government investments since 1900. One noteworthy item is the breakdown of government investment in Brocheux and Hémery (1995: Appendix Table II), whose source appears to be the archives of the Vichy enumeration. Fully 30 per cent of that table's accumulated government investment over 1920–1938 was military expenditures. In light of the fact that the corresponding data for government investment in Pouyanne or Lindblad give parallel totals, perhaps a more realistic evaluation would be a recalculation limited to non-military outlays only.

It may be of interest to note that about half of the investment boom in the 1920s involved firms with head offices in the colony, as opposed to the metropole (Smolski 1929: 805). A more explicit statement relating to a settler-type economy is that of Thompson (1937: 221), "It has been estimated that eight billion francs were subscribed to companies in Indo-China; about half of that sum comes from the French in the colony." Thompson clearly based her analysis on works such as that of Bernard – she proceeded to quote his estimate of FF20 billion as the total indigenous investment. Moreover, she goes on to write, "Of this [eight billion francs] only half has been used for the development of the country; the other half being dissipated in commissions to middlemen, graft..." (op. cit.), which is also a fairly close paraphrase of Bernard (1934: 58).[5] However, Bernard does not state directly that half of the capital was financed from inside the colony, and such a distinction between Frenchmen and colonists may well have been alien to him.[6] In any event, a tentative conclusion of relative equality between the amount of settlers' capital and that of capital from the metropole corresponds to the general impression that settlers were much less important in Indo-China than they were in France's most important colony, Algeria.

Indonesia

The Dutch presence was established in the East Indies in the sixteenth century, during the first wave of European expansion, back when the word *Java* connoted spices. During the entire nineteenth century there was intense Dutch intervention in the economy, under what was called the Cultivation System. À Campo (1996: 90) describes the colonial economy as having reached adulthood before World War I, further suggesting that the booming 1920s could be termed the "Indian summer" of colonial capitalism. Thanks to the thoroughness of the colonial statisticians, and the assiduousness of several contemporary researchers, we have much material to work with about Indonesia. First, mention should be made of the series *Changing Economy of Indonesia* (*CEI*), initially edited by J. Creutzberg, each of whose volumes presents detailed statistics on some topic, for the colonial period. The recently published book by J.T. Lindblad (1998) combines a good selection of the statistical detail of that work with a bold comparative vision, and serves as a model for the general endeavor in this manuscript.

Foreign investment in the Netherlands East Indies was always dominated by the Dutch – although sometimes only nominally, as Van der Eng (1998) points out, because limited liability companies were required to be registered either in Indonesia or in the Netherlands. The data indicate that foreign investment rose through the 1920s, remaining at a plateau during the 1930s. Relative to population or GDP, FDI was higher than in most other colonies, as shown in Table 5.9. Government debt was not large, reflecting mainstream attitudes towards colonial fiscal policy. The end of World War II saw Sukarno emerging as the dominant political figure of a movement that was soon to consolidate independence. Disinvestment by Dutch citizens accelerated, leading to the nationalization of their remaining assets in 1957, and that of British and American firms not long after. After a period of what has been termed "nation building", and which included strongly anti-foreign policies, the regime reversed its policies on FDI, and now Indonesia has a moderate amount of FDI relative to income. In contrast to other south-east Asian countries, the major attraction in Indonesia is petroleum, and not the exportation of manufactured goods. Macroeconomic imbalances have led to major foreign borrowing, and the consequent debt payment problems.

An attempt can be made to establish orders of magnitude of the pre-World War II distribution of wealth; that is, fixed reproducible non-residential assets, although such weighty terms belie the precision of the data, which are presented in Table 5.10. Corporate investment is reported in the *CEI*, whose primary source is an evaluation of Dutch investments made after their nationalization by the government of Indonesia in 1957. The colonial government's investments are well documented, and the magnitudes of investment by foreigners are relatively well known. There is less of a paper trail for investments by Chinese and by "*pribumi*" – indigenous Indonesians.[7] Combining the data on *pribumi* capital in Hart (1982), with the *CEI*'s totals for government and private capital yields the following distribution of the ownership of fixed investment for the late 1930s: government, 16 per cent; Dutch private sector, 44 per cent; other foreigners, 19 per cent; *pribumi*, 16 per cent; and Chinese six per cent. The strikingly low percentage for *pribumi* is arguably consistent with what is known of the distribution of agricultural assets, and the relative importance of agriculture and non-agriculture.[8] The inclusion of land holdings would

Table 5.9 Indonesia: relative size of inward foreign investment stocks, twentieth century

	1900	1914	1930	1937	1947	1970	1980	1990	1995
FI/capita	7	12	16	18		6	17	30	34
FDI/capita	7	11	13	11	4	1	6	12	13
FI/GDP	46	51	82	111		39	38	89	72
FDI/GDP	43	47	66	69	29	9	14	36	27
FI/trade	341	344	485	779		276	136	308	240
FDI/trade	322	313	389	485		65	49	123	89

Sources: Population from Maddison (1995) and *International Financial Statistics Yearbooks.* Foreign Investment: FI and FDI: 1900–1937, from Callis (1942: 36); 1947, FDI datum is the sum of the following – Dutch investment, from Gales and Sluyterman (1993: 65), British investment in 1948, from Bank of England (1950), and US investment, interpolated from data for 1943 and 1950, from US Department of Commerce (1960); 1970, OECD (1973); 1980–1995, *World Investment Report* 1997; FI 1970–1995, the sum of FDI and debt, with debt from various *World Debt Tables.* GDP for 1900, 1913, 1930, and 1939 are Van der Eng's estimated nominal values, as reported by Booth (1998: 255), the 1947 value was interpolated using the real output data of Van der Eng as reported in Maddison (1995), deflated by the US price index; 1970–1995, from the *World Debt Tables.* Trade (the sum of exports and imports): 1900–1947, Mitchell (1995); 1970–1995, *World Debt Tables.*

Notes
It should be noted that Gales and Sluyterman (1993: 65) present an estimate for 1938 of Dutch FDI in the Dutch East Indies, based on work by H. Baudet, which is higher than that used by Callis, and would raise the total FDI by 40 per cent. In addition, Van der Eng's estimated GDP values are one third larger than the earlier, often quoted estimates of Polak in *Changing Economy of Indoensia* Volume 5, Table 1. Virtually none of the FDI involved railroads.

alter that distribution in favor of *pribumi*, because plantations occupied only about 10 to 15 per cent of arable land.[9]

One way to examine the sensitivity of the results from that calculation to the data is to note that, while Callis's data is evidently compatible with Hart's; use of Gales and Sluyterman's higher estimate of Dutch FDI would raise the Dutch share to 56 per cent, correspondingly lowering the other figures, but not changing the major message from that table, namely the relative ordering of holdings of Dutch, other foreign, governmental and local wealth. Similarly, although the most important source of data in Volume 3 of the *CEI* reports only Dutch investment expenditures, the information from business handbooks which has been analysed by Lindblad (1988: 78) and à Campo (1996) suggests that the overall order of magnitude of total corporate investment is correct. Along rather different lines, Booth (1998: 255) compares Indonesia's implicit capital output ratio in 1913 with that of Japan, and concludes that the *CEI* estimates of capital may under-represent total capital by as much as half. This order of magnitude would be difficult to reconcile with Hart's estimate of *pribumi* capital, although the discrepancy disappears if Polak's earlier estimates of income are used instead of Van der Eng's indirect estimates utilized by Booth.

Table 5.10 Indonesia: capital stock, total and foreign owned, 1900–1939 (million guilders)

	1900	1913	1930	1938
Gales & Sluyterman:				
Dutch FDI	763	1,725		4,050
Callis: Foreign Entrepreneur Investment				
Total	750	1,688	4,000	3,528
Dutch				2,225
Island Chinese				375
Other				928
Hart: Private Sector Investment				
Total				4,800
Dutch				2,500
Other Countries				1,080
Indonesians				900
Indies-Chinese				320
CEI: Corporate Investment				
Total	1,000	1,280	4,990	4,430
Private	750	1,000	4,000	3,500
Government Services	250	280	990	929

Sources: Gales and Sluyterman (1993: 65), Callis (1942: 34, 36), Hart (1942: 44), *Changing Economy of Indonesia* Volume 3, Table A.

Notes
Reference years for Callis are 1900, 1914, 1930 and 1937; for Hart the reference is to pre-World War II; for the CEI the reference years are 1900, 1913, 1930 and 1939. The US dollar values in Gales and Sluyterman, and Callis were converted to guilders multiplying by 2.5. Callis is not able to separate Chinese investment for any year except 1937. The estimate of corporate investment for 1930 in Lindblad (1998: 78) is 3,769 million guilders.

It should be remarked that the relative position of Chinese and *pribumi* is not at all clear at an aggregate level. In contrast to Hart's numbers, the analysis of corporate ownership in 1913 by ethnic group, as identified by the name of the company or its directors, in à Campo (1996: 77), indicates that 603 out of 635 local Indonesian firms were in fact Chinese. Lindblad (1988: 73) has similar results for 1930, and the study referenced by Brown (1994: 232) places Chinese capital at an even higher amount. The idea that Chinese dominated local trading firms and other services is very widespread. On the other hand, it is the case that Chinese had less access to land.

Lindblad (1998: 72) speaks gracefully of "shades of alienness" when addressing the issue of foreign ownership in the Netherlands Indies. He presents a table in which Netherlands Indian firms, corresponding to our category of expatriate firms, accounted for less than 15 per cent of total corporate equity in 1930 (page 78). A somewhat different conclusion is reached by Gales and Sluyterman (1998: 296), who estimate that about half of Dutch foreign direct investment was in Free Standing Companies. Furthermore, "One cannot attribute the other half to multinationals or companies working within several parts of the empire. Most of the remainder consisted of investment by companies registered in the East Indies and managed by expatriates." (ibid). The latter authors make the point that investment in colonies was distinct from foreign investment, because of the network of support that the colonial link provided. In effect, therefore, they not only reject the empirical relevance for colonial Indonesia of the "American model" of multinational manufacturing enterprises, they posit something of a continuum between Free Standing Companies and expatriate firms. Furthermore, they cite a study indicating the decline in the percentage of new companies starting operations in the Netherlands East Indies which were registered in the Netherlands, as opposed to being registered locally, over the period 1885–1925. À Campo (1996) describes a chronological sequence of sectors receiving investment, from banking and finance to transportation and subsequently to raw materials, both mining and agriculture. Dutch registered firms were larger, on average. In part, of course, this reflected an increase in smaller, less well financed firms, many of whom did not survive the Depression of the 1930s.

One topic about which these sources are less helpful is reinvestment of profits. Given the context where there is much expatriate investment, especially in agriculture, one hypothesizes that a significant fraction of investment funds comes from reinvested profits, with the corollary that accumulating the merchandise trade surplus underestimates overall foreign/expatriate investment. After noting the "improbably low" level of capital from Indonesia's accumulated balance of payments inflows compared to the estimated accumulation of capital in the inter-war period – as in *CEI* (3: 28) – Lindblad (1991: 188) limits himself to stating: "Much of the capital required for expansion of private business enterprises in the colony was obviously drawn from retained profits." Van der Eng (1998: 18) makes a plausible case that something like two thirds of the value of foreign owned assets in 1938 had been financed with reinvested profits. Unfortunately, the archival records of the Dutch business firms have not yet led to more formal estimates of that ratio.

There is little in the way of official data on the post independence ownership of assets. Hal Hill's estimates, repeated in Table 5.11, suggest that the private domestic sector of the economy produced just over half of total output in the late 1980s, and that the government produced almost one third, leaving foreign interests with 12 per cent. The data reflect our understanding that the nationalization of Dutch and other foreign firms in the early independence era led to the expansion of the public, and not the private sector (Thee 1996).

Korea

Because it had been ruled continuously by the Yi dynasty since the fourteenth century, Korea possessed a national self-identity and historical

Table 5.11 Indonesia: estimated ownership shares of GDP and of the capital stock, total and by sector, late 1980s (percentages)

	Domestic	*Foreign*	*Government*	*Share of GDP*
Total GDP	57	12	31	
Total, Excluding Oil and Gas	71	5	24	
Food, Fish, Forestry	97	1	2	20
Oil & Gas	0	39	61	19
Manufacturing & Other Mining	57	18	25	15
Other Services	77	3	20	38
Central Government	0	0	100	8

	Domestic	*Foreign*	*Government*	*Share of Total Capital*
Total Capital	57	10	33	
Total, Excluding Oil and Gas	66	4	30	
Food, Fish, Forestry	94	2	5	12
Oil & Gas	0	50	50	14
Manufacturing & Other Mining	59	17	24	15
Other Services	75	1	24	50
Central Government	0	0	100	10

	1980	*1985*
Stock of Inward FDI/Capital Stock	6	10

Source: Calculations based on Hill and Hull (1990: 55), Keuning (1991), and *World Investment Report*, 1997.

Note
The first set of data collapses several of the sectors reported by Hill. Apparently, official data on the distribution of ownership only exist for manufacturing, although for several other sectors there is a consensus on likely magnitudes. Booth (1998: 175) presents data indicating that the contribution of government to GDP in 1960 was 21 per cent, and that of smallholder agriculturists was 49 per cent. Foreign investment was not specifically isolated. The second set of data combines the ownership estimates of Hill with the sectoral capital totals reported by Keuning for 1985; the mix of sectors is not exact. The last line simply reports the ratios of FDI to Keuning's capital stock.

continuity practically unique in the Third World. In the late nineteenth century, foreign pressures gradually opened it to trade with the European powers and other external contacts, which eventually resulted in its annexation by Japan in 1910. The following colonial period saw major transformations of the Korean economy, including the establishment of the initial phases of manufacturing. In light of Korea's rapid growth during the second half of the twentieth century, the evaluation of the Japanese colonial experience has generated much interest and sharp debate, as the foundations for growth were established in a context of harsh exploitation. The historical discontinuity represented by Japan's defeat in 1945 was strengthened by the Korean War and the division of the peninsula into two states. Contrary to many predictions, South Korea has flourished, experiencing rapid growth and transformation into a competitive exporter of a broad variety of industrial products. The country's success under such adversity raises the question of the importance of certain cultural attributes that the country shares with or inherited from Japan, particularly in terms of their possible transferability to other countries.

Our calculations of the ratio of FI and FDI to the macroeconomic aggregates are presented in Table 5.12. There was a clear upward trend in foreign investment relative to these variables throughout the colonial period, as the growth of Japan was transmitted to, as well as aided by, that

Table 5.12 Korea: relative size of inward foreign investment stocks, twentieth century

	1914	1920	1929	1931	1938	1962	1967	1971	1980	1990	1995
Inward Investment:											
FI/capita	2	4	11	16	19			12	45	39	
FDI/capita	1	2	3	4	7	$<\frac{1}{2}$	1	1	3	7	11
FI/GDP	14	20	51	84	88			23	31	12	
FDI/GDP	6	10	16	23	32	2	2	3	2	2	2
FI/trade	154	152	238	442	336			130	97	44	
FDI/trade	61	81	73	121	123	21	12	14	6	8	8
FDI/K	9	12	17	24	25						
Outward Investment/GDP									$<\frac{1}{2}$	1	
Outward FDI/GDP									$<\frac{1}{2}$	1	2
Net Inward FDI/GDP									2	1	$<\frac{1}{2}$

Sources: Population, exports and imports: 1914–1938 from Mitchell (1995); 1962–1995, from various issues of the *International Financial Statistics Yearbook*. Inward Foreign investment: 1914–1938, the accumulated long-term capital inflows from Japan, calculated from *Estimates of Long Term Economic Statistics* Volume 14, Table 20. For the period starting in 1970, FI is calculated as the sum of FDI and debt, the latter is taken from the *World Debt Tables*. Inward FDI: 1914–1938, the paid up capital of Japanese firms, from Kaneko (1982); 1967, from OECD (1972), for 1962 subtracts from the 1967 total the accumulated inflows reported by Bishop (1997: 34); for 1971 from OECD (1973); 1980–1995, from *World Investment Report* 1997. Outward FI and FDI: *International Financial Statistics Yearbook*, 1998. GDP: 1914–1938 are the GDE estimates of Mizoguchi and colleagues, as reported in Kimura (1989); 1962–1995, from various issues of the *International Financial Statistics Yearbook*. Capital Stock: Mizoguchi and Umemura (1988: Table 52).

Notes
South Korea after 1950. The FDI measure is paid-up capital of Japanese firms, and is identical to that reported by Chung (1975) and others. Kaneko also provides data on private sector debt ("liquid investments" from Japan – presumably including short-term trade credits) in 1931, which was double the amount of paid-in capital. He also reports disaggregations of balance of payments data on long-term capital inflows, from Mizoguchi, for 1920, 1931, and 1939, which indicate that the accumulated overseas purchase of stock – a minimal version of FDI – equaled about half of the paid up capital. The *World Investment Report* and the *International Financial Statistics* provide data on inward FDI which, while close, appear to differ by more than normal revisions. The tables in the OECD's *International Direct Investments Statistics Yearbook* do not report inward FDI stocks for Korea. Korea is not currently included in the *Global Financial Indicators*, the successor publication of the *World Debt Tables*. Capital stock converted to nominal values using the average of the two price indexes provided in the source.

of her colonies. During World War I, Japan enjoyed a war boom, and that prosperity continued into the 1920s, as the growth areas of Japan's economy continued to evolve. In terms of unemployment and real output, the 1930s Depression was less severe in Japan and her colonies, than in other industrial countries. One noteworthy area of growth in Korea during the 1930s was the defense industries; by that time the Japanese government had decided to utilize its colonies as providers for certain armament related manufacturing goods, such as explosives and aircraft. The major areas for pre-war Japanese private investment in Korea were mining, manufacturing, and electrical utilities.

Because its high population density and severe weather discouraged Japanese settlement, the country's initial role in the burgeoning empire was as a source of rice and other raw materials. With the increased attention during the 1930s to industrialization, some Korean entrepreneurs were allowed to enter manufacturing. Nevertheless, it is quite clear that foreign investment dominated the corporate sphere, with Japanese owning 90 per cent of corporate stock in 1921 and thereafter, up from 32 per cent in 1912, according to Suh (1978: 10) and Chung (1975). Japanese ownership was smaller in other sectors of the colony. Farmland was predominantly in Korean hands; Ho (1984: 373) suggests a figure for Japanese ownership of 20 per cent in the 1920s and 1930s. Although the presumption would be that the percentage of foreign ownership of agricultural capital was higher, it should also be recalled that the country was inhospitable to Japanese agricultural colonists, on personal as well as climatological levels. Wholesale and retail trade were the major non-agricultural areas where Korean ownership was important. The colonial government provided over half of new investment during the quarter century for which data are available, 1911–1936, a major part of which was for railroads (Mizoguchi and Yamamoto 1984). In particular, private sector funds contributed a small fraction of the financing of the railroads.

In light of the dominance by Japan, it is worth noting in Table 5.12 that the pre-World War II level of FDI relative to the aggregate macro-level variables was not high, compared to many other third world areas at that time. Specifically, the maximum ratio of FDI/K in Table 5.12, at about one quarter, is rather low.[10] Several factors contribute to this result. First, the colonial government owned and operated many activities which in other parts of the Third World were in the foreign private sector, while almost all European investment was kept out. Secondly, there is an issue of timing; Korea had been involved in the international economy for a shorter period than Latin America and several parts of Asia and Africa, and Japanese investment was particularly late in arriving, in such global comparative terms. Finally, there is the measurement issue; our indicator of foreign investment is limited to paid-up capital, and does not include the debt of the firms nor reinvested profits, whose inclusion would considerably increase the figures in the Table.[11]

The meager information available in English-language publications suggests that FDI was much smaller than settler investments in Korea. Chung (1973: 90) suggests that accumulated pre-World War II Japanese FDI in Korea was about ¥800 million, compared to a "crude estimate" of total Japanese investments in reproducible capital of three to ¥4 billion.[12] Supporting this vision of the dominance of locally generated capital is the Table in Kaneko (1982: 42), indicating that about three fourths of Japanese corporate investment was attributed to firms with head offices in Korea. Japanese non-governmental loans reported by Kaneko were half again as large as corporate investment, if these had in fact financed non-corporate investment by settlers, then the relative size of the expatriate sector would be comparable to that of Algeria. Settlement of Japanese into Korea was certainly important in aggregate terms; from 1910 on, Korea had the highest number of Japanese overseas residents, compared to Taiwan, other Asian colonies, China and Manchuria, or the Americas (Duus 1995: 290). However, only a small fraction of these immigrants stayed in agriculture and manufacturing, as compared to commerce and government posts, for example. Duus explicitly refers to the low socio-economic status of the emigrants – "The majority were petty merchants, peddlers, construction workers, artisans, and porters." (ibid).

Rather than press the issue of the relative size of colonists' capital relative to FDI in Korea, one might prefer to argue that several considerations lessen the validity of the distinctions between FDI and expatriate investment – or Free Standing Companies, for that matter. Kaneko's Table indicates that only about one quarter of the investment by Japanese firms in Korea was made by firms with head offices outside the colony, which would normally be the criteria for identifying FDI. There was an active presence of Japanese controlled financial institutions in the colony – in contrast to the Free Standing Company's procural of financing in London – and evidently the geographical closeness allowed closer control in Korea. One could point to the greater interest shown by the Japanese government in its colonies, as opposed to the low priority the British and French colonies received in their metropole. Recall also that Japan's financial conditions limited the country's ability to export capital, which led the government to encourage their settlers to generate their financing overseas.

After the disruptions of World War II, the Korean War, and the division of the peninsula into two parts, the amount of direct foreign investment has remained low relative to other macroeconomic indicators. Although this is typically explained as a result of government policies that were hostile to foreign – especially Japanese – firms, one should not overlook that at the same time there was considerable encouragement of joint ventures and similar co-production arrangements. Indeed, the ability of the various governments to direct development successfully has also been the subject of much controversy, with repercussions in policy discussions elsewhere in the Third World. One recent contribution is Haggard, *et al.* (1997), which contains several references to that debate. A contrast is drawn between the longer-term historical analyses of Ahn, Cumings, Eckert, McNamara, and Woo, who see the origin of late twentieth-century Korean development in the structural changes that occurred during the colonial period, versus another set of authors, primarily political scientists and economists, who emphasize the discontinuities during the period beginning with World War II and ending with the coup of 1961, and the subsequent policy changes that were followed by rapid growth. This is a prickly issue, as some scholars are reluctant to be viewed as finding something praiseworthy in Japan's colonialism, and the presence of Korean industrial entrepreneurs (Eckert 1991) puts those people in an awkward position. For our more limited purposes, we can be content here to acknowledge that the perspectives of both historians and political scientists facilitate our understanding of Korea's growth experience.

The historical continuity of government intervention in international economic issues is particularly noteworthy on the subject of FDI by Korean firms. The country became a net exporter of FDI in the 1990s, as indicated above in Table 5.12. Although some of this investment was natural resource seeking, the dominant part has occurred in manufacturing sectors in which the country had been developing competitive advantages. This is certainly reminiscent of what has been called the "American model", but could more usefully be seen as an example of the international product cycle in an intermediate range country, which has also been referred to as the Investment Development Path. The firms investing abroad are parts of *chaebol,* large family-owned conglomerates with a strong resemblance to Japan's pre-war *zaibatsu.* However, in contrast to the implicit context of market-guided growth in the Investment Development Path, the *chaebol* are known to have received considerable government assistance. As pointed out most insightfully by Amsden (1989), the discussion of the role of government policy in facilitating this growth should move beyond simply documenting their receiving sizeable amounts of government subsidies, to explaining how an activist government using unsubtle controls was able to encourage higher rates of investment and technological progress. This is a major question on the research agenda of social scientists at the end of the century, made more acutely important by the recent economic problems afflicting Korea (and Japan), that are quite similar to what would have been predicted by the *laissez faire* school of economics.

Malaysia

Of the south-east Asian countries, Malaysia attracts our interest for several reasons. It is a resource rich area to which the British colonial authorities allowed relatively unfettered access, and the resulting levels of foreign investment were quite high. The process of achieving independence was not accompanied by widespread armed rebellion, and the post-colonial reaction towards the British or other foreigners was correspondingly more muted. It is also the case that ethnic considerations are more palpable in Malaysia, with descendants of Chinese and Indians in some middle ground between the "sons of the soil" *(bumiputra)* and foreigners, leading to a degree of friction which has become violent at times.

As was also the case in India, the geographical area we now call Malaysia includes areas which were autonomously governed during the colonial period; in addition, the most successful part of the colony, Singapore, opted for separation from Malaysia in 1965. The data problems for this area are correspondingly worse. Our choice not to study Singapore responds not just to space and time limitations, but to a sense of the unique nature of its experience, making it of less interest to other areas.

Before World War I, tin and rubber were Malaya's most important exports. The production of tin had been dominated by the Chinese for several decades, while the cultivation of rubber had recently been introduced by the British. Rasiah (1995: 51) has a graph depicting classic product cycle phases for both products over the period 1910–1955; foreign domination of rubber fell as technology dispersed to local elements, while foreign domination of tin rose with the introduction of new, capital intensive technology which the Chinese were unable or unwilling to implement.

Although investment by non-British foreigners was not forbidden before World War II, policies restricting both exports and imports did indirectly discourage investment by outsiders, and Britain accounted for 70 per cent of business investments (Callis 1942). According to UNCTC (1992b: 165), the distribution of accumulated FDI by source countries in 1987 was rather evenly split between four groups, European investors, those from other south-east Asian countries (particularly Singapore), Japan, and others, including the United States. Like so many other ex-colonies, upon achieving independence the Malaysian government embarked on a program to encourage manufacturing; unlike many others, however, the nationalist reaction accompanying this policy was less extreme, and the fundamental strengths of the economy allowed it to weather the inefficiencies which typically have accompanied such an import substitution program. The decline in British investment, especially in traditional areas such as mining, plantation agriculture and export/import trading, was counterbalanced by FDI in new activities, of which export oriented manufacturing in Export Processing Zones was important after 1970. As can be seen in Table 5.13, although current levels of FDI/GDP are lower than pre-World War II levels, they are certainly larger than in most other third world countries.[13] Another aspect of the Malaysian experience, reflected in the Table, is a small relative amount of external indebtedness throughout the century. For example,

Table 5.13 Malaysia: relative size of inward foreign investment stocks, twentieth century

	1914	1929	1937	1970	1980	1990	1995
FI/capita	58	61	50	23	73	85	154
FDI/capita	45	49	41	15	39	44	89
FI/GDP	148	104	79	32	48	67	79
FDI/GDP	115	83	65	22	26	35	52
FI/trade	89	110	140	73	76	79	71
FDI/trade	69	88	115	49	41	40	41

Sources: Population: 1914–1937, author's extrapolation of estimates in McEvedy and Jones (1978), subsequent years from the *International Financial Statistics Yearbook*. FI and FDI: 1914–1937, Callis (1942: 56) – Chinese investments not included; 1970, FDI from OECD (1973); 1980–1995, *World Investment Report*; FI calculated as the sum of FDI and debt, the latter taken from the *World Debt Tables*. GDP: 1913 and 1929, Zimmerman (1962); 1937 estimated by extrapolation between his data for 1929 and 1952/54, all deflated by the US price index; 1970–1995, *World Debt Tables*. Trade (average of exports and imports): 1914–1938, Mitchell (1995); 1970–1995, *World Debt Tables*.

Notes
Malaya before 1950, implying that the earlier figures include investments in Singapore. Lewis (1948) and Callis provide very similar totals for 1938. Callis (1942: 48) implies that the government financed the railroads.

an extensive railroad system was built with public funds, but financed out of current tax revenues.

Data on foreign ownership of the overall economy are not available. Gomez and Jomo (1997: 168) provide data on foreign ownership of share capital in limited liability companies. The *bumiputera* group in 1995 held 21 per cent of the total stock, while Chinese Malaysians held 41 per cent. Between 1970 and 1995, the share of foreigners fell from 63 to 28 per cent, with the increase in local ownership being split between Malays and Chinese. However, this data exaggerates earlier foreign ownership in several ways. Measurement of share holdings will generally miss most of agriculture which was by this time predominantly in local hands, not only rice but rubber production. The data do not include government-owned parastatals. Furthermore, van Helten and Jones (1989: 178) argue that the reduction in foreign holdings had begun early in the post-World War II period, noting that British control was maintained even while equity ownership in trading companies, banks, etc. was shifting to Malaya, Singapore, and Hong Kong. We might conjecture that those legal maneuvers which made possible that minority control probably became less accessible after independence. In any event, while foreign ownership in traditional raw material sectors declined after independence, that of manufacturing increased. Rasiah (1995: 81) presents data indicating that the foreign share of manufacturing assets fell from 53 per cent in 1968 to 19 per cent in 1985, and subsequently rose to 40 per cent in 1991. Our data in Table 5.13 also indicate a sharp up-turn in FDI in recent years, which is generally attributed to increasing investment in export oriented investment, particularly in the Export Processing Zones.

Philippines

The Philippines is the only country considered here which had been a colony of the United States, during the period 1898 to 1946. The United States was the dominant foreign investor in 1935 (Callis 1942: 22), retaining that pre-eminence through 1989 (UNCTC 1992b: 225). According to the data in Table 5.14, the pre-World War II level of foreign direct investment – compared either to GDP or trade – was only slightly higher than an average for third world countries, and certainly not high for south-east Asian countries. Since 1970, these indicators suggest that the Philippines has had low levels of investment, and the increase in FDI after 1990 has been small.

It is often said that, after the dust of the Spanish American War had settled, American investors were rather disappointed with what the Philippines offered. Although early investments were predominantly directed towards raw materials, neither sugar, rubber, nor tin fulfilled initial expectations. There was little foreign investment in railroads. It might also be noted that comments in Callis (1942), Lindblad (1998) and elsewhere suggest an important, but unmeasured, presence of expatriate investment, both by Spaniards and Americans.

During World War II there was widespread destruction in the islands.

Table 5.14 Philippines: relative size of inward foreign investment stocks, twentieth century

	1914	1930	1935	1970	1980	1990	1995
FI/capita	10	14	13	11	19	23	28
FDI/capita	9	11	11	4	2	2	5
FI/GDP	53	68	65	34	31	58	53
FDI/GDP	47	53	54	12	4	5	9
FI/trade	204	301	419	174	110	173	117
FDI/trade	182	234	351	61	13	14	20

Sources: Population from Maddison (1995). FI and FDI: 1914–1935, Callis (1942: 23) – Chinese investments not included; FDI: 1970, OECD (1973); 1980–1995, *World Investment Report*. FI calculated as the sum of FDI and debt; debt from *World Debt Tables*. GDP: 1914 and 1930, calculated using the real output data in Maddison (1995), and the US price deflator; 1938, Brown (1989: 211); 1970–1995, *World Debt Tables*. Trade (average of exports and imports): 1913–1938, Mitchell (1995); 1970–1995, *World Debt Tables*.

Notes
Hooley (1968) provides an estimate of GDP (gross value added in agriculture and non-agriculture) for 1938 which is about one third lower than that used here. The estimates in Zimmerman (1962) are slightly lower than the those used here, while the estimate resulting from projecting backwards from the 1970 datum in the *World Debt Tables*, using Maddison's index – based on Hooley – is about one third higher. According to Callis (1942), only a small part of direct investment was in railroads.

After that war, and independence, there was a significant displacement of older foreign investments, accompanied by expansion in new areas, particularly manufacturing. The description in Yoshihara (1985) of this phase of industrialization highlights the establishment of consumer industries and the American automobile companies. That author also contrasts the Philippines with Malaysia and Indonesia, in terms of the strength of the response to industrialization incentives on the part of domestic, non-Chinese ethnic groups. Although the post-World War II policies were formulated with a US-influenced orientation toward liberal economic policies, Lindblad (1998: 112–13) notes that these were often selectively applied. Moreover, the new incentives favoring FDI that were declared in the 1970s had only marginal effects, as investors were discouraged by the overall political climate and the weak macro performance of the economy. More broadly, Mercado-Aldaba (1994) argues that the protectionist policies followed by the country only attracted import substituting FDI, while the country lacked the most effective incentives for attracting export oriented FDI – political stability and a proper macroeconomic context. It is easily argued that the high levels of indebtedness, as indicated by the large differences between the ratios for FI/GDP and FDI/GDP in Table 5.14, were the proximate causes of that country's debt problems in the late 1980s and thereafter.

Unfortunately, there do not seem to be good studies of overall capital stock in the Philippines, nor of the share in them of foreign holdings.

Taiwan

Taiwan became a colony of Japan after the Sino-Japanese war in 1895. The island was then relatively underdeveloped and even underpopulated, for it had received only marginal attention from the authorities of the Ch'ing dynasty in Beijing. Indeed, the term "frontier" has been used to describe the island at the turn of the century. Correspondingly, there was more intensive Japanese settlement in Taiwan, about 6 per cent of the total population in 1940, according to Kaneko (1982: 35) – double the level of Korea. Although these settlers tended to be people from rural backgrounds, they gravitated towards the cities. Two of the island's agricultural products – sugar and rice – were priority exports to Japan. Their output grew rapidly, the first benefiting from preferential tariffs, while the second was subject to varying political winds emanating from Japan.

Several of the comments made with regard to the Korean case are also applicable to that of Taiwan. There was a marked difference between the levels of foreign investment before and after 1950, when the greater self-reliance in the post-war period reflected widespread resentment towards Taiwan's experience as a raw material, export-oriented colony. The Japanese rulers only became interested in the industrial development of the colony during the 1930s, for provisioning defense related items. Following

Japan's defeat, land held by her citizens was distributed to local farmers, as part of a major land reform which pacified the countryside, facilitating an urban and export-directed growth. During the early post-World War II era there was recourse to a substantial amount of loans, without attracting much FDI, at least compared to the macroeconomic aggregates. Currently, Taiwan's dynamism is a prime example of the "East Asian Miracle", making it the envy of many third world countries. Like Korea, Taiwan is now a net exporter of FDI, predominantly in sectors which grew and matured at home, corresponding to a modified international product cycle scheme.

Equally familiar are a set of differences from the Korean case; Taiwan had not been self-ruled before the Japanese colonial period, the displacement of the Nationalist Chinese government from the mainland to Taiwan in 1949 dramatically affected the island's economy and politics, Taiwan was able to benefit economically from the Korean War, the government has been less active in promoting outward FDI, and of course the political situation of the island is currently sharply contested.

The broad trends of Taiwan's involvement with foreign investment are portrayed in Table 5.15. One noteworthy item is that already by 1914 the ratio FDI/GDP had reached a level comparable to that of many other areas that had been colonies for a longer time, and higher than that of Korea. Moreover, that ratio continued to grow into the 1920s, and remained high until the end of the 1930s. During the post-World War II era this ratio was low, with government control severely curtailing foreign investment. Perhaps more notable is the growth of outward FDI, to the point that the island currently has a positive net outward FDI position.

Fortunately, much work has been produced – in English – on the quantitative aspects of Taiwan's economy during the colonial period. In terms of the ownership of corporate assets, domination by Japanese was nearly complete, as they owned 80 per cent of the island's total stock of joint stock companies in 1929 (Ho 1984: 88). That source also indicates that of the smaller firms, over one third of the capital was owned by Japanese who had established residence on the island. Japanese citizens accounted for between 20 and 25 per cent of cultivated farmland before World War II (Ho 1984: 372). In terms of agriculture, both Taiwan and Korea were less completely "settler colonies" than, for example, Algeria – not to mention Australia. Most Japanese firms were registered in Taiwan. The amount of paid-up corporate stock of Japanese firms actually declined 13 per cent during the 1920s. Although one might suppose that this reflected growing indigenous production, Kaneko (1982: 53–4) suggests consolidation towards larger firms and expansion of control by *zaibatsu*, whose local assets may not have been completely incorporated into the registers of the colonial authorities.

The ratio of FDI to the total capital stock was marginally higher than that of Korea, and Table 5.15 indicates that it grew to reach almost 30 per cent

Table 5.15 Taiwan: relative size of inward foreign investment stocks, twentieth century

	1914	1920	1926	1929	1931	1938	1962	1970	1980	1990	1995
Inward Investment:											
FI/capita	10	13	75	29	35	19		7	13		
FDI/capita	7	15	17	15	16	11	1	3	6	27	36
FI/GDP	37	40	195	79	92	63		11	7		
FDI/GDP	25	45	45	40	43	37	3	5	3	6	6
FI/trade	55	140	619	250	345	164		41	14		
FDI/trade	36	159	143	126	160	97	22	19	6	16	15
FDI/K	20	25	32	26	29	28					
Outward FDI/GDP									$<\frac{1}{2}$	8	9
Net Inward FDI/GDP									3	−2	−3

Sources: Population: 1914–1938, from Mitchell (1995); 1962–1995, various issues of the *Statistical Yearbook of the Republic of China*. Foreign investment: 1914–1938, the accumulated inflows of long-term capital from Japan, as reported in *Estimates of Long Term Economic Statistics*, Volume 14, Table 19. Foreign investment is calculated as the sum of FDI and debt, the latter for 1970 and 1979 (as a proxy for 1980) from the *World Debt Tables* 1978 and 1980. Inward FDI: 1914–1938, the paid up capital of Japanese firms, from Kaneko (1982); 1962–1980, calculated as the accumulated sum of "arrived investments" from Hsüeh (1990: Table A-1); 1990–1995, the *World Investment Report*, 1997. Outward FDI: the *World Investment Report*, 1997. GDP: 1914–1938, the GDE estimates of Mizoguchi and colleagues, as reported in Kimura (1989); 1962–1995, calculated from various issues of the *Statistical Yearbook of the Republic of China*. Trade: 1914–1938, from Mitchell (1995); 1962–1995, various issues of the *Statistical Yearbook of the Republic of China*. Capital Stock (K): Mizoguchi and Umemura (1988: Table 51).

Notes
Kaneko (1982: Table 4) also provides data on total investments by Japanese firms in 1926, which was approximately half again higher than that used here. Loans to the private sector was over half of the FI in 1926. The disaggregation of the balance of payments data in Kaneko indicates that a minimal version of FDI, purchase of stock, equaled about half the value of paid up capital. In addition to this series on "arrived investments" (which may be based on the Balance of Payments of the Bank of China), Hsüeh also reports a series on "approved investments" – as do Lim and Fong (1991), and many others – which is more than twice as large as the series used here. That would appear to be the source for the *World Investment Report*, suggesting that part of the increase in these data, between the years 1980 and 1990, is due to the change in source. Since about 1980, Taiwan is frequently not included in the publications of the World Bank or the International Monetary Fund. The data on capital stocks was converted to current values using the average of the two price indexes provided in

before World War II. As was the case for Korea, this indicator of the foreign presence (paid-in capital of firms registered in the colony) incompletely covers settler investment, which appears to have been several times larger than FDI.[14] The colonial government accounted for less than one third of total investment in the period 1900–1938 (Mizoguchi and Yamamoto 1984: Table 8). This ratio was smaller than the corresponding one for Korea, which is attributed to the greater dynamism of the island's economy and its private sector. Taiwan had also received sizeable transfers from the central government in Japan.

In light of the Korean experience, the question arises as to why Taiwan did not develop an industrial structure dominated by an institution such as the *zaibatsu* and *chaebol.* Fields (1995: 6) cites contemporary data indicating that the top fifty business groups in Korea had sales equivalent to 93.8 per cent of GNP, while the sales of the top 96 business groups in Taiwan was only 31.7 per cent of GNP. There are several historical and economic similarities between Korea and Taiwan – Chinese cultural legacy, the Japanese colonial experience, a scarcity of raw materials, a similar standard of living, and so on. Fields (1995) points out that both Korea and Taiwan were anxious to copy Japan's successful experience with the general trading companies. It turns out that both countries have about the same relative amount of both inward and outward FDI. Fields's explanation for the absence in Taiwan of something like the *chaebol* highlights the different political experiences of the early post-World War II era, with Taiwan receiving a massive inflow of mainlanders who supported Chiang Kai-shek, when Korea was rent by war. According to Fields, Chiang actively opposed bigness, in business as elsewhere, while in Korea, Presidents Rhee and Park were eager to strengthen their regimes by alliances with big business. The jury is still out on the success of the Korean firms, and at the time of this writing (late 1999) Korea is struggling with major reforms necessitated by over-borrowing by several *chaebol.* This leaves Taiwan as the most successful example of an East Asian mode of growth.

Thailand

Thailand/Siam was the only south-east Asian country which avoided becoming a colony. Although the degree of political independence can be exaggerated – the area was in the British sphere of influence, and had signed treaties granting trade rights, extra-territoriality etc., it is the case that Thai policies were generally less welcoming to foreign loans and investment. The indicators of the importance of foreign investment and FDI are correspondingly lower in Table 5.16. Moreover, that table indicates that investment increased relatively up to 1938, and has maintained a lower level in the post-war era. Lindblad (1998: 99) suggests that the change in regime that occurred in 1932 produced a change in policy toward foreign businesses, which became more accentuated after World War II.

In the early part of the century, Britain was the most important source of foreign investment. Faulkus (1989: 155) argues that this was another case of investment via Free Standing Companies, as these firms were especially important in mining and lumber, and indeed the tin mining activity was run by Australians. After World War II, the British position declined, not so much to American and other European investors as to those from Japan, and, most recently, from the Asian NICs.

The landmark study of Suehiro (1996) provides impressive detail about foreign investment and the structure of the Thai economy towards the

Table 5.16 Thailand: relative size of inward foreign investment stocks, twentieth century

	1914	1929	1938	1970	1980	1990	1995
FI/capita	6	5	5	6	12	28	48
FDI/capita	2	3	3	2	2	8	14
FI/GDP	40	37	31	16	21	33	36
FDI/GDP	15	21	22	6	3	9	10
FI/trade	167	190	181	86	68	79	73
FDI/trade	64	108	132	31	10	23	21

Sources: Population from Maddison (1995: 114). FI and FDI, 1914–1938, Callis (1942: 70) – Chinese excluded; FDI: 1970, OECD (1973); 1980–1995, from World Investment Report 1997; debt from various World Debt Tables. GDP: 1914 and 1929, estimated by using Sompop's output data reported in Maddison (1995: 190) and the US price index; 1938, Mitchell (1995); 1970–1995, the World Debt Tables. Trade (average of exports and imports): 1914–1938, Mitchell (1995); 1970–1995, World Debt Tables.

Notes
The GDP datum used here for 1938 is very close to that resulting from projecting backward from the 1950 datum in the International Financial Statistics. According to Callis (1942: 60), the railroads had been built with funds from the government. Lindblad (1998: 35) considers the Callis estimate of Chinese investment in Thailand "hopelessly underestimated".

end of the twentieth century. His data on ownership of enterprises suggests that about half of the large enterprises are owned by Thais in the private sector, and the other half is split between foreigners and the state.[15] The very striking finding in Suehiro's research is the almost total dominance of the contemporary Thai corporate sector by people with Chinese ethnicity, although typically with several generations of residence in Thailand. The importance of Thai-Chinese has been rising gradually through the century. Lindblad (1998: 98–9) places their share of the Thai private sector at scarcely more than one fifth in 1932. Of particular value in Suehiro's work is his tracing the history of Thai-Chinese capital in the country, covering changing attitudes of Thai authorities, while also describing the sectoral changes, from "tax farming" to rice milling to banking.

In the early years of the century the Thai royal family was a major force in the private sector, while today it is people who had been associated with the highest levels of the bureaucracy, and the military, who are the dominant elements of the non-Chinese entrepreneurial sector. These people dominate the public corporations, giving rise to the term "bureaucrat capitalist". It should be clear that such a situation facilitates the use of ethnic considerations to veto privatization, which may account for the slow progress in this direction.

The Middle East and petroleum

The modern petroleum industry started in the United States during the second half of the nineteenth century, and for many years this country was the world's leading producer, consumer, and exporter of hydrocarbon products. Before the outbreak of World War I, Russia had become an important producer, and the industry was starting to grow in Indonesia, Mexico, Romania, and elsewhere. In the Middle East, however, production had only just begun in Persia (Iran). The growth of the automobile industry changed the international market for petroleum, as did the war itself. Armored tanks, powered by gasoline, replaced calvary. Fuel oil was used to power the ships of the British Navy, and its sourcing became a matter of national security. Exploration increased tremendously, and after the break-up of the Ottoman Empire, Iraq was the next major producer in the Middle East. It was only after World War II that wells in Saudi Arabia, Kuwait, Bahrain and other areas of the Persian Gulf began production. A major pipeline to the Mediterranean through Syria involved that country in petroleum geo-politics.

As is well known, in the Middle East, as in Latin America, Indonesia, and Russia, this industry was dominated by foreign investors, primarily from the United States, Great Britain, and the Netherlands. As the industry evolved, payments to the governments became linked to the "posted" export price of petroleum, which was essentially an internal transaction of the oil companies, not determined by markets. Exorbitant profits, hidden behind closed books, became a key focus of conflict, although the discussions of subsequent events touched on broad issues of nationalism.

The major shareholder in Iran's petroleum industry had in fact been the British government. Thus, the 1951 nationalization of the Anglo-Iranian Oil Company (AIOC) involved conflict and negotiation at the highest levels, including strains between Britain and the United States. The AIOC's assets at year-end of 1950 were valued at £269 million. The balance sheet value of AIOC's fixed assets in Iran was £28 million, although their replacement value was asserted to be £300 million. Sales of stock had generated £22 million for AIOC; the rest of their financing having been reinvested profits from Iranian oil (Elm 1992: 107–8). As part of the resolution of the conflict arising out of the 1951 nationalization, an agreement was signed in 1954 between the National Iranian Oil Company and a consortium of foreign oil companies, wherein the latter agreed to produce and market crude oil and refined products, in return for a compensation of £76 million for AIOC's assets (Issawi and Yeganeh 1962: 46). There was to be a sharing of profits between the government and the companies, according to a complex set of rules, which followed recent precedents in Venezuela and Saudi Arabia. Although at the time this agreement was viewed as a loss for Iran, it did serve as an important antecedent for the arrangements that were set up in the 1970s after the OPEC-generated price increases.

Table 5.17 indicates the long-term trends of FI and FDI for some of the oil exporters of the Middle East. The ratio FDI/person rises from literally zero in 1900 to a rather moderate level until the late 1930s. That variable

Table 5.17 Petroleum investment in the Middle East, 1900–1958

	1914	1926	1929	1935	1946	1950	1958
(Million current US$)							
Total	11	100		350	795	1,825	3,325
US Companies			395	403		692	1,138
Per Capita (US$1900)							
Regional Total	$<\frac{1}{2}$	2		8	10	18	21
Iran	1			8		4	7
Iraq		$<\frac{1}{2}$	1	10		13	24
Kuwait							328
Saudi Arabia					13		56

Sources: Population: 1914–1950, interpolated from estimates in McEvedy and Jones (1978); 1958, from the *International Financial Statistics Yearbook*. Investment in Oil, Total: 1914 (only Iran), 1926 and 1935, Issawi and Yenageh (1962: 42); 1946–1958, various issues of Chase Manhattan Bank, *Capital Investments by the World Petroleum Industry*. Investment by US companies, regional total: United States Department of Commerce (1960); in Iran: 1914, Ferrier (1982: 186); 1938, from Lewis (1948), assuming all FDI is in petroleum; 1950, from Issawi and Yenageh (1962: 46); 1958, interpolated from data for 1950 and 1967, from OECD (1972); in Iraq: Issawi and Yenageh (1962: 47–48) for the years 1925, 1928, 1934, 1951, and 1958; in Kuwait: Issawi and Yenageh (1962: 48); in Saudi Arabia: Issawi and Yenageh (1962: 47, 48).

Notes
The regional totals encompass, in principle, all parts of the Arabian Peninsula and the Gulf Emirates, plus Iran and Iraq. The series from Chase Manhattan Bank explicitly refers to oil investment, and therefore could include investment by local governments or domestic firms. The narratives in books such as Issawi and Yenageh (1962) indicate that domestic investment was not significant in these countries before 1950, after which events in Iran and subsequently Iraq increased domestic ownership. Petroleum accounted for 88 to 99 per cent of the FDI in these countries in 1967, according to OECD (1972), and for a similar fraction of US FDI, according to various issues of the *Survey of Current Business* and United States Department of Commerce (1975a). The Chase Manhattan Bank series reported here is gross investment in fixed assets at historic costs. Their net investment figures are about 60 per cent of the gross investment totals; they also report a series on net investment plus liquid assets, which is almost equal to gross investment in fixed assets. Issawi and Yenageh (1962: 26) provide a similar total for pre-World War I FDI in Iran.

accelerates thereafter, due to the investments in Saudi Arabia and the adjoining Gulf states. This is one of the few areas of the Third World where there was no reduction of real values of FDI/person during the Depression and World War II. In addition, note that the accumulated amounts of investment here was not a large fraction of the world total. According to OECD (1972: Table 1), petroleum accounted for one third of total FDI in the Third World in 1967, but the Middle East only had one fourth of that petroleum FDI, less than either Latin America and Africa.

Unfortunately, estimates of GDP for this region only become available after 1950. The ratios of FDI/GDP are shown in Table 5.18, and reveal levels that are not high, even before the nationalizations of the 1970s. Such a result does not correspond to the standard image of petroleum FDI in the Middle East. Certainly many explanations can be suggested. Data problems include treatment of exploration expenses, reinvested

Table 5.18 Relative size of inward stocks of FDI, Middle East, 1950–1995

	1951	1958	1967	1980	1990
FDI/person (US$1900)					
Iran	4	7	5	3	$<\frac{1}{2}$
Iraq	13	24	4	1	1
Kuwait		328	225	22	9
Saudi Arabia		56	31	21	81
FDI/GDP					
Iran		23	9	1	$<\frac{1}{2}$
Iraq	41	45	7	$<\frac{1}{2}$	$<\frac{1}{2}$
Kuwait			25	1	1
Saudi Arabia			30	1	21

Sources: Population and GDP from various *International Financial Statistics Yearbooks*. 1958 GDP for Iran, from Issawi and Yeganeh (1962: 143). FDI: for Iran in 1950, from Issawi and Yeganeh (1962: 46); 1958, this author's rough interpolation between the years 1951 and 1967. FDI in Iraq: 1951 and 1958, Issawi and Yeganeh (1962: 47–48). 1967, for all countries, from OECD (1972). 1980, 1990, the *World Investment Directory* 1996.

Notes
The value of 1950 FDI in Iran utilized here was £90 million. The text indicates a potential range of values from £28 to £300 million.

profits, and depreciation. In terms of the simple arithmetical identities from Table 2.1, one wonders if the productivity of the wells could have been so high as to lead to low capital output ratios – and therefore low FDI/GDP, in spite of a presumably high level of FDI/K. Of course several countries did not possess oil refineries, lowering reported FDI. It is also the case that the stereotype of petroleum dominance is often too widely applied. The very high levels of FDI/person in Kuwait in the early post-World War II era, are indicative of those of several other geographically small countries in the region. In contrast, the low levels of FDI/person in Iran reflect that country's relatively higher population, over 20 million in 1960, compared to Kuwait's 280,000. Although petroleum has dominated exports and the history of economic growth in this region, and there has been limited growth of manufacturing industry activities separate from hydrocarbons, there has been a significant fraction of the population involved in agriculture and other rural pursuits.

During the 1970s, increased oil prices produced high incomes for the various governments of the region, who in turn purchased, or national-ized, the producing companies. The multinational companies maintained their presence in the region, through joint ventures, subcontracting, licensing, and similar arrangements including straightforward bartering, as well as through their direct operations in shipping, refining, and other downstream activities. A description of the intricate relationships between the multinational oil companies and the locally owned petroleum entities is beyond our scope and interest here, in part because the official versions of those contractual links may well have been constructed to disguise a continuing condition of technological dependency. In such a situation, standard FDI data provide an inadequate picture of international contacts. It is the case that the declines reported in Table 5.18 for FDI in Iran and Iraq reflect armed conflict in those two countries, and political regimes that have been hostile towards foreign investment.

Several of the low population Middle East oil exporters have become major sources of capital flows to the rest of the world. The UN data in the *World Investment Directory* indicate that some of this is direct investment, accumulating to about two billion US dollars each for Kuwait and Saudi Arabia in 1995. It is generally understood that a larger amount is represented in banking, finance, real estate, and other activities in the gray area between direct and portfolio investments. The governments of Kuwait and Saudi Arabia established such investment funds in the early 1960s. Although information about them is scarce, the *Middle East Economic Digest* (23 February 1996, page 7) states that Kuwait's "Reserve Fund for Future Generations" had accumulated US$100 billion by 1990, which was four times that year's GDP. Due to the destruction and rebuilding after Kuwait's invasion by Iraq, the same source estimates the amount in this Fund to have declined to US$35 billion in 1995.

Turkey

At the beginning of the twentieth century the Ottoman Empire was declining, in both geographical extension as well as its ability to rule in its customary fashion, due to a weak central government and ethnic conflicts, something the "Young Turks" were unable to remedy. Pamuk (1987) reminds us of the importance of the rivalry of the major European countries in this region, and how "The Ottoman case also provides yet another example of the decline of British hegemony on a world scale" (op. cit., 78), evidence for which is the rising share of German, French and other investors at the expense of the British. The pre-World War I distribution of foreign capital was typical of that of other peripheral countries; government debt was larger than all other capital, and railroads were about two thirds of foreign direct investment. Moreover, for the period just before the Great War there are estimates of national income and its disaggregation, which indicate that foreign capital inflows were only about 10 per cent of total investment (op. cit., 71).

The end of the war brought continued fighting inside the Empire, and eventually resulted in its dismantling. Massive deportations and killings of Armenians, Greeks and other ethnic minorities continued in the area, while a new government formed under Mustafa Kamal – Atatürk – and asserted its authority over the area now called Turkey. The treaty settlements denied Atatürk's government a degree of tax freedom, while imposing on it a significant share of the debt burden of the Ottamans. Hansen (1991: 314) points out that during the 1920s Turkey had a relative openness towards FDI and particularly joint ventures. The year 1929 brought tax and tariff autonomy, the first payments on the debt, and the beginnings of the economic decline related to the world depression. The political response that evolved became known as *etatism*, in which the government assumed a leading role in production and investment, while a policy of what would be known as import substitution industrialization was pursued. Keyder (1987: 106) notes that although this may have been perceived as novel at the time, it was only an early example of what was later to become typical of third world development schemes. Although in principle not hostile to the economic contributions of foreigners, these latter groups did provide convenient scapegoats in times of stress.

This "unwelcome mat" for FDI has essentially remained effective since then, in spite of brief, sporadic, and unsuccessful efforts to the contrary. At the same time, the country has had several debt-related balance of payments crises, which are symptomatic of an inability to achieve a substantial growth of real income per capita.

In aggregate terms, the overall size of pre-World War I levels of foreign investment and foreign direct investment in the Ottoman Empire/Turkey were about average, as shown in Table 5.19. The next year for which some

Table 5.19 Turkey: relative size of inward foreign investment stocks, twentieth century

	1913	1938	1970	1980	1990	1995
FI/capita	41	20	11	31	41	49
FDI/capita	14	3	2	0	1	4
FI/GDP	98	38	17	22	27	37
FDI/GDP	34	6	2	0	1	4
FI/trade	638	513	199	208	189	144
FDI/trade	219	85	27	1	6	12

Sources: Population: 1913 population for the Ottoman Empire from Pamuk (1987); 1938 is author's extrapolation of estimates in McEvedy and Jones (1978), subsequent years from issues of the *International Financial Statistics Yearbook*. Foreign Investment: 1913 FI and its components (including paid-in capital and debentures) for the Ottoman Empire, from Pamuk (1987: 66); 1938, adopted from Lewis (1948); 1970–1995, loans from *World Debt Tables*; FDI: 1971, OECD (1973); 1980–1995, various issues of United Nations, *World Investment Report*. GDP: 1913, Eldem's estimate of the Ottoman Empire's national income as reported in Issawi (1980: 7); 1938, Mitchell (1982); 1970–1995, the *World Debt Tables*. Trade (average of exports and imports): 1913, from Pamuk (1987: 148); 1938 from Mitchell (1982); 1970–1995, the *World Debt Tables*.

Notes
In 1913, railroads accounted for almost two-thirds of foreign direct investment, so that the value of non-railroad FDI/capita was five, non-railroad FDI/GNP was 13, and of non-railroad FDI/trade was 79. The disaggregation of the FI total for 1938 is especially problematic, because although nearly half of the total is described as corporate securities, they were "... issued in settlement of Turkey's quota of the old Ottoman debt". (Lewis 1948: 340.) The conclusion is that there was little new FDI in Turkey after 1914. Comparing Issawi (1980: 6) and Hansen (1991: 308), it appears that pre-World War I per capita income in the Ottoman Empire as a whole was about the same as it was in the area which was to become the Republic of Turkey.

quantitative statement can be made is 1938; there had not been much new investment, and the levels of FI/GDP and FDI/GDP have both dropped substantially. Finally, the table shows quite clearly that foreign investment has not recovered since then, remaining instead at a very low level.

Notes

1 Duus (1989: 67) discusses how the Japanese-owned cotton textile firms in China were generally not extensions of Japanese textile firms, although many did emerge out of trading firms, which might have provided links to textile manufacturing in Japan.

2 In his important work, Bagchi (1972) also notes the regional differences of foreign ownership rates, with the British strong in Bengal, where their political capital initially was located, and weaker in Bombay and the west, which were the more dynamic areas in sectors such as textiles.

3 Nevertheless, Henry (1932: 656) evaluates the agricultural land of indigenous people at 1.6 billion piasters, compared to the corresponding total in Bernard is only 1.2 billion. One might speculate that the difference may have been an attempt to account for falling prices during the depression.

4 Gourou (1943: 8) states "... investment of strictly Indo-Chinese capital in private enterprise is not accurately known, but it is certainly very small in comparison with these enormous sums" (of foreign loans and private investment). Norlund (1994) notes that several textile firms were run by Chinese.

5 Callis cites Thompson on this regard. Perhaps the difference between Callis and Bernard is what fraction of that recent investment they were willing to write off. Although the citation in the text refers to middlemen and graft, these writers were also well aware that during the early 1930s much investment was lost to business failures.

6 Thompson was a frequent writer in the *Far Eastern Survey*, which was published by the New York based Institute of Pacific Relations, an international, non-academic group of research and foreign policy specialists, that was responsible for several of the publications used in this monograph. The Institute was a victim of the anti-communism hysteria of the 1950s.

7 The key document for Table 5.10 is a pamphlet written in a non-academic style and tone during World War II, whose author, a well-respected Dutch official named G.H.C. Hart, cites for his key data, "... figures, calculated recently by a colleague of mine ... [that] appear to me to give a good impression of the proportions of agricultural, mining and industrial investments" (Hart 1942: 44).

8 Lindblad (1998: 78) indicates that agriculture had only about half of corporate investments in 1930. Sugar was dominated by foreigners; this is less clear for rubber; Purwanto (1996) describes a vital smallholder (i.e. *pribumi*) rubber sector. About three fourths of the government assets were accounted for by the railroads.

9 Van der Eng (1993: 33), referring to the island of Java. To establish rough orders of magnitude, suppose that land was one third of total fixed wealth, and that the *pribumi* share of land was 80 per cent. Combining this with the estimates used in the text, the share of *pribumi* in fixed wealth is still less than one third. The land issue quickly becomes complex, not only because of regional differences and the lack of a formal market for land, but because the concept of "ownership" is not appropriate for many tenure contexts in Indonesia.

10 Korea's capital output ratio in 1929 in the Mizoguchi-Umemura (1988) compi-

lation was about equal to unity, which is lower than that encountered for almost any other area; if their capital figure is low, the FDI/K figure in the text is too high.

11 Kaneko (1982) provides data for several years on the paid up capital of Japanese corporate firms registered in Korea. More comprehensive data are provided only for the year 1931; the paid-up capital of ¥323 million can be compared to total corporate investment, including reserves, of ¥434 million, to which possibly could be added "personal investments" of ¥145 million. Furthermore, there are "liquid investments from Japan" (Debentures, Debts, and Others) of ¥652 million, which are separate from Government investments (Kaneko 1982: 42).

12 Gross national expenditure was ¥3 billion (Mizoguchi and Umemura (1988: Table 7). Chung provided no explicit citations. Kaneko (1982) provides some support for the small size of FDI compared to total Japanese corporate capital, while Suh (1978: 129) indicates a similar order of magnitude for the total in 1941. However, the estimated total capital stock reported in Mizoguchi and Umemura (1988: Table 52) is of this same order of magnitude, and at least one third of that was government investment, not to mention Korean capital, corporate and otherwise.

13 The evidence in the table is not completely consistent; FDI per capita or as a fraction of GDP was high in the pre-World War II period, but not the level of FDI/trade. This could reflect an unusually high export propensity in an economy which was admittedly quite open and whose statistics would be distorted by Singapore's entrepôt status, but the more likely explanation is inadequacies in the data.

14 Kaneko (1982: 42) gives the following estimates of Japanese investment in Taiwan for 1926/27, in million Yen: paid up capital by firms with head offices in the colony, 272; total investment by corporate firms, 407; liquid investments from Japan, 832; government bonds, 103.

15 Suehiro's data indicate that foreign firms have a lower ratio of assets to sales than domestic firms, private or state owned, which could be explained by two factors; greater domestic involvement in capital intensive infrastructure, and a higher content of imported inputs in foreign firms.

6 Latin America, the Caribbean, and Canada

There are several distinctive characteristics for this region, compared to other parts of the Third World. At the start of the century, almost all of the region was politically independent; except certain colonies in and bordering on the Caribbean. Many of the countries had begun to industrialize by 1929, and correspondingly, several governments consciously pushed a policy of import substitution industrialization after World War II. Railroads were quite important during the first half of the century, and the role of the private sector, domestic and foreign, was more important here than elsewhere in the Third World. Further introductory generalizations are that the presence of US investment has been strongest in Canada, Mexico, the Caribbean, and certain Andean countries, while that of European investors was more notable in Argentina, Brazil, and in the other countries often referred to as the Southern Cone. During the last two decades of the century outward foreign investment has reached noticeable levels from Mexico and from the Southern Cone countries; for these latter, a regional integration scheme, Mercosur, has provided an important economic stimulus. Since mid-century, a major regional office of the United Nations, known by the various acronyms ECLA, ECLAC, or CEPAL, has documented the region's development, while helping to frame the consideration of development policies. Canada is included in this chapter not only because of some structural similarities with other countries in the hemisphere, but particularly due to the important role that foreign investment has always had in the country. As such, the Canadian case may have lessons for other countries in the region.

Argentina

There are several ways in which Argentina reproduces the characteristics of the countries of recent settlement; the importance of railroads, export oriented grain farming, high per capita income levels, and the massive immigration from Europe.[1] Implicit in that story is the existence of a frontier, which, as was true in North America, Australasia and South Africa, is a euphemism for an area less densely occupied by a racially different people who are displaced or removed by force, disease or whatever. As was true of those other areas of recent settlement, the nature of the Argentine society changed when it reached the end of the frontier early in the twentieth century.

Argentina adhered to free trade up to the 1930s, and had few limits on foreign investment, as well as on immigration. Economic growth slowed during the 1920s, for socio-political as well as economic reasons, and the 1930s are known as the "tragic decade". In retrospect it appears that the stage was set for the appearance of a populist, nationalist dictator, who emerged in the person of Juan Domingo Perón. That tale is too complex to summarize here; his legacy includes the nationalization of the railroad network, a reversal of attitudes towards trade and foreign investment, and an economic instability which each succeeding generation nervously hopes it has finally conquered, as is also true today.

The data in Table 6.1 reflect this vision of a very high level of foreign investment during the first quarter of the century, not only in per capita terms but also relative to income or trade. Railroads dominated that inward investment, and the fact that this sector was foreign owned obscures another fact, that non-railroad FDI was not unusually high. The 1914 Industrial Census reported that two thirds of the industrial establishments had foreign-born owners, but unfortunately, that distribution by value of production is not available (Díaz Alejandro 1970: 215), and one presumes that these were typically small establishments run by immigrants who were permanent residents. The country has little petroleum or mineral wealth, which naturally lowers the overall level of FDI. The data in Table 6.1 also indicate that throughout the second half of the century the levels of the stock of FDI have not been high. The country currently has in place policies which are receptive to FDI, but it has not yet been able to break into the market of exported manufactured goods, for which attracting FDI may well be both cause and effect. Privatization has been quite significant in Argentina, and according to UN-ECLAC (1998), the main attraction for the influx of FDI during the early 1990s was the privatization of several public service enterprises. A final comment about the data in the Table is that, although there was an acceleration of foreign borrowing during the 1970s, the current level of FI/GDP is not large.

The unusually high level of foreign investment early in the century leads us to excavate the long-ignored ECLA document of 1958 for more statistical details about foreign and domestic investment in the Argentine economy during the first half of the twentieth century. For example, one conclusion to be drawn from Table 6.2 is that the peak of either FI or FDI was reached before World War I. At that time, FDI accounted for 38 per cent of total capital, or 27 per cent of physical wealth – capital plus land. The distribution by type of investment changes dramatically during the 1940s, when the country used its accumulated sterling balances to pay off the national debt and to purchase the railroads. Moreover, foreign ownership rates differed

Table 6.1 Argentina: relative size of inward foreign investment stocks, twentieth century

	1900	1913	1929	1938	1950	1970	1980	1990	1995
FI/capita	290	266	140	104	16	28	94	117	152
FDI/capita	176	186	91	80	9	15	15	14	33
Non-RR FDI/capita	56	50	36	36					
FI/GDP	357	248	112	87	12	14	43	53	42
FDI/GDP	216	173	73	67	7	7	7	6	9
Non-RR FDI/GDP	69	47	29	30					
FI/trade	1,035	514	234	593	89	229	239	477	389
FDI/trade	627	358	152	455	51	121	39	59	84
Non-RR FDI/trade	201	97	61	203					
ECLA data:									
FI/GDP		245	145	82	18				
FDI/GDP		194	116	68	18				
Non-RR FDI/GDP		113	65	41	18				

Sources: Population: 1900–1990, *Statistical Abstract of Latin America*, Volume 28; 1995, the *World Development Report*, 1997. GDP: 1900–1970, UN-ECLA (1978); 1980–1995 the *World Debt Tables*. Foreign investment is the sum of Government Debt and Foreign Direct Investment. Government Debt: For 1900, estimated as the sum of that from France, in Rippy (1948) and from the UK from Stone (1987), averaging the data for 1895 and 1905, and following Lewis (1938) in attributing no portfolio investment for the US for 1897; 1913, UN-ECLA (1965: 16); 1929, UN-ECLA (1965: 27); 1938, Lewis (1948); 1950, UN-ECLA (1965: 203); 1970–1995, the *World Debt Tables*. Foreign Direct Investment: 1900–1995, calculated as the sum of FDI stocks from the United Kingdom, the United States, and France (1900–1913 only). From the United Kingdom: up through 1928, data from Rippy (1959); 1938, Lewis (1948); 1950, averaging the amounts of the Bank of England (1950) and Mikesell (1955: 10) – the former referring to 1948, and the latter to 1951. From the US; 1897 through 1929, Lewis (1938) supplemented by UN-ECLA (1965: 32); 1938, Lewis (1948); 1950, US Department of Commerce (1960). From France; 1902 and 1913 business and railroad investments from Rippy (1948); FDI in 1971; UNCTC (1983); 1980–1995, the *World Investment Report*. Non-Railroad FDI: 1900–1938, Lewis (1938 and 1948), Rippy (1959), Bank of England (1950), and various issues of the *South American Journal* for 1928 and 1938. Trade (the average of exports and imports): 1900, US Bureau of Statistics (1909); 1913, Lamartine Yates (1959); 1929–1970, *Statistical Abstract of Latin America* (1980: Table 2731); 1980–1995, *World Debt Tables*.

Notes
The reference dates for the ECLA data are 1913, the average of 1927 and 1931, 1940, and 1953.

significantly; before World War I, railroads were completely dominated by foreigners, while the average for the rest of the economy the ratio was about a third, and varied according to sector. By mid-century, the overall ratio of FDI to domestic capital had fallen to 5 per cent, and the only major sector in which foreign ownership had increased was industry. The relative decline of FI and FDI was gradual, suggestive of the influence of longer-term economic factors rather than major policy switches. An easy example of the former is the gradual substitution of (locally owned) trucks and automobiles for (foreign owned) trains, and indeed by 1939 the railroads accounted for less than half of transport capital.

Table 6.2 Argentina: sectoral distribution of foreign investment, and foreign ownership ratios (per cent)

	1909	1913	1927	1940	1953
Percentage Distribution of Foreign Investment:					
Government Loans	31	33	21	53	0
Railroads	36	21	34	22	0
Other Direct	34	46	44	20	100
FDI/(Capital + Land)		27			
FDI/Capital	28	38	27	15	5
Non-RR FDI/Capital	14	22	15	4	5
FDI/Capital, by sector:					
Railroads	81	93	106	154	0
Other Private Enterprise	37	64	36	9	12
Agriculture	15				1
Industry	5				12
Services	252				28
Residential Housing	0				0
Government	0				0

Source: Author's calculations based on data in UN-ECLA (1958), Annex III and VII, and the 1914 census value of land, from Bunge (1917: 21).

Notes

It is assumed that there was no FDI in housing nor government activities. The category "services" is all other activities. The cases in the Table where the foreign ownership ratio, FDI/K, is larger than 100 per cent, reveal measurement problems. In the case of railroads, a prime candidate is lack of depreciation of FDI, because ECLA reported an absolute decline in the real value of railroads (Cuadro 16 of Annex III). With regard to services in 1909, both FDI and the capital stock have potential problems. The FDI data include financial institutions whose assets are not their own fixed capital. Correspondingly, it is possible that not all service activities were canvassed for the generation of the capital stock data. The implication is that the sectoral and hence total values of FDI/K are too large. The valuation of land converted the Census's 10.6 billion paper pesos to 45 billion pesos at 1950 prices, by comparing GDP for 1914 in Cortés Conde (1994) and UN-ECLA (1958). It would be 60 billion 1950 pesos by comparison of the values of 1914 imports.

A major contributor to the decline in the ratio of FDI/K was the growth of sectors with inherently smaller foreign ownership. Table 6.3 provides the details. Once again there is an easy example – the government sector grew relative to the rest of the economy, and since the foreign-owned share of government capital was zero, this lowered the aggregate ratio. Commerce is another example, somewhat muddied when banking is included in the data.[2] More interesting is the growth of industry. Because this sector initially had a very low foreign ownership ratio, its growth relative to (foreign owned) railroads, for example, will have lowered the overall ratio of FDI/K for the country. Also to be noted in the ECLA data is that dwellings accounted for about one third of total capital, without a major secular trend.[3] Thus, what appears as a significant decline in foreign ownership of the capital stock, from 28 per cent in 1909 to 5 per cent in 1953, is in fact a composite of a dramatic decline in railroads –

Table 6.3 Argentina: sectoral distribution of the capital stock and capital output ratios, 1900–1955

	1900	1913	1929	1940	1955
Distribution: (per cent)					
Agriculture and Livestock	28	18	20	18	15
Industry	8	11	12	13	15
Transport	18	18	14	15	10
Public Utilities	1	2	3	3	3
Commerce and Other Services	2	3	5	4	4
Dwellings	34	37	35	33	33
Government	9	12	11	14	20
Total	100	100	100	100	100
Aggregate K/O Ratio	4.5	5.5	4.4	4.3	3.6
by sector:					
Agriculture and Livestock	4.2	3.9	3.8	3.2	3.1
Manufacturing Industry	2.6	4.1	3.0	2.7	2.3
Transport	21.3	15.3	8.1	8.9	4.0
Public Utilities	9.0	9.2	8.1	7.1	4.3
Commerce and Other Services	0.5	0.6	0.9	0.9	0.9
Dwellings	20.5	35.8	34.1	28.2	25.5
Government	6.9	12.7	9.5	8.8	7.4
K/O Ratio without Railroads	3.9	4.8	4.3	4.3	3.8

Source: Author's calculations, using Annexes I and III of UN-ECLA (1958).

Note
The fraction of total capital accounted for by Livestock declined from 18 per cent to 5 per cent during this period, reflecting the importance of this activity in the early economic history of the Republic.

together with an unexpected decline in agriculture – with rising foreign ownership of industry and services. In either a political (e.g. dependency) or an economic (e.g. technology transfer) evaluation of this data, the sectoral differences are likely to be more important than the trend in the overall average. To rephrase the point; either dependency or technology transfer perspectives might interpret the aggregate data as indicating a decline in their variable of interest, while if either or both schools would focus on industry, they would see an increase in that variable. Such a conclusion will hold in spite of problems with the data, such as the unusually low estimate of the capital stock in services, which is suggested by that sector's very low capital output ratio.[4]

For the first half of the century, the data in Table 6.2 depict a decline in FDI/K which mirrors the more easily measured decline in FDI/GDP in Table 6.1. The difference between those two indicators, as will be recalled, is the capital output ratio (K/O), and this variable plays an important role in our overall analytical framework. It might be worth taking advantage of the thoroughness of the ECLA data to analyse trends in this variable, as well. One working hypothesis would be that the aggregate capital output ratio would rise as a country industrializes. However, the capital output ratio in Table 6.3 reached a peak in 1913, and fell steadily afterwards into the 1950s – by a third overall, by one fifth if railroads are excluded. Thus the working hypothesis is wrong, for at least two reasons that are revealed in the Table. First of all, in the Argentine case the development of infrastructure led that of other sectors. Because railroads and other utilities are very capital intensive, the subsequent growth of other sectors of the economy tended to lower the K/O ratio. In particular, industry has a lower K/O ratio than many other activities, particularly government and residential dwellings, and its K/O ratio was relatively equal to that of agriculture in Argentina (although one would question how representative the country would be in this regard). Finally, a third possibility is that technological change may result in a reduction in the measured K/O ratio. These factors were also important in lowering the K/O ratio in other Latin American countries for which we have data for the first half of the twentieth century.

The economic nationalism associated with Juan Perón was much weaker when he returned to power in the early 1970s, and had essentially disappeared during the presidency of the Peronist party's Carlos Menem, during the 1990s. Calvert's analysis of privatization under Menem is rich in details of the range of problems encountered and solutions found, leading to the conclusion, "... in the Argentine case, privatisation certainly cannot be treated as simply a problem in economic management" (Calvert 1996: 155). The compromises imposed by political restrictions weakened the attractiveness of the process to foreign investors, whatever the intentions of the economic ministers. As the century ends, and after more than a decade of macroeconomic stability, observers in and out of the country are waiting to see if the new political context will generate significant new inflows of foreign investment.

Brazil

The historical pattern of foreign direct investment in Brazil reflects most of the major forces which have shaped the region. At the beginning of the twentieth century, the government had a relatively high level of indebtedness, a good part of which was due to spending on railroads. Direct investment by foreigners in other sectors of the economy, while not large relative to GDP, was in fact growing, with the ratio FDI/GDP peaking around the start of World War I. One factor keeping FDI down was that the country's exports were mainly agricultural, and that sector was predominantly in Brazilian hands. The experience of the Depression and World War II accelerated the process of industrialization, and government intervention became more intense during the 1950s. A military coup in 1964 brought a lasting change in the orientation of policies toward foreign trade and investment, while not, incidentally, achieving any sort of

160   *A Century of Foreign Investment in the Third World*

macroeconomic equilibrium in terms of stable prices and exchange rates. Subsequently, high growth rates of national income have been accompanied by high inflows of FDI, and the ratio of the stock of FDI to GNP is currently rather low, as shown in Table 6.4. In contrast to other Latin American countries, Brazil's attraction for multinational corporations is both for its internal market and for exports. Moreover, many manufac-

Table 6.4 Brazil: relative size of inward foreign investment stocks, twentieth century

	1900	1913	1929	1938	1950	1970	1980	1990	1995
FI/capita	40	59	32	29	10	18	51	48	54
FDI/capita	17	35	17	13	} 8	9	12	14	17
Non-RR FDI/capita	7	17	13	10					
FI/GDP	83	92	65	78	11	24	33	31	28
FDI/GDP	34	54	34	34	} 8	12	8	9	9
Non-RR FDI/GDP	14	26	27	27					
FI/trade	546	546	297	707	144	362	253	337	273
FDI/trade	226	321	155	305	} 110	183	59	95	85
Non-RR FDI/trade	91	158	123	248					
FDI/K		17	16	14	6	3	3		
FDI/(K + L)		9	9		4	2	2		

Sources: Population: 1900–1990, *Statistical Abstract of Latin America*, Volume 28; 1995, from the *World Development Report*, 1997. GDP: 1900–1970, Goldsmith (1986) – based on Haddad for the early years; 1980–1995, the *World Debt Tables*. Foreign investment is the sum of Government Debt and Foreign Direct Investment. Government Debt: 1900, estimated as the sum of that from France, in Rippy (1948), and from the UK, from Stone (1987), averaging the data for 1895 and 1905, and following Lewis (1938) in attributing no portfolio investment for the US for 1897; 1913 and 1929, UN-ECLA (1965); 1938, Lewis (1948); 1950, from UN-ECLA (1965: 203); 1970–1995, the *World Debt Tables*. Foreign Direct Investment: 1900 and 1913, calculated as the sum invested in economic enterprises from the UK, from Rippy (1959), plus the amounts from the US and France from UN-ECLA (1965); 1929, Wythe (1945: 154); 1938, Lewis (1948); 1950, Banco do Brasil *Relatorio* (1950: 162); 1971, OECD (1973); 1980–1990, from various issues of the *Boletim* of the Banco Central do Brasil. Non-Railroad FDI: 1900–1938, For the US, Lewis (1938 and 1948). For the UK, Rippy (1959), Bank of England (1950). For 1938, UK holdings in railroads were extrapolated from the values for 1929 and 1949. Trade (the average of exports and imports, in US dollars): 1900, US Bureau of Statistics (1909); 1913, Lamartine Yates (1959); 1929–1970, *Statistical Abstract of Latin America* (1980: Table 2731); 1980–1995, *World Debt Tables*. Capital (K) – structures and equipment – and total tangible assets (K + L) – structures and equipment, inventories, livestock, consumer durables and land – from Goldsmith (1986: Tables IV-5, IV-34, VI-80), using the 1938 FDI data from our sources listed above. The last three reference years for these two series are 1945, 1972, and 1980.

Notes
The GDP for 1913 and 1929 are two year averages. Alternative estimates of the basic data are available. The total FDI and non-RR FDI reported for 1913 in Castro (1979) are very close to that used in this table, although her totals for 1900 are about one third larger than these. Kindersley's estimate of 1930 FDI is dramatically lower than Rippy's, which is based on the *South American Journal*. The datum for FDI in 1995 as reported by the *World Investment Report* was almost twice that reported by the Banco Central do Brasil, even though the data from the two sources coincided for 1980, 1985, and 1990. The Brazilian source is used here. UN-ECLA (1998: 153), which is based on the Central Bank's census of FDI, reports a total for the 1995 stock of FDI about 10 per cent lower than used here.

tured exports have a minimal component of imported inputs, further strengthening the contrast with her neighbors.

Goldsmith (1986) presented estimates of the total value and fixed value of assets in Brazil from 1913 to 1980. Data availability did not allow him to use a technique as refined as the perpetual inventory method, and the country's long experience of high and varying inflation makes such exercises more suspect than most. Nevertheless, the two series in Table 6.4 provide further support for our conclusion that foreign ownership has declined since the second decade of the century, and that foreign ownership of total assets, however measured, has been rather lower in Brazil than in other third world areas. Foreign investment in railroads was not large,[5] and the available data indicate that the relative decline in foreign ownership occurred broadly throughout the economy.

In 1995 the Brazilian Central Bank carried out a census of foreign investment, two of whose results are of particular interest to us. Consider first the aggregate balance sheets of these firms in Table 6.5. For either majority foreign owned or those with at least 10 per cent foreign ownership, we note once again the wide range of possible empirical specifications of the stock of FDI, from a low of R35 billion (when the *Real* had an exchange rate about equal to one US$1), to a high of R273 billion, as one might choose to look at equity, fixed assets, or total assets. Basing itself on that census, an important recent ECLAC publication (UN-ECLA 1998: 153) used a total equivalent to R46 billion, for the amount of foreign held equity. It is reassuring to note that this was just slightly lower

Table 6.5 Aggregate balance sheet of Brazilian firms with foreign ownership, 1995 (billion reals)

	Foreign Ownership at Least 10%	Majority Foreign Owned
Assets	273	159
Short Term Loans	126	75
Long Term Loans	35	17
Fixed Assets	111	66
Liabilities & Social Capital	273	159
Short Term Debt	104	58
Long Term Debt	63	33
Social Capital		
Residents	43	16
Non-Residents	41	35
Other Accounts	21	17

Source: Downloaded from the Banco Central do Brasil's Web page, May, 1999. Address is: <http://www.bcb.gov.br/htms/censo/menucens>

Note
UN-ECLA (1998: 153) used a total for FDI in Brazil of US$42.5 billion, equivalent to R46.3 billion, with an exchange rate of R/US$0.918.

than what the Central Bank had been estimating, using balance of payments data and direct information from the firms.

The second item derived from the Central Bank's census is the estimate of foreign ownership of capital stock reported in UN-ECLA (1998: 150), in a section written under the guidance of Reinaldo Gonçalves. According to this estimate, as indicated in Table 6.6, the foreign share of Brazilian capital was the same in 1977 and 1995, at 11 per cent. Details of the methodology for estimating the capital stock are not provided in that publication, but in a personal communication Gonçalves has indicated that the capital stock refers to corporations in Brazil. The implied capital output ratio is only a bit over unity, which would appear to be low, suggesting that a substantial amount of capital has not been captured, such as government, residential housing, and non-corporate enterprises, which could have accounted for up to one half of total fixed reproducible capital. The relative constancy in the level of foreign ownership between 1977 and 1995 repeats the message from our Table 6.4, where FDI/GDP was used as a proxy.

Furthermore, it is interesting to note in Table 6.6 the differences by sector in foreign ownership, with the highest levels in manufacturing and wholesale trade, the latter of course is often merely an importing activity. Within the manufacturing sector there are also a wide range of foreign

Table 6.6 Brazil: foreign ownership of domestic capital, total and by sectors, 1977 and 1995 (per cent)

	1977	*1995*
Total	11.1	11.0
Agriculture	5.0	1.7
Mining	8.6	8.2
Manufacturing	23.6	25.6
Food	11.9	11.5
Tobacco	30.5	52.6
Textiles	17.3	16.2
Pharmaceuticals	70.2	67.7
Transport Equipment	51.8	50.6
All Others (unweighted average)	11.1	9.4
Services	4.7	6.9
Wholesale Trade	23.7	22.2
Retail Trade	2.1	3.7
Business Services	16.1	12.7

Source: UN-ECLA (1998: 150).

Note
The data for "All Others" is this author's calculation; not all of the economy's other activities are listed here. According to a personal communication from Reinaldo Gonçalves, a consultant for that UN publication, the capital stock data used for those calculations was based on corporate data from the Ministry of Finance. Presumably, incorporation of government, non-corporate, or residential capital would lower the ratios of FDI/Domestic Capital.

ownership ratios, as is predicted by the OLI paradigm or any such industrial organization perspective. Indeed, many students of Brazil have commented on this; a recent overview by Fritsch and Franco (1991) refers to works by Newfarmer and Mueller, Evans, W. Baer, Bonelli, Malan, and Willmore among others, who relied both on government sources as well as business publications such as *Visão*.[6] These works also reveal the importance of parastatal enterprises in several sectors, such as mining, steel, petroleum and chemicals. This pattern reminds us that in many third world countries, there are three groups of participants in production, the domestic private sector, the government, and the foreign investors. Current efforts at privatization in Brazil are directed at these parastatals, as well as other activities related to social infrastructure that are more traditionally operated by the government.

Canada

Although this country has never been classified as a third world or developing country, its status as an example *par excellence* of a country of recent European settlement makes it an important case for comparative analysis. The Canadian experience is of interest for three themes; as an importer of capital, as a settler economy, and as a capital exporter. Another, nontrivial, attraction is the quality of the country's data. The historical background can be sketched very briefly. Confederation in 1867 gave the country self-governing status in the Dominion. Not long after, Canada began to pursue an industrialization policy, in which highly protectionist tariffs played an important role. Both Britain and the United States had significant amounts of investment there before World War I, about two thirds of the total located in railroads.[7] After that war, Britain's economic dominance receded while that of the United States grew, leaving a residual nationalism which is still present today. In particular, a brief period in the 1970s witnessed a series of measures intended to restrict incoming FDI, which were ultimately reversed by Premier Brian Mulroney after his election in 1984. Currently, of course, the country is a major industrial power, whose exports range from raw materials to high technology products.

The basic set of investment data for Canada are presented in Table 6.7. Although before World War I the country had very high levels of per capita foreign investment, adjusting those numbers for the high per capita income level, and subtracting out government and railroad securities, leaves us with a rather unexceptional level of non-railroad FDI/GDP.[8] The size of that variable grew during the inter-war period, reflecting rapid increases in investment from the United States, in both exporting and import substituting activities. The ratio FDI/GDP grew during the 1950s, after which it slowly declined to levels which are historically low for the country, but still rather high compared to many other countries. The

Table 6.7 Canada: relative size of inward foreign investment stocks, twentieth century

	1900	1913	1926	1930	1939	1950	1960	1970	1980	1990	1995
Inward Investment:											
FI/capita	226	385	313	377	359	225	329	438	647	1,085	1,391
FDI/capita	63	73	87	114	117	90	178	231	237	275	304
FI/GDP	140	146	120	133	126	53	64	58	57	77	90
FDI/GDP	32	23	32	40	41	21	34	31	21	20	20
FI/trade	693	676	560	847	876	322	435	320	232	353	312
FDI/trade	195	128	156	257	286	129	236	169	85	89	68
FI/K	34	33	28	31	28	15	17	17	14		
FDI/K	9	6	8	9	9	6	9	9	5		
Outward Investment/GDP			24	24	32	31	36	31	36	40	51
Outward FDI/GDP			7	7	11	5	9	7	9	15	19
Net Inward FDI/GDP			25	33	30	16	28	23	12	5	$<\frac{1}{2}$

Sources: Population: *Historical Statistics of Canada* and various *International Financial Statistics Yearbooks*. Inward Foreign Investment: 1900–1913, *Historical Statistics of Canada*; 1926–1992, *Canada's International Investment Position*, 1998. Inward FDI: 1900–1913, sum of direct investment from the United Kingdom, from Paterson (1976), and that from the United States, from Lewis (1938); 1926–1992, *Canada's International Investment Position*, 1998. GDP: 1900–1914, Urquhart (1986: 11); 1926–1950, *Historical Statistics of Canada*; 1960–1995, various *International Financial Statistics Yearbooks*. Trade (average of exports and imports): 1900–1960, *Historical Statistics of Canada*; 1960–1995, various *International Financial Statistics Yearbooks*. Outward FI and FDI: 1926–1992, *Canada's International Investment Position*, 1998. Capital Stock (K): 1900–1926, calculated by subtracting from the 1926 value, the gross investment from Urquhart (1993: Table 1.2), subsequent years from Statistics Canada *Fixed Capital Flows and Stocks*, interpolating residential capital 1926–1936.

Notes
From 1926 on, there was virtually no controlling investment in railroads. For that sector, it would be very difficult to separate controlling from portfolio investment before that date, and Paterson did not include railroads in his estimates of FDI. The series in *Canada's International Investment Position* would appear to have included reinvested profits in all the estimates of FDI.

ratios of FI and non-railroad FDI to the fixed stock of capital are also provided in Table 6.7. Throughout the century, FDI/K has always been less than 10 per cent, which many commentators would judge a small level. Furthermore, it is evident that variations in the overall ratio of FDI to capital have been relatively modest.

Canada is the one of the capital importing countries treated in this book which can be considered to have approximated Narula's Investment Development Path, as is suggested by the data in Table 6.7. A country like Canada, with its extensive but remote holdings of raw materials, would be expected to receive an above average amount of inward FDI. Nevertheless, over time its entrepreneurs would develop the skills necessary to be competitive in global markets, and outward FDI would follow. The path that net FDI/GDP has taken is certainly not a symmetrical textbook sinusoidal path, but that does not disqualify the model. Moreover, it is also undoubtedly the case that some of what is listed as outward FDI from

Canada is probably more accurately described as portfolio investments, in areas such as finance and real estate. Nevertheless, Canadians also are very active in mining, wood products, and telecommunications, which have long been exporting sectors for the country. In fact, even before World War I, Canada had become a source of investment funds, and entrepreneurship, in Latin America, particularly in public utilities, a subject explored in depth by Armstrong and Nelles (1988).

One interesting aspect of the pre-1913 period is the disaggregation by modes of external funding to the private sector, outside of railroads. Canada is perhaps the only country covered in this book where published data exist, at least for investment from Great Britain. For most other host countries, stocks and bonds are reported as one total, and often railroads are not separated. For the Canadian case, Paterson (1976) used information on FDI at the firm level, as reported in stock market yearbooks and other business publications. Leaving aside funds in railroads, a comparison of his totals for British FDI, with those for total foreign capital into the private sector, in Paish (1911: 180) for 1910, or in Simon (1970: 246) for 1914, indicates that non-controlling portfolio investment from the United Kingdom amounted to about half of British capital in the private sector. In comparative terms this is a large fraction, as few host countries had been able to attract such a high volume of inherently risky funds. Two obvious explanatory factors are the shared legal and institutional environment, and the importance of loans to settlers from the United Kingdom, whose contacts on the other side of the Atlantic could reassure an otherwise reluctant financial market.

Table 6.8 Canada: foreign control and ownership of non-financial activities, 1926–1987 (percentages)

	1926	1930	1939	1951	1960	1970	1980	1987
Total Control	17	19	21	27	33	36	27	24
Manufacture	35	36	37	48	59	61	51	53
Mining	} 33	38	38	50	{ 61	70	41	30
Petroleum & Gas					73	76	50	35
Railroads	3	3	3	3	2	2	1	0
Other Utilities	23	29	29	21	5	7	3	2
Commerce	5	8	10	9	10	12	10	10
Total Ownership	37	39	38	31	34	35	34	32
Manufacture	39	41	43	44	52	53	48	48
Mining	} 33	38	38	50	{ 60	59	49	40
Petroleum & Gas					62	61	48	40
Railroads	54	58	56	39	26	16	28	40
Other Utilities	31	35	29	18	14	19	29	27
Commerce	10	8	10	9	9	9	9	10

Source: *Canada's International Investment Position* (1992: Table 75).

Note
The determination of control is made by the Canadian officials. It is clear that government regulations guaranteed local control in railroads and utilities.

The official Canadian data on foreign direct investment illustrate very well how markedly different have been both the level and evolution of ratios of foreign ownership and control by economic sectors, in the period since 1926. Table 6.8 indicates how the overall trend in the foreign presence is an average of quite disparate sector specific changes; foreign control of manufacturing and minerals has risen since World War II, while that in the service sectors is lower and follows a declining trend. In such a situation, the behavior of the economy-wide average may be a poor indicator of such fundamental economic factors as competitiveness or technological change.[9] In particular, the long-term growth of services in the economy will lower the aggregate ratio, even while certain sectors experience increases in foreign ownership. As we just saw with Argentina, the Canadian data also indicate this to be a plausible occurrence.

Chile

Mining has always been a major production and export activity in Chile. In the latter years of the nineteenth century, nitrate was the major mineral. Then, shortly before World War I, American companies began to produce copper, using large-scale mines and the capital-intensive techniques which characterized the foreign owned *gran minería*. The growth of the foreign mines dwarfed not only the Chilean mining firms, but also crowded out the externally oriented agricultural sector and domestic manufacturing industry. The response of successive governments was to adopt a classic strategy of import substituting industrialization, using a variety of interventions in the foreign sector. Confrontations over the mines, on policies such as taxes, exchange rates, and profit remittances, eventually led to their expropriation under President Salvador Allende in 1971.[10] A military coup in 1973 led to the complete reversal of these economic and social policies.

Although the Chilean government now welcomes foreign investment and has seen it flourish, the core of what had been the American mining companies remains with the government, in an entity known as CODELCO. The mining sector is open to investments, and this sector presently has over half of the country's accumulated FDI. Moguillansky (1998) mentions several factors explaining the strength of investments into a sector dominated by the government; exploration of new sites, renewed interest in old sites laid dormant during the 1960s and 1970s, favorable prices in the late 1980s, new technology of exploration and refining, a perception of political stability. She highlights the growth of medium sized firms, undertaking "greenfield" investments (as opposed to buying out already existing firms), as well as the expansion of the production of minerals other than copper. In contrast to mining, the manufacturing sector is not attractive to foreign investors, predominantly because the country has low tariffs and the internal market is small. Agriculture has never attracted much outside investment in Chile. There have been well-publicized booms in foreign investment in forestry (Clapp 1995) and in activities related to fishing, which while small in terms of aggregate FDI, may well account for a large fraction of those sectors' total capital.

Furthermore, little of the post-1985 surge in foreign direct investment has been directly related to privatization (UN-ECLA 1998: 104), although a program of debt equity swaps had earlier been instrumental in jump-starting FDI inflows during a balance of payments crisis. It should also be noted that the liberalization of the financial sector has led to many joint ventures in that industry, involving a new mode of foreign presence which this book's emphasis on direct investment will not capture. That dynamism is also fueling an outflow of Chilean FDI, particularly into its neighbors in the southern cone.

The data in Table 6.9 certainly indicate that foreign investment was unusually high in the early years of the century. However, the peak in the

Table 6.9 Chile: relative size of inward foreign investment stocks, twentieth century

	1900	1913	1929	1938	1950	1970	1980	1990	1995
FI/capita	74	114	128	127	47	49	76	102	113
FDI/capita	48	74	72	86	} 30	3	7	42	51
Non-RR FDI/capita	28	51	63	71					
FI/GDP	175	197	152	170	49	34	39	87	58
FDI/GDP	113	127	86	115	} 31	2	3	35	26
Non-RR FDI/GDP	66	87	74	95					
FI/trade	408	369	283	995	370	251	141	225	170
FDI/trade	263	239	160	671	} 236	15	12	91	77
Non-RR FDI/trade	154	164	138	554					

Sources: Population: 1900–1990, *Statistical Abstract of Latin America*, Volume 28; 1995, from the *World Development Report*, 1997. GDP: For 1900–1940, Maddison (1995); 1940–1970, UN-ECLA (1978), 1980–1995, *World Debt Tables*. Foreign investment is the sum of Government Debt and Foreign Direct Investment. Government Debt: 1900, estimated as the sum of that from France, in Rippy (1948) and from the UK from Stone (1987), averaging the data for 1895 and 1905, and following Lewis (1938) in attributing no portfolio investment for the US for 1897; 1913, UN-ECLA (1965: 16); 1929–1950, UN-ECLA (1954: 84); 1970–1995, the *World Debt Tables*. Foreign Direct Investment: 1900–1913, calculated as the sum of FDI stocks from the United Kingdom, the United States, and France. From the UK, data from Rippy (1959); from the US, 1897 through 1914, from Lewis (1938); 1902 and 1913 business and railroad investments from France were taken from Rippy (1948). 1929–1950, UN-ECLA (1954: 84); 1971, from OECD (1973); 1980–1995, the *World Investment Report*. Non-Railroad FDI: 1900–1938, for the US, Lewis (1938 and 1948). For the UK, Rippy (1959), Bank of England (1950), and various issues of the *South American Journal* for 1928 and 1938; for 1938, UK holdings in railroads were extrapolated from the values for 1929 and 1950. Trade (the average of exports and imports): 1900, US Bureau of Statistics (1909); 1913, Lamartine Yates (1959); 1929–1970, *Statistical Abstract of Latin America* (1980: Table 2731); 1980–1995, *World Debt Tables*.

Notes
The data in UN-ECLA (1954) are those of Central Bank of Chile, which were very close to those of the source countries.

ratios of FDI to population, GDP or trade occurred before the major investment by the American mining companies, when the major group of foreigners were British, and the investments centered in nitrate mines, railroads, and urban activities.[11] The calculations in Table 6.9 also clearly indicate the declining trend of FDI before 1970, and that the post-coup recovery has attained levels which are still very much smaller than those of the beginning of the century.

The available data for Chile allow us to pursue these topics along two lines of inquiry; the path of overall foreign ownership of capital, and the sectoral variations of that variable. Estimates made during the 1950s by economists at the recently created ECLA indicated that a peak in the ratio of foreign capital to domestic capital was reached at 33 per cent in 1930, falling to less than half that level by mid-century, as shown in Table 6.10. The Central Bank of Chile's data on foreign investment and FDI indicate a stagnation of the nominal levels during the 1930s, and a decline by a third during the Second World War.

Rather more speculative are our own estimates in Table 6.11 of the sectoral ownership ratios during the first half of the century – unfortunately, no parallel data are available for more recent years. The source for 1928 has often been cited in the literature, and its authors were well informed, but the publication itself accompanied an exposition at an international fair, which may explain why no academic-style citations were offered for the data. The source for 1950 is one of the first of a set of publications by ECLA in its series of country studies whose major publications were titled *Analyses and Projections of Economic Development.*[12] The author of the Chile study was Aníbal Pinto, a well-known academic. Although in one sense all that the data in Table 6.11 are able to demonstrate is that FDI was most important in mining and industry, there may be some value in indicating orders of magnitude of the size of the capital stock in those areas of the economy which traditionally do not receive much FDI. In particular, according to these numbers, the stock of mining capital in Chile was about 10 per cent of the country's total in 1930, and had fallen to 7 per cent in 1951.

Table 6.10 Chile: foreign investment and FDI as percentages of the domestic capital stock, 1925–1951

Period	FI/K	FDI/K
1925–29	36	24
1930–33	52	33
1934–39	40	27
1940–45	25	15
1946–50	21	14
1951	21	15

Source: Author's calculations, based on UN-ECLA (1954: 78, 84).

Table 6.11 Chile: sectoral ownership of the capital stock, 1928 and 1950 (million 1900 US dollars, and percentages)

1928	Capital Stock			Foreign Direct Investment			FDI/K
	Reported Total	Adust.	Revised Total	Reported Total	Adjust.	Revised Total	
Total	1,702	−15	1,687	626	−280	346	21
Agriculture	116	225	341	37	−10	27	8
Mining	609	−280	329	348	−170	178	54
Industry	128	0	128	70	−30	40	31
Transport	112	80	192	39	10	49	26
Commerce	5	60	65	2	20	22	34
Urban Property	733	−300	433	130	−100	30	7
Government	0	200	200	0	0	0	0
1950							
Total	1,293	110	1,403			179	13
Agriculture	213		213			1	10
Mining	55	110	165			124	73
Industry	266		266			10	6
Commerce	29		29			11	45
Urban Property	285		285			} 32	} 6
Transport	241		241				
Government	205		205			0	0

Source: Author's calculations, based on Jara Letelier and Muirhead (1929) and UN-ECLA (1954), adjusted as indicated below.

Notes
1928 data converted from Pesos of 6d using an exchange rate of 8.25 Pesos/US$, and then dividing by 2.09 for 1900 prices. Agriculture: adjusted to correspond to the datum in the *Anuario Estadístico* (*AE*) 1930; this may include land. Mining: adjusted for consistency with data on US mining (Reynolds 1965: 382) and data on British and domestic mining, in *AE* 1923. Industry: data is consistent with the *AE*. Transport: railroad capital in *AE* 1923. Commerce: adjusted for compatibility to the dollar equivalent values in the *AE* for 1915, 1916 and 1923. Urban property (*propriedad raíz*) may well include holding companies, involving some double counting. Government capital: not mentioned in Jara Letelier and Muirhead, assumed here to be roughly one eighth of total. At the 8.25 Peso/US$ exchange rate, the reported total of foreign capital is much higher than that given by the Chilean Central Bank, with the clearest cases of mis-estimates in mining, railroads, and probably urban property.
The total capital for 1950, as given in ECLA's *Economic Survey of Latin America, 1951–52* was converted to 1900 US$ by converting at an exchange rate of 65 Pesos/US$, and deflating by the US price index of 3.3. The distribution of domestic capital is that of UN-ECLA (1954: 65), for 1946–1950. These ECLA publications, as well as Ganz (1959), understate mining capital, compared to Reynolds (1965), and are adjusted accordingly. The distribution of foreign investment is that of UN-ECLA (1954: 82), applied to the total for 1950 in UN-ECLA (1954: 84). The fit of categories is not precise; "urban property" and transport in capital stock are here compared to "services" in FDI. The label of the category for urban property in Ganz (1959: 229) includes housing, but it is not clear if this is included in the other ECLA publications mentioned here.

Lacking any recent study of nation-wide ownership rates, Table 6.12 presents data from different sources on the sectoral distribution of FDI and total capital, so that a ratio of the two numbers will give a rough sense of relative degrees of foreign dominance. Mining still has the largest relative foreign component, while that of manufacturing has been falling. The

Table 6.12 Chile: sectoral shares of capital and FDI, 1960–1995 (per cent)

Sectors	Agric.	Forestry & Fishing	Mining	Manuf.	Services
Percent of FDI					
1984	2	1	43	25	29
1990	1	1	50	19	29
1995	1	2	54	17	25
Percent of Fixed Capital					
1960	13	n.a.	9	13	66
1970	13	n.a.	10	15	59
1982	16	n.a.	13	12	59

Sources: Author's calculations based on Comité de Inversiones Extranjeras (1996) and Coeymans and Mundlak (1993), respectively.

Note
The FDI data represent the accumulated amounts of funds entering the country under DL 600 from 1974. The Coeymans and Mundlak paper does not give much detail on estimating methodology. In particular, it is unclear if residences are included. In Hofman (1992: Tables 9 and 10), residences in Chile amounted to between 28 and 39 per cent of the capital stock in 1980, depending on estimating techniques and categories. Although the value of agricultural land is not included in the data here, according to Coeymans and Mundlak, its value was less than 10 per cent of total fixed capital.

data on services cannot be disaggregated, which is unfortunate in a country as technologically dynamic as Chile.

Colombia

One characteristic of Colombia's economy during the twentieth century was the small role that foreign direct investment played in the country, at least compared to other countries in the region. Leaving aside outmoded attempts to explain this by recourse to cultural characteristics, we can note that railroads were less attractive in this mountainous country, and that the major export, coffee, has always been grown on small, family plots. Unlike its fellow Andean countries to the south, there are no major mines to attract FDI. Bananas and, more recently, petroleum have been the major export-oriented FDI activities.

The statistical support for this vision of limited foreign investment in Colombia is presented in Table 6.13. The mild increase in FDI/GDP during the 1920s can be attributed to its growth having been postponed due to the political fallout of Panama's separation in 1903. Furthermore, not only has FDI been relatively small, but the country has tended to avoid reliance on foreign borrowing, virtually throughout the century. Note also that the low levels of FDI/GDP lead us to expect that the FDI/K ratio will also be small, and this is indeed what is indicated for the first half of the century by the data in Table 6.13, based on one of the early ECLA studies.[13]

Table 6.13 Colombia: relative size of inward foreign investment stocks, twentieth century

	1900	1913	1929	1938	1950	1970	1980	1990	1995
FI/capita	22	10	16	19	15	18	24	34	38
FDI/capita	19	6	19	8	11	7	3	6	12
Non-RR FDI/capita	16	4	9						
FI/GDP	61	25	34	35	24	19	24	55	41
FDI/GDP	53	16	21	16	18	8	3	9	13
Non-RR FDI/GDP	44	10	20						
FI/trade	721	184	118	346	156	276	132	218	177
FDI/trade	626	119	75	163	115	111	17	37	57
Non-RR FDI/trade	521	67	68						
FI/K			12		7				
FDI/K			7		5				

Sources: Population: 1900–1990, *Statistical Abstract of Latin America*, Volume 28; 1995, from the *World Development Report*, 1997. GDP: 1900–1929, estimated as the product of population and GDP/capita, estimating the latter to have grown at 0.5 per cent/annum 1900–1913, and for 1913–29, the 1.2 per cent/annum in Maddison (1995); 1938–1970, UN-ECLA (1978); the *World Debt Tables*. Foreign investment is the sum of Government Debt and Foreign Direct Investment. Government Debt: For 1900, estimated as the sum of that from France, in Rippy (1948), and from the UK from Stone (1987), averaging the data for 1895 and 1905, and following Lewis (1938) in attributing no portfolio investment for the US for 1897. For 1913, UN-ECLA (1965: 16); 1929, UN-ECLA (1965: 27); 1938, Lewis (1948); 1950, UN-ECLA (1965: 203); 1970–1995, the *World Debt Tables*. Foreign Direct Investment: 1900–1950, calculated as the sum of FDI stocks from the UK, the US, and France (1900–1913 only). From the UK: up through 1928, data from Rippy (1959), and UN-ECLA (1965: 9); 1938, Lewis (1948); 1950, United Nations (1955: 65). From the US; 1897 through 1929, from Lewis (1938) supplemented by UN-ECLA (1965: 32) and US Department of Commerce (1960); 1938, Lewis (1948); 1950, US Department of Commerce (1960). 1902 and 1913 business and railroad investments from France were taken from Rippy (1948). 1971, from UNCTC (1983); 1980–1995, the *World Investment Report*. Non-Railroad FDI 1900–1938: For the US, Lewis (1938 and 1948). For the UK, Rippy (1959), Bank of England (1950), and various issues of the *South American Journal* for 1928 and 1938. Trade (the average of exports and imports): 1900, US Bureau of Statistics (1909); 1913, Lamartine Yates (1959); 1929–1970 *Statistical Abstract of Latin America* (1980: Table 2731); 1980–1995, *World Debt Tables*. Data on FI/K for 1930 and 1950 from UN-ECLA (1957a: 30), the FDI/K was calculated by adjusting those figures by this table's ratio of FDI/FI. The measure of the capital stock excludes land, while it includes livestock and inventories, which by themselves accounted for 30 per cent of the value of capital.

The one counter-example to low foreign investment is the data for the year 1900, indicating relatively high levels of FDI. Tracing back the sources of UN-ECLA (1965) and Rippy (1959), we find that the major investor in Colombia was France, which, according to the *Bulletin de Statistique* of the French Ministère des Finances (1902: 479), had most of its funds in the sector "canals and navigation (companies)". Undoubtedly, this was the remnants of de Lesseps's company which had gone bankrupt more than a decade before the turn of the century, leaving behind a very important trans-isthmanian railroad, but no canal.[14] With the separation of Panama from Colombia, the amount of FDI in the latter country evidently fell, as indeed is indicated by Rippy's data for subsequent years.

Cuba

It is common knowledge that the "Pearl of the Antilles" had high levels of foreign investment before the nationalizations decreed by Fidel Castro's newly arrived government around 1960, and it is equally well known that the economy had been dominated by sugar. Perhaps less widely appreciated is that in 1950 the economy had achieved one of the highest levels of per capita income in Latin America, which arguably had characterized it throughout the century. Although there currently is some amount of foreign investment, reflecting a change of attitude by the Cuban authorities, the United States-led blockade has restricted that investment, and we will focus our attention on the pre-Castro period.

The new political circumstances accompanying independence from Spain in 1898 led to competition between investors from the United States and the United Kingdom, most visibly in railroads and sugar. Virtually all of the railroad trackage had been constructed by the private sector, as much as two thirds of it for private use by sugar plantations. The latter represented the core of economic and political power on the island, and were dominated by interests from the United States.

The data on trends in foreign investment, presented in Table 6.14, indicate that Cuba's unusually high levels of FDI per person also translate into high values of FDI/GDP. The maximum value of this indicator was achieved before the Depression. The rapid growth up to 1929 is partially an artifact of our data source, which misleadingly treats all investments owned by Spaniards as local. One reason for the subsequent decline was the growth of the rest of the economy, following the initial investments in social infrastructure such as railroads. Of more interest is the expansion of Cuban control of sugar mills, during the Depression and World War II period. According to the Grupo Cubano de Investigaciones Económicas (1963: 1007), this was due to the worsened prospects in the international sugar market and protectionism against Cuba in its major market, combined with the generally dismal economic conditions in the United States, also the major investor. Although there was some new investment by US interests in the Cuban sugar sector after World War II, it is clear that by that time sugar had lost most of its previous attractions to foreigners. In this sense the Cuban experience of a relative decline of FDI after 1929 parallels our finding for most other Latin American countries. Furthermore, although the island did have some mineral resources which might have received foreign investment if the political history had been different, the overall prospect for mining-based FDI was not positive, given the lack of petroleum and the limited need of related on-site mineral processing.

To what extent can we trace in Cuba the relative control of foreign capital? Jenks (1928: 165) reports an estimate for 1913 of national (i.e. Cuban) capital at US$700 million, as compared to foreign capital of

Table 6.14 Cuba: relative size of inward foreign investment stocks, 1900–1950

	1900	1913	1929	1938	1950
FI/capita	123	175	165	104	43
FDI/capita	64	147	150	90	39
Non-RR FDI/capita	39	93	118	74	35
FI/GDP	102	138	204	170	47
FDI/GDP	53	116	186	148	43
Non-RR FDI/GDP	33	73	146	121	39
FI/trade	315	345	502	639	138
FDI/trade	163	289	457	556	125
Non-RR FDI/trade	101	182	359	455	115

Sources: Population: 1900–1990, *Statistical Abstract of Latin America*, Volume 28; 1995, from the *World Development Report*, 1997. GDP: Current value estimates of NNP were taken from Mitchell (1993). Foreign investment is the sum of Government Debt and Foreign Direct Investment. Government Debt: For 1900, estimated as the sum of that from France, in Rippy (1948) and from the UK from Stone (1987), averaging the data for 1895 and 1905, and following Lewis (1938) in attributing no portfolio investment for the US for 1897. For 1913, UN-ECLA (1965: 16); sum of UK from Rippy (1959), and US from US Department of Commerce (1960: 16), for 1928 and 1930, respectively; 1938, Lewis (1948); 1950, from IBRD (1951: 636). Foreign Direct Investment: 1900–1950, calculated as the sum of FDI stocks from the UK, the US, and France (1900–1913 only). From the UK: up through 1928, data from Rippy (1959), and UN-ECLA (1965, 9); 1938, Lewis (1948); 1950, Bank of England (1950) and Mikesell (1955: 10) – the former referring to 1948, and the latter to 1951. From the US; 1897 through 1929, from Lewis (1938) supplemented by UN-ECLA (1965: 32) and US Department of Commerce (1960); 1938, Lewis (1948); 1950, US Department of Commerce (1960). 1902 and 1913 business and railroad investments from France were taken from Rippy (1948). Non-Railroad Direct investment 1900–1938: For the US, Lewis (1938 and 1948). For the UK, Rippy (1959), Bank of England (1950), and various issues of the *South American Journal* for 1928 and 1938. Trade (the average of exports and imports): 1900, US Bureau of Statistics (1909); 1913, Lamartine Yates (1959); 1929–1950, *Statistical Abstract of Latin America* (1980: Table 2731).

Notes
The *World Investment Report* listed Cuban FDI stocks as US$45 million in 1995. Suchlicki and Jorge (1994: 19) cite an article from the *Financial Times* with a 1993 estimate of FDI of US$500 million.

US$400 million, for a ratio of FDI/K at 36 per cent. A detailed set of estimates of domestic capital in 1957 was prepared by a group of exiled Cuban academics and is summarized in Table 6.15. Combining their data with estimates of FDI suggests that the foreign ownership ratio had fallen to one fourth of private non-residential capital, and perhaps one fifth of fixed capital in the country.[15] Although the procedures for generating the capital stock estimates are not detailed, the data do imply a capital output ratio of slightly over two, which is consistent with estimates from other countries. One check on the estimates of foreign investment is the amount claimed after their expropriation. Sigmund (1980: 36) notes that US investors have claimed US$3.3 billion from Cuba, while the US Foreign Claims Settlement Commission recognizes US$1.8 billion. The latter figure is about one third higher than what had been reported by the US Department of Commerce, which is the core of our estimates.

Table 6.15 Cuba: foreign investment and total capital, 1913, 1929, and 1957 (data in million current US dollars, and per cent)

	1913			1929	1957		
	FDI	*K*	*Per cent Foreign Owned*	*FDI*	*FDI*	*K*	*Per cent Foreign Owned*
Total	440	1,140	38	1,102	864	4,556	19
Agriculture	129			575	268	1,335	20
Fishing and Forestry						245	
Mining and Petroleum				**	200	655	31
Industry				45	101	310	33
Transport, Communications and Utilities		361	282	946	30		
Railroads	136			263			
Utilities	95			98			
Housing						779	0
Government						500	0
Per cent of sugar controlled by US investors		30		63		37	

Sources: 1913, FDI summing UK and US investments, from Stone (1987) and Lewis (1938); domestic stock calculated as the sum of that datum, and national capital, from *Cuba Review* April 1912, p. 82; 1929 and 1957, US FDI from US Department of Commerce (1960), British FDI from Rippy (1959); domestic capital in 1957 from Grupo Cubano de Investigaciones Económicas (1963: 819, 1110). US control of sugar: 1913, average of fractions of total output from US-owned plantations, 1908–1912, in *The Cuba Review* March, 1912; 1926 and 1958, from Baklanoff (1975: 29).

Notes
Blank spaces indicate that the data are not available. The 1957 amount of government capital was assumed to be 11 per cent of the total. This procedure ignores the value of investment by Spaniards in Cuba, some of which, by any criteria, was foreign investment. Consequently, the increase in FDI between 1913 and 1929 is exaggerated. The citation in the *Cuba Review* is to an unspecified newspaper article. However, it should be noted that Jenks (1928) repeats the datum, and that when it is combined with Allenes's income estimate, the corresponding capital output ratio (2.8) is of a credible order of magnitude. Several agricultural processing activities were assigned to the category of agriculture, and not industry; those relating to sugar, tobacco, rice, livestock, and coffee. The datum for capital in housing is the sum of constructions from 1941 through 1958. The datum for foreign control of sugar refers to control of milled sugar. Dye (1998: 60) cites a Cuban government source indicating the following breakdown of ownership of milled sugar for 1913: Cuban, 33; Spanish, 18; United States, 37; other foreign 11 per cent. The *Great Britain Overseas Economic Surveys: Cuba* for 1956 cites data, from the *Cuban Sugar Year Book* indicating that the foreign fraction was 53 per cent in 1953, all but 2 per cent from the United States.
(**) Data on US investment in mining in 1929 was suppressed to protect individual firms. The US government had invested about $100m in a nickel mine according to IBRD (1951: 998) and Crupo Cubano (1963: 1081). The value of industrial capital in Grupo Cubano page 1110 is consistent with the Truslow Commission's estimate in IBRD (1951: 129). The run-down state of the railroad system in 1957 makes any attempt at measuring its value very questionable. IBRD (1951: 252) states: "Both railway systems are today overcapitalized in relation to present or reasonably foreseeable earning power." The Consolidated Railroad had arrears almost equal to the value of outstanding stock, while the British owned United railroads was in receivership. Prices in the United States rose by more than half between 1929 and 1957, and it is likely that any relevant price index in Cuba underwent a similar increase.

Honduras

The case of Honduras is suggestive of that of the other countries in Central America, who pursued an export-oriented growth model, were dependent on agricultural exports, and whose economies were typically dominated by foreign firms, in particular the infamous banana companies. In Honduras the two major agricultural exports were coffee and bananas. The former was produced on small, family farms with strong integration into the local economy, while the latter were produced on plantations which were vertically integrated into the economy of the investor country, often with weak multiplier effects in the local economy. For geographical and climatic reasons Honduras had the smallest proportion of coffee to banana exports in the region. The government sponsored the construction of major railroads, but cheating by the contractors resulted in failure, with the result that the country had few lines available for transportation of the general public. We are fortunate that Honduran economy was analysed in the mid-1950s along the lines of the ECLA series *Analyses and Projections of Economic Development.* Although the work of Emanuel Tosco and his colleagues at the Central Bank of Honduras was not published with the same detail as the studies on especially Colombia and Argentina, their historical research provides unique insights into the evolution of Honduras.

With regard to the foreign investment ratios, we see in Table 6.16 that the size of FDI in Honduras, relative to these other variables, was about average for Latin America. Moreover, the time profile of these indicators of the importance of FDI in Honduras was quite similar to that of many other third world countries; there was a peak in FDI/GDP before the 1930s, and after reaching a trough after 1970, there has been a modest recovery of that ratio recently. Diseases affecting the banana trees, as well as a worsened international market, are reasons often given for the decline in investment during the 1930s. Finally, note that in the early years of the century the Honduran government had incurred high external debts, and something similar has occurred again since 1980.

According to Tosco's data on the capital stock, as presented in Table 6.17, the level of foreign direct investment in Honduras in the late 1920s accounted for over 25 per cent of national capital, which was quite high for the region. Most of that was investment in what are often called banana companies; Tosco more frequently used the term *fruteras*, or fruit companies, in recognition that these companies were involved in the production of several crops. It is noteworthy that the relative size of the *fruteras* declined for the three decades for which we have estimates, and that the biggest increase was achieved by capitalization in other private sector activities; manufacturing, non-government services, and housing; perhaps less in manufacturing, given the small size of the domestic economy and the absence of manufactured exports. Although one may

Table 6.16 Honduras: relative size of inward foreign investment stocks, twentieth century

	1900	1913	1929	1938	1950	1970	1980	1990	1995
FI/capita	43	50	51	28		18	35	43	39
FDI/capita	12	13	37	19	13	12	2	4	5
FI/GDP	156	156	119	88		38	64	148	141
FDI/GDP	44	42	87	61	34	26	4	14	16
FI/trade		593	245	428		143	138	337	45
FDI/trade		160	178	297	120	98	8	31	5

Sources: Population: 1900–1990, *Statistical Abstract of Latin America*, Volume 28; 1995, from the *World Development Report*, 1997. GDP: 1900–1929, estimated as the product of population and GDP/capita; the latter was assumed to grow at 1 per cent per year 1900–1913, and 1.9 per cent for 1913–1929; 1929–1970, UN-ECLA (1978); 1980–1995, *World Debt Tables*. Foreign investment is the sum of Government Debt and Foreign Direct Investment. Government Debt: 1900, estimated as the sum of that from France, in Rippy (1948) and from the UK from Stone (1987), averaging the data for 1895 and 1905, and following Lewis (1938) in attributing no portfolio investment for the US for 1897. For 1913, UN-ECLA (1965: 16); 1938, Lewis (1948); 1970–1995, the *World Debt Tables*. Foreign Direct Investment: 1900–1950, calculated as the sum of FDI stocks from the UK, the US, and France (1900–1913 only). From the UK: up through 1928, data from Rippy (1959), and UN-ECLA (1965: 9); 1938, Lewis (1948). From the US; 1897 through 1929, from Lewis (1938) supplemented by UN-ECLA (1965: 32); 1950, US Department of Commerce (1960); 1938, Lewis (1948). 1902 and 1913 business and railroad investments from France were taken from Rippy (1948). 1971, from UNCTC (1983); 1980–1995, from various issues of the *World Investment Report*. Trade (the average of exports and imports): 1900, US Bureau of Statistics (1909); 1913, Lamartine Yates (1959); 1929–1970 *Statistical Abstract of Latin America* (1980: Table 2731); 1980–1995, *World Debt Tables*.

Notes
The sources do not provide information on the value of railroad investment. It is known that a substantial amount of trackage was in existence. It would appear that the rails were constructed by the banana companies, and a separate accounting for them is generally not available without archival work.

always wish to criticize the underlying data, these calculations do provide support for a vision of an upsurge of foreign investment early in the century stimulating growth in the rest of the economy, however slowly. Any detailed analysis of this issue would need to specify the alternative scenario against which this growth is being compared; the physical isolation of the banana plantations, the companies' freedom from local taxes, and the technology intensive mode of production all argue for low levels of induced growth elsewhere in the economy.

The banana companies began their period of growth at the end of the nineteenth century, responding to several stimuli. On the demand side there was a growing market in the United States and Europe, to be sure, and in terms of the technology of production one reads of better control of pests and improved varieties, as well as control over yellow fever and malaria. Perhaps the most important change was in transport technology – cooling the fruit in the holds of the ships. The major company in Honduras was Standard Fruit, while the biggest banana company in the region

Table 6.17 Honduras: sectoral distribution of the national capital stock, and FDI/K, 1925–1955 (per cent)

	1925	1929	1938	1950	1955
Agriculture/Total	57	55	46	40	36
Fruteras/Total	23	23	11	10	12
Other Ag./Total	34	32	35	29	23
Other Private/Total	17	19	23	29	31
Government/Total	7	7	8	11	13
Housing/Total	10	19	22	21	20
FDI/Total	27	26	14	15	17
Fruteras/FDI	88	88	80	70	75

Source: Author's calculations, based on Tosco (1957).

Note
The term *fruteras* appears to be used by Tosco as synonymous with banana companies.

was known as United Fruit. Each of these shipped fruit from various sites in the Caribbean and, eventually, from South America as well. Both these companies are now parts of much larger food conglomerates, continuing a long-standing process of centralization. The major banana producing areas in the Central American countries were on the eastern or Caribbean side, which had not seen much permanent settlement from the major indigenous populations, who tended to live in the highlands where the climate was more attractive. Thus an argument can be made that in these areas the expansion of banana cultivation did not displace other cultivators; however this conclusion would be less valid for several islands in the Caribbean.

Recent years have seen an expansion of non-traditional agricultural exports from Central America, especially vegetables. Honduras has achieved limited advances in this regard. The processing of manufactured products for re-export, along the lines of the Mexican *maquila* program is a growing activity in the country, and at the end of century the level of FDI/GDP has been slowly rising.

Jamaica

This island in the Caribbean provides a useful counterpoint to the other cases in this chapter, particularly because it was one of the few colonies in the hemisphere during the twentieth century, and its institutions reflect the British legacy.

The century began with the old source of wealth, sugar, in general decay. Its "plantocracy" was reluctant to invest in new processing technology, and was suffering competition from the often subsidized exports of European beet sugar producers. At the same time, the exportation of bananas was beginning using ex-sugar plantations as well as other land in the hands of small farmers. A series of disturbances in 1938 highlighted the seriousness of the issue, but the outbreak of World War II postponed any resolution. Industrialization programs have often been debated for the island, as it has long suffered from overpopulation. Nobel prize winning economist W. Arthur Lewis, who was born and raised in the Caribbean, is generally associated with the position that such industrialization would have to rely on FDI rather than tariff protected factories.

In the early 1950s there was a dramatic change in the productive structure of the economy, caused by massive investments by foreign mining companies producing bauxite/aluminum. As this is a very capital intensive activity, the employment problem persisted. The achievement of independence in 1962 did not change this situation, and Michael Manley was elected in 1972 on a program strongly critical of foreign investment and *laissez faire* capitalism. A declining economy led in 1980 to the election of his political opposite, Edward Seaga, who was not any more successful. As the century ends the country's major earners of foreign exchange are mining and tourism, with export processing activities growing, although confronting competition from Mexico and Central America. The outlook for FDI oriented towards the local market is minimal, due to the small size of the market and the country's lack of protectionism.

At the beginning of the century the ratio FDI/GDP was about 25 per cent in Jamaica as shown in Table 6.18, which is a relatively modest level for a third world area. Investors from Britain showed little interest in the island, with most funds coming from the United States and Canada. Although the availability of estimated stocks of foreign investment is weakest for Jamaica at mid-century, the indications are that this had not risen since the beginning of the Depression, which is not surprising given the problems in the North American economies, the labor unrest of the late 1930s, and the availability of alternative investment locations elsewhere. What is certainly verifiable is the large increase in investment after 1950, involving bauxite mining, by Canadian and US firms (Girvan 1971). The FDI/GDP ratio has since fallen, although at the end of the century it remains higher than in most of the rest of the Third World. There have been several periods of balance of payments crises, and problems of the high debt burden have been difficult to resolve in a country with a relatively well-informed electorate.

British direct investors never showed much interest in the island during the colonial period. In terms of our investment categories, the old sugar plantations should probably be classified as settler run, rather than FDI or Free Standing Companies. It is of interest to note that the Sugar Planters' Association estimated the value of their plantations in 1895 as £1.2 million, which would have been larger than its stock of FDI, and more than 10 per cent of the island's income at the time.[16] Although the US companies exporting bananas and other fruits developed an important

Table 6.18 Jamaica: relative size of inward foreign investment stocks, twentieth century

	1913	1929	1967	1970	1980	1990	1995
FI/capita	31	27		181	124	131	116
FDI/capita	13	14	77	91	62	39	46
FI/GDP	59	57		147	123	148	149
FDI/GDP	25	29	67	74	61	44	59
FI/trade	256	224		454	282	392	245
FDI/trade	109	112	230	229	141	117	105

Sources: Population: 1913–1929, author's extrapolation of census data in Mitchell (1993); 1967–1995, the *International Financial Statistics Yearbooks*. Foreign Investment (the sum of loans and direct investment): 1913 Debt and FDI from Halsey (1918); 1929 debt from *Statistical Abstract for the British Empire* (1929: Table 15), FDI as the sum of amounts from US, in Dickens (1931: 18), from Canada, in Armstrong and Nelles (1988: 252), and an allocation to the UK raising its 1913 level proportionate to the increase in debt; 1967 FDI from OECD (1972); 1971 FDI from OECD (1973); 1980–1995, calculated by adding on the increased stock of FDI for the period from 1970, from *World Investment Report* 1997; 1970–1995, loans from *World Debt Tables*. GDP: 1910 and 1930, Eisner (1960); 1967 from *International Financial Statistics Yearbook*; 1970–95, *World Debt Tables*. Trade (average of exports and imports): 1913–1980, Mitchell (1993); 1990–1995, *International Financial Statistics Yearbook*, 1998.

Notes
The national income estimate for 1930 in Eisner (1960) is essentially identical with the earlier estimate of Deane (1948).

presence on the island, this was predominantly as shippers, and not producers, so that little FDI should be identified with agricultural production. The sporadic efforts at private development of railroads had generally failed, leading to the sector being absorbed by the government. Currently, the bauxite mines are foreign controlled. Of more interest is the tourism industry. Jefferson (1972: 178) estimated that about half of the capital in hotels was foreign owned. The activities in the export processing zones are predominantly foreign owned, with Jamaican firms providing one fourth of total employment (Willmore 1994: 96).

Mexico

Most of the dramatic events that could possibly happen to a country in terms of foreign direct investment occurred in or to Mexico: foreign ownership of an extensive railroad network, a popular uprising that took back land from foreigners, invasion by foreign armed forces to protect their nationals' interests, the nationalization of the foreign-owned petroleum industry, a subsequent reversal of anti-foreign ideology, adoption of labor-intensive foreign-owned industries for export processing, and expansion of outward direct investment in sectors where the local entrepreneurs are world competitors. Such a rich mixture of experiences has led to frequent re-evaluations of the role of foreign investment in the country's history. In particular, the anti-foreign aspect of the 1910 Revolution has tended to get exaggerated with the frequent re-telling of the story, slighting the influence of domestic issues, both economic and political. Nevertheless, a nationalistic position always seemed an easy posture for a politician to take, so that as late as 1973 the foreign investment law was re-written, mandating majority national ownership of firms, when actual domestic practice had clearly abandoned that policy. Within two decades the country had officially abandoned that nationalistic image, by joining the GATT and signing a free trade agreement with Canada and the United States, providing assurances to foreign investors.

Mexico possessed one of the most extensive railway systems in the Third World in 1910, by which time the government of President Díaz had already begun to purchase it from the foreign companies. It is one of the ironies of the country's history that, while the Revolution was being waged during the second decade of the century, petroleum companies were expanding their activities and aggregate level of FDI was in fact increasing. These two companies (one from Britain, one from the United States), were nationalized in 1938, at the end of a long confrontation that many argue could have been resolved amicably but for the miscalculation on the part of the companies' executives of both Mexican resolve and of the supportive stance of the American government. Mexico's relations with the United Kingdom and the United States remained strained after that nationalization and the eventual agreement to pay an indemnity that was judged too small by the investors. Moreover, the experience of Pemex, the governmental entity which took over the petroleum operations, was closely evaluated by friend and foe alike, to see if a third world country's parastatal could thrive in that technologically competitive sector. As things turned out, Pemex did better than most had thought it would, although the country became a net importer of crude oil for a time during the 1970s, before finding new oilfields off the Caribbean coast later in that decade. Accompanying the country's recent moves away from state dominance of productive activities and greater acceptance of free trade and investment, has been a reduced role for Pemex.

While Mexico's nationalization of the foreign oil companies is one landmark in the history of its policy stance toward FDI, notable steps in the opposite direction included the mid-1960s decisions to allow tax-free foreign investment for in-bond manufacturing activities (called *maquila* or *maquiladora*) and to permit 100 per cent foreign-owned investment by major automotive firms. As part of its import substitution program, Mexico had encouraged joint-ownership type investment by the major automobile and trucking firms, but this had ended up stagnating at a level of minimal assembly. Thus, the acceptance of the automobile companies represented another step in the growth of automobile production in Mexico, which had started from the expansion into production by importing firms, slowly increasing domestic content to the point where today, aided by NAFTA, cars produced in Mexico have a growing share of the North American market. This story is best told by Bennett and Sharpe (1985), who emphasize the evolution of the positions of both the Mexican state and the automobile companies; an example of what is referred to as obsolescing bargains. Such a characterization may well be equally valid for petroleum or mining companies, as well as other manufacturing and service activities. The signing of the NAFTA agreement has strengthened the shift in policy on the part of the Mexican authorities, toward greater acceptance of foreign investment, free trade, and privatization. As has happened in other countries of the region, the process of privatization has been accompanied by new forms of foreign involvement, and has occurred during periods when balance of payments crises have threatened the stability of the entire process.

The empirical profile of the century's FDI ratios for Mexico is displayed in Table 6.19. FDI/GDP reached its highest level before the Revolution, after which it continually declined until the 1970s. The recovery of FDI since then has been stronger than in many countries, in relative as well as absolute terms, although not reaching the high levels of the beginning of

Table 6.19 Mexico: relative size of inward foreign investment stocks, twentieth century

	1900	1910	1929	1938	1950	1970	1980	1990	1995
FI/capita	54	88	65	22	12	28	58	75	117
FDI/capita	46	76	42	13	6	8	10	21	34
Non-RR FDI/capita	21	46	26						
FI/GDP	119	126	108	51	23	25	26	48	98
FDI/GDP	101	108	69	30	12	7	4	14	28
Non-RR FDI/GDP	46	67	52						
FI/trade	1,083	1,339	583	573	198	436	165	194	238
FDI/trade	918	1163	373	340	103	127	27	55	68
Non-RR FDI/trade	421	710	230						

Sources: Population: 1900–1990, *Statistical Abstract of Latin America*, Volume 28; 1995, from the *World Development Report*, 1997. GDP: 1900–1970, Cárdenas (1987: 190–1); 1980–1995, *World Debt Tables*. Foreign investment is the sum of Government Debt and Foreign Direct Investment. Government Debt: 1900 and 1911, Turlington (1930: 229, 246); 1929, UN-ECLA (1965: 27); 1938, data from Lewis (1948); 1950, UN-ECLA (1965: 203); 1970–1995, the *World Debt Tables*. Foreign Direct Investment: 1900 and 1911, D'Olwer (1965); 1929, summing totals for the UK and the US from UN-ECLA (1965: 9, 32); 1938–1950, United Nations (1955: 111) reporting data from the Banco de México; 1971, UNCTC (1983); 1980–1995, *World Investment Report*. Non-Railroad Direct investment: 1900–1911 D'Olwer (1965); 1929, Lewis (1938) and Rippy (1959); 1938 United Nations (1955: 111). Trade (the average of exports and imports): 1900, US Bureau of Statistics (1909); 1913, Lamartine Yates (1959); 1929–1970, *Statistical Abstract of Latin America* (1980: Table 2731); 1980–1995, *World Debt Tables*.

Notes
The estimates from the source countries coincide well with those used here from Mexican sources, for 1900, 1911, 1929 and 1950. The discrepancy of the order of three for 1938 presumably results from different treatment of the railroads, mines, and petroleum. The Banco de México's 1938 data is interpreted here as indicating that there was no foreign investment in railroads.

the century.[17] Railroads were clearly an important sector for foreign investment in those early years, with the companies establishing links between their lines in Mexico and in the United States. Moreover, non-railroad FDI appears to have been relatively high in Mexico, as well. The strength of the petroleum investments during the second decade of the century kept the ratio of non-railroad FDI to GDP from falling as rapidly as in most of the rest of the hemisphere. It is the case that the precise timing of the subsequent reduction in FDI cannot be determined easily, due to the contested legal status of the events involving railroad, petroleum, and agricultural enterprises.

Some rough estimates of total capital and its sectoral distribution are presented in Table 6.20. Government and dwellings composed 40 per cent of the total in 1950, according to work done in collaboration with the ECLA teams, and indications from the work of Hofman (1992 and 2000) are that the share of residences has since increased. At the start of the century, railroads comprised a significant share of non-residential, non-government assets, as occurred in other countries as well. Manufacturing industry grew slowly to comprise about 10 per cent of total capital in

Table 6.20 Mexico: reproducible wealth, total and sectoral distribution, 1910–1970

	1910	1930	1940	1950	1960	1970
Total (billion current pesos)	6.7	8	12	91	408	678
Distribution (%)						
Agriculture		15	14	13	7	12
Mines	5	2	5	1	1	1
Petroleum	2	2	2	3	4	4
Industry	2	9	8	9	20	10
Railroads	24	19	14	7	6	4
Non-RR Services	13	13	17	21	17	12
Government		11	10	13	19	
Dwellings				31		
Land/Reproducible Wealth (%)		30	24	23	16	13

Sources: Author's calculations, based on UN-ECLA (1957b) for 1950, and sources for other years as discussed in Twomey (1993: 84) – including D'Olwer (1965), Alanís Patiño (1943), Lamartine Yates (1978), Banco de México (1969 and 1978), and several sector-specific official censuses. GDP from Cárdenas (1987: 190) and *International Financial Statistics Yearbook*, 1998.

Notes
The item reproducible wealth incorporates fixed public and private sector capital (including residential housing), inventories, and farm implements, but not durable consumer goods, nor land. Blank spaces indicate that no estimate had been found in the sources consulted. For the estimation of total non-financial wealth, these items had to be approximated, for which purpose the ratios for nearby years, and those for 1950, were utilized. Thus, the only year for which all the basic data had been published was 1950. The value of land is taken from several agrarian censuses, as reported in Alanís Patiño (1943), and Lamartine Yates (1978: 856). Hofman (1992) does not present sectorally disaggregated estimates of the composition of gross capital stock, but he does calculate that the ratio of dwellings in total gross capital in Mexico has risen from 33 per cent in 1950 to 50 per cent in 1989 (op. cit., 384).

1970.[18] The Table probably understates the values of capital in mining and petroleum for the early years; this is the message when those data are compared to the FDI data, even if allowance is made for the latter's inclusion of outlays for exploration. For the period after 1980, any major changes in the sectoral disaggregation of capital would arise from further decline in agriculture, and expansion of the central government (as opposed to state owned enterprises). As data on these are lacking, the Table stops in 1970.

The sectoral estimates of capital stock can be combined with FDI data to generate sectoral and nation-wide estimates of foreign ownership of capital; these are presented in Table 6.21. The overall trend parallels that of our indicator FDI/GDP in Table 6.19, with foreign ownership declining rather steadily from 40 per cent in 1910 to about 5 per cent during 1960–1970. The initial figure would be rather less than 30 per cent if land is included along with reproducible capital in the denominator. This would be a plausible adjustment, as foreign companies must purchase land as well as buildings and machinery. However, there are other, rather more basic problems with the data whose existence discourages further elaborations, particularly the mismatch between the value of FDI and that

Table 6.21 Mexico: foreign ownership of domestic capital, by sectors, 1910–1970 (percentages)

	1910	1930	1940	1950	1960	1970(a)	1970(b)
Total	42	33	21	5	3	5	13
Agriculture	7		1	$<\frac{1}{2}$	$<\frac{1}{2}$	$<\frac{1}{2}$	$<\frac{1}{2}$
Mines	261	466	92	76	43	32	5
Petroleum	110	617	2	4	2	2	3
Industry	118	20	19	15	9	39	28
Construction				6	3	2	1
Railroads	78	51	0				
Utilities	106		80	35	1	$<\frac{1}{2}$	1
Commerce	22		8	10	9	18	7

Sources: Author's calculations, based on FDI and capital stock data from the sources for Tables 6.19 and 6.20. The last column is from Sepúlveda and Chumacero (1973), and reports percentage of sales due to foreign firms.

Note
Blank spaces indicate data are not available. If FDI and K are measured consistently, then the ratio of FDI/K cannot be greater than 100; cases where it is reflect either or both an underestimation of the capital stock, or an overestimation of FDI. Correction for either error lowers the estimated ratio of the country's total FDI/K. The data reported here for total FDI/K 1910 and 1930 split the differences for mining and petroleum sectors for those two years; the original data yielded estimates of 47 and 44, respectively. If the denominator were tangible capital (capital plus land), then for 1930 and 1940, the values of FDI/K would be 26 and 17, after which the differences with those given in the table are insignificant. Alanís Patiño (1943: 101, 104) provided estimates of foreign ownership at the turn of the century and the mid-1930s, of 20 per cent and 42 per cent, respectively, using a measure of wealth which included financial instruments. Letcher (1912) reproduced Seamon's 1911 estimate of Mexican wealth, which placed foreign holdings at half of the total, but it is clear that capital in certain sectors without much foreign participation were undervalued.

of capital in the two major foreign dominated extractive activities, petroleum and mining. Finally, it should be noted that even in the case of
industry, neither the data in Table 6.21, nor the more extensive review
(Twomey 1993: Table 5.5c) of data from censuses and other informed estimates, indicates a clear trend in foreign ownership of Mexican manufacturing during the twentieth century, with plausible estimates of that
variable at around 20–30 per cent between 1960 and 1985.

Peru

The legacy from the nineteenth century in Peru included an important
network of railways leading to mineral deposits high in the Andes, and
recollections of opulence during the years of easy exports of guano, and –
further back – of grandeur during the colonial era. The first quarter of
the twentieth century was dominated by a modernizing dictator named
Augusto Leguía, and witnessed strong export-led growth, behind a diversi-
fied set of agricultural products (sugar, cotton and rubber), minerals, and
petroleum. The cultivation of cotton has always been locally controlled,
while petroleum production was – until the military coup of 1968 – predominantly in the hands of foreigners. Sugar and mining represent situations where both local and international control have been important,
whose evolution responded to a mix of factors analysed most perceptively
in Thorp and Bertram (1978). The last quarter of the twentieth century
has seen a succession of civilian governments struggle to remedy the
negative legacies of the military regime, which had unsuccessfully confronted Peru's fundamental problem of the geographical and cultural separation of its inhabitants.

The available data suggest that the relative size of foreign direct investment declined continually during the twentieth century, with the trend
recovering upwards only around 1990 – see Table 6.22.[19] The initially high
levels of FDI relative to GDP or trade are mainly a reflection of the high
cost of the railroads and an agreement for paying off the country's
defaulted debt by an early version of a debt-equity swap, but foreign investment in mining had also expanded vigorously before World War I. The
long decline of FDI relative to GDP or trade was somewhat unexpected,
and presumably more detailed data would show a brief reversal during the
1950s, when some expensive mining projects came on line. Such is the
message of the calculations presented by FitzGerald (1979), repeated in
Table 6.23, in which the foreign share of output doubles between 1950
and 1968.[20] FitzGerald's data are also of interest in terms of the economy-
wide impact of the military government's nationalization policies, which
cut the foreigners' share back to where it had previously been; from
22 per cent to 11 per cent of total output. A more detailed analysis of the
Peruvian case would indicate how the military's reforms were gradually
but painfully eroded over time, ricocheting between more extreme

Table 6.22 Peru: relative size of inward foreign investment stocks, twentieth century

	1900	1913	1929	1938	1950	1970	1980	1990	1995
FI/capita	44	40	31	24	12	20	49	53	69
FDI/capita	44	36	21	16	8	9	4	3	11
Non-RR FDI/capita	13	15	13	8					
FI/GDP	168	119	64	46	22	22	52	67	62
FDI/GDP	168	110	44	30	14	10	5	4	10
Non-RR FDI/GDP	50	45	27	16					
FI/trade	800	591	202	423	171	191	208	417	358
FDI/trade	798	543	139	274	112	88	18	25	55
Non-RR FDI/trade	238	221	86	144					

Sources: Population: 1900–1990, *Statistical Abstract of Latin America*, Volume 28; 1995, from the *World Development Report*, 1997. GDP: 1900–1950, Maddison (1995); 1950–1970, UN-ECLA (1978); 1980–1995, *World Debt Tables*. Foreign investment is the sum of Government Debt and Foreign Direct Investment. Government Debt: 1900, estimated as the sum of that from France, in Rippy (1948) and from the UK from Stone (1987), averaging the data for 1895 and 1905, and following Lewis (1938) in attributing no portfolio investment for the US for 1897; 1913, UN-ECLA (1965: 16); 1938, from Lewis (1948); 1950 from UN-ECLA (1965: 203); 1970–1995, the *World Debt Tables*. Foreign Direct Investment: 1900–1950, calculated as the sum of FDI stocks from the UK, the US, and France (1900–1913 only). From the UK: up through 1928, from UN-ECLA (1965: 9); 1938, data from Lewis (1948); 1950 Bank of England (1950) and Mikesell (1955: 10) – the former referring to 1948, and the latter to 1951. From the US: 1897 through 1929, from Lewis (1938) supplemented by UN-ECLA (1965: 32) and US Department of Commerce (1960); 1938, Lewis (1948); 1950, US Department of Commerce (1960); 1902 and 1913 business and railroad investments from France were taken from Rippy (1948). 1971, from UNCTC (1983); 1980–1995, the *World Investment Report*. Non-Railroad Direct investment 1900–1938: for the US, Lewis (1938 and 1948); for the UK, Rippy (1959), Bank of England (1950), and various issues of the *South American Journal* for 1928 and 1938; for 1938, UK holdings in railroads were extrapolated from the values for 1929 and 1950. The breakdown of Peruvian investments into railroads and others follows Rippy (1959: 69) in assigning most of the Peruvian Corporation's investment into the railroad sector. Trade (the average of exports and imports): 1900, US Bureau of Statistics (1909); 1913, Lamartine Yates (1959); 1929–1970, *Statistical Abstract of Latin America* (1980: Table 2731); 1980–1995, *World Debt Tables*.

models of free markets and heterodox stabilization, while internal security deteriorated due to the actions of terrorists.

Returning to the issue of the determinants of the long-term decline of FDI, the fundamental structural problem, emphasized by Thorp and Bertram (1978: Chapter 14), was the exhaustion of export-led growth by the late 1960s. Those authors analysed the physical and economic limitations of expanding not only mining, but also petroleum and irrigated agriculture. Without denying an important counter-example in the case of fishmeal, they are generally critical of the weak response of both domestic entrepreneurs and the state, in creating growth opportunities in non-export sectors, thereby contributing to the overall stagnation of the economy. Implicit in that analysis is the lack of attractions for new FDI into Peru during the period. Moreover, their analysis might be rephrased for our purposes as stating that had the domestic entrepreneurs been

Table 6.23 Peru: foreign ownership of domestic production and employment, 1950–1975 (per cent)

	1950	1968	1975
Share of Domestic Output, Total:	10	22	11
by sector:			
Primary		31	10
Secondary		35	24
Tertiary		9	2
Share of Employment, Total:	4	10	3

Source: Author's calculations, based on FitzGerald (1979: 122, 314).

Note
The estimates for 1950 are stated to be "more tentative" and to be a "rough estimate" Fitz-Gerald (1979: 120, 313). The pre-reform share of foreign firms in manufacturing assets is reported to have been 46 per cent (p. 274), of mining sales at 72 per cent (p. 113, referring to the three major firms), of fishing (corporate sector) and utilities to have been one third (p. 313). The share of FDI in agriculture – as distinct from the share of foreigners who are long-term residents) was small, no more than 2 per cent of 1968 GDP. The foreign share of construction, commerce, and services are described as conservative estimates by FitzGerald (ibid).

more successful, the decline in FDI would have occurred earlier and been more rapid.

Sectorally disaggregated data on the capital stock in Peru are scarce. The UN-ECLA team did generate one estimate of it, which is combined in Table 6.24 with the appropriate FDI data to provide indicators of ownership by sectors in the early 1950s. The low level of foreign investment in

Table 6.24 Peru: foreign ownership of domestic capital, by sectors, 1955 (data in million US dollars, and percentages)

	FDI	Capital	Ratio
Agriculture	15	884	2
Mining	149	439	34
Petroleum	103	388	27
Manufacturing	17	681	2
Transport & Utilities	77	381	20
Commerce	28	} 1,475	2
Other	7		
Total	396	4,249	9

Sources: FDI from United Nations (1955: 134); capital stock from UN-ECLA (1959: 12).

Notes
The FDI data relates to 1953, and the capital stock relates to 1955. Capital stock converted to dollars at 19Sol/$. The US Department of Commerce reported total FDI in Peru in 1950 at $145 million, and in 1957 at $383 million. The UN datum for US investment in 1953 was $295 million, which is consistent with the US source. The capital stock data are: "... very rough estimates, prepared on the basis of indirect criteria and partial statistics". (UN-ECLA 1959: 12.) One presumes that the authors relied less on censuses or official surveys, and more on capital output ratios from other countries. It is unclear if government activities were included in "other sectors".

manufacturing is an indirect result of free trade policies which allowed consumer goods to be imported. The share of FDI in mining capital, 34 per cent, is lower than the corresponding data of 56 per cent of output in Thorp and Bertram (1978: 212), reflecting both the weaker data available to the ECLA team and differences in coverage.

Venezuela

Before petroleum production in Venezuela took off during the second decade of the twentieth century, the country's low population and meager income levels had not attracted much foreign investment. In contrast to Mexico, where so-called independents began the oil industry, the successful development of production in Venezuela waited for the majors – Standard Oil and Royal Dutch/Shell. Petroleum was, and remains, the country's dominant export product, and a key source of government revenue. For several decades, the government made half-hearted attempts to impose controls on the petroleum sector, limiting itself to skirmishes on issues of pricing and taxes during the period from the 1930s through the 1950s (Edwards 1971). A fundamental change in the political system in 1958, set in an evolving international context, eventually led to the purchase of the companies on the last day of 1975. The economic nationalism that is implied by that action has since subsided, and current policy welcomes foreign participation in the sector, albeit in a secondary role. Moreover, government policy encourages foreign investment in other sectors of the economy.

The variable FDI/GDP reached its peak in 1929, according to our calculations in Table 6.25. From that year, the indicator gradually declined, before experiencing a larger drop at the time of nationalization. This indicator has recovered only slightly after 1990. By the time of the nationalization of the foreign oil companies, the value of those firms, compared to the national product – and by implication to the national stock of capital – was not particularly high. Moreover, Venezuela is a good example of a country for which the concept of FDI is rather out of date; no FDI is registered in petroleum, although there continues to be important foreign participation, via modes which are called joint ventures, licensing, and so on. Moreover, balance of payments problems in the 1990s caused by bank mismanagement led to either their outright sale or to the transference of control of important financial areas to foreign interests. These types of involvement fit awkwardly into the FDI category. It should also be mentioned that FDI in manufacturing has grown steadily, if unspectacularly, since mid-century. Finally, we could note that Table 6.25 indicates a rather high level of FDI/GDP in 1900. Basically, this responds to a low initial level of GDP; real GDP/capita tripled between 1913 and 1929, according to Maddison (1995).

The available estimates of the capital stock of Venezuela include two from the central bank – the first following closely the methodology of the

Table 6.25 Venezuela: relative size of inward foreign investment stocks, twentieth century

	1900	1913	1929	1938	1950	1970	1980	1990	1995
FI/capita	30	17	58	49	62	73	169	102	90
FDI/capita	20	10	58	49	62	61	9	11	15
Non-RR FDI/capita	11	4	55						
FI/GDP	126	49	59	49	50	37	44	79	59
FDI/GDP	83	29	58	49	50	31	2	8	10
Non-RR FDI/GDP	47	13	55						
FI/tade		248	181	216	115	196	158	216	201
FDI/trade		152	179	216	115	164	8	23	33
Non-RR FDI/trade		67	170						

Sources: Population: 1900–1990, *Statistical Abstract of Latin America*, Volume 28; 1995, from the *World Development Report*, 1997. GDP: 1900–1913, Baptista (1991: II-2); 1929–1970, Baptista (1991: II-7); 1980–1995, the *World Debt Tables*. Foreign investment is the sum of Government Debt and Foreign Direct Investment. Government Debt: for 1900, estimated as the sum of that from France, in Rippy (1948) and from the UK from Stone (1987), averaging the data for 1895 and 1905, and following Lewis (1938) in attributing no portfolio investment for the US for 1897; for 1913, UN-ECLA (1965: 16); 1938, Marichal (1989); 1950, UN-ECLA (1965: 203); 1970–1995, *World Debt Tables*. Foreign Direct Investment: 1900–1929, calculated as the sum of FDI stocks from the UK, the US, and France (1900–1913 only); from the UK: up through 1928, data from Rippy (1959), and UN-ECLA (1965: 9); from the US: 1897 through 1929, from Lewis (1938); 1938, using the datum for (net) petroleum investment in Rangel (1970: 187), and adjusting for non-petroleum sectors; 1950, the data from the *Memoria* of the Banco Central de Venezuela reported in United Nations (1955: 144), adjusting for depreciated assets as per Table 6.29. 1902 and 1913 business and railroad investments from France were taken from Rippy (1948). 1971, from OECD (1973); 1980–1995, the *World Investment Report*. Non-Railroad Direct investment 1900–1938: for the US Lewis (1938 and 1948); for the UK, Rippy (1959), Bank of England (1950), and various issues of the *South American Journal* for 1928 and 1938. Trade (the average of exports and imports): 1913, Lamartine Yates (1959); 1929–1970, *Statistical Abstract of Latin America* (1980: Table 2731); 1980–1995, *World Debt Tables*.

Notes
The nominal dollar value of GDP, as reported in the *World Debt Tables*, declined between 1970 and 1980, even though the real value of GDP rose. Recalculation of FDI/GDP using the real GDP data reflated by US prices does not change the message that the variable FDI/GDP reached its low point in 1980. Lewis (1948: 333) notes that her data on 1938 United Kingdom investments into Venezuela were "probably greatly understated".

contemporaneous efforts by the ECLA investigators – one by an academic, Asdrubal Baptista, and the recent work of Hofman (2000). Although as Hofman indicates, the central bank study and Baptista have parallel totals for the domestic capital stock in 1950, those two sources differ widely on the importance of petroleum in the total, as indicated in Table 6.26. Government and housing together accounted for about 40 per cent of total capital. These data indicate that while manufacturing did indeed grow relative to the rest of the economy, from 6–9 per cent over 1950 to 1969, the major sectoral growth over that period was in services, from 27–40 per cent.

Because petroleum investment surged during the 1920s (Brown 1985), we are not surprised that the peak level of FDI/K would be reached during this period, even though the ratio of 45 per cent in Table 6.27 is

Table 6.26 Venezuela: sectoral distribution of the domestic capital stock, 1929–1969 (percentages)

	Baptista			Banco Central		
	1929	*1938*	*1950*	*1950*	*1960*	*1969*
Agriculture				12	12	15
Petroleum	35	37	40	11	14	8
Mining				$<\frac{1}{2}$	3	1
Manufacturing				6	7	9
Services				27	29	40
Housing	25	24	18	15	17	21
Government	14	16	21	28	18	7

Sources: Author's calculations based on Baptista (1991) and various issues of Banco Central de Venezuela, *Memoria* and *Informe Económico.*

Notes
The series for petroleum in Baptista may include related activities in other sectors, such as manufacturing.

Table 6.27 Venezuela: foreign ownership of the domestic capital stock, 1929–1969 (percentages)

	Author's FDI			BCV(a)			BCV(b)	
	1929	*1938*	*1950*	*1950*	*1960*	*1967*	*1967*	*1969*
Total	45	33	28	40	40	36	16	17
Agriculture							$<\frac{1}{2}$	$<\frac{1}{2}$
Petroleum				337	254	337	120	125
Mining				280	67	123	63	81
Industry				13	12	43	31	37
All Services				4	5	6	6	6

Sources: Author's calculations based on Baptista (1991) and various issues of Banco Central de Venezuela, *Memoria* and *Informe Económico.*

Notes
The estimates for 1929–1950 use the FDI estimates from Table 6.25, and the capital stock estimates of Baptista. The estimates for 1950–1967 use the earlier BCV series which did not discount for depreciation (a term that in this context may include exploration expenditures), which is expected to be high in petroleum and mining. Foreign investment in banks and insurance companies was not included. If correctly measured, the ownership ratio cannot be greater than 100, and for the BCV(a) series, the problem could well be the lack of depreciation. That the ratio of FDI/K remained greater than 100 for the subsequent BCV series indicates further problems of comparability. To the extent that the problem lies in overestimation of sectoral investment, then adjustment for it would also decrease the overall estimate of FDI/K. For purposes of comparison, the following are the value of FDI for 1967, in million US$, according to the two methodologies of the central bank (BCV), e.g. *Informe Económico* 1969 and 1971, and from the host countries in OECD (1972).

	BCV(a)	BCV(b)	OECD
Total	$5,488	$2,350	$3,495
Petroleum	$4,337	$1,550	$2,548
Non-Petroleum	$1,150	$ 980	$ 947

unusually high, probably upwardly biased due to the inclusion of exploration costs in the numerator but not in the denominator. The relatively rapid decline of that indicator suggests a spreading of the growth impetus to other sectors of the economy, only some of which would have been directly dependent on petroleum. Finally, the Table shows how foreign domination was rather narrowly confined to petroleum and mining.

As described by Sigmund (1980: 243), the compensation to the companies for the 1975 nationalization was based on their own calculations of their own book values, but amounted to only 10 per cent of the replacement value of their assets. The firms were unhappy with this outcome, but were aware that domestic politics in Venezuela was against them, while there would continue to be profitable opportunities for them in the country. The history of Venezuelan oil policy graphically illustrates once again the importance of viewing the links between the firms and the host countries not as one of a fixed contractual relationship, but as one of continuing negotiations leading both sides to hedge their bets – the "obsolescing bargain".

Notes

1 Carlos Díaz Alejandro's classic 1970 book on Argentine economic history has an excellent coverage of immigration issues, along with many other themes. In 1914, one third of the country's population was foreign born, whereas in the United States, the highest ratio ever was 14.4 per cent (p. 25).
2 Although we are most fortunate that the investigators at ECLA provided detailed appendices which appear to be internally consistent, these data are not perfect for our needs. A more important example is the fact that foreign investment in banking, real estate and holding companies is spread throughout the economy, thus exaggerating the impression of FDI in the financial sector.
3 In contrast, Hofman (1992) finds residential capital to have been one half of total fixed capital in 1950. The difference cannot be attributed solely to ECLA's inclusion of livestock and inventories, and it is robust to changes in measurement (national or "international" prices) or definition (gross or net).
4 Their methodology for calculating capital stocks – the perpetual inventory method – was apparently quite representative of the best methodology in the 1950s, but today would be judged rather dated. For a useful overview of the early UN-ECLA work on the quantification of capital stocks (and GDP and other macroeconomic variables) see Hofman (1999).
5 Duncan (1932: 87) estimated that government ownership of railroads was 34 per cent in 1889, 61 per cent in 1914, and 68 per cent in 1930. Data on the nominal value of railroads are available for the pre-World War I period, in Halsey (1916: 79), and for 1929 in official statistics reported by Topik (1987: 122). In both years, railroads accounted for 6 per cent of Goldsmith's estimated total of structures and equipment.
6 The book by Evans (1979) is particularly worth highlighting for the influence of its argument that FDI can result in development, without eliminating dependency.
7 Construction on the first transcontinental railroad in Canada began shortly after Confederation. A second line was built a generation later, some parts of

which were redundant. During the early 1920s the Government engaged in major consolidation of these systems, after which there was virtually no FDI in this sector.

8 In point of fact, the Canadian source (*Canada's International Investment Position – CIIP*) distinguishes between ownership and control; non-controlling equity purchases are included only under ownership. The first year covered by *CIIP*, 1926, was after the reorganization of the railroads.

9 Two important details of this comparison should also be noted. The ratio of FDI/K in Table 6.7 is much lower than those of foreign control or ownership in Table 6.8. The explanation is that the source for the latter, *Canada's International Investment Position*, excludes services, such as the government, education, community buildings, and residences, all of which have negligible foreign investment. These sectors accounted for a growing share of the fixed capital in Canada, representing half of the country's total in 1980, according to the *Fixed Capital Flows and Stocks*.

10 Obviously this is an incendiary issue. Under Allende's predecessor, Eduardo Frei, the Chilean government had begun purchasing ("nationalizing") the *gran minería*. The rationale given for the actions taken by Allende's government was excessive profits during the previous 15 years.

11 Note that the ratio with respect to trade is not as high, relatively, as the ratio with respect to income, and furthermore, that the trade data for 1938 appear to be out of line with the other data in the table. The first official estimate of GNP referred to the year 1940; for most of the middle years of the twentieth century Chile had multiple exchange rates, making any estimate in dollar terms particularly problematical.

12 Independently of one's view of the policies which are associated with Raúl Prebisch and ECLA, one must admire the creativity and energy of these investigators in collecting data and generating analyses and policy proposals specifically focusing on contexts different from those of Europe and North America. An overview and further comments on the early estimates of capital stock in several countries are presented by Hofman (2000).

13 Incidentally, the UN-ECLA study reinforces the message communicated by the less reliable data for several other country studies, that the sectors of the economy in which we would expect to find little FDI – government, housing, and the service sector – account for slightly less than half of the total capital stock.

14 The amount invested from France in "canals and navigation companies" was FF200 million, out of a total from that country of FF246 million, when the total foreign investment into Colombia was about FF400 million. For comparison, McCullough (1977: 235) states that the total expenditure on the construction of the trans-isthmanian canal by de Lesseps's company had been of the order of FF1,435 million.

15 The 1913 estimate of FDI cited in Jenks (1928) is comparable to others from what are today the standard sources. Note that Jenks (1928: 300) asserts that over half of the United States capital in Cuban sugar properties had been generated from retained profits. Thus the estimated US investment in agriculture, from the source for US FDI in Table 6.15, is lower by US$180 million than that of the *Cuban Sugar Year Book*; raising the total estimate of FDI by this amount would not invalidate the text's conclusion that foreign ownership of domestic capital had fallen.

16 Sugar plantations from Royal West India Commission, Appendix A, p. 187, as reproduced in British Parliament *Command Paper* (8655, 50 Appendix A: 137). Income from Eisner (1960). The turn of the century evolution of FDI from the United States and Canada appears in Halsey (1918), who attributes very little to England.

17 Recent Mexican data on FDI has been questioned. Twomey (1993: 52) presents data for the period since the 1970s indicating a widening difference in the official data from Mexico and the United States, with regard to US FDI stocks in Mexico. In Salomón (1998: 806) there is reference to a very recent change in methodology in the Mexican source. One of the problems arises from ignoring the potential difference between "approved" and "realized" investment. Also affecting these measures is the growth of non-controlling equity investment through so-called ADRs, and the difficulty of classifying funds in financial institutions. An argument in favor of the higher Mexican figures would be the fact that one third of US FDI is channeled through the tax havens of the Caribbean, presumably ending up in countries like Mexico.

18 The Table utilizes the Banco de México (1969) estimate for 1960, which is about three times as large as either the census figure, or that of Banco de México (1978). The presumption is that the cited datum on manufacturing capital is too large, so that the 1960 ratio of FDI/K in industry in Table 6.21 is too small.

19 The income data incorporated in Table 6.22 are particularly weak for the first quarter of the century, and it is fortunate that the trend in that Table of FDI/trade parallels that of FDI/GDP.

20 Are these two sets of data compatible? Perhaps not. An assumed spurt of foreign investment after 1950 would arguably have caused the capital output ratio to rise, which would have caused the opposite movement in the two indicators. However, sectoral shifts in production towards mining and industry, would help bridge the two results, as would consideration of the hypothesis that new foreign investment was more leveraged, in the sense of fewer dollars gaining more control.

7 General results

This chapter reviews and synthesizes the information from the previous chapters. We proceed from a summary of long-term trends of FDI/GDP and FDI/K, to several explanations of these patterns. The search for causes looks first at long-term cyclical models, and then investigates both economic and non-economic factors in the sending and receiving countries. The railroad sector receives special attention, and some econometric equations are estimated to answer the question of whether colonies received more investment than independent countries at the start of the century. One unexpected result from the case studies is the weak stimulus that privatization of state-owned companies appears to have given to inflows of FDI, and this also receives some brief comments. After a general summary, the chapter ends with a few speculative comments about future trends of FDI in the Third World.

Long-term trends

The dominant characteristic of the long-term trend of foreign investment into the Third World, both total and direct, was a slackening of the overall levels sometime around the middle of the twentieth century. The reader will recall that the data from the source countries in Chapter 3 on either total investment or FDI presented this pattern. As a complement to this, and based on the detailed information from the host countries, Table 7.1 presents calculations of average levels of investment for these countries over the twentieth century. These are rough measures, as they are unweighted averages, and the coverage is not entirely consistent. Nevertheless, we see that total foreign investment followed a markedly U-shaped pattern, with a low point apparently between 1950 and 1970. Direct foreign investment followed a similar path, although its decline is smaller than that of total investment, because of the greater variations in debt. For both types of investment, the depth of the mid-century decline, and the size of the recovery at the end of century, depend on the choice of denominators – population or GDP. A general increase in per capita income after about 1960 makes the paths resulting from these two

Table 7.1 Twentieth century trends in foreign investment ratios and their dispersion, third world countries

	Year	FI/cap	FDI/cap	FI/GDP	FDI/GDP
Average					
	1914	63	23	94	40
	1930s	49	22	96	51
	1950s	53	22	53	30
	1970	34	18	32	13
	1995	115	29	86	18
Dispersion					
	1914	1.5	1.4	0.7	0.9
	1930s	1.5	1.2	0.8	0.9
	1950s	1.2	1.1	1.0	1.0
	1970	2.3	2.3	0.8	1.1
	1995	2.4	2.3	0.5	0.9

Source: Estimates in the previous chapters.

Note
The measure of dispersion is the ratio of the standard deviation to the mean. The FDI in 1914 is non-railroad FDI. The number of countries varies by year; there are fewest observations for 1950, and there were several cases for the late 1930s when different sources provided dramatically different results. Table 3.5 cites data from the 1997 *World Investment Report*, reporting ratios of FDI/GDP for the entire Third World, rising from 4.3 per cent in 1980 to 15.4 per cent in 1995.

indicators diverge, so that the fall is larger, and the recovery more modest, when deflating by GDP. Because our ultimate goal is to approximate foreign ownership of the total stock of domestic capital, the logic expounded in Chapter 2 indicates that the finding on FDI/GDP is more relevant.

One item of special interest is the potential differences in FDI trends over the century, separating entities according to their political status in 1914 – independent nations or colonies. Latin America accounts for most of the independent third world countries which we have been able to include. Table 7.2 presents these series, using the same data as above, and for simplicity limited to FDI/GDP. The noteworthy result is the divergence in trends between 1914 and the early 1950s. FDI into colonies increased considerably between 1914 and the 1930s, and subsequently fell more dramatically into the 1950s through to 1970, after which the two series are rather similar. Our explanation of this finding centers on behavior in the source countries. As we saw in Chapter 3, the metropolitan countries turned their interests towards their colonies after the Great War, and especially as the prospects for another conflagration became clearer in the 1930s. As the European countries invested more in their own colonies, their attention toward Latin America waned.[1] Moreover, their competitive position in Latin America also declined, due to developments in the domestic economies of that region, and to FDI from the United States.

Table 7.2 Twentieth century trends in FDI/GDP: averages for colonies and independent countries (per cent)

	Total	Colonies	Independent countries
1914	40	42	36
1930s	51	61	37
1950s	30	35	17
1970	13	14	9
1995	18	19	14

Sources: Case studies in Chapters 4 through 6.

Notes
Political status as of 1914. Investment data excludes railroads. Independent countries include all of Latin America except Jamaica, as well as Egypt, Liberia, Turkey, China and Thailand. As noted in the previous Table, the number of cases varies by year, and in some cases rather arbitrary choices were made in choosing between sources, especially for colonies. Data are simple unweighted averages. GDP estimates were not available for several colonies. Approximating their GDP by multiplying the trade totals by an average ratio of GDP/trade increases the sample, and produces an average ratio of 51 for FDI/GDP in colonies in 1914.

Recall that although United States investment in Latin America did increase, the major growth areas during the 1920s for that country's foreign investors were in Canada and Europe. After the Second World War the possession of colonies became progressively untenable, and in most cases the political process leading to independence also resulted in a decline of FDI stocks. That cycle had worked itself out by about 1970. In a subsequent section of this chapter we explore more rigorously the issue of differences in terms of FDI intensity, between colonies and independent countries, for 1913/14. After the war the quality of the data deteriorates, rending less valuable regression estimates on this variable.

Another finding in Table 7.1 above was that deflating by GDP results in a lower dispersion than does deflating by population. The statistical results presented later in this chapter will explain this finding by demonstrating that foreign investment (total or direct) is positively correlated with per capita GDP. This raises the possibility that the ranking of countries by relative amounts of FI or FDI might depend on which deflator – population or GDP – is chosen. A set of rankings for the data on 1914 is shown in Table 7.3. Some countries remain near the bottom for all four indicators, such as China, India, and Korea, while South Africa, Chile, and Cuba are always near the top. But the rankings are sensitive to the indicator chosen. When moving from the rankings by FI to those by FDI, areas which had a low level of loans move up, such as Ghana, Indonesia, Philippines, and Taiwan, while those with high loans, such as Canada and Algeria, move down. When moving from a comparison where the denominator is population, to one where it is GDP (or its proxy, trade times an average ratio of GDP/trade), countries with a relatively high level of GDP

Table 7.3 Rank ordering of third world countries by foreign investment ratios, 1914

FI/cap		Non-RR FDI/cap		FI/GDP		Non-RR FDI/GDP	
Korea	2	FrW Africa	1	Korea	18	Korea	6
Nigeria	3	China	1	China	24	India	10
China	3	Korea	1	Colombia	25	Colombia	10
FrW Africa	4	Nigeria	2	Taiwan	28	Tunisia	11
BrE Africa	6	India	2	India	35	China	11
Thailand	6	Thailand	2	Thailand	40	Turkey	13
India	7	Morocco	4	Tunisia	43	Venezuela	13
BrW Africa	8	FrE Africa	4	Morocco	44	Thailand	15
Taiwan	8	Indo-China	4	Venezuela	49	Algeria	16
Indo-China	9	Colombia	4	Indonesia	51	Morocco	18
Philippines	10	Venezuela	4	Philippines	53	Australia	20
Colombia	10	Zaire	5	Jamaica	59	*FrW Africa*	22
Indonesia	12	Turkey	5	*FrW Africa*	65	Canada	23
Morocco	13	Tunisia	6	*Indo-China*	65	Taiwan	25
FrEAfrica	14	BrW Africa	6	Ghana	75	Jamaica	25
Zaire	14	BrE Africa	6	*Nigeria*	78	Brazil	26
Venezuela	17	Algeria	7	*BrW Africa*	79	*Indo-China*	33
Tunisia	22	Taiwan	7	Australia	80	Honduras	42
Ghana	29	Philippines	9	Brazil	92	Peru	45
Jamaica	31	Indonesia	11	Turkey	98	*Nigeria*	47
Peru	40	Honduras	13	Algeria	103	Indonesia	47
Turkey	41	Jamaica	13	Egypt	105	Philippines	47
Algeria	48	Peru	15	*BrE Africa*	110	Argentina	47
Honduras	50	Brazil	17	Peru	119	Egypt	48
Malaysia	58	Ghana	24	Mexico	126	*BrW Africa*	56
Brazil	59	Egypt	29	Cuba	138	Ghana	60
Egypt	63	Malaysia	45	Canada	146	*FrE Africa*	60
Mexico	88	Mexico	46	Malaysia	148	Mexico	67
Rhodesias	109	Argentina	50	Honduras	156	Cuba	73
Chile	114	Chile	51	Chile	197	Chile	87
Cuba	175	Australia	70	*FrE Africa*	226	*BrE Africa*	106
So Africa	202	Canada	73	So Africa	235	Malaysia	115
Argentina	266	Cuba	93	Argentina	248	*Zaire*	157
Australia	275	So Africa	140	*Rhodesias*	384	So Africa	163
Canada	385			*Zaire*	404		

Note
For the purpose of making comparisons, the GDP was estimated for eight countries by multiplying the trade figure by the average ratio of GDP/trade. These countries are indicated here in italics.

will fall, such as Australia and Canada. Beyond the sensitivity of the rankings to the choice of indicator is the more fundamental point in that Table, of a considerable dispersion of the countries geographically and by political status; neither colonies nor any particular region monopolizes either end of the rankings.

The focus in the subsequent sections of this chapter will be on explaining these findings – particularly that of the path of direct investment.

Total foreign investment followed a similar path, but one can argue that the variable differentiating FI and FDI, portfolio loans, was determined by separate factors which deserve their own analysis. Indeed, the history of the re-entry of third world countries into the international bond markets, leading to various Third World Debt Crises, is rather well known. The determinants of the path of FDI include factors in both the source and the receiving countries. Our analysis of the differences in timing of the initial high points in the early part of the century, and the speed of the subsequent decline, attributes more importance to events in the source countries. After mid-century, the growth of nationalism in the Third World, which was not limited to ex-colonies, accentuated that decline. The wider differences in pace and amount of increased FDI in recent years apparently responds predominantly to specific factors in the host countries.

At the end of the century, there has been much conversation in the mass media about globalization. The finding of small levels of FDI/GDP at this time in the Third World certainly suggests the need for a modification of that belief. To be sure, total foreign investment has regained its levels of a century ago, but as we have seen, the recovery in that variable has been dominated by an increase in lending, and doubts exist about the wisdom of celebrating high levels of debt in weak and/or wasteful governments. Nevertheless, our analysis has provided an alternative interpretation with regard to FDI. Although during the period of nationalizations the reductions of FDI should be considered a reversal of globalization, there are several indications that the current low levels of FDI predominantly reflect the growth of domestic entrepreneurial ability, displacing foreign investors while developing sectors, such as services, with inherently low attractiveness for FDI, as will be discussed below in the context of the Investment Development Path. In this light, there has been a process of globalization, but it is via the spread of technology, not ownership. That the mode of this globalization is via domestic instead of foreign entrepreneurs may well be an insignificant detail. Another consideration which downplays the view of the earlier period's investments as representing globalization is the fact that for most third world areas – especially colonies – those investment flows were primarily bilateral flows from the metropolitan powers, in contrast to the end of century situation which is much more multi-lateral. Furthermore, each of the metropolitan countries had restricted the growth of domestic enterprises, so that the above-mentioned process of globalization as it is currently occurring had not been allowed to develop in the early years of the century.

The presentation of the OLI model in Chapter 2 argued that industrial organization factors will lead to significant differences by economic sector in the levels and trends of foreign ownership ratios. A first part of this demonstration is easy; government capital and residences account for between one third and one half of total capital, and almost by definition these have minimal foreign ownership. Furthermore, we argue that the railroad sector also fits this description very nicely; further details are provided below in this chapter. With regard to other sectors of the economies, evidence was presented for several countries on all three continents, indicating both that there are major differences in sectoral ownership ratios, and that these have varied significantly over time. Furthermore, the case studies indicated that the reasons for these changes involve both market forces and government policy, and indeed their interaction – an example being the development of private sector consulting firms which assist governments in managing large parastatal enterprises, such as the raw materials sector. One implication of this analysis is that the determinants of FDI are distinct from those of portfolio investment, as are the effects of FDI.

Estimates of the foreign ownership of domestic capital

Our work with the country data generated not only numerous estimates of non-railroad FDI/GDP, but also a smaller set of estimates of the ratio FDI/K, foreign direct investment divided by the total domestic stock of capital. These are pulled together in Table 7.4. The major positive conclusion from them is that the ratio FDI/K fell in virtually all countries, during at least the first half of the twentieth century.[2] This result is consistent with our findings about how FDI/GDP was generally falling from a pre-World War II peak, by an amount greater than any plausible decline in the capital output ratio (K/O), so that the ratio of those two variables would fall (FDI/K = FDI/GDP ÷ K/O). Furthermore, these results encourage us to accept FDI/GDP as a valid proxy for the more difficult to observe FDI/K.

Another interesting result is that, in almost all cases, the ratio of foreign capital to total capital was less than half, and actually clusters at a level of about one quarter in the early years. As we saw in Chapter 2's discussion of the sectoral distribution of capital in the industrial countries, something around one half of a country's capital stock is composed of government assets and private residences. Thus the foreign ownership ratios may well be much higher in terms of what might be called business capital, and especially corporate capital. Nevertheless, this data bids us to take caution at mention of an overwhelming degree of foreign ownership of third world countries. It also suggests that most savings comes from domestic sources. Finally, a close reading of the individual country studies in the earlier chapters, or a familiarity with the sources of the data utilized, lead to the disappointing conclusion that in Table 7.4 there is not much credibility to broad cross-country comparisons of these data.

One major surprise in Table 7.4 is the low ratios of non-railroad FDI/K in Australia, Canada, and India. One explanation could be methodological, because for each of these countries the estimate of wealth was

Table 7.4 Estimates of foreign ownership ratios, twentieth century (non-railroad FDI/domestic capital; the "*" indicates settler capital is included per cent)

	1914	1929	1938	1950	1970
Algeria	5 50*				
Egypt		32	22	16	14
Ghana	<50			7	
Kenya				29 56*	
South Africa	<40*	16	11	12	19
Zaire				66	
Zimbabwe					66
Australia	6	5		5	
India	3*	2*	3*	1	<$\frac{1}{2}$
Indo-China		17			
Indonesia			63*		
Korea	9	17	25		
Taiwan	20	26	18		
Argentina	22	15	4	5	
Brazil	17	16	14	4	3
Canada	9	13	13	8	12
Chile		24	27	14	
Colombia		7		5	
Cuba	38			19	
Honduras		26	14	15	
Mexico	42	33	21	5	5
Peru				9	
Venezuela		45	33	28	17

Sources: Respective case studies in Chapters 4–6.

Notes
In the text, it is stated that much caution is need if using these data for cross-country comparisons. The major reason is differences in methodology in estimating capital, and in the underlying data. Because of that, no adjustments have been made here for differences in factors included in the capital stock, such as residences, inventories, or consumer durables. Those estimates of foreign ownership ratios that were clearly limited only to corporations were not included here. Railroads are included in the first estimate for South Africa, and in all of those for Honduras.

generated using the perpetual inventory method. But the estimates for Argentina and Chile also grew out of some version of this approach, although there are indications that the capital stock in their service sectors was underestimated. More importantly, we have seen that the standard image of the above three countries as having received heavy foreign investment is dramatically altered when the comparison is restricted to non-railroad direct investment. The key to this result is that in settler countries such as Canada and Australia the strictly foreign direct investment was probably smaller than the expatriate investment during the twentieth century.

The relative importance of expatriate investment

In spite of the difficulties in distinguishing FDI from expatriate investment, several tentative conclusions can be proposed on the basis of the
material presented in the previous chapters. As a rule, expatriate investment, owned by resident "outsiders" such as settlers, and typically
financed with funds generated locally, such as retained earnings, was
generally more important in the first half of the century, and in colonies.
It was largest in absolute amounts in the self-governing colonies of Great
Britain, and appears to have been relatively more important in the
colonies of at least two other metropolitan countries, the Netherlands and
Japan. The situation in the French colonies is more difficult to decipher.
In part this results from the widespread intermingling of government and
private sector investments, blurring the operationally less important dis-
tinction between FDI and expatriate capital.

European settlers brought some capital with them into their host
territories, and over time generated more themselves. Because Europeans
significantly outnumbered natives in the "areas of recent settlement", it is
probable that accumulated expatriate investment overshadowed native
capital. In these areas it is also plausible that during this century it was
larger than what we now call FDI. The settlers would have had similar
skills to those of their compatriots in the metropole, especially in the era
before FDI in manufacturing became important. Moreover the settlers did
not suffer discrimination *vis-à-vis* the foreign firms, as had the natives. In
general, the settlers' most important activity was farming, where self-
financing was much more typical than financing from abroad, and therefore does not show up in data resulting from balance of payments
statements. Thus, in these regions, not only was investment by expatriates
larger than that coming from other sources, but with succeeding generations and increasing self-governance, that expatriate capital would gradually be considered domestic investment. As a result, the remaining foreign
direct investment would be measured as a correspondingly small fraction
of domestic capital. Of course, the "areas of recent settlement" received
sizeable amounts of foreign loans, but these went predominantly to railroads and other infrastructural projects ultimately under government
control. This, then, is our story for Canada and Australia (and presumably
New Zealand). We argued above that a similar domestication of investment by outsiders occurred in South Africa between the two world wars,
and subsequently in Southern Rhodesia.

Perhaps the most important area of European settlement where the
Europeans did not dominate numerically, nor achieve independence
from the metropolitan country, was Algeria. According to the evidence
reviewed in Chapter 4, settler capital dominated here as well. Our sources
indicated that settler capital was also greater than FDI in Kenya. The
analysis of the case of the Dutch East Indies/Indonesia by Gales and

Sluyterman (1998) splits the outside investment evenly between that of settlers and that in Free Standing Companies, also downplaying FDI on the "American model". Expatriate investment was also of a similar order of magnitude to FDI in India, although neither was large compared to the size of the economy. The available literature in English about Japanese investments in Korea and Taiwan hints at a similar description, but still awaits formal analysis. One independent country where expatriate investment was important was China, but this appears to have been concentrated in the treaty ports, which for this discussion were essentially mini-colonies.

In most colonial contexts, the dominance of domestic capital by outsiders is not surprising, given the mercantilistic elements in colonial strategies, and the limited degree of adoption of western technology by indigenous groups prior to absorption into colonial empires. A major point of this book has been to demonstrate that the amount of (non-railroad) FDI has been rather small, inherently limited by conditions in both source countries and receiving areas. The differences in development between the British colonies of "recent settlement" and virtually all other colonies is thus envisioned as being due to greater levels of expatriate investment in the former, where numerical and hence political dominance by the settlers eventually led to their capital being considered national. Thus for example, the key explanatory factor for a colonial historian who is contrasting the metropolitan contribution to capital formation in Canada with that in Nigeria or Indo-China, is not the low level of FDI in the latter – according to our analysis, that is not even an accurate statement – but the higher level in the former of colonization and its attendant expatriate investment.

Another reason for separately emphasizing expatriate investment is that in colonial settings, the relevant variable, either for political backlash against foreigners or for technology transfer by outsiders, would have been all investment by outsiders, not just FDI. In particular, hostility against foreigners was most clearly motivated by resentment over usurpation of land, not dominance of urban or mining activities where FDI was concentrated. Furthermore, expatriate investment has not been limited to that of European and Japanese colonists, but also included that of Chinese, (east) Indians, and émigrés from the Ottoman Empire. After World War II, independence eliminated expatriate investment by Europeans, but not necessarily that of these other groups. Resentment against them periodically surfaces in different countries. Finally, we should underline that the strength of the expatriate, or settler community was so large in places such as Algeria and Rhodesia that these groups pursued policies against the expressed political wishes of the metropole, to the extent of Southern Rhodesia's unilateral declaration of independence, and a near-secession in Algeria. That these were ultimately unsuccessful, and control reverted to indigenous people, does not lessen our appreciation of the political as well as economic potential of the expatriate sectors in these societies.

Econometric explanation of pre-World War I FDI

One of the motives for generating data for more than three dozen countries is that the accumulated evidence allows us to speak with some confidence about overall patterns. In particular, we use econometric techniques for investigating which countries/areas had above or below average amounts of investment. We look first at direct investment, and later, at total foreign investment. The period chosen was pre-World War I. The availability of data declines after that war, and only becomes satisfactory in 1970, by which time domestic political considerations in the third world countries appear to dominate the economic determinants of direct investment.

The dependent variable is non-railroad FDI, which as we have shown, can be deflated by either population or income. The explanatory variables were per capita income and per capita income squared, a measure of the importance of railways, of mining, and dummy variables for political status. The inclusion of the income variable corresponds to what is called a gravity equation. Its rationale is that larger countries will attract more investment, perhaps because their markets are bigger.[3] Following Narula (1996), non-linearities in the income term are allowed by inclusion of its squared value. The hypothesized value of the coefficient on railways was positive, on the presumption that more infrastructure would attract more investment. The expected sign of the mining variable was also positive, because it was felt that greater raw materials would attract more investment, and that due to technological and financial difficulties, a greater fraction of mining would be performed by foreigners.

The initial hypothesis on the political independence dummy variable, D1, was that its coefficient would be positive, because colonies had been restricted in their development. As was pointed out at our conference in Bellagio, a more informed hypothesis would be that investors from the metropolitan country would be more willing to invest in their colonies, because of similar legal systems, so that the coefficient on political independence would be expected to be negative. Of course, this logic is easily extended to include an hypothesized effect that in the several colonies, foreigners were given privileged treatment, which would give a distinctly different evaluation to such a finding.[4] Finally, experience with the individual country data, as well as initial regression runs, indicated that Australia, Canada, and South Africa were outliers, and so a separate dummy was inserted for them, G1, which we might refer to as the settlement variable.

Table 7.5 reports some estimated equations. Judging by the R^2, the use of Narula's specification of the dependent variable as investment per capita does better than this author's previous work using a formulation with investment/GDP (Twomey 1998). Moreover, Narula's non-linear formulation for GDP/capita is strongly supported. The point of inflection occurs at per capita GDP levels of around $250, depending on the specification of the equation. Note that this is the level of per capita income that separates Canada and Australia from all the other countries. At the median levels of income and investment, the elasticity of FDI is over two. The coefficient of the mining variable had the expected sign, and was significant, while that for railroads was not significant.

With regard to the political variables, the estimated coefficient on the dummy variable reflecting political independence is in fact negative; colonies received more FDI than independent third world countries, other things being equal. In other words, this analysis of cross sectional data supports the model of the investment development path, as it does the hypothesis that there was more investment in colonies. It is also interesting to note that the coefficient for the settlement colonies was much larger in absolute size than that for the colonies as a whole, and was negative. These two countries – Canada and Australia; South Africa was not included in the regression on FDI, due to the difficulty of separating railroad investment – received much *less* non-railroad, direct foreign investment than would have been expected, given the sizes of their economies and the other structural variables. According to the above reasoning about how FDI was being attracted to colonies due to less risk because of similar legal and political traditions, the estimated coefficient for these two colonies should have been positive, and if anything, one would expect the effect of shared culture to be stronger in them than in non-settler colonies. Our explanation for this finding of low FDI in the settler colonies is that the expatriate investment has displaced the explicitly foreign direct investment. Finally, the results in Table 7.5 indicate that the coefficient for the dummy variable representing political independence, D1, is generally not statistically significant, while the "t coefficient" for the coefficient on the settlement dummy does have the required size. This author's previous result, omitting those two countries, is re-estimated here as equation 10 in the Table, using an updated and extended data set, where the econometric importance of omission of the observations on Canada and Australia is demonstrated. The message from the estimated coefficient on the political variable would seem to be that what is more important is being a settler area, and not colonial status by itself.

As a complement to these equations, further regressions were run on total foreign investment, in the two specifications of FI/capita and FI/GDP. These are shown as equations 8 and 9 in Table 7.5. The effect of GDP/capita is similar in these equations to the earlier ones relating to non-railroad FDI, and there is a parallel decline in R^2 for the equation in FI/GDP. The railroad variable has a positive coefficient, reflecting the common, while by no means universal, practice of using external sources

Table 7.5 Regression results

#	Dependent Variable								R^2
1.	NonRRFDI/cap =	−11.91 (2.39)	+0.89 GDP/cap (6.39)	−0.0013 GDP/cap² (3.04)	−0.69 RR (1.88)	+0.45 Min (3.01)	−0.95 D1 (0.19)	−50.0 G1 (1.93)	0.75
2.	NonRRFDI/cap =	−11.41 (2.17)	+0.86 GDP/cap (5.90)	−0.0018 GDP/cap² (4.31)	−0.68 RR (1.74)	+0.44 Min (2.87)	+1.44 D1 (0.28)		0.75
3.	NonRRFDI/cap =	−5.65 (1.07)	+0.55 GDP/cap (5.65)		−0.26 RR (0.64)	+0.35 Min (2.11)	−0.67 D1 (0.12)	−88.44 G1 (3.36)	0.70
4.	NonRRFDI/GDP =	14.90 (1.45)	+0.73 GDP/cap (2.91)	−0.0014 GDP/cap² (1.80)	−0.90 RR (1.34)	+0.88 Min (3.31)	−9.15 D1 (1.01)	−68.3 G1 (1.45)	0.34
5.	NonRRFDI/GDP =	15.58 (1.68)	+0.70 GDP/cap (2.73)	−0.002 GDP/cap² (2.80)	−0.88 RR (1.28)	+0.86 Min (3.20)	−5.89 D1 (0.66)		0.31
6.	NonRRFDI/GDP =	21.62 (2.51)	+0.37 GDP/cap (2.34)		−0.43 RR (0.66)	+0.76 Min (2.85)	−8.85 D1 (0.94)	−109.6 G1 (2.55)	0.28
7.	NonRRFDI =	−36.59 (1.17)	+0.53 GDP (5.69)	−0.00007 GDP² (4.98)	−0.002 RR (0.77)	+1.66 Min (1.91)	+12.66 D1 (0.37)	−188.56 G1 (2.03)	0.82
8.	FI/capita =	−54.34 (4.77)	+1.94 GDP/cap (6.13)	−0.0037 GDP/cap² (4.44)	+2.39 RR (2.83)	−0.51 Min (1.56)	+2.04 D1 (0.18)	+107.2 G1 (3.52)	0.93
9.	FI/GDP =	7.63 (0.48)	+1.04 GDP/cap (2.34)	−0.0034 GDP/cap² (2.89)	+2.92 RR (2.45)	+0.09 Min (0.20)	+9.89 D1 (0.62)	+59.18 G1 (1.38)	0.61

Equation estimated without observations for Australia and Canada

#	Dependent Variable								R^2
10.	NonRRFDI/GDP =	19.02 (2.26)	+0.54 GDP/cap (3.01)		−0.86 RR (1.28)	+0.88 Min (3.32)	−9.51 D1 (1.05)		0.38

Notes

Absolute values of the "t" statistics in parenthesis. The adjusted R^2 value is reported. The number of degrees of freedom was 22 in the first set of equations, and 20 in the last equation. RR is railroad miles divided by GDP; Min is the fraction of exports composed of mining products. D1 is a dummy whose value is unity if the country was independent in 1913, and G1 is a dummy whose value is unity for Australia, Canada and South Africa. South Africa is not included in any of the equations for non-RR FDI, because it is not possible to separate out the railroads.

to finance public or private railroad construction. Similarly, the mining variable now does not have a well-determined coefficient, suggesting that this activity attracted direct investment only. Turning now to the political variables, we see that, for FI, the coefficient of the dummy for independent countries, D1, is now positive, but not statistically significant, providing only a weak indication that independent countries borrowed more. However, the coefficient for the dummy variable for the settlement colonies now has a positive sign, and is quite large in the equation for FI/cap. An interpretation for this finding is that these countries were able to borrow more on international markets because of their cultural similarities with Britain and the rest of Europe. Thus, with regard to these countries of recent European settlement in the pre-World War I period, and by implication for New Zealand as well, there was less need of the entrpreneurial skills which FDI provided, while the cultural affinity facilitated greater portfolio borrowing, with the net impact being an increase in overall foreign investment.

The question to which this leads is, for how long did the settler areas have below average FDI? The answer is that in simple regressions of non-railroad FDI/cap, the sign of the coefficient on the dummy D1 changes from negative to positive by 1938, and fluctuates thereafter. Pursuit of this topic, which is essentially about the settler colonies and not our prime interest, would require more elaborate econometric techniques, and better data, and so will be left for future work.

Finally, we can use the regressions to inquire which countries had above or below average levels of FI or FDI. The results for the latter variable for 1914 are presented in Table 7.6, in which are indicated the residuals (actual minus predicted value) from the corresponding regression equations, each one standardized by comparison to GDP. Without wishing to read too much into these equations, given the weakness of some of the basic data and the tentative nature of the empirical exercises, it is reasonable to interpret situations where the three specifications give similar results as identifying clear situations. Thus, Argentina, Cuba, Honduras, Philippines, and Ghana all had above average amounts of direct investment, while Colombia, Venezuela, Turkey, Morocco and Tunisia had less FDI than would have been expected, given the explanatory variables which are being used.

The relative size of railroads

Because railroads occupied such an important role in the early phase of foreign investment, and in turn represented one of the first major concentrations of capital, there may be some value of sketching out their story in more detail. The basic goal is to indicate how big the railroads were relative to other sectors of the economy, and what was the timing of their rise and eventual decline. The size of railroads is measured either as the

Table 7.6 Observations and residuals from regression equations

	GDP/cap	Non-RR FDI/GDP	R1	R4	R7
Argentina	107	43	11	7	7
Brazil	65	26	−8	−18	−11
Canada	252	26	0	1	3
Chile	58	87	4	9	−17
Colombia	38	10	−18	−32	−30
Cuba	127	73	6	17	31
Guatemala	38	12	1	4	18
Honduras	31	42	27	29	125
Jamaica	55	25	−20	−26	54
Mexico	70	67	9	7	24
Paraguay	42	36	15	7	75
Peru	33	45	1	−8	−33
Uruguay	106	33	−17	−17	3
Venezuela	32	13	−8	−13	−15
Australia	344	21	0	−1	−4
China	13	11	−2	33	1
India	17	10	−9	31	−1
Indonesia	11	47	9	18	−1
Korea	14	6	−15	31	−28
Malaya	45	115	53	45	52
Philippines	27	47	17	17	11
Taiwan	34	25	2	11	11
Thailand	16	15	−6	6	−32
Turkey	40	13	−13	−23	−30
Algeria	47	32	−3	−6	−2
Egypt	48	48	7	0	7
Ghana	38	60	23	16	56
Morocco	23	18	−10	−6	−4
Tunisia	51	11	−55	−55	−75

Source: Regressions reported in Table 7.5 above.

Note
The residuals are from equations 1, 4, and 7 of the set reported in Table 7.5 above. They are presented here as fractions of GDP. South Africa is not included as it is not possible to separate non-railroad investment.

length of track in use, or as the (preferably appropriately discounted) value of the system. Data on the former variable are easily available, while the latter can be estimated for a number of countries, with varying degrees of accuracy. Given our need for cross-country comparisons, the options for scalars remain the same as before: population, which is easily available to the degree of accuracy needed here; GDP, which is available for several countries, the national capital stock – available in very few cases.

In both the United Kingdom and the United States, railroads reached their peak relative size before 1900, with railroad capital accounting for about 20 per cent of national capital, and 25 per cent of fixed non-residential capital.[5] In all the countries of interest in this paper, the railroads attained their highest relative size later in chronological terms, although the degree of relative size was either higher or lower, depending on the country. For example, in Japan, the only other country for which elaborate, authoritative, published estimates of railroad and total capital appear to be available, the growth of railroads started later, peaked in the second decade of this century, and at a level less than half that of the UK and the US.

Our expectations of railroads playing an important role in Argentina,[6] Australia, and Canada,[7] are supported by the calculations based on the available data, which are illustrated in the accompanying Graphs. By our rough estimates, the value of net railroad stock reached over 20 per cent of fixed reproducible capital[8] in these countries. Similar calculations for India, using the best available estimates, suggest that capital in railroads was almost as high a fraction of total capital as anywhere else, frontier country or otherwise.[9] The situation of the size of railroad capital compared to total non-financial wealth, including land, can also be mentioned briefly. The fraction of total tangible wealth accounted for by railways was between 5 and 10 per cent. The major differences among countries were due to the different sizes and trends in the value of land (United Kingdom and India) and residences (Japan), and should not be attributed to the railway systems themselves.

Of the variables illustrated in the Graphs, only railroad kilometer per person (RR km/person) is not subject to important imprecisions in measurement, such as those plaguing capital stocks. The RR km/person peaks around 1913–1917 in Argentina and Australia, while its maximum value occurred around 1929 in India and Canada. Argentina's highest value of RR km/person was about half of that of Australia and Canada. More importantly, the maximum value of RR km/person in India was roughly one tenth of that reached in those other countries, reflecting the high population in India. Thus the case of railroads becomes another useful example of an important development variable whose measurement gives markedly different evaluation depending on whether it is calculated in per capita or as a fraction of GDP or total wealth.

One purpose of making these calculations is to relate the size of railroad capital to that of FDI. For Argentina, Australia and Canada, the value of railroads reached about 60 or 70 per cent of GDP; in India the maximum was closer to 20 per cent. In Table 7.1, the 1914 average value of non-railroad FDI/GDP was about 40 per cent. Thus, the amount of capital invested in railroads, from foreign and domestic sources, was the same order of magnitude as that invested by overseas entrepreneurs in all non-railroad sectors. Such a result implies that it was not the lack of capital which constrained investment by local people, but the lack of technical knowledge or the very riskiness of the activities.

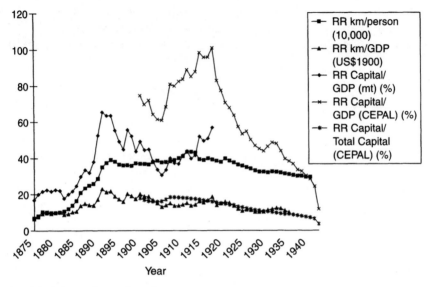

Graph 7.1 Argentina: railroads

Sources: Population, *Statistical Abstract for Latin America,* extrapolating values for years before 1900 based on census data. Railroad kilometers from Mitchell (1983). GDP from UN-ECLA (1958), and for series labeled (mt) from Cortés Conde (1994). Railroad capital in gold pesos from Tornquist (1919: 117); and for the CEPAL series from UN-ECLA (1958). Fixed capital from UN-ECLA (1958).

Notes
The Graph indicates two distinct estimates of Railroad Capital/GDP; as explained in the text, one major contributor to the difference between those estimates would be the distorted relative prices used by CEPAL for 1950.

With regard to cyclical patterns, note that in Argentina, Australia and Canada, both the ratios of railroad kilometers to GDP and that of the stock of railroad capital to GDP seem to have had two peaks; one before 1900, and the other after 1913. Moreover, for these countries, the ratio of railroad capital to total capital had only one peak. This suggests that the second wave of investment in railroads was part of a broader investment surge, of which railroads was a participant, but not necessarily the leader.[10]

One presumes that the South African case would be similar to that of Canada or Australia. The few other countries in Asia and Africa with available estimates of GDP present similarities in both size and timing to the pattern described above for Japan, which we might alternatively call one of "late entrance" to international commerce, or "lesser importance" of railroads. In some of the cases included in Table 7.7, such as Algeria, Taiwan, and Thailand, the peak year for railroads occurred after 1930. In contrast, the Latin American experience more closely approximated that of the "countries of recent settlement". In several Latin American coun-

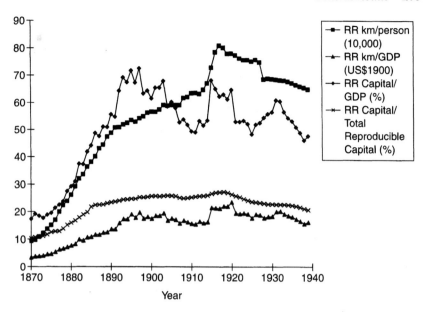

Graph 7.2 Australia: railroads

Sources: Population, from Mitchell (1983). Railroad kilometers from Mitchell (1983). Real GDP from Butlin (1962: 460). Railroad capital and total capital, calculated by summing the annual investment data in Butlin (1962: 460–1), applying a 2.5 per cent annual depreciation rate for railroads and a 4 per cent rate for total capital.

tries the railroads attained levels fully comparable to that of Argentina, at least when measured by railroad mileage/GDP, our only comparison, due to the lack of estimates of the total capital stock. Specifically, this is the case for Brazil and Mexico, and nearly so for Chile and Peru, while the level in Costa Rica was actually much higher. The data in Table 7.7 reveal the sensitivity of the rankings when variables are compared to income instead of population, although there are fewer reversals when one moves from RR km/person to RR km/GDP, than was the case in Table 7.3 when the variable of interest was foreign investment.

A brief summary of these results on the relative size of the railway system can place them in context for a study of twentieth-century trends in foreign investment. We have noted that in most cases, especially in Latin America, railroads had already peaked by 1930, and usually by 1913. So, in a study basically interested in the twentieth century, we must avoid letting declines in railroads hide, in economy-wide averages, potential increases of foreign investment into other sectors. That is the reason for the emphasis in this work on non-railroad FDI. Secondly, in a comparison across continents and historical experiences, railroads were more import- ant in Latin America than elsewhere in the Third World. This leads to the

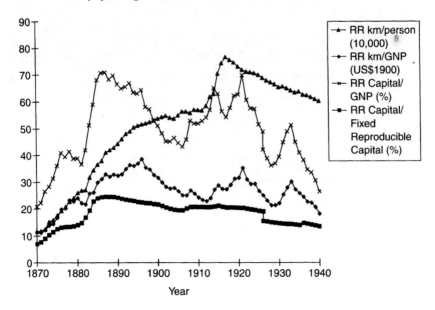

Graph 7.3 Canada: railroads

Sources: Population from *Historical Statistics of Canada*. Railroad kilometers from Mitchell (1983). GDP from Urquhart (1986: 30). Railroad capital and total capital calculated using the investment data in Urquhart (1986: 16), summing the annual data, and applying a 2.5 per cent annual depreciation rate for railroads.

final conclusion; industrialization – as at best a twentieth-century phenomenon in the Third World – essentially has occurred after the high point was reached in railroads. In contrast to today's developed countries, in the Third World the cycles of railroad building and of industrialization have had chronologically distinct effects on total capital stocks.

Railroad financing

A related theme about railroads is their ownership and financing. By 1913 there were few national railway systems that were predominantly owned and operated by the private sector, either domestic or foreign. Argentina and Cuba are well-known exceptions, while in some French colonies, as well as in Manchuria, the separation between foreign private and public was weak. In many areas, the railroads had been started by private interests. The period of transference from private to public often lasted several decades.

Lewis (1983) describes three models of railroad financing confronted by several Latin American countries after the late nineteenth-century exhaustion of the obviously profitable opportunities led to reductions of new construction. At this point, the motive for further expansion was one

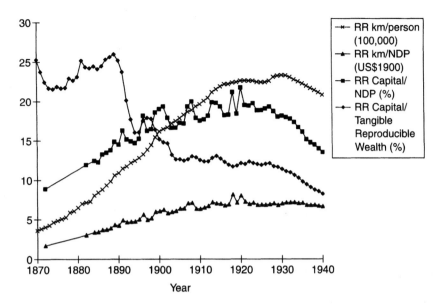

Graph 7.4 India: railroads

Sources: Population, (India only) from Maddison (1995), extrapolating early years. Railroad kilometers, from Morris and Dudley (1975). NDP, Heston (1983: 397–8). Railroad capital, calculated using the annual investment data in Morris and Dudley (1975), deflating by the investment price index in B. Roy (1979 and 1996), and applying an annual depreciation rate of 2.5 per cent. Total reproducible wealth; 1857–1899, from B. Roy (1996), 1900–1951 from B. Roy (1979).

Notes
There are some inconsistencies between the implied values of the nominal capital stock for the early 1900s in Roy's two publications, which may be the result of index number problems accumulated over more than one century, as the 1996 book used 1980 prices. The results from the 1979 book are used here, where possible.

of infrastructural development, as opposed to market generated profits. One approach was that governments stepped in with various forms of financial encouragements (land grants, purchase of shares, subventions, profit guarantees). A second model had the government generating financial capital, from domestic sources or foreign borrowing, and also operating the lines. A third model – labeled the French system – had the government doing the construction and then letting private entities be responsible for the operations. This mixture of public with private funding helped motivate our separation of railroads from other productive sectors, where government involvement was smaller.

Researchers of a generation ago calculated the "social rate of return" to railroad construction, taking into consideration factors such as heavy government subsidies, and dynamic spillovers. These returns were often

Table 7.7 Relative size of railroads in 1913

Country	RR km /person	RR km /GDP	Index of RR km/GDP (L.A. = 1.0)
Argentina	4.3	36	1.2
Brazil	1.0	36	1.2
Chile	2.4	27	0.9
Colombia	0.2	7	0.2
Costa Rica	2.5	51	1.7
Cuba	1.6	18	0.6
El Salvador	0.3	12	0.4
Guatemala	0.6	14	0.5
Honduras	0.4	10	0.3
Mexico	1.8	36	1.2
Nicaragua	0.6	17	0.6
Peru	0.7	28	1.0
Puerto Rico	0.4	5	0.2
Uruguay	2.3	18	0.6
Venezuela	0.4	na	na
Latin America Average	1.4	30	1.0*
Australia	6.9	15	0.5
Canada	6.5	18	0.6
Algeria	0.6	10	0.3
Egypt	0.4	7	0.2
Ghana	0.2	3	0.1
Morocco	0.1	2	0.1
South Africa	2.0	19	0.6
China	<0.1	1	<0.1
India	0.2	8	0.2
Indonesia	0.1	9	0.3
Malaysia	0.5	9	0.3
Philippines	0.1	2	0.1
Thailand	0.1	6	0.2
Turkey (Ottoman Empire)	0.3	5	0.2

Sources: For Latin America, author's calculations using data in Bulmer-Thomas (1994: 107, 432, 444). Others from the sources in the country studies in Chapters 3 and 4.

Notes
The unit for column 2 is kilometers per thousand people; for column 3 it is kilometers per million US dollars in 1913 prices. The data for GDP for the Latin American countries was calcu-lated from Bulmer-Thomas's GDP/cap data and population; the conversion from 1970 dollars to 1913 dollars involved dividing by 4.5, the ratio for the US GDP deflator. * Indicates overall average; the total in Bulmer-Thomas is inconsistent with the data for individual countries. That the level of railroad kilometers/GDP for Argentina in this table is 75 per cent higher than in the corresponding Graph results from the latter's use of the actual GDP, from Cortés Conde.

not high in the United States or Europe. Recent work on several Latin American countries has been more favorable to their railroads.

The Latin American models outlined by Lewis – obviously open to vari-ations – have an important additional alternative scenario when the area under discussion was a colony; namely, whether the funds the colonial governments utilized had been generated in the mother country, or from the colony itself. This decision depended on factors internal to the metropolitan power, many of which were unrelated to the economic feasibility of the project. Historians of Britain speak of the "official mind", and contrast the developmentalist orientation of Chamberlain to the "colonial self-sufficiency" of his predecessors. Changes in official attitudes in France were marked by Albert Sarraut, while a major watershed in Dutch thinking in the late nineteenth century was indicated by the decline of the "culture system". The emphasis Japan placed on railroads for strategic purposes has been mentioned. In the debate been free traders and what might be called neo-mercantilists, the latter sometimes lobbied for infrastructural development. Defense expenditures – against outsiders or rebellious natives – were often the dominant part of the colonial outlays, and railroads played an important supporting role. Other influential metropolitan pressure groups included merchants, mining companies, producers of railroad equipment, and manufacturers of consumer goods such as textiles. Mention should be made of cultural lobbying groups, and missionaries. Overall, our expectation would be that railroad construction in the colonies was less determined by economic factors, and that the list of political factors would be dominated by considerations from the metropole. The overall impact of these considerations on the social profitability of railroads in the colonies has yet to be determined.

The Investment Development Path

Having described the patterns of FI and FDI for a broad cross section of third world countries, and with these comments about the role of railroads, we now turn our attention to possible explanations of the investment patterns. We will look first at purely economic explanations, using Narula's Investment Development Path as our point of departure. It will be recalled that his central idea was to privilege technological change, in a model which extended Vernon's Product Cycle. The key idea is that a country will initially import capital and FDI, but that subsequent increases in technological and entrepreneurial skill will allow it to displace foreign entrepreneurs, and eventually result in being a net exporter of FDI.

Of the countries covered in this study shown in Table 7.8, South Africa and Taiwan have passed through both the net importer and net exporter phases of this Investment Development Path, while Canada and Korea are close to the point of possessing positive net outward FDI stocks. Of the countries which had been major importers of FDI, the case for South Africa differs from that of Canada in the relative importance of a decline in inward FDI/GDP in the former country, as opposed to a rise in outward FDI/GDP in the latter. Our interpretation of the South African case was that not only did improved technology allow its business sector to replace foreign investment and expand elsewhere, but also that political factors such as the international boycotts contributed to a withdrawal by foreign firms, further lowering inward FDI/GDP. Thus this case cannot be seen as a complete confirmation of a cyclical model driven by economic fundamentals. Data on Australia would seem to follow that of Canada, although the cyclical process is less complete. Narula's hypothesis is confirmed that countries with a large natural resource base will remain net importers of FDI for a longer time than those, like Korea and Taiwan, without this factor so attractive to FDI. Indeed, the magnitudes of the changes in the net position of Korea and Taiwan, less than 5 per cent of GDP – as well as the levels of the stocks of inward FDI/GDP – were much smaller than what occurred in South Africa, Canada, and elsewhere, where those changes were more than 10 per cent. Reinforcing our interpretation of the changes in the net investment positions of both Korea and Taiwan as corresponding to the Investment Development Path, is the fact that this occurred during a period when most commentators believe that each country experienced dramatic changes in entrepreneurial skills and human capital accumulation. In summary, these countries' experiences lend considerable support for an interpretation of the rise and fall of net inward FDI/GDP, based on the Investment Development Path, in which technology acquisition is a major factor.

There are a few other third world countries whose outward FDI is appreciable. Table 7.8 also indicates that, not only are they some distance from being net exporters of FDI, but the recent growth of outward FDI/GDP is accompanying that of inward FDI/GDP. The simplest explanation would be that the driving force is a reduction in the controls on capital flows, as part of a political environment more welcoming to FDI, rather than a dramatic improvement in domestic skills. The Chilean case is a noteworthy example. As such, the full paradigm of a technology-driven investment development path would appear less relevant for these countries. Although this certainly does not rule out technology accumulation as the major driving force in explaining the time path of stocks of FDI/GDP, it does make the *a priori* case of the investment development path less attractive.

A different story of how technology affects FDI/GDP or FDI/K should be mentioned, if only in passing. The main idea is that the means for controlling a company have evolved so that this can be accomplished more concisely now than in the past, because of improvements in communications and information science. In this vision, the ratio of FDI/GDP will fall over time, even when foreign control may be rising. This is evidently a plausible idea, but one which has escaped quantification. In our context, of course, the most recent period of rising FDI/GDP demands other explanatory factors.

As a descriptive device, the Narula/Dunning Investment Development Path has been very useful for our study. Nevertheless, we must be careful not to confuse a decline in inward FDI due to technological growth in the

Table 7.8 Stocks of inward and outward FDI/GDP, 1980–1995 (per cent)

	1980	1990	1995
Australia			
Inward FDI/GDP	17	25	27
Outward FDI/GDP	3	15	19
Net Inward FDI/GDP	14	10	8
Canada			
Inward FDI/GDP	21	20	20
Outward FDI/GDP	9	15	19
Net Inward FDI/GDP	12	5	$<\frac{1}{2}$
South Africa			
Inward FDI/GDP	22	10	11
Outward FDI/GDP	8	16	18
Net Inward FDI/GDP	14	−6	−6
Korea			
Inward FDI/GDP	2	2	2
Outward FDI/GDP	$<\frac{1}{2}$	1	2
Net Inward FDI/GDP	2	1	$<\frac{1}{2}$
Malaysia			
Inward FDI/GDP	26	35	52
Outward FDI/GDP	1	2	3
Net Inward FDI/GDP	24	33	49
Taiwan			
Inward FDI/GDP	3	6	6
Outward FDI/GDP	$<\frac{1}{2}$	8	9
Net Inward FDI/GDP	3	−2	−3
Argentina			
Inward FDI/GDP	7	6	9
Outward FDI/GDP	$<\frac{1}{2}$	$<\frac{1}{2}$	$<\frac{1}{2}$
Net Inward FDI/GDP	7	5	9
Brazil			
Inward FDI/GDP	8	9	9
Outward FDI/GDP	$<\frac{1}{2}$	1	1
Net Inward FDI/GDP	7	8	8
Chile			
Inward FDI/GDP	3	35	26
Outward FDI/GDP	$<\frac{1}{2}$	1	5
Net Inward FDI/GDP	3	35	22
Mexico			
Inward FDI/GDP	4	14	28
Outward FDI/GDP	$<\frac{1}{2}$	$<\frac{1}{2}$	1
Net Inward FDI/GDP	4	13	27
Venezuela			
Inward FDI/GDP	2	8	10
Outward FDI/GDP	$<\frac{1}{2}$	3	4
Net Inward FDI/GDP	2	6	5

Sources: Author's calculations, using inward and outward FDI and GDP from the sources listed in the respective country studies in Chapters 4 through 6.

host country, with a decline in FDI due to changes in government policy, such as reduced subsidies to foreigners, or increased nationalistic restrictions in the host country. Although improved technological capabilities have played an important role in lessening FRI in most third world areas during the twentieth century, we will argue below that nationalistic restrictions were the dominant factors affecting FDI during the third quarter of the century.

The "Big Push" and domestic growth

An alternative cyclical story is that the mid-century decline in FDI/GDP, and by implication a fall in FDI/K, simply resulted from a more rapid growth of domestic income and capital in sectors of the economy less attractive to foreign investors, and was not directly due to the displacement of foreign capital by domestic capital. We might borrow an image from the early years of development economics, and speak of a "Big Push" cycle. The relative decline in FDI is then the second phase of the cycle, coming after an initial burst of FDI. The typical scenario would be that new foreign investment leads to important improvements in the economy, such as by opening up a new export product, or establishing infrastructure such as railroads. After that stimulus, the rest of the economy grows, in the first example using the retained foreign exchange generated by the exports, in the second example because the improved transport makes new activities economically feasible. Accompanying the growth of these other sectors will be higher income and eventually more investment. Such a process has received much attention in the theoretical literature in terms of induced investment in some of the endogenous growth models.

The two phases to this Big Push cycle are easily comprehended. The innovation here is the attribution of the decline of FDI, relative to income or capital, to growth in the rest of the economy. Distinguishing empirically between Big Push and Investment Development Path will be difficult, as both processes normally occur simultaneously in a growing economy, and sectoral data on capital stocks and FDI are always scarce. On a theoretical plane the distinction is quite clear, and of course the evaluations are different – the Investment Development Path reveals technological sophistication, while the second phase of the Big Push might consist of growth of housing or petty commerce, and other less dynamic activities. One symptom of the second phase of the Big Push cycle would be strong growth of service activities, which could include either the government or residential housing, in addition to trade and other services.

Perhaps the first place to look for this Big Push phenomenon would be in countries with a low initial capital stock. Indeed, this appears to be an appropriate description of the experience of several sub-Saharan countries during the first half of the twentieth century. The empirical record is predominantly, although not exclusively, limited to the ratio of FDI to trade. Pre-depression levels of this variable were in fact quite high, even while per capita levels of income – and most assuredly the capital stock – was quite low. European investment in tropical Africa was only beginning at the start of the twentieth century, and it is also clear that there had been minimal accumulation by Africans of machine-made capital goods. The development of mines and plantations, and the construction of railroads and other infrastructure, would certainly have created growth prospects, and the above scenario could have played itself out. Indeed what stands out in the experience of several African countries is the slowness of the development of the other sectors of the economies, which makes the bulge in relative FDI more visible to our crude measures.

Support for this story can also be marshaled from the Argentine data of the first half of the century. The corresponding tables in Chapter 6 indicate that the ratio of FDI/K fell after 1913, and that there was an increase in the share of non-railroad services in total capital. Nevertheless, we also presume that the technological processes were at work associated with the Investment Development Path, of which railroads has already been singled out as a key example.

Source country determinants of FDI growth

We now turn to some summary comments of the determinants of the long-term trends in FDI, discussing separately factors originating in the source and host countries.

The reader will recall from the discussion in Chapter 3 that the United Kingdom, France, and Germany were the most important sources of FDI at the beginning of the twentieth century. For several decades, the evolution of FDI into the Third World was a function of events in the source countries. Germany lost its colonies as a result of World War I, and subsequently had little FDI into any part of the Third World until the 1960s. After the First World War, investors in France and the United Kingdom changed the geographical distribution of their overseas portfolios, concentrating on their colonies at the expense of other third world areas, as well as first world countries. British investment into the Third World was stagnant in real terms, and declined relative to growing incomes. In contrast, the Netherlands, Belgium, and Japan all expanded their investments into their colonies rather continually up to World War II, while not having appreciable FDI in the rest of the Third World. France, which had numerous colonies as well as a significant amount of investments in Europe, also redirected its investments towards its colonies, while reducing them in the rest of the Third World.

Finally, during the first half of the century, the United States emerged as a major foreign investor. Although it had investments in Europe, the major recipients of its earliest capital outflows were its near neighbors; Canada, Mexico, and other areas in and around the Caribbean. After

1929, the geographical distribution of United States overseas FDI shifted away from the Third World, towards Canada rather than Europe. The rush of American firms across the Atlantic was strongest later on, with the formation of the European Community.

The net effect of these geographical shifts was to lower FDI into Latin America, as Britain and France concentrated on their colonies, especially those with growing European settler populations. For a short period the decline of French and British investments into that region was outweighed at least in nominal terms by the increase of that from the United States, but this stopped with the depression.

After World War II, several major geopolitical changes occurred. Independence movements appeared and flourished throughout Asia and Africa, while the Cold War raised the stakes in the anti-colonialist movements, as well as among the many Latin Americans who were opposed to what they viewed as dependency and neo-colonialism. The other international force was the creation of the European Union, which attracted foreign investment by multinationals from within and without. One presumes that the opening up of the ex-socialist countries of eastern Europe will also divert some investment that might have gone to the Third World.

It is intriguing to realize that several of the most important economic events that are said to have affected capital movements from the source countries to the Third World – the imbroglio over inter-allied War debts after World War I, the Depression, capital flows as an inter-generational transfer into the areas of recent settlement (Taylor and Williamson 1995) – are all more accurately described as referring to portfolio rather than to direct investment flows. In the above listed cases the two types of capital flows moved together, of course, suggesting a weakness in the initially postulated theoretical distinction between portfolio and direct investment. Similarly, the restrictions on sterling balances after World War II ended up financing the purchase of British overseas investments, in railroads and other sectors as well, which also might be considered to be outside of our implicit theoretical model.

An explanation of the changes in the source countries' portfolios based on an evolving philosophy of treatment towards their colonies is clearest for the case of France. From a position of relative neglect, the empire grew to be viewed as a potential aid in the metropolitan country's own growth and safety, and increased its transfers and subsidies to the colonies. As the century moved on, this attitude progressed to a desire to encourage the growth of the colonies themselves, but the rush of events after 1945 denied this new philosophy much time to show its merits. France's decision to join the European Economic Community marked an important turning away from colonialism, and the support given to French entrepreneurs overseas – especially settlers – correspondingly declined thereafter.

Policies in host countries

The first type of policy in third world countries which comes to mind as affecting the long-term path of FDI is nationalization.[11] This is predominantly a post-World War II phenomenon in Latin America and China, and it had to wait until political independence in the colonies, which was even later. Quantitatively, the largest number of the nationalizations occurred during the 1960s and 1970s. Williams (1975) estimated that one quarter of the value of FDI in the Third World was nationalized between 1956 and 1972, and that the compensation paid was equal to 41 per cent of the value of those assets – 67 per cent if one excludes what he termed "socialist" countries. We might speak of this wave of takeovers being sparked by Egypt's takeover of the Suez Canal in 1956, but important earlier precedents were set by the actions in Mexico after the 1910 Revolution, as well as the events in the fledgling Soviet Union (Williams 1975). In this perspective, what was important about Egypt was that the action was not reversed, in contrast, for example to the nationalization of the petroleum industry in Iran in 1951, which lasted about two years before a counter-coup reinstalled the Shah, or the case of Guatemala in 1954, where a coup reversed a land reform that threatened foreign owned banana companies.

Evidently, most transferences of ownership from foreigners to nationals were not the result of normal legal and institutional processes per se, but rather were the direct byproducts of armed revolution or the easily foreseeable result of independence movements, such as the abandonment of farms and businesses by Europeans in Indonesia, Kenya, and Algeria. Moreover, it is clear that nationalizations were not simply the outgrowth of anti-colonial sentiments, as illustrated by the events in politically independent China, Cuba, and Chile. Furthermore, the juxtaposition of the cases of Iran's nationalization of oil and Egypt's nationalization of the Suez Canal introduces another element overlooked by some authors; changing attitudes in the industrially powerful countries. Britain and the United States eventually acted together in reversing the nationalization in Iran, but it was the United States's refusal to send oil to Britain that forced the latter to accept the results of Egypt's actions.

A helpful distinction is that of Korbin (1984), between massive and selective nationalizations. He suggests the use of the term "massive" when whole sectors of the productive structure are affected, occurring most often after social revolutions, and perhaps also involving the socialization of domestic capital, as well. Thus there may be a specifically ideological element, as distinct from an anti-colonial one. In contrast, selective nationalizations are those which involve individual firms. Korbin (1980: 74) notes the widely accepted view that massive nationalizations were more common before the early 1960s. Although he does not venture into an explanation of this watershed, presumably it would relate to the termination of a particular set of anti-colonial independence movements, as well as a shift in the Cold War balance of power.

The interests of Korbin, Williams, and others writing in this literature center on those nationalizations which are more limited, and perhaps, accompanied by a more transparent rationality. Thus, it is important that they demonstrate that since the early 1960s, selective nationalizations have been more common. Moreover, there has been a decline in the number of selective nationalizations since the mid-1970s, which Minor (1994) shows has continued into the 1990s. Korbin (1984: 338) explains this pattern of selective nationalizations in terms of four interrelated factors: the completion of the takeovers in sectors "where ownership is of the essence, i.e., large scale mining and petroleum ventures"; the growing self confidence of LDC governments and their declining apprehensions *vis-à-vis* foreign firms; growing administrative and technical capabilities in the host countries, resulting in more effective regulatory behavior; and different international economic conditions increasing the cost of nationalistic policies to third world countries, while increasing the benefits of FDI to them. To this last point Minor (1994: 183) adds ". . . interest by developing countries in expropriation has been replaced by disillusion with the typical result of expropriations, the state-owned enterprise".

Korbin's analysis works with many of the same insights as Dunning's eclectic model; most obviously the emphasis on sector- and firm-specific characteristics, and within them, the changing levels of technological competitivity and entrepreneurial advantages. An economist working in Dunning's tradition might quarrel with Korbin's classifying the foreign ownership of oil, mining and utilities as *incompatible* with economic control and national security (Korbin 1984: 329), preferring to interpret the greater volume of takeovers in those sectors as also responding to shifting ownership advantages, given the growth of consulting firms and greater comfort with joint ventures, factors which Korbin also acknowledges. This work on nationalizations also relates to analyses associated with Raymond Vernon in highlighting the usefulness of understanding a cost benefit rationality on the part of host governments, along with that of the foreign entrepreneurs. The distinction between massive and selective, with the attribution of a certain type of rationality to the latter, is also helpful. We emphasize that this contribution is not simply conceptual, but also empirical, and is not diminished by the unresolved problems with the data utilized, which Korbin, Williams and their co-workers have been the first to recognize.

Let us now place the chronological aspect of this empirical work back in the perspective of our broader interests. First of all, it implies that most of the decline of FDI in the Third World before the 1950s was not the result of expropriations. The separation of widespread, ideologically related nationalizations from the other, less spectacular actions in both the years before 1950 and those after 1975, allows us to relate the purchase of railroads in the early part of the century with the numerous specific nationalizations in the later period, associating both phases with a rationalist calculus set in a bargaining context infused with uncertainty, without needing to assert that this is the complete explanation. The reader will recall that the transference of ownership of railroads during the early years of the twentieth century, or the last years of the nineteenth century, involved amounts which, as a fraction of GDP, were generally larger than the post-1950 decline of FDI/GDP.

The fourth factor affecting nationalizations, mentioned by Korbin and elaborated on by Minor, is the changed international macroeconomic situation. However plausible intuitively, this is difficult to handle analytically at their level of generality. One of Minor's examples, "... the growing ability of the World Bank and the International Monetary Fund to change national policies toward FDI and expropriation" (page 182) is less about economics than politics, and that author is anxious to discuss the possibility that the current wave of privatization and liberalization of FDI restrictions may be reversed. Moreover, our data seem to link increased external debt and related balance of payments pressures, with a decreased attractiveness of a country to foreign investors. Minor (1994: 186) is probably correct in pointing out that Korbin did not anticipate sufficiently the "increase in sympathy for market systems" among third world countries.

Location specific advantages in host countries

Dunning's model emphasizes the importance of host country characteristics in attracting foreign investment. One obvious characteristic is the existence of raw materials; let us borrow a term from Carlos Díaz Alejandro and speak of the "commodity lottery". Once again there exists an easy example – petroleum, where the random aspect relates both to where it is located, and when it becomes exploitable commercially. The cases of bananas and rubber work similarly. The point being emphasized is that the host country's governmental policy, wage structure, and so on, have little to do with the determination of when and how much FDI will be attracted. This is probably less true for mining, and our individual country studies mentioned many cases in other sectors, such as agriculture, where government policy was key in making land available to foreigners.

These considerations lead to the question of the role of low cost labor in attracting foreign investment. If the investment were to be for sales into the domestic market, then one would doubt that low wages, as an isolated factor, would be positively correlated with FDI, because the low wages would be associated with low purchasing power. In contrast, investment for sales into international markets might well attract FDI into low wage countries, and it is helpful to discuss how important that has been. In agriculture and mining, wages may well be of secondary importance in attracting

FDI, behind the availability of land, climate, or minerals. So it is in the manufacturing industry that we expect low wages to be crucial. Yet our several country studies revealed that export processing zones, *maquiladoras,* and so on, are of relatively recent development, and of limited geographical extension.

In light of the fact that most FDI occurs among industrially developed, high income countries, low wages cannot be said to play a major role in world investment totals. The incipient nature of FDI in export-oriented manufacturing and service activities also tempers our evaluation of low wages as a determinant of FDI into the Third World. It can also be argued that the major deterrent to the expansion of export-processing FDI is currently the protectionist policies in the industrial countries, not nationalist policies in the Third World.

Privatization and FDI

One topic conspicuous by its absence in the previous chapters is the impact of privatization on increased inflows of FDI. Journalistic reports associate both contemporary phenomena, an increase in FDI and an upsurge of privatization, with a common root, the shift of the economic and political debate in favor of the free market orientation, and away from that of protectionism and interventionism. However, it is the case that recent privatizations have been most important in eastern Europe and a limited number of the middle income countries of Latin America, but not in the rest of the Third World. Indeed, Ramamurti (1999: Table 3) estimated that state-owned enterprises accounted for 13 per cent of the GDP of a sample of 25 developing countries, and that only 12 per cent of the assets of these enterprises had been privatized during the period 1988–96. We will argue that it is incorrect to consider an increased openness to FDI to have resulted from the same shift of policy as the recent privatizations, even though the intellectual rationale for both actions is ultimately the same. Indeed, what is new is not the validity of the neo-liberal position, but rather the relative strengths of several competing actors in the private and public domains in the respective countries. This focus on the political economy of government ownership and divestment informs the recent study on privatizations of the World Bank (1995), entitled *Bureaucrats in Business,* as an explanation for both successes and failures, and more broadly, for the limited scope of such actions in the Third World.

As stressed by both the World Bank and several authors in a recent mini-symposium appearing in *World Development* (January, 1999), many of the recent privatizations occurred not as a move toward the greater microeconomic efficiency supposedly inherent in the private sector, but rather as a reluctant recognition of the unsustainability, from a macroeconomic perspective, of the subsidies afforded to certain high-profile state-owned enterprises. Another point raised in this literature about the limited scope of privatizations is that success is not guaranteed, or less positively, there have been some major failures recently, in the Third World as well as eastern Europe. Many state-owned enterprises operate in non-competitive sectors where the value of the firms is difficult to gauge beforehand, and where some regulation can be expected after privatization. Two components of the successful privatization package are skilled, disinterested public servants, and a propitious macroeconomic context. But the lack of these inputs is often a major contributor to the need for privatization. Except for the cases of macroeconomic crisis, many acknowledge that in unstable environments, the cure of privatization may be worse than the disease of microeconomic inefficiency.

Thus, the policy makers and the general public discourse have only half-accepted the logic of *laissez faire*. As such, those who would be hurt by privatization find it advantageous to raise the flag of nationalism against opening up the process to foreigners. It is as if the political process can approve privatization, at the price of excluding foreigners. Thus, the striking finding in the Latin American cases is the dominance of the domestic private sector in purchases of the state-owned enterprises. Undoubtedly, there has been participation by foreign interests, but this is frequently limited to some sort of joint venture, not stand-alone FDI.[12] A final comment would be that this analysis does not rule out the prospect of greater commitments by foreigners at a later date. In this sense the weak relationship between privatization and FDI may simply be the result of our making the inquiry too early in a lengthy process of re-establishing the pre-eminence of the market mechanism.

Future trends

The switch towards attitudes more favorable to FDI may not be permanent, of course, and it is unlikely that any other such change will occur which will continue to increase the welcome for FDI in the Third World. When looking at potential scenarios for future trends, several economic considerations come to mind, which can be listed if not ranked. The growth of technological sophistication in the host countries is a factor much emphasized in this work. While it is clear that a few of today's industrial countries will maintain their technological superiority in certain very visible activities such as computers and biotechnology, it is also evident that these sectors represent a small fraction of a third world nation's overall production or consumption. In the other, less dynamic sectors, there could be catching up – think of textiles, and perhaps automobiles – which would reduce the incentives for FDI.

The effects of continued trade liberalization in the Third World produce a similarly agnostic prediction about future trends of FDI into these countries. Openness towards FDI has typically accompanied trade liberalization, as part of the attitudinal shift away from the heady nationalism of the 1960s. That does not necessarily imply an increase in FDI, because the lowering of tariffs also reduces the location specific advantages that attract foreign direct investment. This has been demonstrated in the case of four of the larger Latin American countries by Bielschowsky and Stumpo (1995).

Foreseeable changes in productive structures may well have a larger impact. Three facets of these changes are the shift of demand towards services, the greater foreign trade in manufactured inputs, and new forms of cross-national co-ordination. The fact that the ratio of foreign ownership of services is generally much lower than that in sectors producing physical goods, implies that higher growth in this sector will dampen the effect of increases in foreign ownership ratios in each subsector on an economy-wide average.[13] We saw support for this in our analysis of the second phase of the "Big Push" scenario. Greater foreign trade in manufactured inputs will result from more FDI by the final users, and increased trade liberalization in their home countries. There are several countries which have successfully utilized their low wage workers in export processing zones to expand exports. At the present time, the limiting factors for this process certainly appear to be the protectionism of the industrial countries, so that further relaxation of controls on FDI by individual third world countries will not increase the aggregate amount of FDI oriented toward exporting manufacturing inputs.

It is currently fashionable to speak of new forms of foreign direct investment, such as joint ventures and sub-contracting. The pre-eminence of the general trading companies in Japan's overseas ventures is often cited. Improved modes of communication – between enterprises, as well as between enterprises and the general public – suggest that there will be a continuation of the disaggregation of business services. In effect, what is being predicted is another step away from the "American Model", towards decentralization of decision making, placing greater reliance on employees in overseas locations. Inevitably, this reduces the ratio of FDI/K, although it is less clear if such changes should be interpreted as reducing external dependency.

Overall summary

The central finding of this book is that FDI, compared either to GDP or to the available measures of the capital stock, declined steadily in the Third World for a period of 60 to 80 years. The subsequent recovery of FDI compared to either variable has not been strong.

Another major result was the documentation of marked sectoral differences in foreign ownership, in colonial times as well as today. Such differences will lead some scholars – friends or foes of FDI – to reject a macro or economy-wide approach such as what has been used here, in favor of more micro-based investigations.

During the first half of the twentieth century, wars and economic depression reduced the investments coming from the source countries – from Europe, North America, and Japan. Countering this fact was an increase of investment in the years before World War II by the metropolitan countries in their colonies, responding to increased economic and strategic interest in the latter. Direct investments from the United States grew rapidly during the first three decades of the century, and then dominated the world after World War II. At all times, direct investment was much larger among the industrial countries, than it was from them into the Third World.

After the Second World War, political processes unleashed in the Third World reduced investment there. Upon attaining independence, many ex-colonies nationalized assets held by foreigners, whether settlers or not. At the same time, resentment against foreign investment, often combined with a broader rejection of capitalism, led to nationalizations in many independent countries. Political instability was another factor contributing to the reduction of FDI in third world countries during this period, as was a variety of economic policies limiting exchange flows and imposing other restrictions.

Several third world countries experienced a change in attitude towards FDI after, say, 1980, and there has been a relative increase in FDI since then. Several factors contributed to this change of heart, of which the biggest is the ending of the Cold War, which eliminated the most important alternative growth model. Another fundamental cause of a change of heart is the dimming of memories of colonial exploitation. Neither of these factors can be repeated. A third contributor to the changing attractiveness of FDI is a corresponding tarnishing of the luster of domestic political and economic elites who were perceived as alternatives to foreign investors, particularly in ex-colonies. Finally, we can point to an increase in the number of source countries, and the promise of a higher return for the host countries as they more willingly negotiate the conditions of the multinationals' presence and operations. Overall, these considerations certainly point towards a conclusion that FDI from the first world to the third world countries will not grow much, at least relative to the Third World's aggregate macroeconomic variables. But certainly one of the lessons from a review of the histories of third world countries during the twentieth century is to be very sceptical about such long-term predictions.

Notes

1 Recall Marichal's recent (1994: 8) reaffirmation of the characterization of the period 1880–1914 as a "golden age" of foreign capital in Latin America. The dating in Stallings (1987) of the cycles of United States lending to the region is slightly different, responding to the later emergence of the United States as a capital exporter, compared to Europe.

2 The reader will recall that Table 7.4's increase in FDI/K in South Africa after

World War II is predominantly a statistical artifact, reflecting a change in data sources. It is the case that one should expect an increase after 1950, due to inflows of investment in manufacturing, as indeed is registered in Canada. In addition, the decline between 1914 and 1929 in South Africa is exaggerated due to a change in sources.

3 The recent paper by Zhang and Markusen (1999) investigates the link between country size and inward FDI, arguing that threshold effects and scale economies lessen investment in smaller third world countries.

4 A related treatment is that of Hanson (1999), who addresses specifically the issue of shared culture. It might be pointed out here that much more elaborate specifications of investment appear in the literature, and that attention is typically directed towards flows rather than stocks.

5 United Kingdom data from Feinstein (1988). United States data from *Historical Statistics of the United States* and Fishlow (1966). A sobering lesson for empirically oriented investigators is the drastic revision in the initial description of the United States case in Ulmer (1960), which we would have had every reason to consider authoritative, which arose with Fishlow's subsequent work on the country's railroad stocks.

6 An essential part of our understanding of the Argentine case is the question of the representativeness of the data used by the UN-ECLA, where the base year for prices (1950) is generally felt to have exaggerated the relative size of capital goods (see Díaz Alejandro (1970), or Cortés Conde (1994)) because of a distorted relative price of capital goods at that time, resulting from price and exchange rate controls. A helpful check on our calculation of the size of pre-World War I railroad capital stock is the estimate given in 1915 by Tornquist (1919: 255), which, when compared to the available estimates for GDP or GNP for 1914 (such as Cortés Conde, Díaz Alejandro or Randall), also suggests that UN-ECLA's published ratio for railroad capital/GDP is too high. Furthermore, the bias is not so evident when comparing the 1914 ratio of railroad capital to what is referred to as reproducible capital (~15 per cent) in Tornquist or UN-ECLA.

7 The rapid rise in the estimated ratio of railroad capital to GDP or total capital in Canada, although somewhat sensitive to the assumed initial levels in 1870, does correspond to the timing of the construction of the trans-continental railroad. Moreover, the continued construction of railroads in Canada in the early twentieth century led to what was described by J.H. Dales as "a ridiculous amount of overinvestment in railways" (1986: 92). Although this would appear to be the accepted judgement of economic historians of Canada, the paper by Green (1986) attempts to temper that criticism.

8 Even though these calculations require crude assumptions as to initial conditions, the growth was such that those initial conditions had a small effect on long-term ratios, as can be inferred from the published data on annual investments.

9 The Graph for India suggests that railroads were an even higher fraction of total capital before 1900. This is not implausible, in light of the early British interest in that sector in the sub-continent, and the low levels of investment suggested by the area's poverty. However, doubts about the pre-1900 data, from B. Roy (1996), stem from two considerations. That data is presented in terms of 1980–81 prices, and any extension of a price index over eight decades is dubious. More importantly, the data in that book imply a much lower level of the 1913 capital stock than do the data in B. Roy (1976).

10 Contrary to this interpretation for Canada, also presented by Urquhart (1986: 35), the results of Green (1986: Table 15.12) imply two distinct peaks in railroad investment in that country – during the 1880s, and again during World War I – relative either to GDP or to the capital stock.

11 Strictly speaking, one distinguishes between those acts where the owners of the assets are paid a fair price, versus the cases where little or no compensation is paid, and the divestment is made under duress. The former are nationalizations, and the latter should be referred to as expropriations, although the difference between these categories is most difficult to identify in empirical work.

12 The study by the World Bank (1995) pays close attention to how the success of the reforms of state owned enterprises may depend on the type of the resulting contracting arrangements.

13 For a numerical example, consider an economy composed of two sectors, traded and services. The traded goods sector initially accounts for 40 per cent of capital stock. Assume that the foreign ownership ratio in traded goods is 50 per cent, while that of services is only 10 per cent. Then the average ownership ratio for the entire economy is 26 per cent. Suppose now that services grows to be two thirds of the capital stock, while foreign ownership in each sector rises by an absolute amount of 2 per cent, so that it is 52 per cent and 12 per cent, respectively. The average ownership ratio for the economy falls to 25.3 per cent.

Bibliography

Abe, E. (1997) "The Development of Modern Business in Japan", *Business History Review* 71: 299–308.

Adler, R. (1943) "Les Lignes Principales du Problème de la Population d'Égypte et leur Coordination", *L'Égypte Contemporaine* 34, 211: 179–204.

Alanís Patiño, E. (1943) "La Riqueza de México", *El Trimestre Económico*, 10: 97–34. An essentially identical paper appeared as "La Riqueza Nacional", in *Investigación Económica* 1955, XV, 1: 53–82.

Aldrich, R. (1996) *Greater France: A History of French Overseas Expansion*, Houndmills: Macmillan Press.

Amin, S. (1966) *L'Économie du Maghreb: La Colonisation et la Décolonisation*, Volume 1. Paris: Les Editions de Minuit.

—— (1967) *Le developpement du capitalisme en Côte d'Ivoire*, Paris: Les Éditions de Minuit.

Amsden, A.H. (1989) *Asia's Next Giant: South Korea and Late Industrialization*, New York: Oxford University Press.

Armstrong, C. and Nelles, H.V. (1988) *Southern Exposure: Canadian promoters in Latin America and the Caribbean*, Toronto: University of Toronto Press.

Australian Bureau of Statistics (1989) *Foreign Investment Australia 1988–89*, Canberra: Government Publishing Service.

Ayache, A. (1956) *Le Maroc: bilan d'une colonisation*, Paris: Éditions Sociales.

Baer, G. (1962) *A History of Landownership in Modern Egypt 1800–1950*, London: Oxford University Press.

Bagchi, A.K. (1972) *Private Investment in India 1900–1939*, Cambridge: Cambridge University Press.

Baklanoff, E.N. (1975) *Expropriation of U.S. investments in Cuba, Mexico and Chile*, New York: Praeger.

Banco de México (1969) *Cuentas Nacionales y Acervos de Capital, consolidadas y por tipo de actividad económica*, México, D.F.: Banco de México.

—— (1978) *Encuestas: Acervos y formación de capital 1960–1975*, México, D.F.: Banco de México.

Banerji, A.K. (1963) *India's Balance of Payments*, New York: Asia Publishing House.

Bank of England (1950) *United Kingdom Overseas Investments 1938 to 1948*, London: East and Blades, Ltd. Subsequently published annually until 1959.

—— *Board of Trade Journal.*

Banque Centrale du Congo Belge et du Ruanda-Urundi, monthly, *Bulletin* [*BBCCBRU*] Brussels and Leopoldville.

—— (1955) "Essai d'Estimation du Capital Investi au Congo Belge" *BBCCBRU* 4, 8: 289–305.

—— (1956) "Quelques Considérations sur le Développement de l'Economie Congolaise de 1920 a 1954", *BBCCBRU* 5, 3: 99–108.

Baptista, A. (1991) *Bases Cuantitativas de la economía venezolana 1830–1989*, Caracas: Litografía Melvin.

Barber, W.J. (1961) *The Economy of British Central Africa*, London: Oxford University Press.

Belal, A.A. (1976) *L'investissement au Maroc (1912–1964) et ses enseignements en matière de développement économique*, Rabat: Les Editions Maghrebines.

Bennett, D.C. and Sharpe, K.E. (1985) *Transnational Corporations Versus the State: The Political Economy of the Mexican Auto Industry*, Princeton: Princeton University Press.

Bennoune, M. (1988) *The making of contemporary Algeria, 1830–1987*, New York: Cambridge University Press.

Bergsten, C.F., *et al.* (1978) *American Multinationals and American Interests*, Washington, D.C.: The Brookings Institution.

Bernard, P. (1934) *Le problème économique indochinois*, Paris: Nouvelles Editions Latines.

Berry, T.S. (1968) "Production and Population since 1789: Revised GNP Series in Constant Dollars", mimeo, Boswick Papers No. 6.

Bielschowsky, R.A. and Stumpo, G. (1995) "Transnational corporations and structural changes in industry in Argentina, Brazil, Chile and Mexico", *CEPAL Review* 55: 143–69.

Bishop, B. (1997) *Foreign Direct Investment in Korea: The Role of the State*, Aldershot: Ashgate.

Bloch-Laine, F., *et al.* (1956) *La zone franc*, Paris: Presses Universitaires de France.

Bobrie, F. (1976) "Finances publiques et conquête coloniale: Le coût budgétaire de l'expansion française entre 1850 et 1913", *Annales E.S.C.*, 31, 1: 1225–49.

—— (1977) "Le financement des chemins de fer coloniaux: un exemple de l'investissement public outre-mer entre 1860 et 1940", *Cahiers d'Histoire*, 22, 2: 177–201.

Boone, C. (1993) "Commerce in Côte d'Ivoire: Ivoirianisation without Ivoirian Traders", *The Journal of Modern African Studies* 31, 1: 67–92.

Booth, A. (1998) *The Indonesian Economy in the Nineteenth and Twentieth Centuries, A History of Missed Opportunities*, New York: St. Martin's Press.

Bose, A. (1965) "Foreign Capital", in V.B. Singh (ed.) *The Economic History of India 1857–1956*, Bombay: Allied Publishers.

Brocheux, P. and Hémery, D. (1995) *Indochine la colonisation ambiguë (1858–1954)*, Paris: Éditions la Découverte.

Brown, I. (ed.) (1989) *Economies of Africa and Asia in the Interwar Depression*, London: Routledge.

Brown, J.C. (1985) "Why Foreign Oil Companies Shifted Their Production from Mexico to Venezuela during the 1920s", *The American Historical Review* 90, 2: 362–85.

Brown, R.A. (1994) *Capital and Entrepreneurship in South-East Asia*, New York: St. Martin's Press.

Buckley, K. (1955) *Capital Formation in Canada 1896–1930*, Toronto: University of Toronto Press.

Bulmer-Thomas, V. (1994) *The Economic History of Latin America Since Independence,* Cambridge: Cambridge University Press.

Bunge, A.E. (1917) *Riqueza y Renta de la Argentina Su Distribución y su Capacidad Contributiva,* Buenos Aires: Agencia General de Librería y Publicaciones.

Bureau of Industry Economics (1993) *Multinationals and Governments: Issues and Implications for Australia,* Research Report No. 49, Canberra: Australian Government Publishing Service.

Butlin, N.G. (1962) *Australian Domestic Product, Investment and Foreign Borrowing 1861–1938/39,* Cambridge: Cambridge University Press.

Callis, H.G. (1942) *Foreign Capital in Southeast Asia,* New York: Institute of Pacific Relations.

Calvert, P. (1996) "Privatisation in Argentina", *Bulletin of Latin American Research* 15, 2: 145–56.

Campo, J.N.F.M. à. (1995) "Strength, Survival and Success. A Statistical Profile of Corporate Enterprise in Colonial Indonesia 1883–1913", *Jahrbuch für Wirtschaftsgeschichte* 1: 45–74.

—— (1996) "The Rise of Corporate Enterprise in Colonial Indonesia, 1893–1913", in J.T. Lindblad (ed.) *Historical foundations of a national economy in Indonesia, 1890s–1990s,* Amsterdam: North Holland.

Cárdenas, E. (1987) *La industrialización mexicana durante la gran depresión,* México: El Colegio de México.

Castro, A.C. (1979) *As Empresas Estrangeiras no Brasil 1860–1913,* Rio de Janeiro: Zahar Editores.

Changing Economy in Indonesia, [*CEI*], various years and editors, Amsterdam: Royal Tropical Institute. 15 Volumes.

Chao, K. (1977) *The Development of Cotton Textile Production in China,* Cambridge MA: East Asian Research Center and Harvard University Press.

—— (1983) *The Economic Development of Manchuria: The Rise of a Frontier Economy,* Ann Arbor, MI: Center for Chinese Studies.

Chapman, S. (1998) "British Free-Standing Companies and Investment Groups in India and the Far East", in M. Wilkins and H. Schröter (eds.) *The Free-Standing Company in the World Economy 1830–1996,* Oxford: Oxford University Press.

Chege, M. (1998) "Introducing race as a variable into the political economy of Kenya debate: an incendiary idea", *African Affairs,* 97: 209–30.

Chevassu, J.-M. 1997. "Le modèle ivoirien et les obstacles á l'émergence de la petite el moyenne industrie (PMI)", in B. Contamin and H. Memel-Fotê (eds) *Le modèle ivoirien en questions: Crises, ajustements, recompositions,* Paris: Éditions Karthala.

Chung, Y. (1973) "Japanese Investment in Korea, 1904–1945", in A.C. Nahm (ed.), *Korea Under Japanese Colonial Rule,* Kalamazoo: Western Michigan University.

—— (1975) "Korean Investment Under Japanese Rule", in C.I.E. Kim and D.E. Mortimore (eds), *Korea's Response to Japan: The Colonial Period 1910–1945,* Kalamazoo: Western Michigan University.

Clapp, R.A. (1995) "Creating Competitive Advantage: Forest Policy as Industrial Policy in Chile", *Economic Geography* 71, 3: 273–96.

Clarke, D.G. (1980) *Foreign Companies and International Investment in Zimbabwe,* Gwelo, Rhodesia: Mambo Press.

Coeymans, J.E. and Mundlak, Y. (1993) *Sectoral Growth in Chile 1960–1982,* Report # 95, Washington: IFPRI.

Comité de Inversiones Extranjeras (Chile) 1995. *Chile: Inversión Extranjera en Cifras 1974–1995*, Santiago: CIE.

Constantine, S. (1984) *The making of British colonial development policy 1914–1940*, London: Frank Cass.

Coquery-Vidrovitch, C. (1972) *Le Congo au temps des grandes compagnies concessionnaires 1898–1930*, Paris: Mouton & Co.

Corley, T.A.B. (1994) "Britain's Overseas Investments in 1914 Revisited", *Business History* 36, 1: 71–88.

Cortés Conde, R. (1994) "Estimaciones del PBI en la Argentina 1875–1935", unpublished manuscript, Universidad de San Andrés, Argentina.

Crouchley, A.E. (1936) *The Investment of Foreign Capital in Egyptian Companies and Public Debt*, New York: Arno Press, reprinted 1977.

—— (1938) *The Economic Development of Modern Egypt*, London: Longmans, Green and Co.

Cumings, B. (1984) "The Legacy of Japanese Colonialism in Korea", in R.H. Myers and M.R. Peattie (eds) *The Japanese Colonial Empire*, Princeton: Princeton University Press.

Curtis, F. (1991) "Foreign Disinvestment and Investment – South Africa: 1960–1986", in Z.A. Konczacki, *et al. Studies in the Economic History of Southern Africa, Volume 2*, London: Frank Cass.

Dales, J.H. (1986) "Comment" [on Urquhart's "New Estimates of Gross National Product, Canada, 1870–1926"] in S.L. Engerman and R.E. Gallman (eds) *Long Term Factors in American Economic Growth*, Chicago: University of Chicago Press.

Davis, L.E. and Huttenback, R.A. (1986) *Mammon and the pursuit of Empire: The political economy of British imperialism, 1860–1912*, Cambridge: Cambridge University Press.

de Jager, B.L. (1973) "The fixed capital stock and capital output ratio of South Africa from 1946 to 1972", South African Reserve Bank *Quarterly Bulletin*, June: 17–29.

De Villiers, L. (1995) *In Sight of Surrender: The U.S. Sanctions Campaign against South Africa, 1946–1993*, Westport CN: Praeger.

Deane, P. (1948) *The measurement of colonial national incomes*, Occasional Papers No. 12: National Institute of Economic and Social Research. Cambridge University Press.

Deininger, K. and Binswanger, H.P. (1995) "Rent Seeking and the Development of Large-Scale Agriculture in Kenya, South Africa and Zimbabwe", *Economic Development and Cultural Change* 43: 493–522.

Demontès, V. (1922) *L'Algérie[:] Vie technique et industrielle*, Paris.

Díaz Alejandro, C.F. (1970) *Essays on the Economic History of the Argentine Republic*, New Haven: Yale University Press.

Dickens, P.D. (1931) "A New Estimate of American Investments Abroad", United States Department of Commerce *Trade Information Bulletin* No. 767 reprinted by Arno Press (1976) as part of *Estimates of United States Direct Foreign Investment, 1929–43 and 1947*, New York: Arno Press.

—— (1938) "American Direct Investments in Foreign Countries – 1936", United States Department of Commerce *Bulletin* reprinted by Arno Press (1976) as part of *Estimates of United States Direct Foreign Investment, 1929–43 and 1947*, New York: Arno Press.

Doane, R.R. (1933) *The Measurement of American Wealth*, New York: Harper and Brothers.

—— (1957) *World Balance Sheet,* New York: Harper and Brothers.

D'Olwer, L.N. (1965) "Las inversiones extranjeras", Chapter X in D. Cosío Villegas (ed.) *Historia Moderna de México: El Porfiriato. La Vida Económica,* México: Editorial Hermes.

Douël, M. (1930) *Un Siècle de Finances Coloniales,* Paris: Librairie Félix Alcan.

Dresch, J. (1979) *Un géographe au déclin des empires,* Paris: François Maspero.

Ducruet, J. (1964) *Les capitaux Européens au proche-orient,* Paris: Presses Universitaires de France.

Duncan, J.S. (1932) *Public and Private Operation of Railways in Brazil,* New York: Columbia University Press.

Dunning, J.H. (1983) "Changes in the level and structure of international production: the last one hundred years", in M. Casson (ed.) *The Growth of International Business,* London: George Allen & Unwin.

Dunning, J.H. and Cantwell, J. (1987) *IRM Directory of Statistics of International Investment and Production,* Houndmills: Macmillan.

Duus, P. (1984) "Economic Dimensions of Meiji Imperialism: The Case of Korea, 1895–1910", in R.H. Myers and M.R. Peattie (eds) *The Japanese Colonial Empire, 1895–1945,* Princeton: Princeton University Press.

—— (1989) "Zaikabō: Japanese Cotton Mills in China, 1895–1937", in P. Duus, *et al.,* (eds) *The Japanese Informal Empire in China 1895–1937,* Princeton: Princeton University Press.

—— (1995) *The Abacus and the Sword: The Japanese Penetration of Korea 1895–1910,* Berkeley: University of California Press.

Dye, A. (1998) *Cuban Sugar in the Age of Mass Production[:] Technology and the Economics of the Sugar Central, 1899–1929,* Stanford: Stanford University Press.

Eckert, C.J. (1991) *Offspring of Empire: The Koch'ang Kims and the Colonial Origins of Korean Capitalism 1876–1945,* Seattle: University of Washington Press.

Eckstein, A.M. (1991) "Is there a 'Hobson-Lenin thesis' on late nineteenth-century colonial expansion?", *Economic History Review* XLIV, 2: 297–318.

Edelstein, M. (1982) *Overseas Investment in the Age of High Imperialism,* New York: Columbia University Press.

Edwards, G.G. (1971) "Foreign Petroleum Companies and the State in Venezuela", in R.F. Mikesell (ed.) *Foreign Investment in the Petroleum and Mineral Industries,* Baltimore: The Johns Hopkins Press.

Eisner, G. (1960) *Jamaica, 1830–1930: A Study in Economic Growth,* Manchester: Manchester University Press.

Elm, M. (1992) *Oil, Power, and Principle: Iran's Oil Nationalization and Its Aftermath,* Syracuse: Syracuse University Press.

Estimates of Long-Term Economic Statistics of Japan Since 1868, Vols 1–14, under the general editorship of K. Ohkawa. Tokyo: Toyo Keizai Shinposha.

Evans, P. (1979) *Dependent Development: The Alliance of Multinational, State, and Local Capital in Brazil,* Princeton: Princeton University Press.

Falkus, M. (1989) "Early British business in Thailand", in R.P.T. Davenport-Hines and G. Jones (eds) *British Business in Asia since 1860,* Cambridge: Cambridge University Press.

Feinstein, C.H. (1988) "Sources and Methods of Estimation for Domestic Reproducible Fixed Assets and Works in Progress, Overseas Assets, and Land", in C.H. Feinstein and S. Pollard, (eds) *Studies in Capital Formation in the United Kingdom 1750–1920,* Oxford: Clarendon Press.

—— (1990) "Britain's overseas investments in 1913", *Economic History Review* 2nd ser. 43, 2: 288–95.

Ferrier, R.W. (1982) *The History of the British Petroleum Company*, Volume 1. Cambridge: Cambridge University Press.

Feuerwerker, A. (1995) *The Chinese Economy 1870–1949*, Ann Arbor: Center for Chinese Studies, University of Michigan. Slightly revised from an essay in *The Cambridge History of China*, Cambridge University Press, 1980.

Fidel, C. (1915) "Au Maroc au début de la guerre de 1914", *Bulletin du Comité de l'Afrique Française: Renseignements Coloniaux* 3: 38–43.

Fieldhouse, D.K. (1965) *The Colonial Empires: A Comparative Survey from the Eighteenth Century*, 2nd ed. 1982, London: Macmillan Press.

—— (1971) "The Economic Exploitation of Africa: Some British and French Comparisons", in P. Gifford and W.R. Louis, (eds) *France and Britain in Africa*, New Haven: Yale University Press.

—— (1986) "The Economics of French Empire", Review article in *Journal of African History* 27: 169–72.

Fields, K.J. (1995) *Enterprise and the State in Korea and Taiwan*, Ithaca: Cornell University Press.

Fishlow, A. (1966) "Productivity and Technological Change in the Railroad Sector, 1840–1910", in *Output, Employment, and Productivity in the United States After 1800*, Studies in Income and Wealth Volume 30, New York: Columbia University Press.

FitzGerald, E.V.K. (1979) *The political economy of Peru 1956–78*, Cambridge: Cambridge University Press.

France, Ministère des Finances (1902) "La Fortune Française à L'Étranger", *Bulletin de Statistique et de Législation Comparée* 29: 450–85 (Paris: Imprimerie Nationale).

Frankel, S.H. (1938) *Capital Investment in Africa*, London: Oxford University Press.

—— (1967) *Investment and the return to equity capital in the South African gold mining industry 1887–1965*, Oxford: Basil Blackwell.

Franzsen, D.G. and Willers, J.D. (1959) "Capital Accumulation and Economic Growth in South Africa", *Income and Wealth*, Series VIII: 293–322.

French, C. (1915) "Au Maroc au début de la guerre de 1914", *Renseignements Coloniaux: Bulletin du Comité de l'Afrique Française* 3: 38–43.

Fritsch, W. and Franco, G. (1991) *Foreign Direct Investment in Brazil: Its Impact on Industrial Restructuring*, Paris: OECD.

Gales, B.P.A. and Sluyterman, K.E. (1993) "Outward bound. The rise of Dutch multinationals", in G. Jones and H.G. Schröter (eds) *The Rise of Multinationals in Continental Europe*, Aldershot, England: Edward Elgar Publishing Ltd.

—— (1998) "Dutch Free-Standing Companies, 1870–1940", in M. Wilkins and H.G. Schröter (eds) *The Free-Standing Company in the World Economy 1830–1996*, Oxford: Oxford University Press.

Ganz, A. (1959) "Problems and Uses of National Wealth Estimates in Latin America", in *Income and Wealth*, 8: 217–73.

Garland, J.M. and Goldsmith, R.W. (1957) "The National Wealth of Australia", in *Income and Wealth* 8: 323–64.

Gbagbo, L. (1982) *La Côte d'Ivoire: economie et societé à la veille de l'independence*, Paris: Editions L'Harmattan.

Girvan, N. (1971) *Foreign Capital and Economic Underdevelopment in Jamaica*, London: Uniwin Brothers Ltd.

Goldsmith, R.W. (1983) *Financial Development of India, 1860–1977,* New Haven: Yale University Press.

—— (1985) *Comparative National Balance Sheets: A Study of Twenty Countries, 1688–1978,* Chicago: University of Chicago Press.

—— (1986) *Brasil 1850–1984: Desenvolvimento Financeiro sob um Século de Inflação,* São Paulo: Harper & Row do Brasil.

Gomez, E.T. and Jomo, K.S. (1997) *Malaysia's Political Economy: Politics, Patronage and Profits,* Cambridge: Cambridge University Press.

Gourou, P. (1943) *Land Utilization in French Indochina,* photocopy of a translation apparently made privately by the Institute for Pacific Relations.

Gragert, E.H. (1994) *Landownership Under Colonial Rule: Korea's Japanese Experience 1900–1935,* Honolulu: University of Hawaii Press.

Green, A.G. (1986) "Growth and Productivity Change in the Canadian Railway Sector, 1871–1926", in S.L. Engerman and R.E. Gallman (eds) *Long Term Factors in American Economic Growth,* Chicago: University of Chicago Press.

Grupo Cubano de Investigaciones Económicas (1963) *Un estudio sobre Cuba,* Miami: University of Miami Press.

Guillen, P. (1977) "Les investissements français au Maroc de 1912 à 1939", in M. Lévy-Leboyer (ed.), *La position internationale de la France Aspects économiques et financiers XIX–XX siècles,* Paris: École des Hautes Études en Sciences Sociales.

Haggard, S., *et al.* (1997) "Japanese Colonialism and Korean Development: A Critique", *World Development,* 25, 6: 867–81.

Halsey, F.M. (1916) *Railway Expansion in Latin America,* New York: The Moody Magazine and Book Co.

—— (1918) *Investments in Latin America and the British West Indies,* US Department of Commerce Bureau of Foreign and Domestic Commerce, *Special Agents Series* No. 169. Washington, D.C.: GPO.

Hansen, B. (1991) *The Political Economy of Poverty, Equity, and Growth: Egypt and Turkey,* Oxford: Oxford University Press.

Hansen, B. and Marzouk, G.A. (1965) *Development and Economic Policy in the U.A.R. (Egypt),* Amsterdam: North-Holland.

Hanson, J.R. (1999) "Culture Shock and Direct Investment in Poor Countries", *The Journal of Economic History* 59, 1: 1–16.

Hara, T. (1976) "Les investissments ferroviaires français en Algérie au XIX siècle", *Revue D'Histoire Economique et Sociale* 54, 2: 185–211.

Hart, G.H.C. (1942) *Towards Economic Democracy in the Netherlands Indies,* New York: Netherlands Information Bureau.

Henry, Y. (1932) *Économie Agricole de L'Indochine,* Hanoi: Gouvernement General de L'Indochine.

Heston, A. (1983) "National Income" in D. Kumar (ed.) *The Cambridge Economic History of India. Volume 2: c. 1757–c. 1970,* Cambridge: Cambridge University Press.

Hill, H. and Hull, T. (eds) (1990) *Indonesia Assessment 1990,* Canberra: Panther Publishing and Presses.

Himbara, D. (1994) *Kenyan capitalists, the state, and development,* Boulder: Lynne Rienner Publishers.

Ho, S.P.S. (1978) *Economic Development of Taiwan 1860–1970,* New Haven: Yale University Press.

—— (1984) "Colonialism and Development: Korea, Taiwan, and Kwantung", in

R.H. Myers and M.R. Peattie (eds) *The Japanese Colonial Empire, 1895–1945*, Princeton: Princeton University Press.

Hofman, A.A. (1992) "Capital Accumulation in Latin America: A Six Country Comparison for 1950–1989", *The Review of Income and Wealth* 38, 4: 365–401.

—— (1993) "Economic Development in the 20th Century – A Comparative Perspective", in A. Szirmai, *et al.* (eds) *Explaining Economic Growth: Essays in Honour of Angus Maddison*, Amsterdam: North-Holland.

—— (2000) *The Economic Development of Latin America in the Twentieth Century*, Northampton: Edward Elgar.

Hooley, R.W. (1968) "Long-term Growth of the Philippine Economy, 1902–1961", *The Philippine Economic Journal* 8, 1: 1–24.

Hou, C. (1965) *Foreign Investment and Economic Development in China: 1840–1937*, Cambridge: Harvard University Press.

Hsüeh (Schive), C. (1990) *The Foreign Factor: The Multinational Corporation's Contribution to the Economic Modernization of the Republic of China*, Stanford: Hoover Institution Press.

Huybrechts, A. (1970) *Transports et structures de développement au Congo. Etude du progrès économique de 1900 á 1970*, Paris: Mouton et IRES.

India Central Statistical Office (1988) *Estimates of Capital Stock of Indian Economy as on 31 March 1981*, New Delhi (?): Government of India.

Innes, D. (1984) *Anglo-American and the Rise of Modern South Africa*, London: Heinemann Educational Books.

Instituto Brasileiro de Geografia e Estatística (1950) *Recenseamento Geral do Brasil [1940] Volume III. Censos Econômicos: Agrícola, Industrial, Comercial e dos Serviços*, Rio de Janero: Serviciço Gráfico do IBGE.

International Bank for Reconstruction and Development (IBRD) (1951) *Report on Cuba*, Baltimore: The Johns Hopkins Press. [The Truslow Report].

Issawi, C. (1954) *Egypt at Mid-Century: An Economic Survey*, London: Oxford University Press.

—— (1963) *Egypt in Revolution: An Economic Analysis*, London: Oxford University Press.

—— (1980) *The Economic History of Turkey: 1800–1914*, Chicago: University of Chicago Press.

—— and Yeganeh, M. (1962) *The Economics of Middle Eastern Oil*, New York: Praeger.

Jara Letelier, A. and Muirhead, M.G. (1929) *Chile en Sevilla*, Santiago de Chile.

Jefferson, O. (1972) *The Post-war Economic Development of Jamaica*, Jamaica: ISER.

Jenks, L.H. (1928) *Our Cuban Colony: A Study in Sugar*, New York: Vanguard Press.

Kaneko, F. (1982) "Prewar Japanese Investments in Colonized Taiwan, Korea and Manchuria, A Quantitative Analysis", *Annals of the Institute of Social Sciences* 23: 32–64.

Kaplan, D.E. (1983) "The Internationalization of South African Capital: South African Direct Foreign Investment in the Contemporary Period", *African Affairs* 82: 465–94.

Katwala, G.J. (1979) "Export-led Growth: The Copper Sector", in G. Gran (ed.) *Zaire[:] The Political Economy of Underdevelopment*, New York: Praeger.

Keuning, S.J. (1991) "Allocation and Composition of Fixed Capital Stock in Indonesia: An Indirect Estimate Using Incremental Capital Value Added Ratios", *Bulletin of Indonesian Economic Studies* 27, 2: 91–119.

Keyder, Ç. (1987) *State and Class in Turkey: a study in capitalist development*, New York: Verso.

Kimura, M. (1989) "Public Finance in Korea under Japanese Rule: Deficit in the Colonial Account and Colonial Taxation", *Explorations in Economic History* 26: 285–310.

—— (1995) "The economics of Japanese imperialism in Korea, 1910–1939", *Economic History Review* 48, 3: 555–74.

Kindersley, R. (1931) "British Foreign Investments in 1929", *The Economic Journal* 41, 158: 370–84. Reprinted in M. Wilkins (ed.) (1977) *British Overseas Investments: 1907–1948*, New York: Arno Press.

—— (1932) "British Foreign Investments in 1930", *The Economic Journal* 42, 166: 177–95. Reprinted in M. Wilkins (ed.) (1977) *British Overseas Investments: 1907–1948*, New York: Arno Press.

—— (1933) "British Overseas Investments in 1931", *The Economic Journal* 43, 170: 187–204. Reprinted in M. Wilkins (ed.) (1977) *British Overseas Investments: 1907–1948*, New York: Arno Press.

—— (1935) "British Foreign Investments in 1933 and 1934", *The Economic Journal* 45, 179: 439–55. Reprinted in M. Wilkins (ed.) (1977) *British Overseas Investments: 1907–1948*, New York: Arno Press.

—— (1937) "British Foreign Investments in 1935 and 1936", *The Economic Journal* 47, 188: 642–62. Reprinted in M. Wilkins (ed.) (1977) *British Overseas Investments: 1907–1948*, New York: Arno Press.

—— (1939) "British Overseas Investments, 1938", *The Economic Journal* 49, 192: 679–95. Reprinted in M. Wilkins (ed.) (1977) *British Overseas Investments: 1907–1948*, New York: Arno Press.

King, R.G. and Levine, R. (1994) "Capital Fundamentalism, Economic Development, and Economic Growth", *Carnegie-Rochester Conference Series on Public Policy* 40: 259–92.

Kinney, A.R. (1982) *Japanese Investment in Manchurian Manufacturing, Mining, Transportation and Communications 1931–1945*, New York: Garland.

Kirsch, H.W. (1977) *Industrial Development in a Traditional Society*, Gainesville: University of Florida.

Kitching, G. (1985) "Politics, Method, and Evidence in the 'Kenya Debate' ", in H. Berstein and B.K. Campbell (eds) *Contradictions of Accumulation in Africa*, Beverly Hills: Sage.

Korbin, S.J. (1980) "Foreign enterprise and forced divestment in LDCs", *International Organization* 34, 1: 65–88.

—— (1984) "Expropriation as an Attempt to Control Foreign Firms in LDCs: Trends from 1960 to 1979", *International Studies Quarterly* 28: 329–48.

Kumar, N. (1998) "Liberalisation and Changing Patterns of Foreign Direct Investments. Has India's Relative Attractiveness as a Host of FDI Improved?" *Economic and Political Weekly*, 30 May: 1321–29.

Lamartine Yates, P. (1959) *Forty Years of Foreign Trade*, London: George Allen and Unwin.

—— (1978) *El campo mexicano*, México, D.F.: El Caballito.

Leduc, G. (1954) *L'Economie de l'union française d'outre mer*, Paris: Recueil Sirey.

Lefèbvre, J. (1955) *Structures Économiques du Congo Belge et du Ruanda-Urundi*, Bruxelles: Editions du Treurenberg.

Letcher, M. (1912) "Wealth of Mexico", in US Department of Commerce and

Labor, Bureau of Manufactures, *Daily Consular and Trade Reports* #168, Thursday, 8 July, 1912.

Lewis, Cleona (1938) *America's Stake in International Investments*, Washington, D.C.: The Brookings Institution.

—— (1948) *The United States and Foreign Investment Problems*, Washington, D.C.: The Brookings Institution.

Lewis, Colin (1983) "The Financing of Railway Development in Latin America, 1850–1914", *Ibero-Amerikanische Archiv* 9 n.s., 3–4: 255–78.

Lewis, W.A. (1978) *Growth and Fluctuations 1870–1913*, London: George Allen and Unwin.

Leys, C. (1975) *Underdevelopment in Kenya*, Berkeley: University of California Press.

Lim, L.Y.C. and Fong, P.E.F. (1991) *Foreign Direct Investment and Industrialisation in Malaysia, Singapore, Taiwan and Thailand*, Paris: OECD Development Centre.

Lindblad, J.T. (1991) "Foreign Investment in Late-Colonial and Post-Colonial Indonesia", *Economic and Social History in the Netherlands* 3: 183–208.

—— (1998) *Foreign Investment in Southeast Asia in the Twentieth Century*, Houndmills, England: Macmillan Press.

Mabro, R. and Radwan, S. (1976) *The Industrialization of Egypt, 1939–1973. Policy and Performance*, Oxford: Clarendon Press.

Maddison, A. (1995) *Monitoring the World Economy: 1820–1992*, Paris: OECD.

—— and Associates (1992) *The Political Economy of Poverty, Equity and Growth: Brazil and Mexico*, Oxford: Oxford University Press.

Maddock, R. and McLean, I.W. (1987) *The Australian economy in the long run*, Cambridge: Cambridge University Press.

Maldant, B. (1973) *Croissance et conjoncture dans l'Ouest africain*, Paris: Presses Universitaires de France.

Marichal, C. (1994) "Introduction", to C. Marichal (ed.) *Foreign investment in Latin America: impact on economic development, 1850–1930*, Milan: Universita Bocconi.

Mars, J. (1948) "Extra-Territorial Enterprises", in M. Perham (ed.) *The Economics of a Tropical Dependency*, London: Faber and Faber, Ltd.

Marseille, J. (1974) "L'investissement français dans l'Empire colonial: l'enquête du gouvernement de Vichy (1943)", *Revue Historique* 512: 409–32.

—— (1977) "La politique métropolitaine d'investissements coloniaux dans l'entre-deux-guerres", in M. Lévy-Leboyer, (ed.) *La position internationale de la France: Aspects économiques et financiers XXIX–XX siècles*, Paris: École des Hautes Études en Sciences Sociales.

—— (1984) *Empire Colonial et Capitalisme Français: Histoire d'un divorce*, Paris: Albin Michel.

Martin, A. (1975) *Minding Their Own Business: Zambia's struggle against Western control*, Houndsworth: Penguin Books, Ltd.

Matukama, L. (1988) *Les Determinantes de la Repartition des Beneficies des Enterprises au Zaire*, Louvain la Neuve: CIACO.

McCullough, D. (1977) *The Path Between the Seas: The Creation of the Panama Canal 1870–1914*, New York: Simon and Schuster.

McEvedy, C. and Jones, R. (1978) *Atlas of World Population History*, Harmondsworth, N.Y.: Penguin Books.

McLaughlin, R.U. (1966) *Foreign Investment and Development in Liberia*, New York: Praeger.

238

McNamara, D.L. (1990) *The colonial origins of Korean enterprise, 1910–1945*, Cambridge: Cambridge University Press.

Mercado-Aldaba, R.A. (1994) "Foreign Direct Investment in the Philippines: A Reassessment", Philippine Institute for Development Studies *Research Paper Series* No. 94–10.

Meynier, G. (1981) *L'Algérie Révélée*, Paris: Librarie Droz.

Mikesell, R.F. (1955) *Foreign Investments in Latin America*, Washington, D.C.: Pan American Union.

Ministère des Colonies (1955) *Les investissements au Congo Belge et au Ruanda-Urundi*, Brussels.

Mining Industry Year Book Annual publication. Published by the Copper Industry Service Bureau, Ltd. in Zambia. Title varied.

Minor, M.S. (1994) "The Demise of Expropriation as an Instrument of LDC Policy, 1980–1992", *Journal of International Business Studies* First Quarter: 177–88.

Minost, É. (1930) "Essai sur la Richesse Foncière de l'Égype (Propriété Non-Bâtie)", *L'Égype Contemporaine* 121: 334–55.

—— (1931) "Essai sur la Propriété Batie de l'Égype", *L'Égype Contemporaine* 130: 677–96.

Misra, M. (1991) "Politics and Expatriate Enterprise in India: The Inter-war Years", in D. Tripathi (ed.) *Business and Politics in India*, New Delhi: Manohar Pubs.

Mitchell, B.R. (1982) *International Historical Statistics: Africa and Asia*, New York: New York University Press. (2nd edition, 1995.)

—— (1983) *International Historical Statistics: The Americas and Australasia*, London: Macmillan.

—— (1988) *British Historical Statistics*, New York: Cambridge University Press.

—— (1992) *International Historical Statistics: Europe, 1750–1988*, New York: Stockton Press.

—— (1993) *International Historical Statistics – The Americas 1750–1988*, 2nd ed. New York: Stockton Press.

Mizoguchi, T. (1979) "Economic Growth of Korea under the Japanese Occupation – Background of Industrialization of Korea 1911–1940", *Hitotsubashi Journal of Economics* 1: 1–19.

—— and Umemura, M. (1988) *Basic Economic Statistics of Former Japanese Colonies 1895–1938*, Tokyo: Toyo Keizai Shinposha.

—— and Yamamoto, Y. (1984) "Capital Formation in Taiwan and Korea", in R.H. Myers and M.R. Peattie (eds) *The Japanese Colonial Empire, 1895–1945*, Princeton: Princeton University Press.

Moguillansky, G. (1998) *Chile: las inversiones en el sector minero 1980–2000*, Serie Reformas Económicas #3 Santiago: CEPAL.

Morard, L. (1948) "Algérie et Sahara", in *Encyclopedie Coloniale et Maritime*, Paris.

Morris, M.D. and Dudley, C.B. (1975) "Selected Railway Statistics for the Indian Subcontinent: 1853–1946/47", *Artha Vijnana* 17: 187–298.

Moulton, H.G. (1931) *Japan: An economic and financial appraisal*, Washington, D.C.: The Brookings Institution.

—— and Lewis, C. (1925) *The French Debt Problem*, New York: The Macmillan Co.

Mukherjee, M. (1995) *Selected Papers on National Income*, Calcutta: K.P. Bagchi and Co.

—— and Sastry, N.S.R. (1959) "An estimate of tangible wealth in India", *Income and Wealth* 7: 365–87.

Narula, R. (1996) *Multinational Investment and Economic Structure*, London: Rout-
    ledge.
Ndoma-Egba, B. (1974) *Foreign Investment and Economic Transformation in West Africa
    1870–1930*, Ph.D. thesis published by Studentlitteratur: Lund.
Ndongala, T.L. (1982) *Structure Agro-économique du Développement au Zaïre*, Louvain-
    la-Neuve: Université Catholique de Louvain.
Nørlund, I. (1994) *Textile Production in Vietnam 1880–1940[:] Handicraft and Indus-
    try in a Colonial Economy*, unpublished Ph.D. dissertation, Copenhagen Univer-
    sity.
Nzongola-Ntalaja. (1986) "Crisis and Change in Zaire, 1960–1985", in Nzongola-
    Ntalaja (ed.) *The Crisis in Zaire: Myths and Realities*, Trenton, New Jersey: Africa
    World Press.
Omaboe, E.N. (1960) "Ghana's National Income in 1930", *Economic Bulletin of
    Ghana* 4, 8–9: 6–11.
Ord, H.W. (1962) "Private Ownership of Physical Assets in Kenya", *The South
    African Journal of Economics* 30, 4: 327–32.
Organisation for Economic Co-operation and Development [OECD] (1972) *Stock
    of Private Direct Investments by D.A.C. Countries in Developing Countries: End 1967*,
    Paris: OECD.
—— (1973) *Development Co-operation*, Paris: OECD.
—— Annual *International Direct Investments Statistics Yearbook*, Paris: OECD.
Oualid, W. (1910a) "La fortune mobilièr de l'Algérie", *Bulletin de la Réunion
    d'Etudes Algériennes* 12, 1–2: 38–51.
—— (1910b) "Essai d'evaluation du capital privé de l'Algérie", *Revue d'Économie
    Politique* 24: 385–409.
Paish, G. (1911) "Great Britain's Capital Investments in Individual Colonial and
    Foreign Countries", *Journal of the Royal Statistical Society* 74, 2: 167–187.
    Reprinted in M. Wilkins (ed.) (1977) *British Overseas Investments: 1907–1948*,
    New York: Arno Press.
—— (1914) "The Export of Capital and the Cost of Living", *The Statist Supplement*
    79: I–viii. Reprinted in M. Wilkins (ed.) (1977) *British Overseas Investments:
    1907–1948*, New York: Arno Press.
Pamuk, S. (1987) *The Ottoman Empire and European Capitalism, 1820–1913*, Cam-
    bridge: Cambridge University Press.
Paterson, D.G. (1976) *British Direct Investment in Canada, 1890–1914*, Toronto: Uni-
    versity of Toronto Press.
Peattie, M.R. (1984) "Introduction", and "Japanese Attitudes Toward Colonialism,
    1895–1945" in R.H. Myers and M.R. Peattie (eds) *The Japanese Colonial Empire,
    1895–1945*, Princeton: Princeton University Press.
Peemans, J.P. (1975) "Capital accumulation in the Congo under colonialism: the
    role of the state", in P. Duignan and L.H. Gann (eds) *Colonialism in Africa
    1870–1960: Vol. 4, The Economics of Colonialism*, Cambridge: Cambridge Univer-
    sity Press.
—— (1980) "Belgium – Economics of Decolonization", *Journal of Contemporary
    History* 15, 2: 257–86.
Picquemal, M. (1957) "Les exportations de capitaux français dans les colonies",
    Economie et Politique 37–38: 66–75.
Platt, D.C.M. (1986) *Britain's investment overseas on the eve of the First World War*,
    Houndmills: Macmillan Press Ltd.

Poggi, J. (1931) *Les chemins de fer d'intérêt général de l'Algérie*, Paris: Larose.

Poquin, J.J. (1957) *Les Relations Économiques Extérieures des Pays D'Afrique Noire de L'Union Française 1925–1955*, Paris: Librairie Armand Colin.

Pouyanne, A.A. (1926) *Les travaux publics de l'Indochine*, Hanoi: Imprimerie D'Extrême-Orient.

Purwanto, B. (1996) "The economy of Indonesian smallholder rubber, 1890s–1940", in J.T. Lindblad, (ed.) *Historical foundations of a national economy in Indonesia, 1890s–1990s*, Amsterdam: North-Holland.

Radwan, S. (1974) *Capital Formation in Egyptian Industry & Agriculture*, London: Ithaca Press.

Ramamurti, R. (1999) "Why Haven't Developing Countries Privatized Deeper and Faster?", *World Development* 27, 1: 137–55.

Ramstetter, E.D. (ed.) (1991) *Direct Foreign Investment in Asia's Developing Economies and Structural Change in the Asia-Pacific Region*, Boulder: Westview Press.

Rangel, D.A. (1970) *Capital y desarrollo Tomo II*, Caracas: Instituto de Investigaciones Económicas y Sociales, Universidad Central de Venezuela.

Rapley, J. (1993) *Ivoirien Capitalism: African Entrepreneurs in Côte d'Ivoire*, Boulder: Lynne Rienner.

Rasiah, R. (1995) *Foreign Capital and Industrialization in Malaysia*, Houndsmills: St. Martin's Press.

Remer, C.F. (1933) *Foreign Investments in China*, New York: The Macmillan Co.

Reserve Bank of India (1950) *Census of India's Foreign Liabilities and Assets*, Bombay: Examiner Press.

—— (1954) *Banking and Monetary Statistics of India*, Bombay: Reserve Bank of India.

—— (1957) *Survey of India's Foreign Liabilities and Assets*, Bombay: Reserve Bank of India.

—— (1964) *India's Foreign Liabilities and Assets, 1961*, Bombay: Reserve Bank of India.

—— (1985) "India's International Investment Position 1977–78 to 1979–80", *Reserve Bank of India Bulletin* April: 269–92.

Reynolds, C.W. (1965) "Development Problems of an Export Economy: The Case of Chile and Copper", in M. Mamalakis and C.W. Reynolds, *Essays on the Chilean Economy*, Homewood, Ill.: Richard D. Irwin, Inc.

Rippy, J.F. (1948) "French Investments in Latin America", *Inter-American Economic Affairs* 52–71.

—— (1959) *British Investments in Latin America, 1822–1949*, Hamden, CT.: Archon Books.

Robequain, C. (1944) *The Economic Development of French Indo-China*, London: Oxford University Press. Translation of the French edition published in 1939.

Roy, B. (1979) *Capital Formation in India*, Calcutta: Das Gupta and Co.

—— (1996) *An Analysis of Long Term Growth of National Income and Capital Formation in India (1850:51 to 1950:51)*, Calcutta: Firma KLM Private Limited.

Roy, T. (ed.) (1996) *Cloth & Commerce: Textiles in Colonial India*, New Delhi: Sage Publications India.

Salomón, A. (1998) "Inversión extranjera directa en México en los noventa", *Comercio Exterior* October: 804–8.

Salvatore, D. (1998) *International Economics*, 6th edition, Upper Saddle River, New Jersey: Prentice Hall.

Samuels, B.C. (1990) *Managing Risk in Developing Countries: National Demand and Multinational Response*, Princeton: Princeton University Press.

Schröter, H. (1998) "Continental European Free-Standing Companies: The Case of Belgium, Germany, and Switzerland", in M. Wilkins and H. Schröter (eds) *The Free-Standing Company in the World Economy 1830–1996*, Oxford: Oxford University Press.

Sepúlveda, B. and Chumacero A. (1973) *La inversión extranjera en México* México, D.F.: Fondo de Cultura Económica.

Sigmund, P.E. (1980) *Multinationals in Latin America: The Politics of Nationalization*, Madison: University of Wisconsin Press.

Simon, M. (1970) "New British Investment in Canada, 1865–1914", *Canadian Journal of Economics* 3, 2: 238–54.

Sivasubramonian, S. (1997) "Revised estimates of the national income of India, 1900–1901 to 1946–47", *The Indian Economic and Social History Review*, 34, 2: 113–68.

Smolski, T. (1929) "Les investissements de capitaux privés el les émissions de valeurs mobiliérs en Indochine, au cours de la période quinquennale 1924–1928", *Bulletin Economique de l'Indochine* 803–20.

South African Reserve Bank (1958) "The Foreign Liabilities and Assets of the Union of South Africa: Final Results of the 1956 Census", *Supplement to the Quarterly Bulletin of Statistics*, December.

Southworth, C. (1931) *The French Colonial Venture*, London: P.S. King & Son.

Staley, E. (1935) *War and the Private Investor*, Garden City: Doubleday, Doran & Co.

Stallings, B. (1987) *Banker to the Third World: U.S. Portfolio Investment in Latin America, 1900–1986*, Berkeley: University of California Press.

Statistics Canada (annual) *Canada's International Investment Position, [CIIP]* Ottawa: Information Canada. Catalogue 67–202.

Statistics Canada (annual) *Fixed capital flows and stocks, [FCFS]* Ottawa: Minister of Supply and Services Canada. Catalogue 13–568.

Stone, I. (1987) *The Composition and Distribution of British Investment in Latin America, 1865 to 1913*, (Reprint of the author's Ph.D. thesis of 1962). New York: Garland Publishing.

—— (1999) *The Global Export of Capital from Great Britain, 1865–1914 [:] A Statistical Survey*, Houndsmills: Macmillan Press.

Stoneman, C. (1976) "Foreign Capital and the Prospects for Zimbabwe", *World Development* 4, 1: 25–58.

Stopford, J. and Dunning, J. (1983) *The World Directory of International Business*, Vol. 3. Detroit: Gale Research Co.

Suchlicki, J. and Jorge, A. (1994) *Investing in Cuba: Problems and Prospects*, New Brunswick: Transaction Publishers.

Suehiro, A. (1996) *Capital Accumulation in Thailand 1855–1985*, Bangkok: Silkworm Books. [First published in Tokyo in 1989].

Suh, S.C. (1978). *Growth and Structural Changes in the Korean Economy 1910–1940*, Cambridge: Harvard University Press.

Suret-Canale, J. (1971) *French Colonialism in Tropical Africa 1900–1915*, London: C. Hurst. Translation of *Afrique Noire* Volume II, copyright 1964.

—— (1972) *Afrique noire occidentale et centrale*, Tome 3, Paris: Editions Sociales.

—— (1987) *Afrique et capitaux: Géographie es capitaux et des investissements en Afrique tropicale d'expression française*, Tome 2. Montreuil-sur-bois(?): L'Arbe verdoyant Editeur.

Svedberg, P. (1978) "The Portfolio-Direct Composition of Private Foreign Investment in 1914 Revisited", *The Economic Journal* 88: 763–77.

Swainson, N. (1980) *The development of corporate capitalism in Kenya 1918–1977*,
London: Heinemann Educational Books.

Swearingern, W.D. (1987) *Moroccan Mirages: Agrarian Dreams and Deceptions,
1912–1986*, Princeton: Princeton University Press.

Szereszewski, R. (1963) "Capital and Output in Ghana", *Economic Bulletin of Ghana*
7, 4: 33–41.

—— (1965) *Structural Changes in the Economy of Ghana 1891–1911*, London: Wei-
denfeld and Nicolson.

—— (1966) "Capital", in W. Birmingham, *et al., A Study of Contemporary Ghana*,
Vol. 1, London: George Allen and Unwin Ltd.

Taylor, A.M. and Williamson, J.G. (1994) "Capital Flows to the New World as an
Intergenerational Transfer", *Journal of Political Economy* 102: 348–71.

Thee, K.W (1996) "Economic Policies in Indonesia during the Period 1950–1965,
in Particular with Respect to Foreing Investment", in J.T. Lindblad (ed.), *Historical foundations in a national economy in Indonesia, 1890s–1990s*, Amsterdam:
North Holland.

Thobie, J. (1982) *La France Impériale 1880–1914*, Paris: Editions Mégrelis.

Thompson, V. (1937) *French Indo-China*, New York: Macmillan.

Thorner, D. (1951) "Great Britain and the Development of India's Railways",
Journal of Economic History 51, 4: 389–402.

Thorp, R. and Bertram, G. (1978) *Peru 1890–1977: Growth and Policy in an Open
Economy*, London: Macmillan Press.

Tignor, R.L. (1984) *State, Private Enterprise, and Economic Change in Egypt, 1918–52*,
Princeton: Princeton University Press.

—— (1989) *Egyptian Textiles and British Capital 1930–1956*, Cairo: American University in Cairo Press.

—— (1998) *Capitalism and Nationalism at the End of Empire: State and Business in
Decolonizing Egypt, Nigeria, and Kenya, 1945–63*, Princeton: Princeton University
Press.

Tomlinson, B.R. (1978) "Foreign Private Investment in India 1920–1950", *Modern
Asian Studies*, 12, 4: 655–77.

—— (1979) *The political economy of the Raj, 1914–1947*, London: Macmillan Press.

—— (1993) *The New Cambridge History of India III The Economy of Modern India
1860–1970*, Cambridge: Cambridge University Press.

Topik, S. (1987) *The Political Economy of the Brazilian State, 1889–1930*, Austin: University of Texas Press.

Topuz, L. (1948) "Les Capitaux Étrangers en Egypte", *La Revue d'Égypte Economique
& Financiere*, No. 836, August 21, pp. 7–8, 18.

Tornquist, E. (1919) *The Economic Development of the Argentine Republic in the Last
Fifty Years*, Buenos Aires: Ernesto Tornquist & Co., Limited.

Tosco, E. (1957) "Capital Existente de Honduras, C.A.", mimeo, published by the
Departamento de Estudios Económicos of the Banco Central de Honduras.

Turlington, E. (1930) *Mexico and her Foreign Creditors*, New York: Columbia University Press.

Twomey, M.J. (1993) *Multinational Corporations and the North American Free Trade
Agreement* Westport: Praeger.

—— (1998) "Patterns of Foreign Investment in Latin America in the Twentieth

Century", in J.H. Coatsworth and A.M. Taylor (eds) *Latin America and the World Economy Since 1800,* Harvard: David Rockefeller Center for Latin American Studies and the Harvard University Press.

Ulmer, M.J. (1960) *Capital in Transportation, Communications, and Public Utilities: Its Formation and Financing,* Princeton: Princeton University Press.

United Africa Company (1949) "Some Financial Aspects of Trading in West Africa", in their *Statistical & Economic Review* No. 4, September, pp. 50–58.

United Nations (1953) *Review of Economic Conditions in the Middle East 1951–52,* New York(?): United Nations. Sales No. 1953.II.C.1.

—— (1954) *The International Flow of Private Capital 1946–52,* New York: United Nations.

—— (1955) *Foreign Capital in Latin America,* New York: United Nations.

—— (1958) *Yearbook of National Accounts Statistics,* New York: United Nations.

—— (1959) *Economic Survey of Africa since 1950,* New York: United Nations. Sales No. 59.II.K.1.

United Nations Centre on Transnational Corporations [UNCTC] (1983) *Transnational Corporations in World Development. Third Survey,* New York: United Nations.

—— (1988) *Transnational Corporations in World Development: Trends and Prospects,* New York: United Nations.

—— (1989) *Foreign Direct Investment and Transnational Corporations in Services,* New York: United Nations. Sales No. E.89.II.A.1.

—— (1992a) *The Determinants of Foreign Direct Investment: A Survey of the Evidence,* New York: United Nations.

—— (1992b) *World Investment Directory 1992: Foreign Direct Investment, Legal Framework and Corporate Data. Volume I. Asia and the Pacific,* New York: United Nations.

United Nations Conference on Trade and Development [UNCTAD] (1993) *World Investment Report 1993. Transnational Corporations and Integrated International Production,* New York: United Nations.

—— (1994a) *World Investment Directory: Foreign Direct Investment, Legal Framework and Corporate Data. Volume IV Latin America and the Caribbean,* New York: United Nations.

—— (1994b) *World Investment Report 1994: Transnational Corporations, Employment and the Workplace,* New York: United Nations.

—— (1996) *World Investment Directory Volume V, Africa,* New York: United Nations.

—— (1997) *World Investment Report, 1997 TNCs, Market Structure and Competition Policy,* New York: United Nations.

United Nations, Department of Economic and Social Affairs (1955) *Foreign Capital in Latin America,* New York: United Nations.

United Nations Economic Committee on Latin America [UN-ECLA] (1954) *Antecedentes sobre el desarrollo de la economía chilena, 1925–52,* Santiago Chile: Editorial del Pacifico.

—— (1957a) *Analyses and Projections of Economic Development III. The Economic Development of Colombia,* Geneva: United Nations. Statisistical Appendix reprinted by Departamento Administrativo Nacional de Estadística, Bogotá, Colombia. E/CN.12/365.

—— (1957b) *External Disequilibrium in the Economic Development of Latin America: The Case of Mexico Volume 1,* La Paz Bolivia(?): United Nations. Sales No. E/CN.12/428.

—— (1958) *Analisis y proyecciones del desarrollo económico: El desarrollo económico de la Argentina*, México: United Nations.

—— (1959) *Analyses and Projections of Economic Devlopment VI. The Industrial Development of Peru*, Mexico: United Nations. Sales No. E/CN.12/493.

—— (1965) *External Financing in Latin America*, New York: United Nations.

—— (1978) *Series históricas del crecimiento de América Latina. Cuadernos de la CEPAL* #130. Santiago de Chile: United Nations.

—— (1998) *Foreign investment in Latin America and the Caribbean 1998 Report*, Santiago de Chile: United Nations.

United States Bureau of Statistics (1909) *Statistical Abstract of Foreign Countries*, Washington, D.C.: GPO.

United States Department of Commerce (1960) *U.S. Business Investments in Foreign Countries*, Washington, D.C.: USGPO.

—— (1975a) *U.S. Direct Investment Abroad, 1966: Final Data*, Washington, D.C.: USGPO.

—— (1975b) *Historical Statistics of the United Sates, Colonial Times to 1970*, Washington, D.C.: USGPO.

—— (1981) *U.S. Direct Investment Abroad, 1977*, Washington, D.C.: USGPO.

—— (1986) *U.S. Direct Investment Abroad: 1982 Benchmark Survey Data*, Washington, D.C.: USGPO.

—— (1991) *U.S. Direct Investment Abroad: 1989 Benchmark Survey*, Washington, D.C.: USGPO.

—— (1998) *U.S. Direct Investment Abroad: 1994 Benchmark Survey*, Washington, D.C.: USGPO.

Urquhart, M.C. (1986) "New Estimates of Gross National Product, Canada, 1870–1926: Some Implications for Canadian Development", in S.L. Engerman and R.E. Gallman, (eds) *Long Term Factors in American Economic Growth*, Chicago: University of Chicago Press.

—— (1993) *Gross National Product, Canada, 1870–1926. The Derivation of the Estimates*, Kingston: McGill-Queen's University Press.

Van de Velde, M.W. (1936) *Economie Belge et Congo Belge*, Anvers: Éditions "Lloyd Anversois".

Van der Eng, P. (1993) *Agricultural Growth in Indonesia*, Groningen: Universiteitsdrukkerij, Rijksuniversiteit Groningen.

—— (1998) "Economic Benefits from Colonial Assets: The Case of the Netherlands and Indonesia 1870–1958", Research Memorandum GD-39, University of Groningen.

Van der Steen, D. (1977) "Echanges économiques extérieurs du Zaire: dépendance et développment", *Les Cahiers du CEDAF* 4/5.

Van Helten, J.J. and Jones, G. (1989) "British business in Malaysia and Singapore since the 1870s", in R.P.T. Davenport-Hines and G. Jones (eds) *British Business in Asia since 1860*, Cambridge: Cambridge University Press.

Viner, J. (1975) [1924] *Canada's Balance of International Indebtedness, 1900–1913*, Toronto: McClelland and Stewart.

West, R.L. (1965) "Estimates of National Accounts for Kenya 1923–1939," *East African Economic Review* 1, 3: 23–45.

Wheelwright, E.L. (1963) "Overseas Investment in Australia", in A. Hunter (ed.) *The Economics of Australian Industry*, Melbourne: Melbourne University Press.

Wilkins, M. (ed.) (1977) *British Overseas Investments: 1907–1948*, New York: Arno Press.

—— (1988) "The free-standing company, 1870–1914: an important type of British foreign direct investment", *Economic History Review*, 2nd ser., 41, 2: 259–82.

—— and Schröter, H. (eds) (1998) *The Free Standing Company in the World Economy 1830–1996*, Oxford: Oxford University Press.

Will, H.A. (1970) "Colonial Policy and Economic Development in the British West Indies, 1895–1903", *Economic History Review* 2nd Series, 43, 1: 129–47.

Williams, M.L. (1975) "The Extent and Significance of the Nationalization of Foreign-Owned Assets in Developing Countries, 1956–72", *Oxford Economic Papers* 27: 260–73.

Willmore, L. (1994) "Export processing in the Caribbean: the Jamaican experience", *CEPAL Review* 52: 91–104.

Woodruff, W. (1967) *Impact of Western Man: A Study of Europe's Role in the World Economy 1750–1960*, New York: St. Martin's Press.

World Bank (annual), *World Debt Tables*. Washington, D.C.: The World Bank. Subsequently titled *Global Financial Indicators*.

World Bank (1995) *Bureaucrats in Business: The Economics and Politics of Government Ownership*, New York: Oxford University Press.

Wythe, G. (1945) *Industry in Latin America*, New York: Columbia University Press.

Yoshihara, K. (1985) *Philippine Industrialization: Foreign and Domestic Capital*, Manila: Ateneo de Manila University Press and Oxford University Press.

Zhang, K.H. and Markusen, J.R. (1999) "Vertical multinationals and host-country characteristics", *Journal of Development Economics* 59: 233–52.

Zimmerman, L.J. (1962) "The Distribution of World Income 1860–1960", in E. de Vries (ed.) *Essays on Unbalanced Growth*, The Hague: Mouton & Co.

Index